THE ROOTS OF TERRORISM

From Cuban Terrorism
To
Islamic Terrorism

THE ROOTS OF TERRORISM

From Cuban Terrorism
To
Islamic Terrorism

Juan F. Benemelis
2013

The Roots of Terrorism
From Cuban Terrorism to Islamic Terrorism

© Juan F. Benemelis

First English edition 2016
Translated by: Mariela de los Ríos

Publishers: The Ceiba Institute.
Miami, Florida.

About the Author:

Juan F. Benemelis was a principal Africa specialist to Cuba's foreign ministry for many years. He was a Cuban diplomat to Ghana and Tanzania, and operated extensively in Africa and the Middle East. He served as advisor to Yemen President Salem Robaya Ali, between 1976 and 1978.

An award-winning historian both in Cuba and abroad, and author of more than 40 books and hundreds of essays concerning politics, terrorism, espionage, history and philosophy, Benemelis is considered in Spanish language the foremost expert in Africa, Islamic culture, international politics and terrorism.

He is also a refined poet and an excellent painter. A very real renaissance personality.

INDEX

Archeology of a geo-strategy

Asia and the Middle East:
a time bomb in the post-Cold War.

The countries and ethnic groups in the Islamic world, more than in any other region, have been caught in the duels and maneuvers of the world powers.

During the first half of the 19th century, the Arab neck of land was in hands of the Wahhabi fundamentalists, while the Egyptian monarchy and the adjacent Sudan were under firm English safeguard. The German Kaiser, Wilhelm II, masterminded a railroad from Berlin to Baghdad, to reach the Arabian Gulf. But London obstructed that design creating the buffer state of Iraq, snatched from Istanbul, adding the oil zone of Mosul. Through the Sykes-Picot secret agreement[1] in 1916, England and France divided the decayed Ottoman Empire. Only Egypt and Iran remained untouched.

Thus were born, the republics of Syria and Lebanon protected by France, and the Hashemite Kingdom of Transjordan by England. The Anglo-French fragmentation of the Fertile Crescent was compensated with the unification of the Arabian Peninsula under the pro-English Abdul-Aziz Ibn-Saud. Meanwhile, across the Pacific, two forces were raising: The Japanese Mikado and the United States, with its navy deployed at Pearl Harbor and a chain of stations in Midway, Guam, Wake and Corregidor.

England then decentralized its empire into three zones: Europe, the Middle East, and the Hong Kong-Singapore axis. In the Mediterranean France kept the North African mainland under the terms of the Treaty of Utrecht; England kept the sea with Gibraltar, Malta, Cyprus and Suez. The Middle East was manipulated from Suez in Egypt, Aden in eastern Arabia and the Sultanate of Kuwait in the Gulf. In Asia, the "perfidious

Albion" safeguarded its possessions with a ring of naval and aerial bastions: Ceylon, India, Hong Kong, Penang and Singapore.

The Second World War and the decolonization process, triggered by the *Atlantic Charter*, totally upset this strategic design. The English dilemma to defend the Far East or the Middle East was settled in 1942 by the "tiger of Malaysia", the Japanese Marshal Tomoyuki Yamashita, when he easily occupied the so called impregnable Singapore. Then, the British iron belt retreated around the Suez Canal and with it the Empire that Rudyard Kipling had glorified.

In a polygon in Siberia, in June 1949, finished the U.S. nuclear monopoly and started the Cold War. In a historic speech three years early, on March 5, 1946, at Westminster College, Fulton, Missouri, premier Winston Churchill coined his famous phrase "from Stettin in the Baltic to Trieste in the Adriatic, an iron curtain has descended across the continent." This "Iron curtain" fell over Eastern Europe and the correlation of forces changed dramatically when new countries gained independence and the great colonial powers moved to a second echelon.

After the independence of India, Burma and Ceylon, United States warned England not to allow a military vacuum in their former colonial space. In 1951 they sponsored the (Dean) "Acheson plan", with a defense command centered at the colossal Egyptian air base of Mers El-Kebir. From where, if necessary, an attack could be launch to the Soviet industrial poles and the refineries of the Donets basin and the Siberian south, controlling also the Bulgaria, Caucasus and Turkestan air spaces.

NATO considered the Zagros Mountains, in Turkey, as natural wall for the Mediterranean; not without reason, the acute warrior mind of General Dwight Eisenhower prophesied that future tanks battles would be fought on the sands of Islam, from the Nile to Kurdistan. But not everything went perfect for Washington.

In 1951, Josef Stalin accelerated rearmament to counter this strategy, and strove to gain access to the Indian Ocean wading Iran or Baluchistan, via Afghanistan. United States immediately stationed an atomic arsenal in Darkhan, Saudi Arabia.

The United States supported the continuity of British bases in the Suez Canal Zone, saying[2] "it would be essential to our common strategic plans to have the British on the spot'. Pentagon officials insisted on endorsing Britain's position in Egypt and pointed out that 'any action that threatens Britain's control of the Suez Canal and deprives her of a sizeable portion of the Middle East oil fields threatens the position of the United States as a world power".

United States Secretary of State David Acheson plan who helped design the Marshall Plan and played a central role in the development of the Truman Doctrine and creation of the North Atlantic Treaty Organization. Secretary Acheson included Egypt as part of the all-important "defense perimeter" of the United States. But the Egyptian monarch Faruk Al-Awwal contested the "Acheson plan".

The denial of Egypt led the US Vice President Richard Nixon to design the Bagdad Pact, wherein Karachi not only occupied the role as a bridge between Europe (NATO) and the Manila Pact (OTASO), but it supplanted the Middle East headquarters of Egypt and served as a seat to the American strategic air command.

However, the current Arab world dilemma was set in motion long before. Likewise, rivalries between the sultanates and disparities among countries, alongside the political motives, had oil extraction as a common factor.

London opposed the Dean Acheson policy for aid to Greece, Turkey and Iran, and interfered in the creation of the State of Israel.

The British transformed the port-city of Aden as the pivot of all their Middle East military might, supported by the

Amman air base in Iraq, and the legendary Jordanian Arab Legion commanded by the English General Glubb Pasha. United States supplemented this trench from the Aleutian to Japan, Ryukyu and the Philippine Islands.

With their oil assets the Persian Gulf acquired a strategic and economic magnitude greater than the Suez Canal, shifting the Middle East focus to their original points of the Islamic medieval expansion, recovering in addition its global relevance. In the eighties, the financial reserves of the Gulf Arab States and Saudi Arabia exceeded the hundred billions of dollars, a third of the world at the time.

During those years, 50% of United States oil imports came from that region, a fact that implied a greater military and political commitment. On the other hand, the Arab world saw a sharp opposition and division between its "progressives" and "moderates" states. Parallel to that, the Arab-Israeli conflict every so often turned into armed confrontation with international connotation.

The British credence in Saudi Arabia was waning with the appearance and activity of the American oil cartel ARAMCO, which lodged solidly in the Peninsula, being a big chunk of their total national income. So therefore, it was not difficult for United States to develop in Saudi territory, the atomic base of Darkhan, transforming the area into a strategic territory, essential for the defense of the "free world".

But the British didn´t stand still. On March 1947, the Anglo Iranian Oil Co., the Standard Oil Co., and the Socony Vacuum Oil, formed a huge corporation, the Middle East Pipeline, to build and operate a thousand-mile pipeline from the oil fields of Iran and Kuwait to the Mediterranean. The purpose was to oppose to the one being built by ARAMCO, from Saudi Arabia to the Mediterranean, at a cost of $ 300 million.

In May 1951, a crisis took place between England and Iran that shook the world. The Iranian Prime Minister, Mohammed Mossadegh, decreed the nationalization of the oil monopoly Anglo-Iranian Oil Company, compromising the British future in the area. Additional to this conflict and deepening the rift was the emergence of the Palestinian movement and the Egyptian nationalist eruption headed by Gamal Abdul Nasser. England was caught between its financial uncertainty, an empire that was torn to pieces, and the Arab League that was proving to be an unwieldy instrument.

The orientation of the monopoly Iraq Petroleum Concessions Ltd., (IPC) in all of South Arabia settled in the search of the hegemony of prospecting to, at the appropriate time, pursuit its intensive exploitation. The IPC estimated that, should there be oil in the Aden protectorates, such sites would be considered as a reserve for an emergency situation, since remaining petroleum stockpiles in the area were very easy to exploit.

The IPC popularized the idea that South Arabia was still politically too unstable to launch a large scale prospect and data indicated that the deposits were too deep. This was a smokescreen to discourage competitors. In 1954, the IPC explored several areas discovering in them possible deposits, especially in Shabwah, provoking the immediate claim of the Yemeni Government.

When the "Mossadegh affair" entered the paroxysm, English cartels developed a double strategy. On one hand, they focused their efforts on prospecting and exploitation in Kuwait.

On the other hand, the Imam protested when a concession was granted to a subsidiary of British Petroleum to scrutinize the Kamaran Island in the Red Sea. In 1955, oil was discovered also in Thamud, North of Aden. Then, in 1959, the IPC concluded direct negotiations with the sultanates of Hadramaut, a region in the colonized South Arabian sultanates, but these efforts didn't crystallize.

A year later, a subsidiary of the giant Standard Oil of Indiana contacted the sultans of the Hadramaut so they granted them consent to carry out mining and oil explorations. The English colonial Government temporarily blocked the American intentions.

In that decade, British oil monopolies extracted from the area more than $9.000 million. British Petroleum (BP) decided to build a refinery in Aden to process crude oil from the Arabian Gulf and Saudi Arabia, to meet its military needs. It would have an initial capacity of 7 million tons per year, at a cost of $ 130 million, of which 15 million were invested in port facilities. 2500 engineers and specialists and 10000 Arab, Indian and Somali workers, erected the refinery in a time record of 21 months.

The activity of the colonial port of Aden, in Yemen, which exceeded 30 million tons and received an average of 5.800 ships per year, surpassed that of Marseilles. This, considering that French ships used their facilities in colonial Djibouti, and United States has access to Europe across the Atlantic and to Asia through the Pacific.

Meanwhile, Kuwait grew in less than ten years from a traditional fishing port to world financial muscle, to the point of becoming the fourth largest oil producer in the world. The speed of change brought about by sudden oil wealth had its effect in the production boost achieved by the Kuwait Oil Company, and the highest statistic per capita in the world. This immediately raised the border dispute with Iraq, the expected military clashes with the English, the well-known and unfinished emergency sessions of the Arab League, the UN, and so on.

The second strategic coefficient lay and still lies in the oil. In the mid-fifties, American oil investments in Arabia surpassed a billion dollars, setting up the military base of Al–Zahran at the same time.

The growth of the relations between Saudi Arabia and the United States would be relevant in the fifties, when Ibn-Saud, due to the English rejection, sought the support of Washington creating a Federation which covers Kuwait and Bahrain, and thus becoming the world's largest producer of oil.

Another relevant factor was the political arena which in Egypt played a key role. The area radiated its conflicts on the

North African region and the rest of Asia. Thus, any local dispute was linked to NATO's plans, the military bases, the Cold War, oil, transnational corporations, religious affairs, British vital interests and the Israeli issue.

The Middle East has been the political graveyard of many Western leaders. Since 1949, each of the U.S. Presidents has pointed out to the Persian Gulf as a strategic area and part of their national security, due to the oil price, trying to controls the energy sources and looking for the integrity of its borders.

During the visit of Soviet premier Nikita S. Khrushchev to London in 1956, his British colleague, Sir Anthony Eden clarified that the Arabian Peninsula, particularly the South Arabian, was of vital importance to his country. Eden stated that he was even ready to face a war in order to defend their interests in the Middle East. He also expressed to Nikita Khrushchev the importance for the Soviet Union not to get involved in a crisis in that area.

In March 1957, at the Bermuda Conference with President Dwight Eisenhower, the British Prime Minister Harold MacMillan agreed to deploy the *Polaris* submarines in Scotland, placing his country under the American nuclear umbrella. This put an end to the London efforts to be an independent nuclear power, since their ballistic project Blue Streak was both costly and complex.

Convinced that the Soviet Union possessed the lead in long-range ballistic missiles, United States implemented the so-called "Eisenhower doctrine", which surrounded the Soviet Union with several strategic bases from Okinawa to the North Sea. President John F. Kennedy then formed the famous "triad", separating its nuclear forces in three bodies: The *Polaris* submarines in the Navy, the *Minuteman* intercontinental ballistic missiles in the Army, and the strategic B-52's bombers in the Air Force.

By 1962, the Soviet southern flank (the Middle East) was their most vulnerable strip, seeded with American´s

Thunderbird and Polaris hot rods with nuclear warheads. In this scheme, England, from her headquarters in the port of Aden had conventional and nuclear responsibility from Libya to Pakistan and from the Caspian Sea to the Island of Madagascar, with 200 thousand soldiers and a thousand aircrafts.

Subordinate to this global military structure and overwhelmed in addition by military expenditures, UK´s Laborist Premier Harold Wilson ordered in 1966 the removal of the whole command "East of Suez", leaving as a token, only several squadrons of bombers in Bahrain, and the Islands of Massirah, Gann and Coco.

In 1967, the American discomfort increased when London dismantled his aerodrome in Khormaksar, Aden, seat of the Canberra nuclear bombers, stringed against the groundswell of Soviet tanks and artillery of the Caspian and Central Asia, and vigil of the 400 million tons of oil that franked the Suez Canal. Faced with the breakdown of the Baghdad and the OTASO pacts, United States had to reorganize all its military deployment and with it the Middle East geopolitics.

In the Mediterranean the pro-West coup d'état of Athens granted more latitude to the American Sixth Fleet and allow to assemble a mobile defense for North Africa and the Middle East. The Israeli air force took over the commission of doing away the Soviet naval fleet in the Black Sea and Eastern Mediterranean in case of war.

In Asia, the United States assigned to Japan and Indonesia the containment of China. It commissioned to Iran the guardianship of the Arabian Gulf, and to Saudi Arabia the supervision of Iraq, Yemen and the United Arab Emirates.

In the Indian Ocean, United States took possession of the English telecommunications hubs and enclaves; and forced Great Britain to, at least, militarize the islands of Diego Garcia, Aldabra, Farquhar and Desrodes, for the use of its Pacific Seventh Fleet.

All these decisions proved to be timely four decades after in the Gulf War and the offensive on Afghanistan, where the

B-52, from the island of Diego Garcia, the F-16 from Bahrain and Farquhar, and the F-117 Stealth from Turkey, were the backbone of every one of the air assaults.

In the midst of the armed clash between India-Pakistan in 1971, President Richard Nixon considered the use of tactical nuclear weapons against India, a judgment that precipitated the Atomic career of both Asiatic nations.

As soon as they were withdrawing from Vietnam, United States noticed how the soviets spring to the Indian Ocean, an area where they almost didn´t have allies since the departure of the British.

The "Arab weapon", meaning the policy concerning oil prices, which had previously failed, at the moment proved to be a powerful economic and psychological force. Aside from the economic recession the capitalist world was facing, the so-called "oil war" with all its sequels, embargoes. The price of oil jump representing the most dangerous blow to the international trade balance, since the United States emerged as a world power in World War I. Also, this fact demonstrated the role played by raw material from the colonies in the development of the industrial economies.

The oil war would threaten the Japanese, Brazilian and German miracles, and would lead to a vast readjustment of industrial economies, faced with the threat of an energy shortage. The measures taken by the oil producer cartel, the OPEC, prompted an aggressive response by the rulers of the developed Western world, who demanded price reductions and blame them for the global inflation. The West threaten to retaliate increasing the cost of food and even more, letting know with apocalyptic tone that such attitude entailed the danger of war.

After the oil crisis of 1973-1974, United States develops its own energy policy, trying to balance the role of the Arab States petroleum on the world stage. The objective was to curb the harmful consequences of the enslavement of the world capitalist system to the Arab Peninsula wells, and to prevent that such menace spread to other raw material producers.

As top exporter and third largest producer of oil in the planet in 1974, Saudi Arabia already possess the fourth currency reserve of the world[3] and its greatest oil deposits, estimated at 156,000 million barrels. In 1975, their petroleum revenues amounted to $30,000 million dollars. This powerful financial position let the Saudis to modify its policy in the area.

In concord with the United States, the Saudi policy in the region showed its double-edged sword. The Saudis soothed their disagreement with Abu-Dhabi attaining inalienable rights of the Liwa oasis, where oil prospecting was set up immediately, obtaining at the same time a corridor to the sea.

On June 1974, Feisal II signed a military and economic agreement with the United States by which it turn into the main pillar of the Pentagon in the area. Under the terms, Saudi Arabia obtained military equipment and industrial supply that would transform it into a powerful nation, capable to exert pressure on the Indian Ocean, and counterbalance the Soviet military presence.

The Saudis, in concert with Abu-Dhabi, acquired 32 French Mirages fighters, which would be piloted by Pakistanis. In May 1975, the Saudis concluded agreements with Egypt, Qatar and the United Arab Emirates to establish a combined armament industry in Egypt at a cost of $11 billion dollars.

In its new policy Saudi Arabia faced a development program to reduce future imports and use the gas in an industry of massive exports of capital goods. The program - which included 13 refineries, a similar number of petrochemical plants, aluminum processing, iron and steel industries, fertilizers and cement plants- rose to $140 billion by the five-year period of 1976-1980.

In the course of 1975, after the assassination of Faisal II, his half-brother Khaled Ben Abdul-Aziz ascended to the throne establishing an internal balance in a Royal Court of five

Princes, and implementing a new policy for the entire Arab Peninsula. A new team emerged with the talented Ahmed Zaki Yamani as the Tsar of oil. From that moment on, Saudi Arabia strengthened its position in the whole Middle East, especially after the Egyptian political regression and its Saudi financial dependency.

The Western powers looked at the problems of the Arab Peninsula and Gulf with the same ruthless logic used in Southeast Asia. For a long time, they would prevent the shift of the so call Third World from providers of raw materials to producer economies, as well as obstructing the much needed agricultural revolution.

President Anwar El-Sadat, of Egypt, and other Arab countries were willing to make concessions in order to wrap up a separately peace agreement with Israel, obtaining back the crucial corridors of Mitla and Giddy in the Sinai desert, as well as the Abu Rudeis oil fields. This agreement would counteract the pressure that Arab countries could exert on Israel.

The efforts made by the American Chancellor Henry Kissinger achieved its objectives in the Israeli-Egyptian accord signed on January 18, 1974, at kilometer 101 of the Cairo-Suez highway, and the agreement of the ceasefire signed in March 1975. Syria chose to follow Al-Sadat path and endorsed also an agreement with Israel in May 1974.

The bilateral pacts with Israel entitled preliminary steps for comprehensive peace agreements. Behind all these approach was present United States, especially after re-establishing diplomatic relations with Egypt in February 1975 and with Syria, in June of that same year.

The Egyptian President Anwar El-Sadat decided to pursue a policy of several options, supported by a huge financial aid from the U.S. He was urged to free up high military budget, face inflation and avoid internal problems. At the same time, he develops plans for the economic reconstruction, and look for credits to buy technology and machinery. Sadat lunched a privatization process creating free trade areas on both banks of the Suez Canal: Cairo and Alexandria.

American financial institutions immediately began operations in the Egyptian capital. At the same time, Egypt increasingly oriented its trade towards the prosperous region of the Arabian Peninsula and the Gulf.

Although the President El-Sadat sought a new attempt at reunification with Libya and Sudan, he accepted the "Rodgers' plan" of a temporary cease-fire in the Suez Canal and, later, a unilateral peace treaty with Israel. As a result of the Egyptian peace campaign, a string of European Foreign Ministers would visit Cairo, and El-Sadat would be the first Egyptian President to visit France, fact that occurred in January 1975.

Under the influence of Saudi Arabia and Egypt a flexible block of moderate countries was established mainly in the periphery of the Middle East, the Arab world. In April of that year, the Presidents El-Sadat, of Egypt, and Hafez El-Assad of Syria, conferred with the new Saudi monarch, Khaled, to smooth over the political differences arisen by El-Sadat initiatives.

Syria decided to implement the type of mixed economy experienced by President El-Sadat, compensating some of the companies that were nationalized in 1960. The climax of this whole diplomatic offensive of El-Sadat was the visit by U.S. President Richard Nixon to Egypt, after touring the area, in June of that year.

Iran was incorporated in the new Egyptian Middle East policy. The Shah of Iran, Mohammed Reza Pahlavi, and the President Sadat exchanged visits in January and April 1975, achieving an accord to ensure concurrence among oil producers.

In 1973, as a result of the oil crisis, the Iran army was further strengthened and the number of American military advisers increased dramatically. At a cost of $3 billion dollars, the Shah acquired French ground to ground missiles, anti-tank TOW rockets; the tank arsenal was upgraded with 800

British Centurions. The air force was modernized with 180 fighter aircraft F-4, a hundred F-5E fighters, plus F-14 fighter aircrafts. Also, a set of KC-135 aerial refueling tankers, and more than 700 helicopters were added. A small navy was formed with 8 destroyers, 4 frigates and 12 torpedoes.

Iran was managing to sanctify his position in the Persian Gulf by signing an agreement with Iraq where they pledged to not further encourage the rebellion of the Kurds. On the other hand, the Shah reached certain commitment with King Khalid bin Abdul-Aziz Al-Saud of Saudi Arabia, which included performing joint pressures to eliminate the guerrillas in the region of Dhofar, in Oman, and neutralize the political influence of South Yemen.

The Soviet Union achieved nuclear parity with the United States with a huge inventory of intercontinental atomic missiles. The Kremlin gambit included getting hold of Yemen, Somalia and Ethiopia, the other way in of Suez. From the airports of Asmara in Eritrea and Khormaksar in Aden, they would dominate the air space of the Western Indian Ocean.

Followed this, the Soviet counterbalanced the U.S. *Poseidon* submarine fleet and naval base of Chagos, in the Indian Ocean, by introducing a fleet of *Echo* nuclear submarines in the Mozambique Channel, escorting the aircraft carriers *Kiev*, and destroyers *Burevestnik*, and enabling the Dahlak Archipelago in the Red Sea.

The solution was to realign all the countries in the area. They reinforced Iran militarily and increased naval patrolling; linking its naval bases to the British comm-system *Skynet* covering Singapore, Bahrain, Gann and Cyprus, and speeding up its nuclear ballistic program for submarines.

United States added its navy squad in Bahrain to the remaining points of support that England retained, such as the Maldives, Seychelles and Mauritius, and transformed the Chagos Archipelago in a gigantic military, nuclear and communications system.

With the subsequent Soviet lightning blitz to Afghanistan the Central Asian region was cut in two, flanking the regional military configuration built by United States, in a tweeze movement that engulfed Southeast Asia on one hand (from Kabul to the east: Cam-Rhan-Bay in Viet Nam) and the Middle East on the other (from Kabul to the west: Aden in Yemen and Massawa in Eritrea).

The fall of the Shah of Iran in 1979, left United States without a subrogate regional power in the area, except for Turkey in the North. But the Soviet Union could not take advantage of this tactical reversal, having collapsed as a state and social system in less than a decade.

But it is irrefutable that the atomic chess game between Washington and Moscow, engaged in a final of medium range missile pawns, where the Kremlin was technically lost. The duel between the Soviet SS-20, and American Pershing-II and Cruisers missiles[4] set forth by President Ronald Reagan, was the detonator of the Soviet collapse. The final blow was given by the White House projected "Star War", which left irrelevant all the Soviet military apparatus and rules of engagement.

The warlike doctrine of facing a wave of artillery and heavy tanks, which for decades had guided the behavior of the superpowers in the Cold War, entered into crisis in the Gulf war. This regional conflict forced the United States to develop a campaign of annihilation, with sweeping aerial strikes and smart weapons (*tomahawk*). In order to accomplish the operation, they needed to deploy speedily the aircraft carriers, a critical mass of soldiers, war arsenal and logistics. This electronic warfare was guided from a structure favored by an array of satellites, electronic intelligence and global positioning systems.

Despite the new American orientation in Asia, NATO rushed to develop a physical presence in the Indian Ocean. U.K. retained the *Skynet* system involving Singapore, Bahrain, Gann and Cyprus, with bases in a number of strategic islets with center in the Maldives, Mauritius, Vacoas, Simonstown, in South Africa, and the security zones of Iran and Saudi Arabia.

It was also added the American naval formation of the Seventh Fleet. This new type of lightning war requires that the United States should engage in new alliances (with Pakistan, India and the future Afghanistan) that make possible to launch quick action responses. Everything point out to the Middle, Center and Far East as main theaters of such actions.

The West didn´t trust entirely the advances achieved by its diplomacy on the Arab flank, maintaining its policy of strengthening Israel militarily. In April 1975 it was estimated that Israel already had more than 2,000 tanks and about 520 combat jet fighters; In addition, Israel kept equipping with Lance and Jericho ballistic missiles while Egypt and Syria did the same with Frog and Scud ballistic missiles.

For the industrialized West, large consumers of the raw material of the area, it was vital to ensure freedom of navigation through the Indian Ocean and control its shipping and air routes. Western strategists immediately profiled the Indian Ocean and the Persian Gulf as a future focus of conflicts due to oil issues and the Soviet presence in South Yemen and Somalia.

All this simultaneously with the importance of other cardinal raw materials in the area, like the Indian cotton, Tin and rubber from Malaysia and Indonesia, copper, gold and diamonds in Africa and the Strait of Bab-El-Mandeb, input and output of the Red Sea. This way, the oil, the states of the Gulf and Israel would be the parallels for Western military strategy and policy.

The era of military bases and secret military pacts has not ended. For this reason, the current Afghan scenario will cover much more than the eradication of the Taliban.

The long-standing duel between Pakistan and India is flavored with atomic weapons, a promise to get more complicated. China is growing at an alarming rate in the military sphere and thus, their demands on Taiwan.

The former soviet republics of the Caucasus and Central Asia are a powder keg. The Turkey-Armenian clash is only a matter of time, as it is Georgia with Azerbaijan, and Azerbaijan with Iran. On the other hand, Turkey wants to regain the Mosul oil, now part of Iraq.

Iran aspires to gobble up the Persian Gulf emirates. The Kurdish issue is not resolved, as it is not the feud between Islamic and Christians in the Sudan. Lastly, Yemen, Syria and Iraq are candidates to fragment under ethnic traces.

Cuba: Terrorism within the Revolution

Any formulation of the world major political and military powers policy concerning the fight against terrorism would be incomplete without in-depth analysis and understanding the nature and extent of Cuba's terrorist and subversive activities that had taken place out of the public view.

You cannot fight terrorism without taking in account Castro´s Cuba. You cannot understand terrorism without studying Cuban last five decades. You cannot stop terrorism ignoring the dealings of Havana. But ironically, Cuba's campaign of violence is not actually of great concern to many countries, including the United States, a big mistake.

Cuba is clearly not the sole source of violence and instability in the third world, but was the most important one and is the most experience, and its activities had militarized and internationalize what would otherwise be local conflicts. A country-by-country examination during the last five decades of Cuba's activities in Latin America, the Caribbean, Africa and countries in the Middle East makes clear that Cuba has campaigned to promote actual insurgencies and terrorism.

Unlike the attention the subject has received in the West, Cuban global interaction with terrorist and revolutionary groups has generated relatively little research. Because the Cuban government carefully guards hard data regarding its subversive and terrorist activities, Cuban scholarly research on the subject has not surfaced[1].

Moreover, the scarcity of research conducted by Afro Asian themselves deprives us of a valuable mirror, in which we could view both the extent and effectiveness of Cuban subversive initiatives in the region as well as Cuba's undermine to a major concern in the case of Latin America and Middle East: stability. Unfortunately, one is left to wonder that this is because they find Cuba's role in those regions less significant than their counterparts in the West: another big mistake.

Most works on the subject previously tended to focus on Cuba's relations with the Soviet Union in order to explain Cuba's objectives as well as the seeming degree of independence Cuba enjoys in those areas This level of analysis is used mainly because Cuba's relatively wide international projection is unusual for a country with such limited resources. It is generally accepted that decades ago, in Africa, Latin America or the Middle East Cuba was neither a proxy of the Soviet Union nor a totally autonomous actor.

Despite the lack of a comprehensive view of Cuba's involvement in other continents, this is perhaps the key factor that explains its visibility on the international scene. Contact with Africa, Latin America and the Middle East, one of the most significant initiatives of the Cuban Revolution, has extended the scope and reach of Cuba's international relations further than ever before.

Apart from the major powers, and the extinct Soviet Union no other Latin American country not even Brazil which also has a dynamic international policy has yet matched Cuba's far-reaching commitments.

There is not any country in the world, not a political elite, or a head of state during the XX century that could match the terrorist and subversive projection of Castro´s brother Cuba; not even the extinct Soviet Union, or yet the Libya of mercurial Muamar Khadafy, or the Assad dynasty of Syria, or the eccentrics of North Korea, or the arachnid movements of Yasser Arafat PLO.

None of these countries, not any of these movements, no one of those terrorist bosses deployed such a vast organization, limitless material resources, intelligence mechanisms, trained personnel, targets and policies than Havana's Castro brother terrorist and subversive actions.

In places whose primary needs are for economic development, social equity, and greater democracy, Cuba compounded the existing problems by encouraging violence.

Havana's terrorist activities rarely make headlines and nearly always avoid serious inquiry. The Cuban leadership has avoided any mention of the subject even in their propaganda, style that contrasts sharply with the Middle East terrorist organizations.

Cuba has worked to unite traditionally splintered radical groups behind a commitment to armed struggle with Cuban advice and material assistance. Cuba has trained committed cadres in urban and rural guerrilla warfare to assume power by force; supplied or arranged for the supply of weapons; encouraged terrorism in the hope of provoking indiscriminate violence and repression; used military aid and advisors to gain influence over violent factions and radical governments.

Cuba has provided advise, safe haven, communications, training, and some financial support to several violent international organizations. Cuba is quick to exploit legitimate grievances for its own ends. But its strategy is not based on appeals to the "people." Instead, Cuba concentrates on developing self-proclaimed "vanguards" committed to violent action.

Until Fidel Castro's ascent to power, Cuba lacked a national foreign policy tradition. Cuba has reached a prominent position in international arena as well as exercising military and political influence at the regional level. Castro's emphasis on the development of a proactive foreign policy has taken precedence over the actual needs of the Cuban people and has without any doubt, become Castro's most important achievement next to militarization. Cuba's influence in Central America, the Caribbean, the southern cone of Africa, and the Gulf of Aden is comparable only to that exercised by the major Western powers.

Castro's international prestige resulted from his own personality. Within the ethical structure the revolution, he was the political and moral leader to Cuba's power elite. His ability to lead derives from his stature as the triumphant leader of his country's revolution, his skills as manipulator of the Cuban masses, and his role as ideological fountain to the revolutionary elite and the Cuban nation.

Fidel Castro's foreign policy can be seen as an extension of his own climb to power, symbolized by the "voluntarism" of armed violence irrespective of the existence of "objective conditions." Yet the history of Cuba's foreign policy must be couched within the context both of its domestic structural considerations and the dynamics of external political conditions. It is precisely the internal and external dimensions, and not a rigidly-held orthodox theory, which have historically shaped Cuba's foreign policy initiatives.

Castro's brother resentment of the United States, their espousal of Marxist-Leninist ideology and alliance with the former Soviet Union became the forces that steered the Revolution's foreign policy. Within these parameters, Cuba has sought to maneuver in ways that enhance the elite domestic power and international prestige as well as contribute to expanding Cuba's presence and influence in world affairs.

Fidel and Raul Castro's Cuba presents a constant dichotomy. On the one hand, the nation's internal socio-economic process corresponds to the traditional limitations of an underdeveloped country. These limitations correspond to a pre-industrial mode of production, a mono-cultural agricultural system; demographic imbalances; scarcity of energy resources; low levels of technical and scientific development; and, weak or undeveloped political institutionalization.

Additionally, the Castro's regime has been confronted with a series of economic crises leading to the continuing pauperization of an already underdeveloped economy. Superimposed on these internal factors is the leadership's drive to exert a global foreign policy. Simply put, Cuba does not count with either the internal resources nor with a "historical national will" to undertake foreign initiatives dictated by the Castro's worldview.

The development and continuity of Cuba's relations with numerous foreign countries have to a great extent been facilitated by Castro's brother long tenure in power. Other Latin American countries also attempted diplomatic initiatives toward Afroasian's newly independent countries in the early sixties, but their initiatives were soon thwarted when their countries suffered abrupt changes in government[2].

Any analysis of Cuba's international military involvement must take into account the potential constraints of Cuba's domestic situation. Cuba's internal economy imposes serious strategic limitations on Castro's expansionist political strategies. Fidel and Raul Castro's range of international options is further constrained by the following internal factors:

The ever-increasing popular dissatisfaction with the regime; the Soviet Union's growing influence inside Cuba's institutions, especially the military, in the three first decades; Castro's brother loss of credibility vis-a-vis Cuba's post-revolutionary generation; and, the regime's unfulfilled economic promises.

Castro's strategy for dealing with Cuba's internal crisis is the development of a militaristic foreign policy which augments his personal prestige and power at home. Cuba's ever-increase economic and military dependence, first on the Soviet Union, later on Venezuela is a consequence of this strategy of military involvement in the Third World.

We may, therefore, assume that Fidel and Raul Castro's proactive foreign policy and his ever-increasing ties to tile the former Soviet Union and actual Venezuela are directly related to their needs to consolidate their power base at home.

Sponsorship of terrorism is a longstanding and major part of Cuba's foreign policy. Training and supporting small bands of terrorists, often with third country weapons (such as from Vietnam) costs relatively little. The American anti-terrorist campaign was never directed at Cuba, but at more obvious offenders.

Despite its long involvement in promoting violence, Havana has never been spotlighted as have Libya's Muammar Khadafy or Iran's Ayatollah Khomeini, been more dangerous than them because the U.S. public is not aware of it.

At best, we may enumerate certain primary motivations of Cuba's foreign policy during Fidel and Raul Castro's decades in power. These include the consolidation of military and political power inside Cuba. The internationalization of the Cuban experience as a way of breaking continental isolation. The promotion of Castro's prestige and influence in the international arena; and the obtainment of ever-increasing levels of Soviet (fist) and Venezuela (later) economic assistance.

Concerning the US. the Cuban strategy has been the creation of anti-capitalist totalitarian states in Latin America and the promotion of subversive and terrorist movements in the Hemisphere. Also, the diffusion of U.S. military power away from Cuba and to other geographical areas. The erosion of the Inter-American defense system.

By 1959, the Soviet Union had firmly consolidated its position as one of the two superpowers in a bipolar world. As such, the preservation of this position was the primary driving force behind its foreign policy.

This fact of life was extremely difficult for Fidel Castro to understand; he could not comprehend the Soviet Union's caution in providing support to insurrectionary movements around the world.

In spite of the fact that Cuba's economy became increasingly dependent on the Soviet Union during the 1960's, 1970's and 1980's the former maintained a foreign policy often at odds with that of the latter. This fact may lead us to assume that the mere existence of increasing economic dependence does not, by itself, explain the differences and similarities between the USSR's and Cuba's foreign policies.

The theory which claims that Castro has tried to maintain a totally independent foreign policy on those years fails to explain certain phenomena such as the "merger" between both intelligence agencies, the KGB and the DGI, the jointly coordinated USSR-Cuba military action in Angola (cover) Ethiopia, and Cuba's active support for the Afghanistan invasion, the Palestinians, the Libyan Khadafy and the South Yemen regime.

Castro's attempts in the 1960's to bring revolutionary, anti-American regimes to power failed. His support for guerrillas and terrorist groups in Guatemala, Venezuela, and Bolivia only produced violence and suffering to those countries and their people, which repudiated violence as a means to achieve power. Violence resulted in military regimes coming to power in several Latin American countries[3].

Likewise, those who consider that Cuba's foreign policy is totally reactive to the coercion of the United States fail to explain the former's involvement in Angola, Ethiopia, Venezuela, Nicaragua, and Ecuador at a critical time of wide-ranging negotiations with the latter.

If anything, it becomes quite difficult to establish "principles" or "rules of conduct" which dominate Cuba state-to-state relations (or the latter's involvement in, and support of, guerrillas and terrorist cells).

Furthermore, certain additional factors must be analyzed to gain a clearer understanding of Cuba foreign policy relationship. Among these are: the role of the U.S. in the post-Vietnam period; the influence of decolonization and the non-aligned movement; de-Stalinization and the Sino-Soviet split; East-West military relations; Middle East crisis.

In addition, more recent factors to consider include: the political instability in Latin America; the lack of U.S. interest in Latin America and Africa; the US. military problems in Afghanistan and Iraq; and the global economic crisis, among others.

In order to understand Castro-Soviet friction, you have to deal with the soviet power structure infight. Between the Russians and the non-Russians between the different international strategies and the groups around them.

There was never a Castro-Soviet friction. There were frictions between Castro and some groups inside the USSR. Castro had his problem with Nikita Khrushchev's group, but he had the total support of Mikhail Suslov, Alexander Shelepin, Boris Ponomarev, Marshall Andrei Grechko, etc. Castro played inside the soviet politics infight.

He was cautious during the first years of Leonid Brezhnev, until Leonid made a deal with Mikhail Suslov-Grechko (the partners of Castro). That is why Castro went all the way with the Czech invasion in 1968, because it was in Suslov-Grechko agenda.

In 1964, during a meeting between Castro and Suslov, together with the heads of Latin American Communist Parties, it was decided to handed Latin America to the Cubans, and in 1968, the KGB decided to replace totally the Czechs with the Cuban Intelligence Directorate and Army Intelligence for their world operation.

Although it may be said that Cuba foreign policy overall rate of success in the last decades has been quite impressive. Furthermore, Cuba's foreign relations have served as a catalyst for its transformation in to an international intelligence and political power.

Likewise, the Soviet Union's and Venezuelan's levels of assistance to Cuba may be considered low in relation to the political rewards gained by the formers. Fidel and Raul Castro's preeminence in Cuban politics will continue to dictate a foreign policy beyond the socio-economic possibilities of the Cuban nation.

Any on-going inquiry in to Cuba's future involvement in subversion, terrorism and US destabilization, especially now in Latin America, must include new factors and perspectives that have been, heretofore, largely overlooked by most of the international specialist on terrorism and intelligence agencies.

Among Cuba's wide-ranging activities in Africa, Latin America and the Middle East some more successful than others military involvement and civilian internationalist cooperation figure as the most prominent. These two aspects of Cuban activities have involved guerrilla training to "liberation movement" combatants, the deployment of thousands of soldiers, as well as the provision of teachers, doctors, technicians, construction workers, etc., to several Latin America, Africa and Middle East countries.

The regime's early efforts to duplicate the Cuban model failed in both Africa and Latin America. Nevertheless, Cuba's contacts with guerrilla groups in the sixties reaped rewards in the seventies. The infrastructure that had been created in terms of personal relationships, intelligence gathering and logistical support allowed Cuba to respond boldly to new targets of opportunity especially in Guinea-Bissau, in Angola, in the Caribbean, in Venezuela, in Ecuador and Bolivia.

It should be emphasized that in addition to violence and terrorism, Cuba have been for more than five decades, the most vocal and active proponents of anti Americanism. Despite the collapse of the Soviet Union, Castro continues to undermine U.S. policies in the Middle East in several ways: a) by portraying U.S. actions and diplomacy in the region as those of an aggressor, seeking to impose hegemony by force, particularly in Iraq and the perpetration of unjustified economic sanctions on Iraq and Iran; b) by portraying the U.S. as the main obstacle to a peaceful settlement of the Israel/Arab conflict; and c) by discrediting U.S. policies and seeking support for Cuba at the U.N.[4]

Most of the covert operations in support of this strategy are planned and coordinated by several intelligence departments that brought together the expertise of the Cuban military and the General Directorate of Intelligence into operations that included secret training camps, networks for covert movement of personnel and materiel between Cuba and abroad, and sophisticated propaganda support.

The bureaucratic apparatus directly responsible for foreign policy, and legal and illegal policy (except the MINFAR), has 8,000 to 10,000 persons. He is in charge of diplomatic, consular, trade, military, technical, and public liaison, as well as intelligence agents; the promotion of subversion; guerrilla training; propaganda; front organizations; illegal trade; contraband; drugs; and special commands with deadly missions.

Cuba's espionage apparatus (the DGI), one of the largest and most efficient on the planet, with more than 10,000 spies, analysts, technical personnel, etc., has been active on a global scale. Cuban intelligence officers are present in every Cuban diplomatic mission encouraging terrorism and any kind of violence in the hope of provoking indiscriminate belligerence and repression and generalized legitimacy and attract new converts.

The DGI rapidly dominated not only the setting up of undercover operations, but also the falsification of documents, cryptography, training of operatives, theft of secret information, the implantation of illegal centers, the penetration of governments and armed forces, disinformation, assassination of political figures, and technological transfers.

Initially, the DGI concentrated its activities on counterintelligence activities and information gathering. During the 1970s, in Europe, Africa, Latin America, and the United States, the DGI established both legal and underground networks. Its efforts were concentrated on operational support activities by means of technical support, underground groups, and specialized, instructional and informational services. At the same time, it undertook operational duties through its underground network and legal centers and the Department of Liberation.

According to DGI defector Hidalgo Castro, under terms of agreements the operations of the DGI would be closely coordinated with the KGB, a fact of special value to Moscow in regard to operations in the United States, where DGI had been utilizing the stream of Cuban refugees as a cover for the infiltration of agents. The most powerful of all these departments has been Liberation which was responsible for subversion and international terrorism. It trained guerrillas and those units that would eventually be incorporated into other theaters of operation such as in the Congo and Guinea Bissau. It has also trained militias in Guinea and Congo Brazzaville.

Throughout this whole period, the Castro government sent Cuban contingents of troops who served as praetorian guards to the presidents and such figures as Sekou Toure of Guinea, Siaka Stevens of Sierra Leone, Salvador Allende of Chile, Agostino Neto and Eduardo Dos Santos of Angola, Francisco Macias Nguema of Guinea, Mengistu Haile Mariam in Ethiopia, Massemba Debat in Congo Brazzaville, Gaston Soumialot of Zaire, Lula da Silva of Brazil, Hugo Chavez of Venezuela.

Liberation has also worked alongside Marxist organizations and groups, as well as with Maoists (such as the Zanzibar UMMA party), Trotskyites (in Guatemala, Peru, Nigeria, and the Congo), radical nationalists, terrorists and even religious groups.

During the Cold War, the DGI joined the KGB for the gathering of economic, technological, and military information from U.S., European, and NATO sources. Specialized Cuban well trained agents were planted undercover in the United States, Spain, Italy, and Canada.

The target of the DGI in the U.S. has been the White House, the CIA, the FBI, the Department of State, the Congress, the Immigration Department and the anti-Castro organizations. As for Western Europe, the intelligence service has been the target, namely that of France, Germany, Italy, Spain and Great Britain. The DGI has accomplished its objectives through the recruitment of governmental officials and agents and contact with citizens, universities, and the press.

Castro in 1974 created another intelligence arm, the America Department, under his direct control. The AD with around 300 agents has been working in carefully selected target countries within the Western Hemisphere, including Cuba's interests section in Washington, D.C and Cuba's mission to the United Nations in New York City[5].

The Americas' Department is an intelligence organization that maintains overt and covert operations in the United States and Latin America. The Department of Americas, on the other hand, operated under less supervision and pressure from Moscow. The America Department has developed successful large scale operations in the Caribbean and Central America.

While it works parallel to the DGI, on occasions the two overlap. For example, in the government of Salvador Allende in Chile, the DGI and the Americas' Department worked through two different groups. The DGI supported the MIR, while the Americas' Department was in charge of the left wing of the Socialist Party. The Department of the Americas has suffered several defeats abroad, namely in Chile, Jamaica, Surinam, and Grenada.

Contact with all countries is maintained through a network of embassies, consulates, trade centers, cultural houses, and Latin American press offices, military and civil missions that serve simultaneously as information, recruitment, and subversion centers. Where a representative from Cuba is not available, that country will fall under the auspices of a neighboring office.

Military missions are not connected to embassies and maintain their own communications network with Havana; likewise, DGI and Department of America posts also answer directly to Havana. Occasionally, an envoy sent to a country is responsible for all state-to-state relations such as in the cases of Algiers, Tanzania, Congo Brazzaville, Angola and Ethiopia in the 1970s and even more recently in Venezuela, Nicaragua, Bolivia and Ecuador.

Up to recently, the Cuban armed forces became a formidable offensive military machine. The Ministry of Armed Forces is the second or third most important military force on the continent. The structure of this Cuban army is typically Latin American.

After the 1970s, this massive and sluggish army became a highly specialized force with high fire-power and mobility. It has nine regular divisions and eighteen reserves and is presently an important element in the implementation of Cuba's foreign policy. The MINFAR command is guided by a group of graduates from Soviet war colleges.

Raul Castro, actual head of state, has taken over the security and intelligence operations of the MININT and the MINFAR. Foreign policy decisions are undertaken in a compartmentalized manner by Fidel Castro before and Raul Castro currently, in conjunction with specific persons and institutions.

Cuban military intelligence personnel selected for clandestine operations in Latin America, Africa, and the Middle East went through an elaborate training program conducted by Cuban instructors in Havana, with special sessions in surrounding cities. In addition to the language and customs of the area to which they are assigned, and typical intelligence operation such as infiltration procedures and photograph techniques, the Cubans instructs in handling explosives.

Several camps in Cuba are dedicated specifically to military training, in Pinar del Rio Province and Guanabo, east of Havana. The camps can accommodate several hundred trainees. Many Cuban instructors are officers and veterans of Cuban expeditionary forces in Africa. Training consists of instruction by Cuban cadres in sabotage, explosives, military tactics, and weapon use. Groups from El Salvador, Nicaragua, Guatemala, Costa Rica, Honduras, Colombia, Grenada, the Dominican Republic, Jamaica, Haiti, Chile, and Uruguay have been trained in these facilities.

Each year Cuba offers hundreds of scholarships to carefully selected foreign students on the Isle of Youth alone. In sum, in their systematic, long-range campaign to destabilize governments through violent revolutionary agitation and terrorism Cuba's infrastructure is a multifaceted yet carefully coordinated mechanism

A review of Cuba's international involvement, provide some background for the promotion of terrorism and revolutions. Most studies on Cuba's foreign policy conclude that one of its primary objectives has been to ensure the survival of the revolutionary power elite.

The maneuverings and alignments deemed necessary to achieve that end have been made in accordance with the moment in history in which the Revolution took place and with the Cuban leadership's interpretation of the international situation it has confronted at any given moment. The policy towards Latin America, Africa and Middle East, to different degrees and through different means, reflects this survivalist objective.

Cuban history is sated with terrorism, notably since the early 1930s when several such organizations fought against Dictator General Gerardo Machado, for nearly a decade. The most lethal, called the ABC, was the one who invented many of the techniques of modern urban terrorism, such as coordinated bombing, experience that later the Cubans have passed on in training camps around the world to thousands of Argentineans, Brazilians, Chileans, Colombians, Ecuadorans, Hondurans, Nicaraguans, Salvadorans, and Uruguayans, to name a few in Latin America, and to Basques, Namibians, Palestinians West Germans, and Yemenis.

Since 1948 when, as a young student, Fidel Castro participated in the violence that rocked Colombian society and distributed anti-U.S. propaganda, he has been guided by two objectives: a commitment to violence and a virulent anti-Americanism. His struggle since and his rule in Cuba have been characterized primarily by these goals[6].

Fidel Castro and his brother Raul Castro wrote and spoke publicly of terrorism even before their insurrection against Cuban dictator, General Fulgencio Batista, who seized power in April 1952.

During Castro's fight for power, his 26th of July organization committed acts of urban terrorism as did his Rebel Army operating in the mountains. Fidel Castro would use every aspect of modem terrorism: American hostages, kidnappings of public figures, political assassinations, rural guerrillas, urban terrorism, extortion of businessmen and air piracy[7].

After Castro's Department of Rebel Intelligence learned in late May 1958 that two of dictator Batista's airplanes had been loaded with U.S. arms and ammunition in the U.S. Naval Base at Guantánamo, the Castro brothers began planning a major terrorist operation against Americans in Cuba. That summer, 26th of July Movement (M-26) terrorists under Raul Castro's command kidnapped fifty-seven North Americans, including a busload of twenty-seven U.S. sailors and Marines, and two Canadians[8]. The ensuing international hostage crisis threatened to result in U.S. military action against the M-26, an event that could have thwarted Castro's seizure of power.

Raul Castro also organized the first history's international plane hijackings, which resulted in the wreck of the aircraft and the deaths of 17 people in 1958.

The exportation of armed revolution and terrorism was also present since the onset of Castroism. When it first came to power, the Castro regime was looking to reproduce elsewhere the rural-based guerrilla warfare experience of Castro's 26th of July Movement in Cuba.

There are an untold number of states in Latin America, Africa Asia and the Middle East where, for the past decades in which Cuba has intervened and fomented terrorist groups, guerrillas and coup d'états by supplying weapons, training, and financing espionage and material assistance.

Castro's targets for subversion and terrorism have included Latin American military dictators like General Rafael Trujillo of the Dominican Republic as well as democratic leaders Romulo Betancourt of Venezuela and Jose Napoleon Duarte of El Salvador.

Much of what is known about the Cuban government supports of terrorism has been gleaned by U.S. and other Western intelligence agencies from a handful of defectors. According to the testimony of Cuban defector Orlando Hidalgo, Castro's intelligence apparatus recruits the potential guerrillas and terrorists, and fly them to Cuba from Latin America via Paris.

In Paris they were provided with false documentation for further travel, either Russian or Czech visas. From Paris, the men would fly to Moscow or Prague and from there to Havana where they would be assigned to training camps[9].

The Cuban training camps instructed as many as 1,500 men a year in guerrilla and terrorist techniques. The various nationalities generally were kept apart for security reasons. A Venezuelan, Juan de Dios Marin, received his training in late 1960, in a seaside estate named Tarara and later at the Cold Mines camp in the Sierra Maestra. He received instruction in weapons, explosives, robbing banks, grabbing payrolls, destroying factories, and killing policemen.

Cuba retained its clandestine ties with remnants of the insurgents and other pro-Cuban elements in Latin America, Africa and the Middle East. Cuba, has acted as the middle man for terrorist groups, in order to arrange arms supply. The terrorists and are normally provided false documentation by

Cuban agents in third countries and are flown to Cuba on civil aircraft under cover.

Panama has been used as a regular transit point for the Hemisphere to and from military training in Cuba, especially as a transit point for Colombian guerrillas coming from Havana. Cuba has taken advantage of Mexico's open society and its extensive presence there to carry out support activities for insurgencies in other countries. Mexico is a principal base for Cuban contacts logistical support, and international activities.

Cuban agents in Mexico engaged in bank robberies to finance several terrorist groups from Latin America operating out of Mexico. Several dozen Mexicans received training in terrorism and guerrilla warfare in Sierra del Rosario, Pinar del Rio Province and in Guanabo beach, in eastern Cuba.

In his first years Castro got involve in the anti-colonial struggle, but also subverted democratically elected governments, participated in African civil wars, and promoted air piracy as well as drug trafficking.

In Africa, Castro exported his armed brigades during the Cold War. Cuban military personnel were involved in the Vietnam War, providing assistance in training but, most significantly, numerous captured American pilots were tortured by specialized English-speaking Cuban intelligence personnel.

And during the Vietnam War, Castro dispatched his henchmen to Hanoi to viciously torture U.S. POWs as documented by the historians Stuart Rochester and Frederick Riley's book *Honor Bound*. The most notorious of these torturers was known by the pseudonym of "Fidel", and has been identified by one of the formers POWs, Vecino Alegret, who was Cuba's Minister of Education for over ten years[10].

In the course of five decades, more than 30,000 militants of various continents and political affiliations -of these, 10,000 were Latin American- have been trained in guerrilla tactics and terrorism in Cuba.

Havana has provided sanctuary, communications, training and funds to every anti-American or anti-Western clandestine organization that employs or employed violence, such as the Italian Red Brigades, the Tupamaros of Uruguay, the Montoneros of Argentina, the Chilean MIR (Revolutionary Left Movement), the Palestinian commandos of George Habash; the Puerto Rican Macheteros, the armed factions of the Palestinian Liberation Organization (PLO), the Liberation Front of Carlos Semprun, Irish nationalists, Belgium's communist cells, Shiite militants from Hizb-Allah.

The first cadres of the Basque organization ETA (Euzkadi Ta Askatasuna) Basque Land and Freedom were instructed in the culture of terrorism by Cuba in 1964.

These courses have graduated a chilling international gallery that include the killer of Rue Marbeuf: Ilich Ramirez Sanchez (Carlos, The Jackal), Abu Nidal, Leila Khaled, Luis de la Puente Uceda, Mohammed Budia (the man of a thousand faces), the Colombians Manuel Marulanda (alias Straight shoot) and Jaime Bateman, the Nicaraguan Daniel Ortega, the Italian Gian Giacomo Feltrinelli, the Dominican Francisco Caamaño, and the Salvadoran Cayetano Carpio.

A religion of war

The Islam is a religion of war; the war as a way of spreading faith; and, the Quranic God is truly a "God's Army." It is a dramatic truth launched by the Islamic terrorists: "You of West know how to confront life, we the Islamic ones know how to confront death". In the *Bible*, the army is made of angels, in the Islam it belongs to Moslem fighters.

The religious characteristic of the Islam was always unknown for the Christianity, which conceives war as defensive and does not see its spiritual mission. Christianity accepted war as a reality of a world dominated by the sin of violence, but never saw the death in battle as the Supreme gesture, the highest act of faith. Opposite to Islam, Christianity sees love as the Supreme Act of faith, the most divine of its attitude. Although the Catholic Church has recognized the Christian fighter, it rarely extols it at the altar level.

The same as the patristic Christianity, Islam believes that the blood of the martyr is the semen of the religion. The profound meaning of the last attestation of faith, as Quintus Tertullian (155-230 a.c.) defined, points out that the injustice of one was the demonstration of the innocence of the other: forgiveness to the killer. "*Father, forgive them; for they know not what they do*", as Christ would say on the cross: "*Sanguis marthyrum, semen christianorum*", distorted in the conduct of the Turkish sultan Mehmet II, which with the decapitated head of a child set fire to the church of St. Sophia in Constantinople, one unfortunate day of 1453.

Now it is Islam who accumulates martyrs; they are today's kamikaze, the wind of God of the Japanese. The *Quran* praises and blesses their martyrs, to the point that the martyrdom that bears witness to faith is a central pilaster of the religion[1]. But there is a huge difference between this martyr and that of the Christian. The Christian martyr didn't fight or went to war, it was the ram sacrificed before injustice, like Christ: a meek lamb to the slaughter house to offer his life for a sin that annihilates him; that's why Jesus offers himself to be crucified for humanity.

For the *Quran* the martyr is a combatant, who spreads the Jihad over the world; human life is only a means on the hand of Allah. The Islamic martyr is not defenseless but causes death to another and does not offer his as a sacrifice for others. It is the bottomless abyss that separates a proposal of love and a destructive arrogance; the confrontation between sweetness and barbarism, the contrast between love and hate.

There are those who suggest that the Jihad culture will face in this new century a new, potentially constructive phase, a period of renewal of the Muslim world to modernity, the globalization of markets and communication from the Western world.

To the "moderate" or opposing elites in power in the Islamic world, and to the new generation of this elite, from Mohammed VI of Morocco to Jordan's Abdullah II Bin Al-Hussein, from the technocracy and Algerian military layer to the Indonesian President Wahid Gus Dur, all were posed with the choice to govern before the opportunity provided by history or disappear from the political scene.

If these elite bows to a current political unfavorable situation of political Islamism, the Muslim world must face a new explosion as much of confessional cast as ethnic and racial. Islam has absorbed from the West the idea of revolution and terrorism, but has rejected the peaceful and creative dimension of human reality that Christianity promotes as the positive vision on life. Also, it has not assimilated the creative value of work and the concept of enterprise on which the cultural and social development of the modern era was founded.

This is the reason why the company ethic and technique work the "pagan" world[2] assumed by contact with the West is incomprehensible in the Islamic world. It is precisely this concept of life versus death where lies the difference between the Western world and Islam, between the Islamic and Christian culture.

Terrorist, anarchist and nationalist groups traces the history of the West and has been an instrument of revolutions, which have influenced the life of their institutions. Terrorism embodied in the West was not a suicide event, although its performers may risk their lives. An instrument of the "pagan west", same as individual terrorism has become an element of the masses in the Islamic community. Islamic terrorism has expanded the meaning and power of the gesture in a scenario of global scale thanks to the communications system that shows events in real time, and is something that the entire Islamic community understands.

Islamic Jihad is one of the most significant phenomena of the twenty century and one of the unpredictable mysteries of the twenty-first century. From Wahhabism in Saudi Arabia to the fundamentalist Muslim Brotherhood organization, from ethnic tensions in Malaysia to the Pakistani dictatorship of generals, from the Integral Iranian regime of Ayatollah to the Palestinian Intifada, from the Algerian Muslim extremists to the Afghan regime of the Taliban, from Al-Qaeda and Hamas to the struggle between laicism and fundamentalism in Turkey.

The Islamic attack against the Christian world is sprouting across the globe: from Timor to the Moluccas and Mindanao. In Nigeria the Northern Muslims extort the Southern Christian lands. In Sudan the fundamentalist Hassan Abd-Allah Turabi is no longer present, but the persecutions against the Christians of the South continue. Why is this fact not a religious problem for the Catholic Church and other churches? Why is it so difficult to the Western world to acknowledge that Islam has replaced communism as their main political problem?

The caricature in the Western world is that terrorism is the absolute work of Al-Qaeda and the dead Osama Bin Laden, and in the West as well as the Islamic world the existence of a terrorist organization funded by the treasury of Saudi millionaires is taken for granted. Organized terror, capable of spreading death and horror throughout the world is not reduced to the extreme nihilism and religious hatred gestated by the Mullah in the mosques.

But Al Qaeda, as a branch of the Moslem Brotherhood, is just a mafia organization, a conglomerate that exercises the extortion in its Middle East environment. Considered the "holy war" is not practiced only with bombs and suicide bombers, but that has a financial circuit that runs through the world in several directions, from Europe to the United States from Indonesia to Australia, of the African continent to Russia.

The war of Islamic radicalism against the West can be seen, moreover, as an economic war, a conflict in which the Mujahidin do not necessarily carries the explosive under the tunic, but it is a well-educated youth who browses the Internet and practices its rating in the Western financial system.

This holy war is also a war of money, of the trade of gold and precious stones, the abduction of persons, the recycling of dirty money made through complex operations. It is the action of organizations which are neither transparent nor charitable and that mixed with skill crime and charity. Unlike the West Non-Governmental Organizations (NGOs), Saudi "charity", although of religious imprint, focuses exclusively their assistance to their coreligionists, and the color with which the message of the Quran is carried.

The Muslim perception of God is not that of the *Bible*. For the Islam, God is impossible to know ultimately. While it expresses its willingness in the Quran, never reveals himself; it is not a deity of love or benevolence, as the *Bible's*. The

Christian Jesus is Prophet and Son of God and Savior of mankind simultaneously, while Muhammad is only the transmitter of the divine word, because in Islam the human was not born with original sin and does not require a Redeemer.

The story, to Christianity, is a personal relationship of a human with God, in which the freedom of belief is guaranteed. Christianity is a personal religion, in which the freedom of God respects that of the human. The Christian God is "Father", not "Patriarch", and in the final analysis, the divine will of the Christian God only imposes on the human the will of the believer.

Islam worships the Biblical God but fights Christianity for considering it a falsification of the word of God. The *Bible* is the book of God's revelation that communicates freely with the human. Therefore, the status of the *Quran* is not the same as the Bible's. The *Quran's* God describes himself as "action" and communicates when he commands the believer[3]. Unlike Christianity, which accepts the distinction between Church and State, Islam does not distinguish the religious fact of the political and social, undeniably constituting a different universe of reference.

The difference between the two touches the roots of the dilemma of individual freedom that stays in parentheses in Islam, between the Christian "obedience" and the Islamic "subjugation." Islamic loyalty is substantially the passive type. Therefore, the theological, cultural and civil differences between Christianity and Islam affect the very structure of how the human lives, and the relationship of the human condition with the divine[4].

The model of the "Dialogic" approach of God's freedom and that of the human runs the entire biblical economy and therein is always autonomous before its God. To do the "will" of God is always choice of the believer. While the action of the

Christian God requires the free and voluntary collaboration of the creature, the *Quran* God claims it. The will of the *Quran* God will be imperative and is presented to the human in prescribed manner. There is no need for collaboration, but it imposes passive obedience; his divine will does not allow the human will.

The God of Mohammed is missing the humanism and the philanthropy of the divine God of Jesus, the Christ. The *Quran* God is not touched by the suffering of the human, does not love him, it only requires obedience[5]. The element that identifies and characterizes the rapport between Allah and the Muslim is the subjection, the outer dimension of the submission that subjugates its interior, while Christian obedience is found in the interior, which transcends the exterior[6]. Between Allah and the Muslim has been established, from the outset, a unilateral approach where the subjectivity of the believer is suppressed and thus the possibility of an exercise of thought, freedom and genuine will.

The divergence is not between Arabs and the West, but between Islam and Christianity, because the reason that divides them is theological and always thought about in conflict. Islam is instituted on the model of the "one", while Christianity is based on the "being", which consists of plurality, in the concept of the distinction of God and creation, which is autonomous.

For the Islam, the *Quran* revelation is the beginning of a world civility since it arranges the whole social framework, the Moslem world community, on behalf of God and as a result of its word. Christianity could distinguish in what dimension the faith and the culture interweave, something that allowed it to adapt itself to the cultural diversities and distinguish between the individual and the society, nature and the divine grace.

Creation is a fundamental concept of Christianity as a reality apart from God, although in God has its origin and foundation. For Islam, creation only exists as a steady production of the divine will: God is the only cause of all the events and, therefore, the concept of nature has no autonomy and is different from that of Christianity.

Christianity, like Judaism, has established with such as a foundation the idea of a bilateral fulfillment with God, of an "Alliance", a participation in which the human remains as such, and can deal with the divine nature. Islam, on the other hand, cannot conceive anything other than total subjection and does not base the bilateral in its relationship with God. Christian Scripture is the word of God and men at the same time, and the *Quran* is only an act of God in which the Mohammedan does not intervene; hence the Islamic monism is total.

The *Quran* assumes the single reality in which God manifests itself and such a thing as a human is not an act of God's revelation, but a desire for obedience to his word. The *Quran*, then, is more than just a creation and does not establish a communion with God, but a subjection of the human to the single cause of the world, the recognition that God is the lonely reality. Islam maintains pantheism, the totality of the divine, but entirely excludes God from nature; it cites the biblical text but excludes the *Bible*. Biblical memory is entirely included in the only revealing Act of God, which is the Quran.

The infidel has a false existence, which does not recognize nature and its radical dependency on the exclusive divine causality. The infidel contradicts the ontology of the single God-cause, that is the essence of the Quranic revelation. Islam has been able to absorb two dualistic religions as the manichaeism[7] and the zoroastrianism[8] because it has introduced dualism in the distinction between the existence of the Muslim, according to the only God, and the malignant existence of the non-Muslim, which is null for not recognizing it. That is why the presence of the infidel, the non-believer, should be denied to affirm the only reality, that of divine causality.

There is no ontology of the created entity in Islam; the idea of evil does not concur, but sprouts a definition of negativity, an impugnation to the uniqueness of the divine cause, who rebels against the only reason of its existence. The whole word of the *Quran* is a verb that recounts a Christian story but is separated from it by a powerful religious institution in which the only God has become the single cause and the reality of the existence.

The political spectrum of the present era centers in the new totalitarian threat. The totalitarianism of the XX century was the communist and fascist, at present very difficult to replicate. But this does not mean that the totalitarian danger has vanished definitively, as its essence, its potential and essentially impalpable spectrum, a substance that is perennially emerging to negatively affect the individual, the concrete possibility of the power of a man over a man, still remains.

If communism was projected as a form of political totalitarianism, Islam can be represented as a concrete way of religious totalitarianism. The totalitarian danger for the third millennium is characterized by the fanaticism and the terrorism of radical Islam. But is a fanaticism that has nothing to do with the religious, although it formally uses religion in the absence of an ideology capable of legitimizing its fiercest violence. This totalitarianism aims its destructive force not only in the direction of the Western liberal-democratic, but it also confronts the 'moderate Islam'.

We are then facing a bipolar division between the Islamic and the non-Islamic world. The western rational still proclaims that this is not a war of religions, as evidenced by the pathetic willingness of the Vatican to insist on 'dialogue', as in the Synod of Vescovi.

The Muslim does not distinguish between Christianity and the West; moreover, the Islamists have not censored suicide in battle, because they consider it a religious act, an act of "holy war" and not a simple war; faced to the heroism of the fanatic decided to give his life,

This is the subtle form of nihilism that permeates the Islamic thought and that projects its annihilating consummation: the action of war, its characteristic of civil and social action. Simultaneously, annulment, death in battle, is the way by which the Muslim enters the second space of creation and is not, as Christianity, God's life but an award-winning existence.

The West modernity with its technological universe, with its philosophy of life, of freedom, of democracy, asphyxiates the Islamic people and only produces tension inside the Islamic power structures. In front of this mimesis the terror war is the only instrument to confront and deny the development of the "infidel" West as a model.

While the Moslem Brotherhood and Al-Qaeda blesses the crusade against United States, the catholic world sees in Islamism the vindication of the globalization of those excluded from power. It's the popular Church that supported the Sandinista movement, for example, fascinated by the "righteous sword of Islam" and is qualified as the fifth anti-Western column by the theological Church, which preludes a schism within Catholicism through his Gnostic heresy[9].

The history of the XX century teaches that democracies were fearful and remitting to totalitarianism and the result was very sad. One of the lessons is that peace is born from violence and, like freedom, is a treasure that has to be fought for with all available means. It is a terrifying but necessary anomaly.

The unsatisfied Western "left" hoists the motto of fighting for peace and freedom, but such a political gesture reveals in its depth the negative will to oppose their own diktat of the peace and of the freedom (to defend itself with everything available), of which it finishes like its most staunchest nemesis.

Deprived of ideas, disappointed of its own historical socialistic ideal and confused in the criterion of what to adopt to solve the present dilemma, this "left" tries then to justify the unjustifiable presenting it as a victim of their own totalitarian danger personified in the fanatic and the terrorist. We are in a situation in which in the end of the last century Muslim totalitarian power (embodied in the Iraqi Saddam Hussein, Ayatollah, etc.) annihilated millions of people before the silent moral darkness of the international left.

In the middle of its confusion, the "left" proposes the slogans, the flags and the rhetoric, like the only action to defend the cause of the peace, forgetting that the ideological pacifism of the 1960´s and 1970´s also was granting the victim's role to Soviet Josef Stalin, to the Chinese Mao Zedong and to the Cambodian Pol-Pot.

The evil for the West is not the "yellow danger", but its incapability to understand the reality of which we have turned into "Islamic land", ground in which the Muslim must exercise the jihad, the war for the faith, for claiming the Islamic law[10] instead of the law of the State. That's why, the war launched by the political Islam is against the concept of the State, and the way it is conducted depends on the circumstances. The jihad is not the "Islamization" of the Islamic, but the "Islamization" of the Western society[11].

In our secular concept of "multi-ethnic" to consider Islam as such is a mistake, as this is a religious and social totality, a "multi-juridical" reality that denies the Westal concept of state and not a culture in the Western sense. Political Islam considers Christianity as a dead body and the West as its real enemy; if it is dangerous to ignore the first consideration; more lethal is to ignore the second.

The essence of the western way of life is the respect for the lifestyle of the fellow man, in other words: the civil liberty of worship, speech, minority rights, of suffrage, the political will of the majority, market, trade unionism, the movement of the person, and so on. This has not been achieved peacefully or without paying a price; it has cost wars and bloody revolutions, and challenges from totalitarian ideologies like fascism and communism.

The Islamic "charity" is not aim to alleviate the suffering of the poor, but to promote the preaching of Islam, and in this perspective "humanitarian" funding is a vehicle less noble than the "other", as it occurs in Afghanistan, Chechnya, Palestine and Kashmir. This tricky situation into humanitarian action constitutes an Islamic economic project hostile to the West, in which the love for the neighbor is based on proselytism via radicalism.

The Western World denies its link with the Islam avoiding the reappear of coexistence in fear of a contamination in the religion. This viscerally anti-religious *res-public* is considered by the Islam as an anti-Islamic project, from a foreign culture that rests in the concept of secularized theology, of civil religion, through which one lives excluding severely God and religion.

The current alarm with the Islamic world does not reside in historical and social causes. For Islam, the European multiculturalism is only about how to guarantee the values of polytheism. For the Islam it is a question of a religious war against a Greco-Roman civil culture, a lustful way of life and a freedom without roots.

The Islamic intellectuals in Europe, like Tariq Ramadan, are preachers of a political Islamism that targets the religious conquest of Europe, of what we can call euro-Islam[12]. Thanks to their rhetorical capacity they have been capable of grouping the Islamic youth in Europe within an anti-globalist religious identity, with an anti-western version originated from the third-world baggage.

They portray themselves as champions of the so-called intercultural dialogue, masters of a "moderate" Islam, capable of spreading Islamic doctrine within a religious reformist record.

These "moderate" Islamic preachers have been praised by intellectuals such as Bernard Kouchner and Bernard-Henry Lévy with their anti-Semite disguised propensities. Also, theologians like Olivier Clement, who considers them important in the affirmation of the Muslim identity in Europe. Andre Glucksmann has published in Italian newspapers that such preachers, like Ramadan, are not Taliban's or supporters of the Algerian Islamic extremists but teachers with which one can talk about Aristotle and René Descartes.

But under their academic varnish hides masters of integral nationalism that grants no space to modernity, except to introduce a "moratorium" to the stoning of the adulteress.

For those preachers Islam will not "Europeanize" but will convert to Islam. According to them, in the course of one or two generations, the current Europe, imprisoned in its self-denial, will have to dispose of secularity, to embrace a theoretical vision inspired by Quran laws. In the actual 21st century, the European "Umma", composed by millions of Muslims, will be a continent "des-territorialized" by traditional Islam.

The cardinal debate of ideas focuses on Islam, in its urgent mission of transcendence and intolerance to human freedom has just begun. Those who are wrapped in a frivolous and cinematic vision of a multi-cultural world tutored by postmodernism deny this fact, emphasizing alleged pluralism in Islam. The minority nature of his *Drang nach Western*, simply ignore the challenge of ideas that is imposed on civilization.

They ignore this religion with its unprecedented and poetic prophetic mission; with its warrior spirit founded on the divine; its "nomadism" and "communalism" derived from its spiritual School of death. They ignore from Islam its moral basis without appeal, its fragmented instruction of interpretations, and its discourse without dialogue. It is ignored, why they dynamite the statues of the Buddha, covers women with veils, and decapitates in the name of Allah.

Islam: tribe and plutocracy

*There is no Islamic or Arab nation
as there is not a Christian.*

The Oriental despotism as outcome of the hydraulic character of ancient societies was one of the many provocative ideas of Karl Marx. But it would be Karl Wittfogel in its text *Oriental Despotism,* who would detail the oppressive bureaucratic nature of these hydraulic societies that made them different from those of the medieval Europe[1]. Bureaucratic tyrannies characterized by colossal defensive constructions and immense architectural works.

Both the Soviet Josef Stalin and the Chinese Mao Zedong dismantled the former Asian hydraulic cultures in their territories. But even with the brutality of their procedures in both cases, the results were still two hydraulic despotic models, pharaonic in their application of the terror.

Stalin and Mao communism not only showed to be a failure in the 20th century, incapable of overcoming the despotic character in their cultures in direct lineage with the ancient hydraulic societies. Theirs was only the intention of implanting the large-scale industrialization with emphasis on monumental public construction projects with slave or prisoner labor.

They proved wrong Marx's analysis that the socialist statism is the final destination of the Middle and Far East civilizations. But these cultures, for so long sedentary and perpetually tyrannized, rarely altered their distinctive traits and personalities, even under the most extreme methods. That was the case also of the Nile River culture, a social milieu where African, Arab and Mediterranean civilizations merged; and that is still a decisive step in the history of mankind.

After the Islamic conquest of Egypt in the year 642, this trend towards gigantism was abandoned, because like the Eastern Orthodox Christianity in Ethiopia, Romania and Slavic areas, Islam was transfigured into a state religion.

But Egypt was too old to change drastically, and it found during the Nasserism, in the 1960´s, that pharaonic version of oriental despotic socialist realism under President Gamal Abdul Nasser, who would undertake the construction of the colossal dam of Aswan, across the Nile River at a cost of about $1 billion. The current state of Egypt, with its million bureaucrats, is a calcified monolith, accustomed to execute the orders of the pharaoh (Gamal Abdul Nasser, Anwar El-Sadat, Hosni Mubarak, etc.).

The purely "hydraulic" nature of Egyptian society has intensified compared to its antiquity. Egypt is still a riparian civilization where roads, railways and telephone routes run along the Nile; where 95% of its population lives in this coastal corridor 600 miles long and 10 miles wide, qualified by the Greek writer Nikos Kazantzakis as a multicolored human anthill.

The Nile is shared with Ethiopia and Sudan[2], and this dispute may be the cause for the next regional war strife, because the needs of agro-industrial and drinking water in these three countries are higher than what the river can provide.

While Egyptians have been historically sedentary and passive, lack of resources and population growth -without considering the possible climate change-, with their excessive needs, has unleash the actual political chaos. The chances that the Egyptian State will control its environment without deepening its despotism are doubtful.

The Egyptian geo-economic constraints (overpopulation, less water and agricultural land, environmental poisoning) will keep on inducing praetorian systems and societies of chronic internal conflicts. With a despotic millennial practice and poverty and in such an environment, democracy can only bring the Islamic fundamentalism in power.

In what way can it impose its territorial responsibility over Libya, avoid the dissolution of Sudan[3] and obtain the lion's share of the waters of the Nile?

During its 1300-year history, from the theocracy established by the "prophet of Allah", Islam has been manipulated politically, and has been presented in as many varieties as the countries that profess it. The unity of its world is as fictitious as its creed. Therefore, there is no Islamic or Arab nation, as there is not a Christian one. There, family, clan and tribal interests always precede that of the nation.

The petroleum phenomenon on the Islamic map -from Indonesia to Morocco- will become an awkward event when large pits of the oil wealth will be confiscated by clans and camel keeper families. But the oil possession didn't restore Islamic supremacy that still stands as a planetary piece where the industry has not developed and where oil extraction has engendered both childish arrogance and scandalous inequalities.

One cannot understand the political process of the area, and the presence of terrorist groups, their associations and philosophies without pinpoint in a transcendent plane the dynamics of the family clans, the linkages of blood within any organization. An analysis by country and movement didn't escape this key element.

That's why is not possible to apprehend the deep trace of the tribalism in the current political behavior of the Middle East if such a phenomenon is not analyzed from its purest origins.

An archaic society where every tribe assumes the natural law of surviving at the expense of the weakest, without external mediators or governments to apply the law, and where the harmed one is erected judge and executor, and is defined by this old Arab proverb:

"I and my brother against my cousin".

"I, my brother and my cousin against the neighbor".

"I, my brother, my cousin and my neighbor against the stranger".

The first reason for which such conflicts of tribal court abound is in view of the fact that numerous people of this region -including the Jews of Israel- have not broken entirely with their essential nomadic identities, although they live in what hollowly can be considered to be modern nations-states.

These are newly created entities but in many senses are still abstractions, and that is why its regents prescribe with serenity the slaughter of inhabitants inside its borders, for the simple reason of not considering them to be parts of their community, but followers of an alien tribe.

The clans, sects, neighborhoods, cities and regions, in constant struggles, could not find a formula to balance intimacy and tribal-group cohesion, within the frameworks and requirements of a nation-state. Because a nation-state requires neutral laws to act and values that should be obeyed by all. Clans –mafia style- aided by technology and the modern European style state, have exerted a brutal central control.

The multiplicity of villages in the area was and is a difficulty to reach a scope of compliance necessary for this prototype of policy. Abnormal was the clan or sect that is spontaneously subordinated to another and inconceivable even the town or city that voluntarily gave in the control of another region, or vice versa

The power elites usually respond to a tribe, as the Jordanian Bedouin monarchy or the Emirates of the Persian Gulf; or to a clan, such as the brutal military dictatorship of Syria-Alawites clan or of the Lebanon Maronites (Christians); or linkages of pairing between the clans in the vein of the Taliban; a religious sect, such as the Wahhabis of Saudi Arabia, or the Sudanese Mahdis, or the Imamate of Yemen.

The is also the family plutocracy of a locality, such as was the town of Tikrit of Saddam Hussein in Iraq; or of a region, as the coastal plains in Algeria or the south of Pakistan.

Sometimes it is the gang of a neighborhood, like the Christian phalange of Amin Gemayel in Lebanon; or colleagues of a military unit, such as Nasser's Egypt, the Iraq of Karim Kassem, or Libya's Muammar Gaddafi; and in other cases it is a combination of the above patterns.

The Taliban clans are interrelated. So Laden is a prominent clan in the region of Hadramaut in Yemen, which traces its genealogy to the days of the Prophet, ingredient that gives it an aura of "authenticity" exploited by Osama Bin-Laden, whom intentionally ignored his name and assumed that of his clan.

What they all have in common is that their members are twinned by a spirit of solidarity and fraternity, of total obligation and mutual loyalty which takes precedence above the fidelity to a wider national community, including that of nation-State. Today there are governments of regional oligarchies in close proximity to the bulk of the population in Lebanon, Jordan, Syria, Israel, Kuwait, Saudi Arabia, Iraq, and Pakistan.

Egyptians historic rivalry with Iraq for the Islamic world hegemony, wrestles with the dilemma of becoming a modern State within the essence of the Islamic heritage. But the modern world is only possible to achieve sacrificing their Islamic tribal values.

For this reason, current state systems, with their political nerves in Damascus, Baghdad and Cairo, only replicate the antagonism between the medieval caliphates, Umayyad, Abbasid and Fatimid, respectively based in such cities, with a network of City-States linked by trade routes.

When such terms as Arabic, Lebanese, Syrian, Palestinian, Afghan, are proclaimed, one does not speak about stable entities, but highly volatile interpretations subjected to dissimilar definitions of political domains with shifting foundations. The other reason deeply rooted in the political tradition of the Middle East, and remarkable from Morocco to Pakistan, is the authoritarianism: the concentration of power in a single individual or elite, free of any constitutional restriction.

In the Islamic world does not be there an explicit and formal mechanism for the transfer of power, nor even in the erroneously called monarchies. The usual authoritarian ruler assumes or inherits the throne by means of the sword, to which it is expected that its subjects, courtiers or people, submit. Violence as well, has been the only mean of the Islamic world for the enthronement of changes.

The long-standing authoritarian tradition in the Islamic politics is connected by the persistence of the tribal affiliations. The people of the Middle East rarely have created by *motu proprio* the states-nations to be ruled and to confront its enemies, as consequence of the tribal archetypes governing emphatically the allegiances and individual identities, and the political attitudes.

As historian Gerard Chaliand would suggest in its book *Revolution in the Third World*, the struggle for liberation in the Third World only produced autocrat systems dominated by state apparatus, corrupt bureaucracies and repressive police force[4].

The pattern will be that of tribes or military groups exercising their power over clans, tribes and cities in other regions, in which case the guardianship imposed from above by antonomasia is dictatorial, with an insurmountable gap between ringleader and subject, because the ringleader will always be a strange, frightening someone, cause for riots, and rarely revered.

But these mercantile empires needed a corpus of political theory to promote obedience to the illegitimacy and justified the brutal authoritarianism of Islamic despots, despite the fact that it is contrary to the Quran.

The founders of the Ottoman dynasty implanted their authority by force in the Islamic world; but they never could placate southern Palestine and the desert of the Negev (Israel and the West Bank), populated by bellicose Bedouin tribes that constantly slaughtered each other. It was only at the end of the 19th century, that the Ottoman Governor Rüstem Pasha managed to pacify the region.

This way the annals of the area will be replete with complaints of a high level of brutality and savageness, next to which the Palestine-Israeli issue is a gentlemen's elegant duel if it is compared with the Armenian genocide on the part of the Turks at the beginning of the 20th century, which almost annihilates this nation; or the bloodthirsty coup d'état against the military regime of Karim Kassem in Iraq, with its almost hundreds of thousands dead persons; or the bloodless civil strife in North Yemen in the 1960´s; or the Lebanese civil war in the 197C and 1980 decades.

To this situation also they register the anti-Soviet war in Afghanistan, which ended in a civil war creating a social chaos, the plundering and the tribal looting from which emerged the dark night of the Taliban; the Kurds' massacres on the hand of the Iraqi Muslims and the Turks; the immolation in mass of the "divine mobs" of the ayatollah Khomeini in the front line with Iraq; the entire eradication of the city of Hama on the part of the Syrian Hafez Al-Assad; the butchering of southern Sudanese Christians by the hands of the Moslem government of the north; the complicated uncivil war of Somalia; the holy jihad of the Algerian fundamentalists with its cut-throat of women and girls.

Authoritarianism has transcended the current events of the Middle East. In more homogeneous Islamic countries -Egypt and Tunisia- and in those like the monarchies of Jordan, Morocco, Saudi Arabia, Oman, or the Emirates of the Persian Gulf, the rulers enjoyed a high degree of consent. This margin of legitimacy allows the sword, though latent, to be kept sheathed for the power to be distributed, tolerates some freedom of the press and of expression and build a slightly more relaxed atmosphere, while and if the autocrat is not in question.

However, in those Islamic countries where societies are highly fragmented among various sects, clans, cities and tribes, and where the modern government management has not gained authenticity (Syria, Iraq, Lebanon, Yemen, Sudan, and Somalia) one bears witness to the most emaciated and cruel profile of despotic practice. Here the sobriety and magnanimity are luxury items and judges are not sheltered in their armchairs.

What makes these authoritarianisms more dangerous is that they respond with devastating armaments. But tribalism and authoritarianism by themselves may not clarify the vast and complex political phenomena of the Middle East. There is another dynamic element in play, which was an importation in the 20th century of the nation-State by colonial invaders; a new concept in an area of long authoritarian dynastic roots.

Countries and nations existed with their names, but were not perceived as defined political alloys, capable of bringing together alliances in the Western sense. Islamic empires were political objects erected on the basis of religious affiliation and clannish, tribal or regional loyalty.

Since the Babylonian Empire of bloodthirsty Nebuchadnezzar more than two millennia ago above the old map, never the Middle East has exerted such attraction[5]. The Islamic world has furiously become a vast front of rejection of the Western world.

Ultra-Religious or lay, wrapped in the mysterious decline of their immense and old civilization, the Middle East continues to embrace suicidal confrontations: terrorism, theocracy, challenging the modern. The secret of such frustration, of this collective hysteria, goes back a dozen of centuries, to the great pomp of its history that has engendered an infuriating religious paranoia, archaically nationalist.

While in different periods of its existence the Middle East was the center of civilization, this past has propelled and compelled the artificial reproduction of such greatness, trying to recreate the days of medieval Islam when it was political heart of the Abbasid Empire, from the Pyrenees to Asia Minor. The splendor with which the Islam shone with the caliphate of Cordova, with the Baghdad of Harun Al-Rashid or the Istanbul of Suleiman the Magnificent, made it possible to offer the "barbarian" West, lessons of civilization. But, from the 12th century on, the victories of its conquerors (Persian, Turkish, Tartar, Kurdish), do not conclude with a Renaissance, Enlightenment, or the "machinist" or the scientific revolution that was fruitful in Europe.

The rise of the Baas political movement in the 1930s, which was born from the rubble of the Arab revolt brought about by the enigmatic and legendary British spy, Thomas Edward Lawrence (Lawrence of Arabia), marked the appearance of a tricky nationalist concept of an isolationist cut, which today embraces Islamic space.

These intellectuals from Damascus, regulars at cafe La Habana, where the Maronite Michael Aflak, the Sunni Salah Bitar and the Alawite Zaki Arsuzi concurred, forged not only the future of the bulk of the States of the area (Egypt, Iraq, Syria, Lebanon, Tunisia), but also its intellectuals and politicians (Gamal Abdul Nasser, George Habash, Saddam Hussein, Abdul Fatah Ismail).

Based on a vague national-socialism and a secular tilt, the Baas movement advocated a restitution of the past: the unity of the Arab people (language, culture and history) and awareness of a common (fallacious) identity. Thus, they swept with the airs of Westalism and linkages with the educated elite of Europe, plotting the expulsion of foreigners from the Arab homeland.

It could be deemed, falsely, Islam and the Arab entity as catastrophic trends intimately imbricate; but between militant Islam and Arabism there is a distinction that, unless set, it is sometimes dangerous. To consider the "Arabs" as an entity is falling squarely in the racist faith and, inversely, denounce radical Islam as the only culprit of the horrors we have seen in recent decades, is to isolate the religious factor, which is only an expression of crisis and not its cause: the anguish of a civilization that has refused to accept its failure, which occurred more than five centuries ago.

The Western supremacy after the 17th century turned out to be incomprehensible for the Islamic firmament, and hence its mirage of superiority and its frenzy of pursuit; that is why its rejection wall to the technology, to the secular state, to the civil laws, for originating from the unbelievers. In its book *Cultural Schizophrenia,* the exiled Iranian writer, Daryush Shayegan[6] diagnosed the "hemiplegic memory" of the Arab-Islamic that tries to conceal its face from the West, tying structurally the theological with the political problems.

Since the Egyptian Mohammed Said Al-Ashmawy[7] would synthesize: "God watched for Islam to be a religion, but the men have turn it into politics; to do politics on behalf of the religion is to transform the last one into endless wars, in divisions without end".

For that reason, the miracle of the "Arab unity" will only know the secular scimitar or the devout stoning; whereas the modernity of the West is a "poisoned gift" for an Islam that cannot match it in technological capacity, in science and in military power; and attempts to safeguard its spirituality Khomeini style or the Taliban way; where culture is allergic to the idea of the modern nation, merchandise from the former 'barbarian' neighbor.

Thus, Islam as a religion is dogmatized, freezing the Arab culture, assuming the stale and nostalgic religious Arabism, founder and unitary, that took the scimitar and the Crescent to Poitiers, through the West, and to the walls of Vienna by the European East. Therefore, restoring the Arab nation is something like rebuilding the Catholic Europe that was mobilized around the papal flag and fought the believers of other confessions. Within such nebula, not everything is Arabic or Islamic; the Arab-Islamic universe, in its various gradations, is simply the federated shadow of a world that already disappeared.

Thus, the far-reaching Islamic body in a prolonged coma within a region full of historical injustices and ethnic aberrations -many legacy of colonialism, the Ottoman Empire and petroleum- cyclically propagates chronic anti-West ranting. The propaganda of almost all the Islamic States manipulates this distant past, opposing it in ingenuous way to the West, which shows a disharmony between the current reality and the archaic Babylonian Persian or of Cordoba magnificence.

Every blow to the modern West is, therefore, the restoration of a phantasmagoric archaism, the escape to a political reality, to its slow decline, to the incapability to accept that the West challenge won centuries ago. This way, the photos of a Gamal Abdul Nasser, Houari Boumediene, Saddam Hussein, Muammar Gaddafi or Osama Bin Laden, interfere with the effigies of Saladdin, the Assyrian Assurbanipal or the Persian Dario.

It is not a matter of singing the virtues of an angelical West opposite to a diabolical East, especially in moments when the modern West implants irreversibly "its" civilization in the whole planet. Adolf Hitler didn't justify Saddam Hussein or Bin Laden, nor Josef Stalin or Slobodan Milosevic justified the Taliban; and the colonial wars already belong to the past.

The track is uninterrupted from the Algerian Moslem Brotherhood defeat to the civil Kurds gassed by Iraq, the scandal of the *Satanic Verses* of Salman Rushdie[8], the feminine subjection, the hostages, the terrorist attacks, the pendulums of Baghdad, the prophets by own choice like Osama Bin Laden, and the diamonds of the emirs.

Its human resources and intelligence do not matter, and it is demonstrated in its substantial Diaspora, precisely towards the hated capitalist neon capitals. The doctors of the Islamic faith have never formally condemned either the terrorist butchering or the airliner hijackings or the gender abuse or the 'contracts' against Rushdie.

Like the lay uniform of Saddam Hussein, who seduced several western capitals in its war against the Shiite fundamentalism, the religious Al-Qaeda's holy war against the West, is not anything other than what the Egyptian Writer Said Al-Ashmawy explained: a parade of grotesque values and symbols, riding on the ghost of invincible Muhammad, Saladdin or Nebuchadnezzar II.

Islam:
state and nation

Is Islam a more "primitive" religion than Christianity and Judaism? How it is possible that the formerly splendid Islamic civilization today it presents itself with the Afghan Taliban or the Yemeni Imamate as the most intransigent?

Is the Arab-Islamic world a monolithic political and social bloc (the Arab League) where a state of 'modern' cut such as the Tunisian and other medieval like Qatar are fused?

What in this universe allows the persistence of enlightened individuals, who drag multitudes, whether they be renowned politics like the Syrian Hafez Basher and the Irani Mohammed Ahmadineyad; tribal groups such as in the Arabic Peninsula; or simpletons transfigured into prophets by own choice, like the Berber Almohad guide of the 12th century Hassan Ibn Tumart, the Iran ayatollah Khomeini, the Taliban supreme leader mullah Mohammad Omar and the topmost Al-Qaeda ruler Osama Bin-Laden, with the right to excommunicate by a fatwa?

The three universal religions of West (Judaism, Christianity, and Islam) are from Judaic origin and emerged in the Middle East. All three have their vernacular language (Latin, Hebrew and Arabic) and their holy books (*Bible, Talmud* and *Quran*). The three worship the same God by different names (Yahweh or Allah) and are messianic; Jesus is the Messiah for Christianity, Islam's is Muhammad, and that of Judaism is still to arrive.

There are more similarities than differences between them, to the point that, for centuries, Islam was looked as a revamped and more 'intellectual' edition, a Christian heresy. They considered Jesus of Nazareth one of their many prophets, and housed the scientific and philosophical thought of its time, alongside the scholastic body. There the Averroes and the Ibn-Khaldun didn't have to appear at a court of inquisition.

Then, what has happened? In contrast to Christianity, Islam does not have religious governance frameworks (such as the Vatican), or central authorities whose verb is the posthumous sanction in theological matters. Hence the "will of God" has been defined by any of the faithful, either a doctor from the Islamic faith of any mosque (a mullah such as the Taliban Omar), a head of State (such as the Saudi Fahd bin Abdul-Aziz), or a simple water carrier of the untamed Morocco.

All have the right to be heard; that is why a hotbed of 'interpreters' of the faith (Protestant usage) swarms polluting the horizon of the believer. This could be considered an advantage when compared with the dogmatic Christian Papacy (remember Martin Luther King) except that in Islam the equation doesn't work, for the simple fact that state and religion are not separated; instead, they adapt a theocratic formula[1], as in the Spain of cruel Isabella, the Catholic.

From there it takes the 'will of the nation' as in the Iran of the ayatollahs, which is a chapel of 'auto-elected' with the reins of power in their hands. The discrepancy with the West resides in that anodyne matter; the advantage (the luck!) in Europe is that on the shoulders of Francis Bacon, Isaac Newton and Oliver Cromwell, the modern state is rocked the priestly folds.

Other one of the widespread fallacies is that of identifying the Arab ethnic group with the Islamic civilization. The marauding horde that accompanied Muhammad stayed in the way, dissolving in the cities that were sprouting from Cordova to Samarqand. The "Arab" unity is rhetoric; the ethnic differences between a Moroccan and an Egyptian, or between a Yemenite and a Tunisian, or between a Persian and a Sudanese, are as substantial as those of the Portuguese with the Slavs.

The problem of the state boundaries is another matter of misunderstanding between Islamic culture and the West. Sometimes one forgets that the Middle East has inherited from the colonialism a terrible legacy of border, territorial and nationality problems.

The countries and ethnic groups of the Islamic world, more than any other region have been pieces on the duels and maneuvers of the world powers. In other words, many of the states of the Middle East -Egypt is the exception- do not owe their existence to their own people, or an organic development from a historical, ethnic, cultural or linguistic memory, and didn't emerge from a social contract between rulers and ruled.

A Western state coincides with the nation, not so an Islamic, where states are artificial creations, such as Kuwait, Jordan, Lebanon, and Iraq. This is exacerbated by not adjusting the boundaries of the existing states with the cultural areas of old civilizations, marking the shortcomings of nations created by European colonial metropolis, and the illusory portrayal that once the colonial ties are dissolved the most pressing difficulties of their archaic societies automatically resolve.

Its structures and borders were designed to the European custom by the imperial pen of England and France from the remains of the Ottoman Empire, to serve to its foreign policies, transportation, commerce, communications and the energy needs. This is the reason that helps to understand the action of Iraq against Kuwait, that of drawing a new political map, new countries that replace the ones created by the Anglo-French agreement of 1916, which dismembered the Ottoman Empire.

Kaiser William II forged the intention of entering the Persian Gulf through a railway from Berlin to Baghdad, but London obstructed it creating Iraq, a buffer state taken from Istanbul, which also absorbed the oil area of Mosul. England and France distributed the worm-eaten Ottoman Empire; only Egypt and Iran were left untouched. The Ottoman Empire and those portions of it, which fell into the hands of the West, were governed in principle by minorities, whose local interests allied them to the colonial power.

In the year 1920, after months of fruitless negotiations, a completely intoxicated Sir Percy Cox, one night in his tent in the Arabic desert, traced in pencil on a world map the frontier rims of the Middle East. Thus were born, protected by France, the Republics of Syria and Lebanon, and by England, the Hashemite of Transjordan. The Anglo-French fragmentation of the Fertile Crescent was compensated with the unification of the Arab Peninsula under the pro-English Ibn-Saud.

Its borders consisted of perfect polygons, with straight angles that contrasted violently with the chaotic reality of the area. As result, such states have constituted big slices where miscellanies of ethnic and religious communities were threaded, each one with its historical memory and its specific game laws.

The current states of Syria, Lebanon, Iraq, Palestine, Jordan and the multiple oil states of the Persian Gulf, were planned in this process, and these foreigners imposed the even names in almost the whole Middle East. This is exacerbated by not adjusting the boundaries of the existing states with the cultural areas of old civilizations, marking the deficiencies of the nations and the false interpretation that once dissolved the colonial ties the most pressing difficulties of their archaic societies would resolve automatically.

These models of nation-state in the Middle East had no precedent in their ancient or medieval world, created without paying attention to tribal, ethnic, religious or linguistic continuities as a nonsensical agglomeration with only a flag in common. Loyalty to the Islamic faith would be more solid that the state, which would fail to resolve this dichotomy. That is why a unique and unified Islamic Community[2] will never be created, nor a single Arab nation, even in the hypothetical case that the purification sects lay down the quasi secular governments of the Middle East.

What happened in the 20th century, after these nation-states were created, was that in each of them a tribal or ethnic particular group was made or was put in the power, and then it sought about how to expand its dominance on others. These states will also be 'confessional' in a sense, on having been integrated by minorities and by a domineering sect that will refuse any ethnic diversity.

This way, the Saudi tribe in Saudi Arabia emerged as domineering, and its current King Fahd bin Abdul-Aziz abrogated the title of 'custodian of two tabernacles' to assign Moslem authority to its government[3]. In the Lebanon, for example, it was the Maronites who took the power, the Alawites in Syria, in the Iraq of Saddam Hussein it was the Tikrit settlers, and in Jordan the British put the Hashemite Abdullah Ibn Hussein, great-grandfather of the current monarch. It allowed these families or specific groups to dominate initially its societies and to construct the governmental bureaucracies with the solidarity of its tribes or clans.

This way the area would tear in tribal contests like those of Yemen or Afghanistan, or that of the Kurds who never surrendered to Turkey, to Iran or to Iraq; military coups would rush like those of Gamal Abdul Nasser and Saddam Hussein; cause would be given for turbulent frontier relations, like those of Morocco and Algeria, Turkey with Iran, and those of Iraq with Kuwait and with Saudi Arabia.

This way, what moves Syria in the Lebanese Bekaa Valley is not its solidarity with the Palestinians, but the control of the Lebanese ports, and the old aspiration of reconstructing "the great Syria", with part of the Lebanon and Israel. Saddam Hussein didn't declare the war on Iran and Kuwait for mere military exercise, but looking desperately for an outlet to Iraq in the Persian Gulf.

The Iranian theocracy also harbored designs to swallow the Lilliputians oil Emirates of the Persian Gulf; and the Libya's Qaddafi aspired to do the same with the North of Chad. These tragic adventures have illustrated the trouble of setting up a state, a geographically and socially stable structure over the smoldering ruins of the colonial empires.

But, subsequent to Ayatollah Khomeini, the scepter was challenged by fundamentalist trends. Al-Qaeda and Ahmadineyad are the lasts of those who, like Saddam Hussein, Muamar Khadafy, and Basher Assad, claimed the political mantle of Gama Abdel Nasser, to fight against foreign domination and throw Israel into the sea, and for the "defense" of the poor Arabs before the oligarchies of the Gulf, whose nations qualify as "oil wells with flag".

But this comparison, which will always have ethical and moral overtones and is target of the ayatollahs, the Taliban, the Moslem Brotherhood and Al-Qaeda, does no justice to the financial ability of the Gulf's oil sheikhs, since a country like Libya's Khadafy, full of black gold, was sunk in poverty; also, the model of "Arab socialism" invented by Nasser, and applied left and right, has transformed such economies in "bureaucratic elephants".

In the same way the colonial administrations and elites imposed "westernized" political institutions of liberal democracy in each of these states including parliaments, constitutions, national anthems, political parties and cabinets. The trauma was that the imperial powers left the area prior to such structures to be rooted, and before these societies experienced the economic, political and social reforms necessary to confer some meaning to the same.

In the subsequent years to decolonization, the Islamic world repudiated both socialism and democracy, as outsiders. It is true that Muslim believers never forgave a Turkish Mustafa Kendal Ataturk for having abolished the Caliphate to establish a Western-style Republic, and why his bust is kept in some *Quran* schools with the only purpose of being spit on by students[4].

On the other hand, the West still sees the Middle East in terms of strategy and energy resources. There is no illustration of reconstruction policy for the Middle East, equal to that which unfolds in Eastern Europe. In almost all these countries the bureaucracy has concluded to solidify the fragile nation-states. That is why the "party-style democracies" of West fashion does not prevail.

The search for a degree of state legitimacy has involved initiatives that despite being defective mostly benefited the generality, as economic development plans, civil constructions, houses and roads, intensive forestation and irrigation systems, ports, the expansion of education and health, and electricity and telephone services. Therefore, the reluctance towards this new state bundle entails a rejection to modernity –like the Islamic fundamentalism- and the affirmation of the secular Republic, which is why autocrats like Saddam Hussein, Muammar Kaddafi or the Basher Assad enjoyed broad popular support.

Political masters like the Iraqi Saddam Hussein, the Egyptian Hosni Mubarak and the Syrian Hafez Al-Assad did not deceive themselves on the tribal and fractional nature and the autocratic character of their societies, and distinguished the differences between urban cosmopolitanism and tribal faction, between the rhetorical patterns they assumed and authenticity, and calculated that the central power they occupied only prevailed by reason of force, leaving the rest to the commentators.

It is uncertain if the artificial borders and institutions that govern the Islamic world will be consolidated to the point of forging real social contracts with their respective populations, and creating public spheres, neutral spaces where individuals may be deprived of their tribal memories to be treated under common laws as equal citizens.

The politicization of Islam has put an end to real devotion, as the identification. Cardinal clip of this Islamic world overwhelmed by violence is not Israel, but the authoritarianism that has stalled their economies, and the absence of creativity and scientific and philosophical education.

The so-called Pan-Arabism has brought only violent resentment to the Islamic countries, the hottest of them the duel with Israel, taken as an insult set up by the West. First with the Gulf War, and the current campaign against terrorism, this portion of the planet is facing a capital transition, where a group of countries with wide diversity of interests (Pakistan and Saudi Arabia, for example), are forced to search for new ideas and political structures, while flirting with certain forms of Islamic fundamentalism at the same time; and where the totalitarian vision like Hussein's, enters in decline.

To project any intra-Islamic conflict as a difference of bad and good is too simplistic. One cannot lose of sight that, with the current alignment (that began with the Gulf War and was expressed in all Islamic head of state meetings), the "Arabs" basically face themselves a violent crisis of identity, where several myths evaporate, and ends the illusory idea that the crises of the area (Palestine, the fundamentalism) can be solved within the Islamic world; and where the outdated practice of portraying only one face to the non-Islamized world is cracking.

The Arabs still keep on blaming the Turks and the Europeans for the conditions of backwardness of their region, but neither the Ottomans nor the Europeans dominated poverty-stricken Yemen. In the whole Middle East, civil institutions exist only in Turkey, Israel and in a certain sense in Jordan.

Islamic societies are falling behind increasingly, in scientific, technological and economic field. The globalization, the economic progress of the modern world and its smug euphoria, has not annulled the religious or nationalistic passions, nor has the post-industrial world flooded to the Middle East.

A handful decades ago the ring of the Pacific Ocean was among the poorest on the planet, but its new entrepreneurship is nowhere in sight in the Middle East, that is why many suggest that there is a correlation between underdevelopment and Islam.

The Soviet Union evaporated; Israel has proved that it can confront the military challenges of all the Arab States combined; Iran has unleashed and legitimized what the secular nationalists were ridiculing: politics ruled by religion. Malek Bennabi, the Algerian thinker, has written a book where confront the reasoning for the failure of the Arab society to build powerful economic and social institutions[5].

Theocracy or any of the forms of Government "conceived by Allah" and proposed by Islamic extremists does not work in the modern world, as its structure, rules and settings cannot be questioned or reasoned. Religious isolationist attempts -type Iran, Yemen or Saudi Arabia- are no longer permissible to build a pure nation, as they were in France or Germany.

It could be that a future disintegration of Iraq after the withdraw of American troops is alike to the ancient Ottoman Turkish provinces of the Kurdish Mosul in the north, the Baghdad Sunnite in the center, and Shiite Basra in the south, which might lead to the revival of the Hashemite influence in the Sunni Baghdad, for the first time from 1958.

At the heart of the Arab culture is the conventional Islamic belief; this is where the current problems are. Islam is a civilization of museum; its policy has not changed since ancient times. For centuries the Islamic world has maintained its closed mind, but if it wants to overcome its stagnation it has to stop constantly repeating itself in order to be open to other influences.

It is because the modernity produces scares and puzzlement that it refuses to adapt to the rapid changes of the planet, and that is why pessimism impregnates powerfully its culture; that is why the social hierarchies, the values and the traditions serves as psychological security.

How can such coded barbarity participate in a world that is increasingly global and more competitive, if it excludes half the population -the women- on having adopted as its legal code the Sharia Law? How can the economy flourish if the Arab women are evaluated for being 'bearers of men' and not by their intellectual capacity?

But there is outlined, precisely, the tragedy of the Arab defeat to seek realistic solutions, since the world that supposedly moves the Islamic fundamentalism was sentenced by the march of history. This is the main reason why the scream of its crisis, of admitting that it has lost its targets, it is found in terrorism and in the stampede of its unemployed youth towards the West.

Like it or not, she is part of a dynamic universe where no culture, no matter how conservative, can stop the changes, nor isolate themselves to the impact of technology on human values, unless Muslim society wants to remain as a pristine island of observation of faith no matter what happens in the sea that surrounds it. In the state in which technology evolves today, the nation-state can only work if it is interlocked with the vast world beyond its borders. And the ones that exist in Central Asia and the Middle East are fossilized proto-industrial nations.

A Jewish State

Between the ghetto and the nation:
Israel or the dilemma of the Promised Land

For the West, the East is all this vast space that lies behind the imaginary line that runs from Greece to Turkey, with exotic places populated by indifferent masses with their mentality, culture, politics and racial characteristics. A myriad of conquerors took Palestine, and countless Diasporas enslaved and dispersed the Hebrew tribes. The Pharaohs were the first and the English the last. The autonomy of the Jewish State in history only lasted 60 years, and ceased to exist with the revolt of Masada at the hands of the Romans.

Palestine was closed to Jews after the birth of Islam, and the region was included as a province of the Ottoman Empire in 1516. Within the confines of the Western Christian Europe, Jews were persecuted until England opened the doors with the glorious revolution of the 17th century.

Eastward their fate would be easier due to the shortage of skilled artisans and writers, protected in urban neighborhoods, Jewish "ghettos". Fifty generations had to pass so the obsession with returning to the land which God bestowed "his people" ceased to be a romantic myth.

The Renaissance, the Protestant Reformation (terribly anti-Semite in its early days), and the Industrial Revolution opened the doors of universities, politics and trade to the Jews. National borders began to change and European culture embarked on a brutal transformation. But in Russia and Poland, where Western democratic ideas never took root, that closed community that had helped Jews survive in the Middle Ages was transformed into a trap. Anti-Semitic terror that destroyed the European Jewry who yearned to return to the "promised land" (Theodor Herzl, Maurice de Hirsch) conceived Zionism; and those seeking to assimilate into European society (Moses Hess, Karl Marx) devised communism.

Hertz and Hirsch with their Association of Jewish Colonization were negotiating the emigration towards Argentina or Brazil, and bargained a territory in Africa. Hertz in its "The Jewish State" was pushing the assimilation back in favor of the national home, obviating the settlers of Palestine[1]. Without a massive migration the Jewish State would remain like a romantic dream, that's why the British were struggling with the Jewish settlement project in Jerusalem, pushed back, clearly, by the Turkish sultans.

Before the First World War, Palestine was a province within the Ottoman Empire and at the conclusion of the war fell in the area of British influence. The Arabs claimed Palestine, promised by the British, but London was abiding by the agreement with France and Russia to internationalize this territory. Loyal to their old tradition of divide and conquer, the British promised Palestine to the Arabs through T. E. Lawrence and the Jews through the "Balfour declaration", sowing the seeds of the current Arab-Israeli conflict[2].

If the Jewish identity has its roots in Antiquity, the condition of the Palestinians is born to the post-war period. The Arabs embrace the notion of a historical right absolute and immutable, without changes of territorial occupants, and where the empire meltdowns do not count. In the West, this right is revocable and can be lost in history, as happened with the Romans, with Byzantium, with the Turkish Empire and as has happened precisely to the Arabs of Palestine. This means that the Arabs do not grant legitimacy to building a new state on territory of another, such as Israel, while the West rejects the timelessness and legitimate present a *fait accompli.*

The Arab reaction to Zionism never was nor has been completely monolithic. The powerful clan of the deceased Saddam Hussein, whose patriarch was heading the Moslem Supreme Council in Jerusalem was opposed to the immigration of the Jews, but the prominent clan of the Nashasibi was favoring it, promulgating policy of engagement and even the division of Palestine between Jewish and Arabs.

Assuming the cultural typology of an irascible Europe in confrontation with the Westal redemption, the Judaic spiritual prejudgment spread as counterpart to the hostility of its neighbors, challenge with the dilemma to grant equity to a Palestine govern by extremists. Prophesying the storm already in the 1930s, a seasoned politician like David Ben-Gurion proposed the "Salomonic" partition of Palestine into two states, one Jewish and one Arab.

The orthodox wing headed by his archrival Menachem Begin stubbornly rejected this accommodation with the reality, persisting in the restoration of the Greater Israel, from the Mediterranean to the Jordan River, and even beyond. To the walls built by the Islamic theology, the raised ones by the Jews would be added.

We have to remember that before Moses would lead them through the desert to receive the Torah in the Mount Sinai, already the Hebrew tribes had turned into nation in Egypt. Nevertheless, the Haredim becomes absorbed in investigating only the revelations of the Sinai and avoids its history and previous Egyptian memory. To them, the Jewish world begins and concludes with the Sinai, forgetting that the Easter is secular and that it precedes the Shavuot.

If for the Islamic fundamentalists the Sharia -sacred law- must be the *Corpus Juridicus* of the state, for the orthodox Jews it must be the Torah. The politics that the Haredim and Gush Emunim (Bloc of the Faithful) offer like the only forms of legitimate life, assuming as key of its tradition an incompatible Torah with the future, are actually in front of a dilemma.

The modern State of Israel was founded by secular Jews and rabbis, rebels to the traditionalism of their grandparents, who aspired to build a democratic state in the Promised Land, and not to rebuild the Judaic Synagogue from the ghettos of Eastern Europe. The Orthodox rabbis from Eastern Europe have problem to accommodate their theology and sacraments to the demands of the technological age, and has not totally accepted democracy as a Jewish value.

In Israel the abyss expands between the critic and defenders of the territorial demand for Samaria and Judea. But the orthodox advocate considered of rigueur continuing with such integration to comply with their elderly patriarchal predictions, where the containment of the pre-Hebrew tribes of the Canaan is the remedy to apply to the Palestinians. The Jewish religious tradition, Christian or Islamic, cannot longer flourish without the political sovereignty of the post-renaissance state, nor can it establish the collective guides of the nation.

Multiple interpretations of Judaism exist and of what it means to be a Jew. Its doctrine was not of redemption of the soul, like the Christian, and it didn't look forward to send the believer to Paradise. Judaism does not have to be transformed -as it is wanted today- in a sort of 'savior faith', with rules of the daily life in search of a Messianic kingdom ruled by the Torah. This is a tradition invented pursue by the orthodox rabbis who overstate the assignment of Israel and its tribe in the history.

Even when the Zionists were successful in their migratory patterns and in the subsequent construction of a nation, the Israel previous to 1967, that of Tel-Aviv and of Haifa, was not the idea for these orthodox, because it is in Samaria and Judea where lie the sacred grounds of evangelical Jerusalem, Nablus, Jericho, Jordan and Hebron, where the Hebrew history began and served as necropolis to the patriarchs Abraham, Isaac and Jacob.

The State of Israel does not conform a unified ethnic grouping, but a mosaic with so many religious communities and cultures as their points of origin: Jew, non-Jew; European

Jew, Jew of Israel, Sephardic, European Ashkenazi, Middle East Ashkenazi, Russian immigrant, Ethiopian Falasha, etc. The born in Israel already presents a less euro-central socio-cultural profile, more Middle Eastern than its congener of the Diasporas.

The current Jewish do not descend from those Hebrews, which Moses towed through the desert, or the ones the Babylonians abused in its Tower of Babel. The wars of extermination, the lengthy captivities and enslavement, the assimilation many times forced to other cultures and religions caused the pure Hebrew to be lost in history, to be superseded in expatriation by converts from other races.

For this reason, one of the deeper cultural revolutions of the 20th century was the emergence of the State of Israel, with its culture, its language and its literature, from an ethnic kaleidoscope. That is why Jews assume dissimilar visions about the nature and the aim of their state and its security.

The military triumph against the Arabs in the 1967 and 1973 wars confused the interpretation about the characteristics of their state; this immediate appreciation led them to move from their previous vulnerability to primacy. In their projection for the future they have involved the Biblical messianic environment with experimental rationalism, and which the only redemption was awarded to the ancient Israel.

Apart from terrorism, the existence of the Palestinian organizations, embodying a displaced population, and declaring continuously that Palestine does not belong to the Jews, created an embarrassing existential scenario for the Zionists. With the invasion of Lebanon in 1982, Ariel Sharon proposed *Manu military* to resolve the dilemma of a Jewish country with an extensive Palestinian population. At that moment, he hoped to destroy the PLO and press the residents of Gaza and the West Bank in order to accept the new arrangement, and at the same time, draw to a close the international reproach as oppressors.

The strategy from Menachem Begin until Sharon was to build a new habitat in the absorbed territories buying land

and creating Jewish districts, and suppress any memory of the Occupied Territories in 1967 -with PLO and all- for which such Palestinians would negotiate peacefully their independence.

Therefore, the seat of Jewish settlements, especially on the West Bank, does not respond to survival but to the erection of a homeland de facto. But at the beginning of the nineties Gulf war showed that this 'strategic depth' didn't protect Israel from the danger of terrorism, weapons of mass destruction and long-range missiles. With this change of equation, land for peace would no longer be a favor to the PLO, but something vital to its national security.

This strategy turned into a political dead end of Israel, especially when the topic about the character of their state was reconsidered as derivation of history and military *realpolitik* and the Arab demographic pressures, and when this fusion program collapsed due to domestic tensions, American coercion and peace treaties with Egypt and Jordan. A large Jewish population segment began to demand a negotiated solution with the Palestinians of Gaza and the West Bank, as well as the reverse of the settlements.

But, the anti-Palestinian posture is not born from the ideological dogmatism; very much is owed to the military coercion and political pressure that has exercised the Arab world, and the widespread denial to grant legitimacy to the Jewish State. It should be recognized in an Israel virtually deprived of non-violent options, of formulas to isolate the domestic (Palestinians) from international (Arabs).

It can be understood as the wave of terrorism prevented Israel to implement equality to the Palestinians in their state, and to the West Bank and Gaza, even more so when the PLO and Hamas lit up the meadow with their violence.

From the invasion of Lebanon in 1982 the European press began to point to Israel as the offender, therefore the controversy star in its population over what kind of society they wanted, and which values to be subjected to.

The dilemma is as follows: A Jewish state ruling eternally the Palestinians, a Prussia intimidating the neighbors or a state which fulfilled the terms of security, democracy and peace with these? With which borders: with the 1947 originals, the priors to the 1967 war, or the Biblical ones? With which system of division of power and ethical values: one for the citizens and the non-citizens alike, or one only to Israeli territory and a different one for the conquered?

At this point, a Jewish nation with all biblical lands would inevitably confront immense difficulties to grant the political rights of its non-Jewish inhabitants and justify it with religion. A democratic nation requires being detached from Gaza and the West Bank[3], or facing the constant jihad Palestine, thereby risking losing its alliance with the United States.

Another option is that of including Jews and non-Jews in the multiethnic state, with all the political rights divided equally, with the alternative that, in decades, the Islamic vote will overcome the Jew vote. Instead of choosing between these possibilities, the Israeli politicians would fight for the transiency, bequeathing to the Middle East and to the international community an undecipherable theorem.

The Zionist revolution was forged to liberate the Jews of its eternal ghetto mentality, that of martyred and helpless people. It was conceived to compose a political history of its own, and to revive the Hebrew language. The surprising cultures assembled in Israel granted them a new identity reason, rescuing its civil rights; it offered to its Diaspora a direction of progress and meta-historical destination. Observing the magnitude of the obstacles and calamities, the achievements reached by the Jews in the 20th century are truly admirable.

Despite creating all these instruments and institutions from the ashes of the Holocaust, the tragedy of Zionism lies in having not eradicated from the collective imagination the

Jewish victim the adverse destiny, the uncertain mornings. Thus, the Zionist revolution ended in a modern Warsaw ghetto that not toppled the tragic soul of its past, and its rulers would not make its history, but they react to events with a political expression that is extracted from the Torah and the Holocaust in its collective unconscious.

The pilgrimage is no longer to Degania Aleph, the once famous kibbutzim where youngsters of the first-generation laughed, sang, studied, trained and manufactured a dream, and for which the Holocaust was only a trauma[4]. It is now at the memorial in the hills of Yad Vashem, to the death camps of Auschwitz, Majdanek or Treblinka, confirming that the Holocaust has been transformed from trauma into the collective pathology of the entire nation.

The subliminal message is that such pathology concurs what ultimately embodies and defines the breath of the State of Israel. Perhaps the third Temple will be only transience in the history of a nation that, turned into a state, has been unable to break its auto- flagellant cycle; meanwhile, the Aliyah is a remembrance as the Jews of the Diaspora are less and less returning to Israel[5].

For Israel, peace involves the Jewish character of its state, with a status quo that prevents it from being simultaneously Jewish, democratic and stable. Of continuing the current impasse, Israel not only will not disappear as a State but it will continue its disconcerting advance, but at a price: of remaining surrounded with hostile Arabs and weak Palestinian states, and under international criticism[6].

The actual dilemma created by terrorism is to remain in the biblical confines and deal with the Palestinian problem, while they are waiting for the Messiah, or to decide on pragmatic borders and deal with the existential nightmare that means to face constant attacks from West Bank and Gaza. Peace could create a unique Israeli identity, half-way between West and East that would play for the Islamic countries a role similar to that of the Medieval Jewish groupings: financial intermediaries between the rival tribes, and providers of services to the cities-states.

The Israeli majority is the only one that can change the history of the region and finish this communal struggle completely or not at all, remodeling unilaterally its safety and delivering to the Palestinians a mini-state, which is not going to be the super-state to which they have aspired or the sovereignty they have wished, if they insist in deny the right of Israel to exist.

The United States has to submerge in the Islamic world, but cannot do it without solving the Israel–Palestine dilemma beforehand. If Washington turns its back on the area, it not only will mark the end of the diplomatic solutions in the Middle East but the victory of the Islamic fundamentalists over the Israelites, in a tribal war with the tribal solution to the strongest, where in the end Israel will alter the political geography of the Middle East. But the Israelis are walking through, they are in their country and the Palestinians, for their part, are tied tightly to their homeland. Palestinians and Jews have more to gain on a shared stage that in a perpetual antagonism.

In an era where the nineteenth-century pogroms and the Nazi genocide are still very close, engaging in the balanced analysis of the Middle East problems is entering a field of irrational emotionalism. Two obsessions: Islamic anti-Semitism and Islam phobia in the West turned the geopolitics of the area and the Arab-Israeli dilemma in a bloody feud that has hijacked international events.

But we are directly in one of those cases of plausible history that should not happen as they did. If the State of Israel that Zionists were negotiating had not ended up in Palestine, then that territory with its Islamic population would has absorbed in one of the Arab countries neighbors.

If the Arab regimes were to assimilate the Palestinian refugees in 1948, or the partition proposed by the UN of a Jew and a Palestinian State was to materialize, they would not be included in the gallery of the insoluble problems of the planet. That is why peace here involves a deep and simultaneous granting of sovereignty and homeland, something for which none of the two sides is ready.

Dogma is not the only element in the Palestinian disagreement that not only involves two irreconcilable religious sides with an endless theological overview of antagonism. It is not, therefore, a simple discussion of how airtight the Jews behave in a venue that was formerly called Palestine or the Palestinians in a feud that certainly time ago was Israel.

There is no doubt that since ancient times the Jew has been identified with biblical sites, or that their genealogy is full of suffering, moral and intellectual greatness and that, throughout their history, it has survived one of the most tragic destinies that people would endure amid an execrated Diaspora.

But the Jewish State didn't take shape in a geographical abstraction, but in a region occupied by another community, and a territory claimed by other Arab states: Egypt, Lebanon, Jordan and Syria. It cannot be denied the Israeli military control of Palestinian territories, or the existence of four million Palestinians on those areas. The Palestinians assumed themselves as a humanity stripped, in exile and without a country; its insistent claim to a nation is not out of context, but its demand for the whole land, including the actual state of Israel, is a political aberration.

Therefore, the crisis is both a cause and a place, and the identity is not only of Arabs who start to call themselves Palestinians, but also of Jews forced to share the acquired. Here the big topics cannot be formulated in a parochial context of bidding between peoples of the Middle East, but in a territorial alignment where two nations that are considered in exile claim the same space, involving the world in their complaint.

With the Romans, the Arabs Abbasids and the Ottoman Turks until its collapse in 1947, Palestine never enjoyed autonomy or independence, and its people would never be identified with its territory. Its inhabitants were recognized as part of the Arab nation and, under the British mandate, as naturals from colonial Syria: Palestine, Lebanon, Syria, and Jordan. The Palestinians (Syrians from the south) regulated under the archaic feudal-tribal didn´t have sufficient consistency to cope with the three major crises the twentieth century raised: The British mandate over the territory, the state of Israel and modernization.

Palestinian nationalism was born by challenging the Jewish State, which consolidates by fighting Arab states. It is the result of a war between two mixed communities, two peoples, two nations and two tribes, aware that survival is at stake and where one of the sides, the Palestinian, does not distinguish between civilians and soldiers, enemies and neighbors; where each member of the other guild is a potential enemy.

It is a wasps' nest where the Palestinians argue that their resistance cannot be labeled as terrorist, and the Israelis repute of benign their occupation; where for the Palestinian the dead do not exist but the 'martyrs', where the Jewish Orthodox assume that the redemption resides in the holy places of the West Bank; and the Palestinian fundamentalists only believe in the prayer of the rifles to erase Israel from the map.

The agenda is not about equality between two groups, but an affirmation and a denial; it is the site of the shock and the rivalry between a culture in progress (Jewish) basically euro-Westal, a minority in the rest of the countries of the world and that demands its right to be majority in a country (Israel), and the traditional tenaciously and relatively outdated native Arab presence, which is in majority in 18 states of the Middle East, and that being a minority in Palestine pretends to act as if it were the majority.

For the Palestinians has been impossible to understand the reasons of the immolated by the anti-Semitism or that they see in Zionism more than a diatribe with the colonizing non-Jew. For them, Israel appears like a European advanced post artificially financed by the United States, and the Jews like a religious sect that was always under the Islam sword. A post-holocaust phenomenon lodged in the Middle East for West, which will disappear eventually like other colonial establishments.

One of its oldest myths underlines that they constituted "people without land" earmarked "a land without people". But, in reality, the Palestinians was a plot in this indeterminate Arab mass settler of the world levy of the Morocco to the Iraq, without cultural, historical or ethnic identity, and for being anything less a nation, without control over the territory they were occupying.

In the literature and humanist thought favorable to the Zionism the Holy Land was essentially unpopulated (as in the puritan vision of the United States), not by absence of inhabitants, but because the dogma in the Victorian human status of non-Europeans was systematically denied, and the only viable option was a colonial mission *civilizatrice*.

The "empty" territory of Palestine was flavored with the restoration of the Promised Land of the Zionists, who, assisted by the great powers, pursued establish the enlightenment and progress. At its most intimate spiritual, the Jews never lost the Promised Land, preposterous abstraction for the Arabs, who conquered it from Byzantium more than fourteen centuries ago.

That is why the Iraqi Baas considered that the confusion of the West on the Arab policy responded to the archeology of colonial mentality. They accept as true that ethnocentrism - the notion that the non-European world has been there to be claimed and its natives to be directed-, influenced the Zionist project that in essence, for the Arabs resembled a colonial factory in the Orient, arguing that was not a coincidence their convergence in time and space with the territorial expansion and imperial hegemony of Europe.

The obsession of the West media with the Israeli issue is disproportionate, and cannot be explained only by the millennial Jew wandering in Europe or the manipulation of the imperial machinery. In the Christian collective memory haunts the trauma of rejection of the Jew, centuries of marginalization, persecution and abandonment; the horrendous Tsarist pogroms, the common graves of Babi-Yar and the bodies stacked in the Nazi concentration camps. If subconscious Islamic Israel is also treading sacred ground for the Christians it is incomprehensible that the Islamists are offending biblical grounds.

The area of the drama is transcendental to Christianity, by settling precisely in Jewish sources the background to the revelation of the New Testament; being they, precisely, who inaugurated a universal code of moral justice detached from divine tables received on Mount Sinai, and that molded the psyche, the cultural environment and the ethnic values of Westal gnosis.

That the Jews returned to Evangelical grounds makes their State, with Jerusalem as its capital, another of the biblical episodes and the heir of a happening of three millennia, which re-established communion with the Judeo-Christian believer with this biblical faith. Israel is so entwined with the religious movements of the Christian genealogy -as Puritan that populated United States and preached to erect the "New Jerusalem"- embodying the hope canon.

The astonishing Israeli victory in the Six Day War in 1967 crowned in the media information and press of the West the certainty of its tenacity and its military prowess. After refusing to return their conquests, began the "bad press" against Israel, especially in Germany, France, Spain and Italy, who later would represent them as a brutal winner, a new Prussia.

The old continent embraced the Palestinian cause not by compassion, but because it would allow it to shake off its debt of conscience with the Jew, misleadingly involving them with the massacres of Palestinians at Sabra and Chatilla, at the hand of the Lebanese and at the same time exonerating the cruelty of the Nazis, by pointing out that there have always been nations that massacre other nations.

The terrorist apostolate of Yasser Arafat´s Al-Fatah, or Hamas, would never be questioned with the same intensity as the responses from the Jewish State. That their enemies were Jews and the battlefield the Holy Land has provided more visibility to the Palestinians than any other community of refugees or other defeated peoples of the planet.

His case does not stand the comparison with other disasters ignored by the West, such as the Armenian genocide, the slaughter of Kurds, the disappearance of Tibet as a State, the carnage of a million people from the Ibo tribes in Nigeria, the atrocious duels between Watusi and Hutus in Rwanda and Burundi, the immolation of the Iranian "divine mobs" in the war with Iraq, the tragic fate of Chechnya, the struggle for Kashmir, the ruin of the Somali nation by the warlords.

Nobody blames Syria for occupying Lebanon! There is no one to lift their finger over the fate of the Christianity of Sudan. What about those who recognize the revelation of the Congo, whose civil war has claimed the creepy figure of 3 million dead?

Caught between the passion and the tribe on one hand, and modernity and economic expansion on the other, Palestinians and Israelis opted for first thing. The Israelis claim Jerusalem as their capital and the Palestinians also; the Israelis demand Haifa and the Palestinians as well; many Israelis are demanding the West Bank and the Palestinians also; the Palestinians want Jaffa, which is in Israeli hands. There are no Palestinians in Israeli fantasy world, and there are no Israelis in the Palestinian's.

Both Arabs and Israelis have to rid of paralysis marked by their tribal worlds, where the ancestors define the present and each side thinks they can get everything. The first obstacle is clinging to the alleged "legitimate rights" granted by tradition, the biblical Yahweh, or by the Quranic Allah, preventing the appearance of "legitimate interests" based *realpolitik*. That is why a rational appreciation is to innovate the terms and approaches that today seem to be insoluble, reformulating the same rights for both sides. So did Anwar Al-Sadat by recognizing the State of Israel, in order to recover the Sinai Peninsula.

The machinery of war in policing will never grant the Israelis the peace and tranquility they so avidly seek, but the historical paradox is that no state has voluntarily ceded a portion of territory for ideological reasons or national security. The price of peace rises every year, exacerbated by the non-existence of attractive alternatives for the two contenders, especially when life and the political destiny of the two are inextricably interwoven.

The future encloses different results: for the Jews implies getting rid of oppressive biblical hypnotism, in the aftermath of Nazi anti-Semitism, from fear to its Arab neighbors; for Palestinians it is to redeem themselves from exile, exceed their cultural and psychological fringe and rid of the discriminated context in which they exist.

The Six Day War had devastating effects on the Palestinian militancy, much of which left the fight convinced that was impossible to defeat Israel militarily. The Israelite mistake was not having negotiated with the Arabs, with international arbitration, a regional peace, immediately after their speedy 1967 victory. The "Palestinian agenda" would have deflated, and Arab communities in Gaza and the West Bank would have been peacefully assimilated to Egypt and Jordan, of Palestinian refugees in other Arab States would have the nationality of residency.

Until 1967 the central theme in the area was the dispute between the Arab States and Israel, and the Palestinian issue was only secondary. Each Arab State sought to have a quick voice among the Palestinians to benefit from powerful legitimacy that in the eyes of the Arab masses from their respective countries granted to be linked to the so called Palestinian struggle. However, with the conquest of Gaza and the West Bank in the Six Day War of June 1967, it was no longer possible to ignore in the Palestinian dilemma, when a bi-national existence between Jews and Arabs was produced.

After the impact of the 1967 war the Egyptians virtually abandoned the Palestinians, and transcended the inter-Arab struggles, reconsidered their relationship with the Baas and Nasserites program of expulsion of the Jews and unification of all the Palestinian territory, in favor of the variant of two states, one Jewish and the other Palestinian secular and democratic, and with a greater militancy toward the PLO and the Communist Party.

¿A tribal conflict?

Israel and Palestine:
two "exiled" nations converge in the Holy Land.

Of the territory comprising Palestine, the British created two entities in 1921. One of them, to the east of the Jordan River, was called Transjordan, or more simply Jordan, and was transferred to the Bedouin chief Abdullah Ibn Hussein. The other one comprised the stripe from the Jordan to the Mediterranean, where the Palestinian Arabs and the Jews were struggling for control under the British Order. Between 1922 and 1947 the crisis in Palestine was not essentially a fight between native Arabs and Jewish settlers, but between the latter and the British authorities.

Two Jewish personalities from opposite slopes, the Communist Lev Dadidovich Bronstein, alias Trotsky, and the Zionist Vladimir Yevgeneyevich Zhabotinsky, predicted the terrible consequences for the Jews and for the international community in its entire dimension that would bring the rise to power of the Nazi Party in Germany. The Arabs counted on the German victory for independence from France and England, and shut down the Jewish emigration to Palestine. Palestinians rebels like Al-Husayni, Grand Mufti of Jerusalem, allied to Adolf Hitler's Germany where they received support for their plan against the Jews of Palestine, including radio facilities from Berlin.

The XXII Zionist Congress, which met in Basel in December 1942, was forced to decide that the State of Israel[1] would have to be established in the middle of a territorial compromise at the price of a partition. The Zionists thought the way to establish a Jewish state was, on one hand to force the British to lift the restrictions on immigration to Palestine, and the other to strengthen Jewish paramilitary forces of self-defense, as the Hagenah, the Irgun and the Stern Gang.

The strategy of the Hagenah rested in waiting for the British promise of surrendering Palestine to materialize. For its part, the "Stern Band" founded by Abraham Stern, was the most violent group on the Zionist rainbow. The Irgun was a mixture of Orthodox Oriental Jews, mainly Polish, basically anti-Marxists and imbued with a fierce messianic fervor. Menachem Begin, former prisoner of Josef Stalin, became the natural leader of this lethal underground organization.

The Jews were against the wall not only in the Europe occupied by the Nazis, who threatened to extinguish the entire Jewish population, but also in Palestine in the midst of an antagonistic ocean of Arabs who, in case of a mass attack, could also destroy them. For Begin, it was impossible to achieve a state without a Jewish Praetorian guard amid a hostile territory and against the wishes of the British colonial authorities.

The Zionists never discussed what to do with the Arab population living in the confines of Palestine. The Jewish Council considered with candor that Arabs would be integrated into the Jewish State. This indecision was an important element used by Britain to justify the mandate and maintain a low quote of immigrants, constraint that in the eyes of the world turned cruel after the German collapse was known the horror of the "final solution". The Arabs, on the other hand, shaped their old strategy in which an Arab Palestinian State would be created with some Jewish communities, but excluding refugees from European concentration camps.

British politicians underestimated the Zionist leaders, and to increased pressure, the Irgun of Begin responded escalating acts of terrorism. The British responded by hanging the Irgun militants, and these in turn hanged English soldiers. The British settled the Jewish refugees in dismantled concentration camps in Germany. The world was horrified by the British moral insensitivity and an outraged President of

United States Harry S. Truman influenced British Prime Minister Clement Attlee not give in to Arab pressures and evacuates the territory.

The UN then announced a plan for the division of Palestine. In debates the Soviet Union supported the partition plan and the creation of the State of Israel. Stalin was the second head of State (after President Truman) to recognize the State of Israel. In his speech the Soviet delegate Andrei Gromyko pointed out that this decision meets the legitimate demands of the Jewish nation, where hundreds of thousands of Jews lacked a national home.

On 15 May 1948, David Ben-Gurion, as Prime Minister, declared the existence of the State of Israel, and the United Nations nominated Swedish Aristocrat Folke Bernadotte to mediate the Palestine partition. For the first time, the millennial Jewish fate of living in the Diaspora was reverted.

The impact on the world's conscience that had the virtual destruction of the European Jewry in the German crematories finally relented Palestine to the survivors of the Holocaust. Thus, the legacy of Hitler far of being the Elimination of Jews ironically resulted in the formation of the Jewish State.

But the British would leave an embryonic state to their fate, surrounded by Arab enemies in the conviction that there would be a war that would sweep with the poor Jewish combatant forces and with it the illusion of a homeland in Palestine. London was washing their hands. This way and on purpose, the English created the Arab-Jew dilemma in Palestine.

On November 29, 1947 the UN adopted the partition of Western Palestine into two States: one for the Jews comprising the Negev desert, coastal Tel- Aviv to Haifa and part of Galilee, and another to the Palestinian Arabs that consisted of the Western Bank of the Jordan[2], the District of Gaza, Jaffa, and Arab sectors of Galilee. Jerusalem, requested by Jews and Muslims as being the "sacred city" for both, supposedly was to become an international enclave under UN trusteeship.

The demographic imperative plus the political reality was what legitimized the claim of the Jews about its origin, precisely when they implemented their State. It has not been unusual historical incident where their enemies define individuals and communities, and this is particularly true with Palestinians, catalyzed by a non-Arabic society.

What is today known as Palestine was articulated by the warmongering Arab response to Jewish immigration tide. And that traumatic encounter pointed out an identity that is cemented simultaneously to the Israeli, equally brought from international hand.

The Arab States didn't attempt to resettle the Palestinians, preferring to keep them in refugee camps as a public reminder to the rest of the world of the creation of the State of Israel in their "holy lands".

After the war of 1948 of the Arabs against Jews, Palestine has been cleared as a geographical entity and as people; they requested almost all of the territory between Israel, Jordan and Egypt. Part of the Palestinians remained in Israel and the majority was confined to refuges in the Lebanon and Syria. After 1948 Palestinian exiles and those who remained within Israel adopted a policy of accommodation to the situation. Those who stayed inside accepted the policy of the Israeli State.

The campaign of Palestinian expatriates in favor of their right to return was launched by the former Arab monarchs of Egypt (Farouk I), Jordan (Hassan II) and Saudi Arabia (Faisal), precisely authors of the fields of Palestine refugees for their anti-Israeli Crusades.

In the fifties, Egypt and a handful of Arabs in exile only hoisted Palestinian rights. It was the Egyptian President Abdul Nasser who, on 12 April 1955, masterminded the Palestinian cause, having gathered in Cairo the Arab leaders of Gaza, with views to organize, train, arm and finance the

Palestinian Fedayeen and join them in a military structure that would allow them to fight for a "home in Palestine", battle in which the Egyptians would assume the forefront.

Al-Fatah was founded by Palestinians from the universities of Cairo and Alexandria and headed by a then anonymous character called Yasser Arafat that preached a return to Palestine through violence. The head of the Egyptian intelligence in Jordan, Colonel Salah Mustafa, took over the training of 700 Fedayeen who spent their baptism of fire in August 1955. Mustafa, who was a close friend of Nasser and didn't conceal his admiration for the Nazis, was blown to pieces in Jerusalem by a bomb hidden in the memoirs of Marshal Gerd von Rundstedt: *The Commander and the Man*, which he had received by mail[3].

It was around that time that the foundation of al–Fatah took place, where Yasser Arafat participated. Arafat came from a family with a long tradition of anti-Zionist struggle; his father and brother had fought against the Jewish communities in Palestine. His tribal clan, el Hussein had embraced the Nazi supporting the Grand Mufti of Jerusalem creed. In the fifties Arafat received training at the Military Academy in Egypt and became an expert in explosives.

In 1956, several small groups attacked some military posts in Gaza. Under orders from Nasser, Fedayeen commands took part in the Suez war in 1957 where the Israeli armored destroyed them. By the end of the decade there was a hotbed of small organizations in exile engaged in the fight against Israel. The "Palestinian entity" as it was called became a certainty in 1959, when it began to be recognized by the members of the Arab League.

In 1963, under the patronage of President Nasser, the main Palestinian groups were forced to establish a formal Alliance between them and join an umbrella organization, the Palestine Liberation Organization (PLO), which would be the Palestinian armed wing. In theory, at least, these groups were represented on the Central Committee of the PLO, and its alliances would be maintained or weaken depending on the progress of the political and military situation of the struggle.

Palestinian intellectuals from Beirut, Lebanon, rejected the PLO from the first moment, which was seen as an extension of the Egyptians. These Palestinian intellectuals -George Habash style- advocated a modern Marxist revolution that placed them at the forefront of the Arab Nations. The Arab League accepted the PLO in 1964, as an umbrella institution that banded and "channeled" the belligerence of refugee organizations.

The main groups within the PLO would be Al-Fatah, the most important; the As-Saiqa Organization, engendered by Syria; the Popular Front of liberation of Palestine (PFLP) which called for an Arab revolution to recover Palestine and was diametrically opposed to any settlement with Israel, the United States or the "Arab reaction"; the Democratic Popular Front of liberation of Palestine (PDFLP), one of the staunchest Arafat opponents, was founded in 1969, nuked Marxist trends and would be the first to propose the establishment of a national Palestinian Authority in any part of the territory evacuated by Israel.

Arafat, known as "the old man", would deploy a centrist philosophy within the Palestine political range and doctrinally would express his rejection of everything that could legitimize the presence of the State of Israel in Palestine. From the Balfour Declaration, the 1947 Partition Plan, to Camp David, the Soviets, Cubans, the Syrians and Iraqis played an important role in the development of the PLO as a terrorist organization with more financial resources, better trained, equipped with modern weaponry and multiple bases and sanctuaries.

But in times of crisis the Egyptian Secret Service was the firmest Allied Forces of the PLO; then it extended bonds with Saudi Arabia and the Libya of Muammar Kaddafi. The PLO received more military and financial resources than other rival Palestinian organizations.

It was not until 1965 that the modern phase of clashes between Israel and the Palestinians started when Al-Fatah, the armed wing of Yasser Arafat, delivered a coup within Israel. In that year, the Syrian President Amin Al-Hafez and his secret services conceived the project to unite various factions of Palestinian refugee activists under a coordinated terrorist organization and provided them with secret training in their military bases, by copying the experience of the Algerian Fedayeen to "expel the Jews as Algerians expelled the French colonists of North Africa"[4]. Al-Fatah launched armed actions against Israel from Jordan, although sometimes from the Lebanon territory until 1967.

With such self-discovery, tensions between the Palestinian organizations and the Arab States would be increased since then. Subsequent to its first leader, Ahmad Shukairy, Yasser Arafat, who initially was seen as an instrument of the Egyptian President Gamal Abdul Nasser, dominated PLO. But under Arafat Palestinian politics would move from the periphery (the control of Arab countries) towards the center of the international consensus.

With the war of 1967, the Palestinians got rid of its Arab patterns. Like the refugees in Lebanon, Jordan and Syria (which from disenfranchised became political forces), those in Gaza and the West Bank rose with their own voice. It was thus, paradoxically, that the Israeli occupation reunified the geography of Palestine again, and unusually the same communities (Jewish and Palestinian) resumed the same struggle that, for the same territory –Palestine under British mandate- their grandparents undertook.

If their parents were "egypsized or jordanized", the new generations of Palestinian in Gaza and West Bank emphasized their affiliation and modeled new cultural roots, now that the previous protectors –Egypt and Jordan- lay defeated. And this budded, from evening to morning: the hope to forge a state.

The balance of Arafat as Palestinian leader would not be entire favorable. But after the Six Day War in 1967, dire for the Arabs, Arafat began his struggle to attain political autonomy of the same, although the inflections of his politics have been marked by those who at every moment are its sources of funding, which have not been confined to professing Sunni Islam countries.

Used by the Arabs, defeated by the Jews and forgotten by the rest of the world, Palestinians were extracted from this stagnation by work and grace of Arafat, who liberated them from their guardians, gave them an international infrastructure and made them sadly famous as terrorists. An avenging political arm would symbolize their collective willingness: the PLO, first in exile and later in Gaza and the West Bank. With a chameleon skin, Arafat tiptoed by the nest of snakes of the intra-Arab policy, spurring the Syrians against Jordanians, Iraqis against the Egyptians and reserving a spot to operate with clear autonomy.

The financial strength of the petro-Arabs and with them their favorite cause (Palestine) cannot be underestimated, since it is the most sacred in Islam. Underpinned by their "Islamic brothers" and heading to the third world, Arafat had the sagacity of transubstantiate himself in a sort of Arabic Pope, and didn't find it difficult that the PLO would win the recognition of the UN and a hundred countries.

After assembling a critical mass that consolidated his almost dictatorial leadership, and uniqueness of the PLO, he managed to keep under his fist the activist mafias by favors, corruption, with an ideology of simple terms and refusing to put at the service of a particular Arabic block.

It is true that he knew how to maneuver in the midst of the bloody internal struggle of the movement; he could raise a winner in the contest to be the only representative of the refugees and resident Arabs in Israel; that, if well battered, he survived his clashes with Arab regimes, and it has managed to maneuver through the crevices of the United States-Europe Alliance.

Terrorism had its initial push by a handful of Palestinian organizations. One of the first to distinguish Islamic violence as the wave of the future was the ringleader military PLO Jalil Al-Wazir, the dreaded Abu-Jihad. The area is further clouded with the use of oil as a political weapon, with the erratic imprint of the then Libyan President Muamar Qaddafi, and the collapse of Lebanon as a nation. Thus, the emergence of the Palestinian movement of the PLO after the Six-Day War was promoted by the desire to compensate for the disastrous performance of the Arab armies against Israel[5].

The Al-Fatah organization in particular was the most vociferous in its position of no-commitment with Israel, rejecting November of 1967 resolution of the UN. The PLO declared war on United States for its support to Israel, a country that from their point of view should not exist. Al-Fatah urged the rest of the Palestinians to press with violence and ultimately destroy Israel through clandestine operations from Jordan and Lebanon.

Palestinian exiles, organized into parish confraternities subordinate to the intra-Arab dynamics, respond more to the cultures of their local residence (Tunisia, Lebanon, Jordan, Syria), and the revolutionary climate of the sixties, than to their ancestral land. During its time in Jordan (1967-1971), Lebanon (1972-1984) and Tunisia (1984-1994), the PLO had their base of support and the source of its guerrillas in refugees, disinterested in the fate of Gaza or the West Bank, for reasons of distance and myopia before reality, more inclined to extreme solutions, such as to push the Jews into the sea.

Palestinian violence and terrorism against Israel acquired notoriety in late sixties and early seventies. The policy of the Palestinians until 1967 had moved parallel to currents of the Islamic universe where Arafat also preside the serious Palestinian misery. He wanted to do nothing to negotiate the recovery of the territories lost in the Arab-Israeli war of 1967 on the "West Bank", Gaza, and East Jerusalem.

For them, who left their homes in Jaffa, Haifa and Galilee, to recognize Israel implies that their sufferings and their dead were in vain. That was the reason the agitators, ideologues and guerrillas have been the most dynamic element of their policy. It was the Islamic psychology in denial to add to the contemporary progress, with their complex inferiority and megalomania, lost in their dreams of holy war.

Despite this metamorphosis of unsettled refugees of a nation in search of sovereignty, Palestinians discover in Beirut and later in Jerusalem -following the peace agreements- that the attributes of Arafat as leader[4], who brought out them of darkness, were now precisely the obstacles to the creation of his State.

The Soviets saw in the guerrillas a means of drawing closer to the rest of the Arab world and as instruments that could serve many of their purposes. Arafat, next to the Marxist George Habash and the most senior Palestinian leaders travelled at the beginning of 1968 to Moscow where the soviets offered resources and the experience of the KGB[6] to start new terrorist training camps in Jordan[7]. But at the same time a too public linkage with Al-Fatah meant compromising their current earnings with those Arab States they were putting together.

The Soviets began to grow distance from them expressing "sympathy for its resistance" but doubts about their methods to unseat Israel[8] as Al-Fatah prestige was growing as his operations became more audacious and he was receiving substantial financial support from the moderate Arabs of the Persian Gulf and Saudi Arabia.

The Soviets practiced an ambivalent policy between Arafat and the Arab States. In the months after the Six Day War, the Soviet Union showed its support to Palestinian guerrilla commands, especially in actions within the occupied territories.

The PLO began to receive arms from the former Soviet bloc and financial support from the region, turning into a dangerous enemy for Israel. Several groups proclaimed their "independence" from Arafat taking responsibility for the terrorist attacks, but the secret services of the Western countries knew that it was a ploy to exempt the PLO's international repudiation.

The UN approved self-determination of Palestine in 1969 and the PLO would receive the recognition of two thirds of the states of the planet, as the legitimate representative of the Palestinian people, despite the fact that United States and Israel have not admitted it officially.

In March 1968 the PLO obtains its baptism of fire on having executed an independent action when it holds a long meeting with Israeli regular forces in Karameh, in Israel. Sometime after the Fedayeen of the PLO had formed *quasi* states inside Jordan and the Lebanon, against which they would clash.

Throughout Europe, PLO terrorists moved to attack any individual, entity or installation representing Israel. On July 22, 1968 the terrorist group headed by Ahmed Yibril abducted the Rome-Tel Aviv flight of the Israeli airway company El-Al. On December 26 of that year, his organization again attacked an aircraft of El-Al in plain sight at the full track of flight in Athens.

In February 1969 it would be the turn of another Israeli aircraft in Zurich. In August, the Palestinian command "Che Guevara" hijacked the TWA Flight bound for Libya, diverting it to Syria. The 29th of that month, a time bomb exploded at the offices of the ZIM in London; September 8th, two bombs simultaneously exploded in the Israeli embassies of Hague and Bonn; on November 27 a grenade detonated amid a crowd gathered at the Athenian offices of the El-Al airlines.

The number of aircraft hijackings of in those years rose to hundreds. The PLO negotiated operational neutrality with some European countries (Greece and Italy) under the commitment they would not operate against them, even though they used them as hiding places in a clandestine fashion.

Behind scenes the Soviet diplomacy exerted tremendous pressure on Arab Governments so they would control and discipline the guerrillas of Arafat. In December 1969 at the Conference of Arab heads of State in Rabat, Arafat blocked the Soviet-Egyptian proposal of a unified policy toward the Palestinian problem. The visit of Arafat to Moscow in February 1970 went without sorrows or glories, to be handled by a second category officer.

In 1970 Egypt accepted the plan proposed by United States Secretary of State William Rogers of a ceasefire for three months. Arafat accused President Nasser of having "capitulated" to the Rogers agenda, definitively distancing the PLO from the Egyptian protection, losing its broadcasting spaces on Radio Cairo.

Also, the confrontation before the political manipulation of the Arab States "brothers" acquires dramatic profiles when Arafat assumes the foolish decision to challenge in Jordan the power of King Hussein, and Habash Palestinian commands flew three hijacked planes that had landed in Jordan, in a celebration of carnage.

This was too much for King Hussein, whose senior Bedouin official begged for the Palestinians to be expelled. The violent manner with which President Nasser reacted to the PLO led King Hussein of Jordan to order his Arab Legion on September 15 to attack the refugee camps and Palestinian guerrillas, in a massacre that killed thousands of Palestinians in a fight that lasted two weeks and almost eliminated the PLO. This was known as Black September.

On the other hand, the Syrians, determined to aid the Palestinians, but were stopped by Israel under the threat of intervention. This civil war in Jordan marked the beginning of the end of the power of the Palestinian Fedayeen in the Arab world. The Soviet Union maintained strict neutrality in this encounter, reserving their toughest epithets for Israel.

The Soviets hoped to supplant the United States as arbiter of the peace negotiations in the area, and so believed they had the support of Sadat. While terrorist bosses Mohammed Boudia (first), and Ilitch Ramirez or Carlos "the Jackal" (second) were the heads in Europe of the operations of the PFLP, Palestinian novelist and refined poet Ghassan Kanafani appeared as their brain in the terrorist attacks until in July 18, 1972 when turning on his car, an Israeli bomb exploded instantly killing him[9].

As a screen structure of Al-Fath a new terrorist movement was created: Black September, headed by Mohammad Youssef Al-Najjar, second aboard of Arafat. Black September received training and advice from the KGB, and the Cubans, which enabled a powerful center of intelligence in Cyprus for such matters.

As revenge against King Hussein, Black September killed the Jordanian Prime Minister, Wasfi Al-Tal when leaving the hotel Sheraton in Cairo. Black September installed their winter quarters in Sweden and Norway using the glare of its intellectuals and editors towards Tiers Monde, the "new left", and the ineffable ingenuity and financial largesse of its rulers toward Palestinian refugees. It was the criterion of Al-Fatah that Israel could be defeated if the Palestinians untied a pitiless and intense terrorist war.

In turn, the armed infiltration of Abu Abbas on Israel take place, and other spookiest adventures that includes two of the most outrageous as the murder of Leon Klinghoffer committed by Abu Abbas in the Achille Lauro in 1985, and the assault on the beaches of Tel- Aviv in 1990.

This strategy of Palestinian terror brought a punitive behavior of counter-attack no less violent, by Israel. After the infamous massacre of 11 Israeli athletes by Palestinian gunmen lead by Ali Hassan Salameh at the Munich Olympics, Israeli premier, Golda Meir, outlined the strategy to fight terror with terror.

On 9 April 1973 Israel mounted a landing command in Beirut annihilating almost all the leadership of Al-Fatah and Black September. Valuable documents seized showed the close linkage of the KGB with all the terrorist framework and Palestinian plans to liquidate the "moderate" Arab leaders. Israel transferred the information to such Governments, who took action against Arafat[10].

Both in Jordan, Lebanon and elsewhere, the PLO used the practice of establishing its commanders, barracks and arms depots in neighboring buildings to schools or hospitals. The bloody clashes between the Palestinian factions in Damascus, Beirut and Baghdad passed unnoticed to the prejudiced news media. The Palestinians of terrorists Abu Nidal in Iraq and Wadie Haddad in South Yemen, natural born killers, mounted attacks on the PLO men prominent in Europe trying to make their way via bombings towards the PLO leaders.

The terrorist fight against Israel, which didn't provide to be a solution to the Palestinian cause, left the PLO virtually leaderless after it disappeared -except Arafat- much of its historic leadership: Ghassan Kanafani, Gamal Nasser, Kamal Adwan, Yusuf Najjar, Abu Al-Walid, Abu Jihad, Abu Iyad and Abu Nidal.

As a result of the agreements of the Sinai in 1974 and 1975, US Secretary of State Henry Kissinger´s strategy rested on forcing each Arab country affected to negotiate with Israel on a bilateral basis, avoiding the Arab organizations[11]. Simultaneously, the European countries decided to back the idea that was incumbent to the Palestinians: to negotiate the peace process with Israel, rejecting Egypt acting for the Palestinians and United States speaking for Israel.

After emerging as the first Arab political movement, his leadership came to the conclusion in 1974 that the Arab Palestinian could never be recreated, but that a type of arrangement was possible with Israel. On spite of that reality, in 1974 around a hundred members in the UN corroborated the Resolution of 1969 confirming the PLO as the legitimate representative of the Palestinian people.

For the first time in the Palestinian National Council meeting in Rabat, in 1974, the Arab Summit accepted the PLO as the representative of the Palestinian people and Arafat spoke of accepting a Palestinian State in Gaza and the West Bank. Arafat was immediately accused of capitulating to Zionism.

After the conferences of the Palestinian National Council in 1977, most headed by PLO confirmed its position in favor of the Palestinian State in the "occupied territories", against fierce opposition from the militant minority that argued for the complete liberation of the territory, including Jaffa, Haifa and Galilee. What tipped the balance in favor of Arafat was the incorporation of the centrist line of Palestinians in Gaza and the West Bank who to achieve peace where settling for a mini-state with common borders, a regular exchange and mutual understanding policy.

The Palestinians have projected an Arab nationalism, which didn't always manage to preserve their godparents of the Islamic world. All the Palestinian organizations without exception have proved to be a headache, among other reasons for the marriage of the Palestinian struggle with the numerous opposition movements in both the Persian Gulf region as in the Fertile Crescent and in north Africa, from the Marxist Egyptians, the Nasserites, the Islamic militant groups up to the myriad of large and small parties, political undesirables, and political currents heretics.

With a budget bulging from donations of Palestinian residents in the wealthy Arab States, as well as the contribution of Saudi Arabia, Kuwait and other oil countries, services, logistics, training and arms control were covered, as well as attention to almost a million Palestinians, the PLO became bourgeois and transformed into a bureaucracy where student organizations, women and trade unions, schools, social care system and veterans, health and supplies were managed.

Between 1977 and 1979 the Iraqis orchestrated a discredit campaign against Egypt and its peace agreement with Israel, while the PLO was plunged into a bloody internal war as Al-Fatah and pro-Iraqis groups in 1978. In 1978, Said Hammami the representative of the PLO in London, who proposed to negotiate directly with the Israelis, was killed by a member of the circle of Abu Nidal, also agent of the Iraqi Secret Service[12].

The peace treaty caused oil Arab countries to cancel their contracts of employment to millions of Egyptians, which remitted an amount in excess to $30,000 million dollars annually, the most important income of the country[13]. For its part the Government of Premier Begin unleashed an offensive against the PLO camps in Lebanon, and refused to apply the autonomy to Gaza and the West Bank, further discrediting Egypt across the Middle East.

In July 1977, the head of the Mossad (Israeli service secret), General Yitzhak Hacka Hofi alerted President Menachem Begin that Libyan President Muammar Gaddafi had infiltrated a Palestinian command to assassinate the Egyptian President Anwar El-Sadat. The Palestinian conspirators not only were arrested in Cairo making possible the historic Sadat trip to Tel-Aviv. He was so impressed that he determined to go one step beyond, and entered into an Alliance with the Israelis that would disrupt enemies and allies, but without which Sadat could not assume its policy of recognition of Israel.

Among the secret agreements of Camp David promoted by United States stipulated the cooperation of the two most powerful secret services of the area: The Israeli Mossad and the Directorate General of Intelligence Egyptian (knower of all secrets of the PLO), factor that in fact was what altered the balance of regional power and sealed the fate of the Palestine armed resistance[14].

It was precisely this covenant of intelligence what dismantled the PLO as an effective terrorist organization, marking a catastrophe more formidable that the Jordanian Black September 1970 or the Lebanese disaster of the following decade. The bulk of the political and military leadership of the PLO were creatures of the Egyptian secret service, which had infiltrated the organization much more than the Israelites. For this reason, in the media intelligence and of the sub-world international clandestine it was learned that Arafat had sentenced to death the Egyptian President Anwar El-Sadat[15].

Even before his death, the preceding Egyptian President Nasser had done the contortion of a traditional intransigence to the arrangement with the United States and the recognition of Israel. As the initiator of this realistic strategy (wrongly attributed to Anwar El-Sadat), Nasser, with its prestige and sagacity would have achieve to drag with him the Arab moderate countries, avoiding the isolation than a bland Sadat brought to Egypt, and dodging the failure of Arab-Israeli reconciliation.

The effect that this political mutation had on the Palestiniars, especially the PLO which angrily opposed any type of settlement, resulted in the crisis against the monarchy of Jordan in 1970-1971 and the Lebanon in 1975-1976, with an enormous cost in human lives.

The Guerrilla Foco

In the early years of their rule, Castro and his closest followers were wedded to the rural guerrillas. In the 1960s, the majority of Cuban-promoted insurgencies in Latin America were rural based. Almost every significant Latin American terrorist group of left wing orientation has had or has today links with Cuba.

In January of 1959, Ernest "Che" Guevara defined what would become until today the central tenet of political violence: "A small group of determined men, without fear of death, if death were necessary, can dominate a disciplined conventional army and defeat it decisively."

Soon after seizing power in 1959, Castro organized a series of groups to subvert the stability of the Dominican Republic, Haiti, Nicaragua, Guatemala and Panama. He trained Dominican nationals in the mountains of Pinar del Rio, and at the Jamaica military camp on the outskirts of Havana, more than 500 Haitians received training. The Castro regime clandestinely acquired weapons in the United States which were also introduced in Costa Rica to overthrow that country's President Mario Echandi.

Particularly troubling for governments in the region was the landing of eighty-four guerrillas in Panama on April 16, 1959 to fight against the elected government of Ernesto de LaGuardia, carrying out the first act of external aggression. The group included only one Panamanian plus a U.S. citizen; the rest were all Cubans[1].

The Dominican Republic assault followed on June 14, 1959. In August, Operation Haiti began. Destabilization of the

Salvadorian government came next. A bit later Peru confirmed Cuba's financing of the insurrectional movement.

In May of 1960 "Che" Guevara and Fidel Castro decided to assume the direction of budding guerrilla and terrorist activities in Colombia. It was at that time that Castro's plan went global. Cuba decided to engage in Africa and the Middle East.

In January of 1961, in Cuba's Sierra Maestra Mountains, Castro organized a Latin American brigade that included Guatemalans, Paraguayans, Colombians, Costa Ricans, and a large number of Venezuelans and established, simultaneously, clandestine weapons assembly stations in the Amazon, along the Venezuelan belt of Garabato, to supply urban guerrillas and terrorist groups[2].

In January 1962, reacting to an Interamerican Peace Committee report demonstrating that the Government of Cuba was violating the rights of the Cuban people and promoting subversion in Latin America, the member states of the Organization of American States overwhelmingly voted to expel Cuba from participating in the Interamerican system, the reason being the incompatibility of a Marxist Leninist state with the Interamerican system[3].

After the missile crisis and reassured by the Soviet's protective umbrella, the Cuban regime continued its subversive efforts. The Cubans rejected orthodox Communist parties, which they regarded as ineffectual. Instead, they lent their support to more militant groups dedicated to armed violence.

During the early and mid-1960s, Guatemala, Colombia, Venezuela, Peru, and Bolivia all faced serious Cuban-baked attempts to develop guerrilla *focus*. The regime placed special emphasis on Venezuela, providing men and materials, to coordinate and support guerrilla uprisings, attacks to military barracks, and sabotage of U.S. property[4].

In Venezuela, a war raged against democratically elected governments between 1961 and 1963 by the so-called Armed Forces of National Liberation (FALN) trained and armed by

Havana, featuring some of the bloodiest acts of urban terrorism committed in Latin America.

In November 1963, four tons of arms provided by Cuba were found by security forces in a cache on Venezuela's lonely northwest coast. The arms had been smuggled aboard a boat belonging to the Cuban Institute of Agrarian Reform.

In August of 1963, the Arrecifes gas pipe and the Ulcamay oil pipeline were blown up, and a Cuban plan to assassinate the presidents of Venezuela and Colombia was uncovered. Intending to ruin Venezuela's December elections, Castro-trained terrorists threatened voters with death if they showed up at the polls.

In July of 1965, a commando team of Cubans and Venezuelars, led by General Arnaldo T. Ochoa, landed in Venezuela to establish a major guerrilla operations base in the country.

In a series of diversionary actions, groups of Venezuelan terrorists blasted the Gulf Oil, Mobil Oil, Texas Petroleum and Socony Oil pipelines[5].

By mid-1964 the extent of Cuba's subversive activities in the region were such that at the Meeting of Consultation of the Ministers of Foreign Affairs of the Organization of American States, convened by Venezuela, a continent-wide embargo was imposed against Cuba. By the end of that year, all countries of the Western Hemisphere had broken relations with Cuba, except Mexico[6].

In 1965, with Cuban support, insurrection increased in Peru along the eastern ridge of the Andes, under the leadership of Luis de La Puente Uceda, head of the MIR and closely linked to Cuba. This was to be followed by "Che" Guevara's major guerrilla effort in Bolivia, a major component of Castro's effort to create "one, two, three, many Viet Nams" in Latin America.

At the Tricontinent Conference, held in January 1966 and attended by 513 predominantly Castroite leaders of eighty-three Third World radical movements and CPs, Castro promised the delegates that any revolutionary movement anywhere in the world can count on Cuba's unconditional support[7].

Claire Sterling, testified that various groups which emerged around 1968, and which were committed to revolution by violence, "were given first access to the guerrilla training camps in Cuba, around Havana, which had opened first for guerrilla fighters from Latin America and Africa."

Mrs. Sterling's testimony point to the Tricontinent Conference in Havana, to devise a global strategy against American or Western "imperialism." The 1966 meeting of the Tricontinent was a program and a schedule for the well planned and equally well-financed terrorist and destabilization operations which have occurred since that time. Mrs. Sterling testified that some of the most important figures on the terrorist scene, including Carlos, were trained in Cuba.

In July 1967, FALN terrorists kidnapped and subsequently murdered the brother of the Venezuelan foreign minister. Though the murder was denounced by the Venezuelan Communist Party, the Cuban press printed the FALN statement on the killing without any show of disapproval, and Castro denounced the PCV for "betraying" the revolution.

Their fundamentalist belief in the "guerrilla focus" was shaken when Castro's close associate "Che" Guevara made his quixotic stab at guerrilla warfare in Bolivia in 1967.

Castro was convinced that a revolution in impoverished Bolivia would ignite a continental revolution. But his small band of Cubans failed to attract the support of the Indian peasants they supposedly were liberating, and the local communist party ignored them. "Che" Guevara and his dwindling band were tracked down by army rangers and decimated in a series of skirmishes.

On the summer of 1958 in the Sierra Maestra Mountains he wrote to his closest confident Celia Sanchez[8]: "I have sworn to myself that Americans are going to pay dearly for what they are doing. When this war is over, a much wider and bigger war will begin for me, the war I am going to wage against them. I realize that is going to be my true destiny".

In 1980, in Monimbo, Nicaragua Fidel Castro said[9]: "We have agents all over the United States who are ready to undertake whatever actions are necessary at the time of our choosing. The Yankees cannot even begin to imagine the capabilitie4s we have in their country. You al read about the riots in Miami (the racial disturbances of Liberty City). We can accomplish things that would make the riots in Florida look like a sun shower".

In 1983, After President Ronald Reagan sent troops to Grenada, Fidel Castro told to General Rafael del Pino, at that time Deputy Chief of Cuba's Air Force, to program his squadron of Cuban Mig-23sto be ready to bomb the Turkey Point Nuclear Plant south of Miami[10]: "I don't have nuclear bombs, but I can produce nuclear explosions".

Lee Harvey Oswald, President John F. Kennedy's assassin, was a member of the "Committee", he was the secretary of the New Orleans chapter and the he had distributed Committee pamphlets in favor of Castro[11].

In August 1964 a group of Afro-Americans arrived from Cuba at New York's airport. The group's spokesman Charles Bernard announced that the 14 Afro-Americans that participated were officially organizing themselves under the name "Black Liberation Front".

On February 18, 1965, the chief of the NYPD, Michael Murphy and the FBI upended a conspiracy destined to create a large-scale campaign of terror in the United States, which would have started with the destruction of 3 national monuments: The Statue of Liberty in New York, The Philadelphia Liberty Bell and the Washington Monument in the nation's capital.

The conspirators were members of the "Black Liberation Front" (Robert Steele Collier leader of the group, Walter Augustus Bowe and Khaicel Sultan Sayyed) and a French-

Canadian woman (Michelle Duclos) supporter of Quebec's independence from Canada. Ms. Duclos had offered her 3 co-conspirators a hiding place until they could find a way to seek refuge in Cuba. Collier went on a trip to Cuba in August of 1964[12].

Raymond A. Wood, a Police spy discovered the conspiracy. The plan to explode the Statue of Liberty was hatched in a meeting between Collier and the Cuban Ernesto "Che" Guevara in the headquarters of the United Nations. The conspirators were members of the "Committee for the Fair Treatment for Cuba", financed by the Cuban Embassy at the United Nations, organization where Lee Harvey Oswald was also a member[13].

In 1966, Castro called for a conference, in Havana, of guerrilla movements and Third World terrorists: The Tri-Continental, attended by 513 delegates of 83 groups from Asia, Africa and Latin America[14]. At the Tricontinent Conference, Cuba sought to enlist North Vietnam and North Korea and create a more aggressive revolutionary internationalism.

From its general headquarters in Havana, the international terrorist network would become the Cuban mechanism for organizing terrorist campaigns, low intensity conflicts, and espionage. The French secret service stated that it was the Tri-Continental conference that established the international coordination of terrorist networks on different continents[15].

Cuba also fostered terrorism in Europe. A close relationship was established with the Red Brigades from its earliest days.

In April of 1965, Alessandro Beltramini, Josefa Ventosa and Clara Bartic, members of the Red Brigades, were arrested in Caracas. They, along with Maurizio Folini and Oreste Scalzone, acted as liaisons with Havana and were providers of military supplies for the terrorist groups such as the Cameroon People's Union (UPC) and the Popular Front for the Liberation of Palestine () and Cuba continued under Mario Moretti and Toni Negri[16].

Since the decade of the sixties, Castro facilitated ties between the African states and groups of black Americans like Max Stanford's Black Revolutionary Action. At the Tricontinent Conference, Cuba also promoted terrorist actions inside the United States with the radical Americans who arrived in Cuba, lured by the revolution. Thusly, an agreement was consolidated in Havana in July of 1969 between the SDS faction (Students for a Democratic Society) of the Weatherman Movement, specifically with their spokespersons, Mark Rudd, Bernadine Dohrn, Peter Clapp, Carlos Aponte and Jeff Jones[17].

Members of the Cuban Mission at the UN in New York were involved in financing black militant groups and in giving propaganda materials for fund-raising to Mark Rudd and Jeff Jones, members of the violent Weather Underground Organization (WUO).

Cuban intelligence was a leading factor in the financing of H. Rap Brown and Huey P. Newton's Black Panthers Party, and of the Students National Coordinating Committee (SNCC) to "take the war home," that is to say, to the United States. The fruits of these assignments were evidenced by the constant violent riots, towards the end of the decade of the 60's, in the main urban centers in the United States.

One Black Panther who personally developed the Cuba contact was Tony Bryant. Bryant even skyjacked a commercial airliner, directed it to Cuba and was welcomed by Castro. Eventually he was released, fled Cuba and joined Cuban freedom fighters Tony Cuesta and Eugenio Llamera, among others, in the struggle against Castro.

Also, Castro would offer the territory of Cuba to Radio Free Dixie so they would transmit their message of subversion to the Afro-American population. Their main speaker was communist Robert F. Williams, who had escaped to Cuba with an order of arrest for kidnapping.

U.S. Communist Party member Angela Davis was a constant presence in Havana in the seventies, to the point of delivering speeches along with Castro in the Revolution

Square in Havana. Davis made the FBI's Most Wanted List for providing the weapons used in the kidnapping attempt of a federal judge, staged as a demand for the release of George Jackson, one of the "Soledad Brothers."

The attempt, led by George Jackson's 17-year-old brother Jonathan Jackson, ended with all kidnappers and hostages shot to death by the police[18]. After receiving a visit from Angela Davis, George Jackson was killed during an armed attempted escape.

Cuba continued to provide safe haven to several terrorist fugitives from the U.S. They include: Black Liberation Army leader Joanne Chesimard *aka* Assata Shakur, one of New Jersey's most wanted fugitives for killing a New Jersey State trooper in 1973 and Charlie Hill a member of the Republic of New Afrika Movement wanted for the hijacking of TWA 727 and the murder of a New Mexico State trooper.

Some interesting aspects of Cuba's involvement with the Black Panthers and other radical groups are well detailed in the book *Soul on Ice*, written by Eldridge Cleaver, Minister of Information for the Black Panthers Party, after he broke with the Castro regime.

Ladislav Bittman, member of the Czechoslovakian secret service (STB) who deserted to the West, gave the following testimony: "the Weather Underground in the United States maintained contact with communist intelligence for years, especially Cuban, as well as with East Germany and North Korea. They supported the Weather Underground with money, equipment and places to hide.

A so called "We Shall Win Brigade" organized by Cuba in the 1970's to invite students and university professors to visit the Island, was a cover handled by the DGI, whose objective were and are the recruitment of American young individuals politically oriented, and who someday could obtain an elective position or appointive, somewhere in the US Government, and which would provide the Cuban government with access to political, economic and military intelligence[19].

The DGI had provided various forms of special training to some individuals from each "Brigade" contingent, in urban guerrilla warfare, techniques including the use of arms and explosives. This type of training is given only to who specifically requested it and only when the Cubans were convinced they were not agents of American intelligence.

The "Brigade" trips to Cuba were handled by leaders of the SDS who became later militants of the Weathermen. According to Julie Nichamin, a principal organizer of the trips to Cuba and a member of SDS as well as of the Weather Organization, interviewed in Cuban newspaper Granma, December 10, 1969: "We want people to understand that the battle of the Cuban people, like the battle of the Vietnamese people is the same battle to which to which we are committed, a battle against American imperialism".

According to Larry Grathwohl, an FBI informant in the Weather Underground Organization, referring to the recruitment by Cuba in the "Brigade", he and others were to find persons who could benefit from a trip to Cuba and "They were referring to insurgency type training, guerrilla type training, and this is point blank exactly what was told to me by Dionne Donghi, a leader of the SDS and member of the WUO who was in Cuba in July 1969[20].

Grathwohl also knew of several individuals who had received training in Cuba in the use of the AK-47, grenades, or infrared scopes (used for sniper shooting in darkness). Naomi Jaffe Dionne Donghi and Corky Benedict were members of the Weather Underground Organization had received guerrilla training in Cuba. The Weather Underground leader Bill Ayers told Grathwohl in February, 1970, that the contacts with other Weather members could be made through the Cuban Embassy in Canada and that a code system for communications had been established by the Cubans. The FBI Report also quoted a column by Georgie Anne Geyer and Keyes Beach of October, 1970, which discussed contacts between SDS and the Cuban UN Mission in New York in 1969[21].

In her column Georgie Anne Geyer cited the case of two mission diplomats Alberto Hidalgo Gato and Lazaro Eddy Espinosa Bonet who were declared *persona non grata* in 1969 because of what was described by intelligence agents as establishing permanent contacts with radicals and provided them with explosives. Also, at the time there was evidence and information from reliable sources alleging that the Weather Underground involved with the two Cuban agents were plotting to assassinate President Richard Nixon[22]

In an enigmatic speech criticizing President William "Bill" Clinton, delivered on January 28th 1997, Fidel Castro express a lethal threat[23]: "This lamb you will not ever be able to devour, neither with airplanes, nor smart bombs, because this lamb has more intelligence than you and in its blood there is and always will be poison for you".

Dr. Ken Alibek, a Soviet colonel who was deputy director for the agency involved with the development of germ warfare, in his book Biohazard, makes reference to the statement made by his superior, General Yury Tikhonovich Kalinin, upon returning from Cuba in the late eighties that the Cubans had developed a germ warfare capability. In the Cuban Center for Biotechnology work more than 1,000 thousand employees and technical personnel and around 200 scientists, with an initial investment of more than 1 billion dollars.

Following "Che" Guevara's defeat in 1967, efforts were also centered on Bolivia, Brazil, Colombia and Guatemala. The ELN of Bolivia received arms and training from Cuba and included some Bolivians and Peruvians. One of the Bolivian ELN's principal commandos was Monica "Irmilla" Ertl, who assassinated the Bolivian consul in Hamburg, Germany, on April 1, 1971, using a weapon provided by

Giangiacomo Feltrinelli, who was deeply involved with European terrorism and with the Cuban Tricontinent.

In October, 1968, the Brazilian terrorist organization, the VPR of Carlos Marighella murdered Captain Charles Chandler of the U.S. in Sao Paulo and on September 4, 1969, the other Maoist and rural/based terrorist organization, the ALN kidnapped the U.S. Ambassador Charles Burke Elbrick who was released after 78 hours in exchange for 15 political prisoners, most of whom soon went to Cuba.

A vast network of subversive elements directed by Castro, with an agenda to disrupt numerous Latin American countries and seize power, was uncovered in June of 1968 by the secret services of Colombia and Venezuela[24].

The Colombian Popular Liberation Army (ELP), a terrorist Trotskyst organization trained by Cuba, exploded a bomb at the residence of the U.S. Embassy Marine guards in Bogota on May 1, 1979, wounding a US marine and two American women. In July, the Colombian government revealed that M-19 has Cuban and Swedish advisers that it works with the FSLN in Nicaragua and Costa Rica, and with Castroite groups in El Salvador, Uruguay, and Guatemala.

Cuban-aided terrorism helped destroy Uruguayan democracy for a decade. In 1965 Cuba helped create the Tupamaro movement in Uruguay. The Tupamaros was an urban terrorist organization, totally linked to Havana, which succeeded in destabilizing Uruguay. Massive ransoms were collected. Bombings and explosions became commonplace.

Its members, including Raul Sendic, Marcos Rosencof Silverman, Maria "La Parda" Topolansky and Engler Golofchenco, looked upon Castro as their Maximum Leader.

Cuba organized the Tupamaros down to the last detail, even providing small explosives factories and light weapons, which greatly facilitated flexibility and autonomy of international operations. In a coordinated operation with Cuban services, the Tupamaros captured and executed American security expert Dan Mitrione[25]. Havana published the conversations of Dan Mitrione, the American security expert in Montevideo, with his Tupamaro captors, and cast the kidnapping as a heroic action.

After the failure of the urban insurgent organized in the early 1970s by the National Liberation Movement (MLN-Tupamaros), several hundred Tupamaros went to Cuba. During the mid-1970s, Cuba provided some of them with training in military and terrorist tactics, weapons, and intelligence.

Several of these former Tupamaros subsequently assisted Cuba in running intelligence operations in Europe and Latin America. Some participated in the Cuban-organized "internationalist brigade" that fought in the Nicaraguan civil war. Cuba continues to provide propaganda support for the Tupamaros and the Uruguayan Communist Party.

The Cubans unleashed a wave of leftist terrorism that swept Argentina in the early and mid-1970s, the Montoneros and the People's Revolutionary Army (ERP). In 1970 the Montonero movement became a force in Argentina more Americans were kidnapped, more were executed. They used the Cuban Embassy in Buenos Aires as a direct liaison with Argentine terrorists.

The Cuban assisted them with travel and communications, supplying false documentation and access to Cuban diplomatic pouches. Havana arranged that the Montoneros trained in Palestinian camps in guerrilla warfare. The Montoneros also have the support of the PLO and the Baader-Meinhof Gang (Red Army Fraction).

The Montoneros, led by Mario Firmenich, were virtually crushed by the end of 1977, and Firmenich fled to Europe. He has admitted to the murder of the Provisional President of Argentina, Pedro E. Aramburu, in 1970.

In 1978, Castro relocated in Havana the Montonero's headquarters, top command, its labor organization, and its intelligence organization, among other units. In 1979 small groups of Montoneros reinfiltrate Argentina and were able to carry out several terrorist actions, including assassinations act.

Also, Cuban-trained Montoneros, including their leader Mario Firmenich, were among members of the "internationalist brigade" that Cuba entered in Nicaragua in 1979. Also Montoneros broadcasted from Costa Rica Cuban propaganda to Central and South America.

At least the militants of the Southern Cone terrorist organizations were carefully preserved to carry out assignments in other parts of the world as part of Cuba's growing international network of terror and subversion. Not surprisingly then, by the late 1970s, South American terrorists were showing up in Central America and even the Middle East in the pay and under the discipline of Havana.

Castro Africanus

Cuba initially established contacts with African countries in search of Third World solidarity with the Cuban Revolution. When the Revolution triumphed in 1959, the Cuban leadership viewed the international situation as entering a new, "essentially revolutionary" era, one that offered new alternatives for the underdeveloped world. Just four years earlier, in the midst of the Cold War, a group of leaders who had emerged from the recent anti-colonial struggles waged in Africa and Asia met in Bandung, Indonesia, to declare their resistance to the centripetal force of the major powers.

They proclaimed that all small countries had the right to self-determination, to remain neutral in the face of the East-West conflict, and to be respected and not threatened by the major powers. These leaders agreed on the need for solidarity among the underdeveloped countries. In this spirit, shortly after their meeting, these countries sided first with Egypt during the Suez Canal Crisis (1956), and later with the insurgents in the Algerian war (1954-1962).

Idealistic and nationalistic Cuban officials were encouraged by these developments. They felt that their revolution was not an isolated case. In fact, they found similarities between the Cuban Revolution and those in Vietnam, Indonesia and China, among others, in terms of their anti-imperialist struggle and desire to transform Cuban society. They drew a parallel between their plan for the Cuban economy and Egypt's nationalization of the Suez Canal, and they felt a kinship between their own revolutionary government and those liberation movements seeking to end colonialism in Africa, particularly with the Algerian struggle against French rule[1].

The fact that a young, inexperienced but charismatic Fidel Castro suddenly shared the world stage with such contemporary Third World leaders as Ghana's Kwame Nkrumah, India's Jawaharlal Nehru, Egypt's Gamal Abdel Nasser, Yugoslavia's Josef Broz "Tito" and Indonesia's Ahmed Soekarno, and that the Revolution was favorably received by the Afro-Asian countries, enthused Cuban revolutionaries[2].

As the "self-fulfilling prophesy" of inevitable conflict with its immediate and most powerful neighbor rapidly materialized[3], Cuba sought solidarity with the Afro-Asian world, hoping its support would help to safeguard the Revolution in the face of aggression. "Cuba needs solidarity," the chief of the regional department of the Cuban foreign ministry explained in 1960, "and has to find it among all the countries that are joined by the same [colonial] patterns of economic penetration, disrespect for sovereignty, pressure, and vassalage to which all underdeveloped countries are subject."

Cuba also reached toward Africa to comply with the objectives of its new independent foreign policy. Two fundamental objectives of the new policy were the expansion of markets and of Cuba's diplomatic and cultural links with all countries[5].

As early as June 1959, Cuba's legendary revolutionary, Ernesto "Che" Guevara, traveled to several of the nonaligned Afro-Asian countries, Egypt, India, Indonesia and Yugoslavia, among others. The purpose of Guevara's trip was to search for markets for Cuba's sugar in anticipation of a cut in the U.S. quota, to acquire weapons in Yugoslavia, and to secure Nasser's and the Arab world's support of Cuba.

As part of the new foreign policy, Cuba also committed itself to supporting those issues that concerned the Afro-Asian world. At his first attendance at the United Nations General Assembly in September 1959, Foreign Minister Raul Roa joined the rest of the Afro-Asian countries in calling for the elimination of apartheid in South Africa and in supporting the self-determination of the other African colonies, particularly the struggle of the peoples of Angola, Mozambique and Guinea (Bissau) against Portugal.

Moreover, in 1961, when the Afro-Asian leaders took the initiative in creating the Non-Aligned Movement, Cuba attended the first conference held in Belgrade, Yugoslavia, becoming the only Latin American country to request membership at the time.

Despite growing ties to the Afro-Asian world, this solidarity was not enough to deter the threat of U.S. aggression as perceived by the Cuban leadership. In the early sixties, at the Organization of American States, many Latin American nations were supporting the United States in its attempt to isolate Cuba from the region.

Because of its geographical location, it is highly unlikely that Cuba could have, in the early sixties, cut its economic, political and military ties with the United States and sustained a nonaligned position as did Egypt, India or Ghana. By mid-1960, when Soviet leader Nikita Khrushchev said that the Soviet Union would defend Cuba in the event of U.S. aggression, the Cuban leaders highlighted that, among those socialist countries was becoming more evident every day[6].

Cuba's policy toward Africa, initially an essential part of Cuba's effort to expand its international role and secure solidarity and foreign support for the Cuban Revolution, was soon radicalized. Although many African colonies attained independence in 1960 (e.g., Dahomey, Upper Volta, Cameroon, Chad, Congo, Gabon, Ivory Coast, Madagascar, Mali, Mauritania, Niger, Nigeria, Senegal, Somalia, Togo and Congo-Kinshasa), Cuba did not immediately seek ties with all of them; it only established relations with those countries that were seen as truly revolutionary, namely Guinea, Mali and Ghana.

After the 1961 victory at the Bay of Pigs, Cuban leaders became more belligerent toward the United States and any country supporting U.S. policies. Fidel Castro redefined the objectives of Cuba's foreign policy, and Havana committed itself to the anti-imperialist struggle[7]: "We cannot consider ourselves at peace with an imperialism that constantly increases its efforts to strangle us. And this situation will determine our international conduct. They are our enemies and we will know how to be their enemies. This situation will determine our policy on the international scene, in the United Nations, and everywhere else."

Between 1959 and 1963, however, Cuba's foreign policy was inconsistent. The undisputed Cuban leader and main architect of Cuba's foreign policy, Fidel Castro, struggled between the need to insure his personal power internally and the search for logistical support for what would become Cuba's internationalist foreign policy. Nonetheless, the policy toward Africa received increasing attention as Cuba became isolated from the Western Hemisphere[8].

Cuba's initial support to guerrilla groups in Africa delayed the establishment of formal diplomatic, political and economic relations with most countries in the region. Frustrated by Latin America's growing support for the U.S. attempt to isolate Cuba, Fidel Castro embarked on a cross-regional policy of supporting subversive activities. The global interests of the world powers did not include Africa as a priority area, which allowed Castro greater room to maneuver in that region.

Through Cuba's actions in Africa and Latin America, Castro at- tempted to validate the guerrilla "foco" theory as a means to reach power. These activities were also expected to be the catalyst that would alter subjective conditions and promote revolutions. They also were to create the image that Cuba was independent from the Soviet Union, as well as offer Africa a development alternative, the Cuban model: The path of the Revolution, the path followed by Cuba, although it may be long and hard, is the only path that promises the people a secure future, a great and stable future[9].

Revolutions similar to the Cuban were expected to take place in Latin America, but conditions in Africa were also viewed as propitious for armed struggle. On one hand, many of the remaining colonies were struggling for independence. On the other, in most African nations, independence awakened the hopes and expectations of the masses and their leaders. Scvereignty was expected to be a magic formula that would automatically promote or generate social and economic development.

Shortly after independence, the masses began to demand immediate material solutions and with few exceptions, the new elites were unprepared to confront the complexity and magnitude of the social, economic and political problems inherited from the colonizers. Marxist economic theories of centralization and freedom from the capitalist international division of labor appeared easy and attractive solutions. Extremist groups also pressured for armed struggle against institutional powers.

Since the early 1960s, hundreds of Africans, from the Congo, Equatorial Guinea, South Africa, Zanzibar and the Namibian Southwest Africa People's Organization (SWAPO) began training on the island of Cuba, and with Cuba support, terrorist bases were opened in Algiers, Tanzania and Brazzaville Congo[10].

Cuba did not develop its relations with Sub-Saharan Africa with ease. Cuban revolutionaries failed to understand African socialism. The symbolism, naturalism and agrarian communal spirit of the African masses could not be categorized under strict Marxist-Leninist ideology.

Cuba established diplomatic relations with only those countries identified as the most "progressive", both because of their support for the deposed Congolese leader, Patricio Lumumba, and because of their opposition to the Western powers meddling in the Belgium Congo, today Zaire.

This lack of understanding of African realities accounts for many of Cuba's decisions reflecting poor judgment, such as

Cuba's miscalculation on the prospect of guerrilla warfare in Congo; paternalism toward Ghana's Kwame Nkrumah and the inability to convince francophone African leaders, such as Senegal's Leopold Sedar Senghor and Ivory Coast's Felix Houphuet Boigny, of Cuba's independence from the Soviet Union.

Cuba was willing to assist those in Africa who were committed to the armed struggle. By 1962, Fidel Castro had cemented close ties with Algeria's leader Ahmed Ben Bella. Because of Algeria's then recent success in its liberation struggle, that country became a main center for the training of guerrillas in Africa.

It was there, as well as later in Tanzania and in the Congo-Brazzaville, that Cubans participated in the training of insurgents from Namibia, Rhodesia, Zanzibar, Senegal, Cameroon, Nigeria, South Africa, the Belgium Congo and others. Some of these nationals struggled against the colonial regime in their countries; others opposed the post-independence governments in power.

In 1964, the involvement of the Western countries in the Congo crisis convinced Cuban officials they needed a greater presence in Africa. "Che" Guevara dropped out of sight in March 1965 and fought covertly, along with about 300 Cubans, in Zaire (then called the Belgian Congo) for the next 12 months or so[11].

The objective of the subversion in the Congo was to cut supplies to the Katanga uranium mines, vital to the US's uranium reserves[12].

Beginning in 1964, Cuban ambassador Pablo Rivalta organized the guerrilla training of the Mozambique Liberation Front in Tanzania and Algiers.

Also, seditious revolts were promoted in Cameroon with Woungly Massawa's United People of Cameroon, in the Ivory Coast with the separatist movement of the Sanwi tribe, in Niger with the Bakary Dyibo movement, and in Senegal, with the African Party of Independence of Casamance. It was

Castro who installed the Umma Party[13] of Abdurrahman Mohammed "Babu" in Zanzibar in 1964.

Commanding 1,000 Cuban troops in 1967, and from the base of Dolissie, in Congo Brazzaville, General Arnaldo T. Ochoa trained the South West African People's Organization of Namibia, the Zimbabwe African people's Union of Zimbabwe and the FRELIMO (Mozambique Liberation Front) of Mozambique[14].

The guerrilla offensives of the sixties did not achieve the expected results either in Africa or in Latin America. Unlike "Che" Guevara's attempts during the 1960s, Cuban subversion and terrorism today is backed by an extensive secret intelligence which oversees far-flung operations that include secret training camps in Cuba and abroad, the deployment of Special Forces units, and a large and sophisticated propaganda network. Radio Havana, for example publicized statements in Arab language in short wave.

The *focus* approach of the 1960s has given way to a more sophisticated strategy involving extensive commitments and risks, sponsoring teams in the field enough to spark insurrection and terrorism. Furthermore, these activities countered the Soviet policy of expanding peaceful roads to power. Thus, starting in 1972, Cuba began to align itself more closely with the Soviet line and initiated its first diplomatic initiative toward Africa.

In the seventies, Cuba launched its major diplomatic offensive toward Africa. More closely aligned to the Soviet policy of developing formal ties with most African countries, Cuba established diplomatic relations with many states that had obtained independence in the early sixties but that it had previously viewed as "reactionaries".

For instance, in 1972 Cuba formalized relations with Sierra Leone, Somalia, Zambia, Mauritania and Equatorial Guinea. In 1974 it established diplomatic relations with Dahomey (Benin), Burundi, Gabon, Madagascar, Zaire, Liberia, Uganda, Nigeria, Senegal, Cameroon and Guinea-Bissau.

Cuba became a super power in low intensity operations, deploying troops to the Southern Cone of Africa, the African Horn and the strait of Bab-el-Mandeb. But, both Cuba and the Soviet Union-in close coordination- substantially increased military assistance to African liberation movements in the early seventies.

As Portugal's empire in Africa crumbled in 1974, Cuba sent a small military contingent to support the African Party for the Independence of Guinea-Bissau and Cape Verde (PAlGC), modestly assisted Mozambique's Liberation Front (FRELIMO).

After its independence, Angola became the centerpiece of Cuban policy in Africa. In 1975, Cuba intervened with an expeditionary force of 47,000 soldiers in favor of the Marxist Popular Movement for the Liberation of Angola which had the strongest ties to Moscow of the three movements competing for power after Portugal's withdraw.

Havana became involved in an extended civil conflict which even included the use of chemical weapons by Cuban military forces, supported by Soviet logistics and materiel.

After 1975, Cuba became more willing to establish relations with newly independent nations. Angola, Mozambique and Cape Verde were rapidly recognized as new, independent nations in 1975. Cuba also established relations with Ethiopia in 1975, following the overthrow of Emperor Haile Selassie I.

This flexibility allowed Cuba to practically complete its initial objective of expanding relations in the mid-eighties. In fact, the increased emphasis on pragmatism has allowed for ties certainly unthought-of of in the past.

The extensive list of agreements signed in 1976 depicts the depth of Cuba's relations with the new nation. In subsequent years, Cuba has continued to strengthen its intergovernmental relations with Angola, and has found in

Angola one of its most important sources of interlocution in Africa[15].

Between 1976 and 1979, Cuba established relations with most of the remaining African countries: Libya, Niger, Chad, Mauritius, Comoros, Botswana, Maldives, Seychelles, Gambia, Lesotho, Rwanda and Togo. In 1980, Cuba immediately recognized Zimbabwe when it became independent.

Between 1977-78, Cuban troops were sent to assist Ethiopia in its dispute with Somalia over the Ogaden region. Here, the integration of Soviet and Cuban operations was even more complete, with the Soviets providing overall command and control, materiel, and transportation Cuban troops fighting.

Cuba sent a full tank division and 32,000 troops to the Ogaden desert, under the command of General Ochoa and Soviet bloc marshals and generals, the Cuban armored units defeated half a million Somalian soldiers, consolidating the military junta (the "Derg") in Ethiopia[16].

These African campaigns legitimized what had until then been a loose concept: internationalism.

In 1976, the Cuban constitution formalized internationalism as the guiding principle of the nation's foreign policy. Defined not only as an ideology but also as a course of action that guides Cuba's international behavior, Cuban officials explain that internationalism assumes an anti-imperialist nature because of Cuba's close alliance with the Soviet Union. Internationalism is based on an appreciation of the real course of the historical development of class struggle at the local and international level[17]. According to Fidel Castro, the sacred duty of a revolutionary in no longer just to make revolutions, but rather to be an "internationalist[18].

The successful commitment to internationalism, as seen in the recent Angolan and Ethiopian military operations, increased Cuba's confidence in its policy toward Africa.

Nevertheless, Cuba surprisingly did not return to the earlier policy of fomenting revolutions or supporting almost any group that opposed perceived reactionary governments.

Instead, Cuba became more selective and only supported specific groups such as the African National Congress, the Southwest Africa People's Organization, the Polisario Front, the Zimbabwe African People's Union, and later the Zimbabwe African National Union all classified as liberation movements. All these movements enjoyed the recognition and support of most African countries. Cuban policy was increasingly geared toward nurturing the revolutionary governments that espoused Marxism-Leninism as their country's ideology and toward the expansion of state-to-state relation with all the African countries[19].

The term "internationalism," however, now encompasses an extremely complex amalgam of nongovernmental and intergovernmental relations that daily flood the Cuban media. It is frequently used by the Cuban leadership primarily to exalt the unselfishness of the Cuban Revolution and to exact support from its population. While initially understood to mean Cuba's generous support to liberation movements or to governments in the process of consolidating a socialist movement, since the mid-seventies the term also has been used to refer to activities generally known as export of services.

Ironically, Cuba does not boast about its staunchest gestures of internationalist solidarity. Activities such as procuring weapons from the Palestinians to ensure a constant flow to the Nicaraguan government and to El Salvador's guerrillas are rarely exposed in the Cuban media.

Nevertheless, Cuba's ties with Africa are impressive. Havana maintains diplomatic relations with more than 40 African countries and has embassies in not less than 30 of them. This record is unmatched by any other Latin American country, much less by those with resources as limited as Cuba. While the cost of these ties may seem prohibitive for Cuba, such a presence in Africa provides it with firsthand information on the internal situations of many countries in the region. It also serves to convince the Cuban population that in spite of being isolated, Cuba has many friends in the Third World.

For example, Cuba intensified its technical-scientific cooperation with Mobuto Sese Sekou's government in Zaire, and in 1986 it established diplomatic relations with Felix Houphuet Boigny's government in the Ivory Coast. Both leaders of these non-revolutionary governments were staunch foes of Cuba in the sixties what is more, in the eighties both Zaire and the Ivory Coast were known to be major supporters of the Union for the Total Independence of Angola (UNITA), the insurgents combating the Cuban-supported MPLA government in Angola.

Cuba does not maintain close ties with all of them. In terms of political links, Cuba remains closer to countries whose governments espouse at least some socialist orientation, such as Angola, Mali, Mozambique, Guinea-Bissau, Tanzania and Zimbabwe[20].

By the mid-eighties, Cuba abstained from breaking relations with countries when a close ally was deposed. For example, when Thomas Sankara, leader of Burkina Faso's revolution and Cuba's close friend, was assassinated in October 1987 by his close collaborator Blaise Campoare, Cuba did not break relations with that country. Cuba condemned the lack of unity among revolutionaries but continued relations with the new government[21].

Another example of this state-to-state relations regardless of changing leaders is Cuba's relationship with Uganda. These relations have been unaffected by coup d'états, regardless of the ideologies they have imposed Cuba's African policy has earned significant political returns at the international level

Many African countries have supported Cuban positions at international organizations on such issues as U.S. control of the Guantanamo base, support for the Nicaraguan government, Puerto Rican independence and other topics that have directly opposed U.S. policies. Most significantly, it was the support of the African nations that awarded Fidel Castro the chairmanship of the Non-Aligned Movement in 1979. Also, at the Organization of African Unity, member states consistently supported the Cuban position.

In addition, African and Latin American heads of states frequent visit Cuba. The Cuban media portray these visits as manifestations of the degree of solidarity Cuba has obtained with the world.

Castro´s offensive in Latin America

In 1970, Havana finalized the details of the infamous Round Table that grouped the Tupamaros and the FARO (Revolutionary Wide Front) of Uruguay, the MIR (Revolutionary Left Movement) of Chile, the ELN (National Liberation Army) of Bolivia with "Chato" Peredo, the Montoneros, the FAR (Revolutionary Armed Forces) and FAP (Popular Action Front) from Argentina, the ELC (National Liberation Army) of Colombia, and Douglas Bravo's FALN (Armed Forces for National Liberation) of Venezuela.

Cuba was supporting primarily urban-based insurgencies but careful never to endorse such urban terrorist groups as Brazils Carlos Marighella, the Uruguayan Tupamaros, and the Chilean Movimiento Izquierdista Revolucionaria (MIR).

Toward 1971, Cuban intelligence, in connivance with the KGB, trained both the Mexican faction of Fabricio Gomez Sousa (Movimiento de Accion Revolucionaria) and the Chilean MIR in North Korea, for the purpose of carrying out a wave of terrorist strikes in both countries[1].

The Guatemalan Rebel Armed Forces (FAR) was founded in 1963 as a Cuban-style rural guerrilla group. Besides being trained by Cuba for some years, first the FAR and later the EGP had the services of Cuban killer experts, to work with them, in order to coordinate the assassinations of several government officials and international targets.

On August 28, 1968, FAR assassinated U.S. Ambassador-John G. Mein, the first U.S. ambassador ever assassinated, and in 1973 kidnapped Roberto Galvez, an executive of an American-owned company who was later released for 50,000 ransom.

In 1975, the Guerrilla Army of the Poor (EGP) emerged as a serious terrorist threat, under the leadership of Cesar Montes and with the backing of Havana. The EGP obtained all its support from Cuba, including instructors in the field, alongside the fighters.

Coronel Antonio "Tony" De La Guardia was Fidel Castro's Golden boy. In 1973 he led a covert mission to Spain to study the possible retrieval of former Cuban dictator Fulgencio Batista. In 1975 De La Guardia laundered sixty million dollars that Argentina's Montoneros guerrillas had obtained in the sensational kidnapping of George and Juan Born.

In 1976 De La Guardia was stationed as head of Cuba's special troops that provided military support to leftist Prime Minister Michael Manly. In 1978 De La Guardia directed the first group of Cuban military advisors that became involved in the Nicaraguan war. After his arrival in Costa Rica he facilitated the funneling of Cuban weapons for the Nicaraguan rebel southern front led by Eden Pastora. In 1978 he helped take President Anastasio Somoza's presidential palace. When he returned to Cuba in 1979 he was placed in charge of Cuban exile community affairs. He even visited Miami and remarkably had ample contact with the Federal Bureau of Investigation during his stay.

In 1971, following the victory of Salvador Allende in Chile, De La Guardia headed the first Cuban special troops contingent to provide military assistance and support to Allende's government. After two years of military, logistic and political support, Cuban special troops commanded by Antonio de la Guardia helped to create havoc for the Nicaraguan National Guard, played a leading role in the assault of Nicaraguan dictator Anastasio Somoza's bunker, and helped to install the Sandinistas in power.

Cuba contributed greatly to the erosion of Chile's democratic institutions under Salvador Allende. Between 1970 and 1973, Cuba's security services moved arms and agents into Chile.

In Chile the Castro regime followed a two-track strategy even under the left wing rule of Salvador Allende. The Cubans supplied the radical left in Chile with large quantities of Soviet and Czechoslovakian-made weapons delivered by Cuban Airline and Cuban merchant ships[2].

The Cubans gave material support and training to the ultra-left MIR, headed by Miguel Enriquez and Pascal Allende, without Allende's knowledge. The MIR openly promoted and attempted to carry out a violent revolution even when Allende was in power.

As in Buenos Aires, the Cuban embassy in Santiago was actively involved in subversive activities, but on a much larger scale. From their coordinating center in Santiago, the Cubans maintained liaison with "liberation movements" in Argentina, Bolivia and Uruguay[3].

According to Robert Moss, about three-quarters of the 150-member Cuban embassy staff "were thought to be involved in intelligence work[4].

The Cuban support apparatus extended to La Moneda, the presidential palace. Moss reported that Cuban operative Fernandez de Oña worked in La Moneda and that a senior DGI officer directly supervised Allende's foreign communications. Fernandez had married Allende's daughter Beatriz Allende, who later was reported to have committed suicide in Havana.

At the same time, Cubans helped organize President Salvador Allende's personal security and trained many leaders of the Chilean Movement of the Revolutionary Left.

In Chile, the DGI and the Americas Department, under the direction of Cuban agent Juan Carretero, develop the infamous "Z Plan" to consolidate ultra radical elements within Salvador Allende's party and subsequent government, and then use that country as a platform to launch subversive actions throughout South America[5].

While emphasizing that Chilean President Salvador Allende had tried to move too far, too fast," before he had adequately neutralized opposition in the armed forces, the economy, and the opinion media, the Cubans (and the Soviets) by the mid-1970s had come to believe that "wars of national liberation (guerrilla warfare and terrorism) would be vital instruments for the destruction of "North American imperialism in Latin America. According to Brian Crozier, Director of the Institute for the Study of Conflict in London[6].

After President Salvador Allende's fall in 1973, Castro promised Chilean radicals "all the aid in Cuba's power to provide." Although Cuban officials maintained regular contact with many Chilean exiles, divisions among the exiles inhibited major operations. The Moscow-line Chilean Communist Party (PCCH), holding the position that revolutionary change could be accomplished by non-violent means, was critical of "left-wing forces" like the Movement of the Revolutionary Left (MIR) with which Cuba had close relations.

Throughout the 1970s, members of the MIR received training in Cuba and in some cases instructed other Latin American revolutionaries. This training ranged from political indoctrination and instruction in small arms use to sophisticated courses in document fabrication, explosives, code writing, photography, and disguise. In addition, Cuban instruction trained MIR activists in the Mideast and Africa.

With its renewed commitment to armed struggle, Cuba increased its training of Chileans beginning in 1979 under the impression that the government of President Augusto Pinochet was in trouble.

Castro renewed high-level support for the MIR and the armed wing of the newly militant Chilean Communist Party (PCCH) including the provision of training and arms. By mid-1979, the MIR had recruited several hundred Chilean exiles and sent them to Cuba for training and eventual infiltration. At the same time, members of the MIR who had been living and working in Cuba since Allende's overthrown began to receive also training in urban guerrilla warfare techniques.

Once training was completed, Cuba helped the terrorist return to Chile, providing false passports and false identification documents. By late 1980, at least 100 highly trained MIR terrorists had reentered Chile and the MIR had claimed responsibility for a number of bombings and bank robberies. Cuba's official newspaper, *Granma*, wrote in February 1981 that the "Chilean Resistance:" forces had successfully conducted more than 100 "armed actions" in Chile in 1980.

The Chilean Communist Party was reevaluating its position in light of events in Nicaragua, where the fragmented Nicaraguan Communist Party emerged from the civil war subservient to the Sandinista. In December 1980, Chilean Communist boss Luis Corvalan held talks with Fidel Castro, who urged Corvalan to establish a unified Chilean opposition.

Corvalan delivered a speech which sketched a new party line calling for armed struggle to overthrown the Chilean Government and for coordination of efforts by all parties, including the violent left. In January 1981, Corvalan commended MIR terrorist acts as "helpful" and stated that the PCCH was willing not only to talk with MIR representatives but also to sign agreements with the group. Several days after this offer, Corvalan signed a unity agreement with several Chilean extremist groups, including MIR.

Until January 1981, when the new Chilean Communist Party policy evidently had been ironed out and validated by the agreement for a broad opposition coalition, Corvalan's statements were issued from such places as Czechoslovakia, East Germany, Cuba, and Peru.

Terrorist activities by MIR commandos operating in Chile increased substantially after that. These have included increased efforts by MIR activities to establish clandestine bases for rural insurgency, killings of policemen, and a number of assassination attempts against high government officials.

The terrorist campaign would escalate in 1984 following a clandestine infiltration that originated in Cuba. From 1985 to 1986, Chilean terrorists committed more than 1,700 attacks.

On August 6, 1986, hidden in several places on the sparsely populated desert country of Chile´s northern coast, the government discovered a 70-ton cache of arms belonging to the Manuel Rodriguez Patriotic Front. The cache, supplied by Havana, was the largest arsenal ever in the hands of any Latin American subversive group[7].

The weapons had been brought by Cuban fishing boats and were destined for the armed wing of the Chilean Communist Party to unleashed a campaign of terror designed to further polarize Chile, an making difficult the transition toward full democracy.

Across from Saint Lucia, there is a rocky islet named Rat Island. In 1976 at a secret meeting, Cuban intelligence and Maurice Bishop and Bernard Coard of the island of Grenada, George Oidium of Saint Lucia, Marxist Tim Hector of Antigua and others, devised a plan to overthrow the heads of state of Eastern Caribbean islands and replace them with communist's rulers.

The plan was originally to begin in Antigua, but it actually began in Grenada when the New Jewel movement, aided by Cuban emissary Oscar Cardenas Junquera, carried out a coup d'état in March of 1979, that carried Maurice Bishop to power as prime minister[8].

So, Cubans participated in the expertly planned and executed overthrow of Eric Gairy's unpopular regime by a few dozen members of Maurice Bishop's New Jewel Movement (NJM) in March 1979.

Cuban influence in Grenada mushroomed almost immediately after the March 1979 coup led by the New Jewel Movement of Maurice Bishop. Bishop and his closest colleagues were Western-educated Marxist radicals, and they turned for help to Fidel Castro, who proved willing to provide assistance.

Grenada under Maurice Bishop who seized power in 1979 with the help of the Cubans was being turned into an arsenal principally by the Cubans and Soviets for arms export to the vulnerable democratic governments of the region.

A senior intelligence officer from the America Department, Julian Torres Rizo, was sent to Grenada as ambassador. Torres Rizo has maintained intimate relations with Bishop and other People's Revolutionary Government ministers, such as Bernard Coard.

Cuban aid to Grenada was most extensive in those areas which affected the security of its client government and the island's strategic usefulness to Cuba. Cuba had advisers on the island offering military, technical, security, and propaganda assistance to the Bishop government. Many Grenadians had been sent to Cuba for training in these areas.

Cuba aided the construction of a 75-kilowatt transmitter for Radio Free Granada. Grenada's state-controlled press, provided facilities for beaming Cuban supplied propaganda into the Caribbean and South America.

Cuba's largest project in Grenada was the construction of a major airfield at Point Salines on the southern tip of the island. The planned 9,800-foot Point Saline's runway, moreover, had military objectives allowing operations of every aircraft in the Soviet/Cuban inventory. Cuba's MiG aircraft and troop transports were supposed to enjoy a greater radius of operation with that airport, giving Cuba a guaranteed refueling stop for military flights to Africa and the Middle East.

Bishop gave implicit endorsement of future military use of the airfield. A March 31, 1980 *Newsweek* report quoted Bishop's comments to a U.S. reporter: "Suppose there's a war next door in Trinidad, where the forces of Fascism are about to take control and the Trinidadians need external assistance, why should we oppose anybody passing through Grenada to assist them?"

The special units of twin brothers Patricio and Antonio de La Guardia trained Prime Minister Michael Manley's security forces, while at the same time approximately 1400 Jamaicans received education and military training in Cuba.

Cuban activities in support of Suriname dictator Desy Bouterse's security and military forces began growing after the arrival in September 1982 of the new Cuban ambassador, Oscar Cárdenas[9].

Only three months after his arrival, Bouterse's Cuban-trained and advised security forces rounded up and massacred fifteen prominent political opponents under the pretext of a coup attempt. With the subsequent cut-off of Dutch assistance to Suriname, Cuban influence increased. During the year that he spent in Paramaribo, Cárdenas reportedly became involved in almost every aspect of government business[10]. He also maintained close ties to the Marxist-oriented People's Revolutionary Party (RVP)[11]. Cuban Advisers-allowed to come and go freely-trained Bouterse's personal bodyguard and advised the Suriname Ministries of Information and People's Mobilization[12].

In the 1970s, Jamaica became a special target for Cuba. Fidel Castro and other Cuban officials developed close relations with important members of the People's National Party. Most of the embassy staff, including former Ambassador Ulises Estrada, was Cuban intelligence agents. Cuban security personnel trained Jamaican security officers in Cuba and Jamaica, including members of the security force of the office of the Prime Minister.

The projected plan was a takeover by Michael Manley, who had openly announced his intentions to abolish Parliamentary rule. The efforts, coordinated by Cuban Ambassador Ulises Estrada, included a Cuban construction brigade, already in Jamaica "to build a high school", similar to the one that fought later in Grenada.

A Cuban front corporation, Moonex International, registered in Lichtenstein, with subsidiaries in Panama and Jamaica was discovered in May 1980 to be the designated recipient of a shipment of 200,000 shotgun shells and .38 caliber pistol ammunition shipped illegally to Jamaica from

Miami. The M-16s found in Jamaica have the same numerical series captured in Vietnam.

They were to be supported by Cuban forces airlifted to Mandelville, ten miles west of Kingston. CIA renegade Philip Agee appeared in Kingston to denounce a CIA plot against Prime Minister Michael Manley, as an excuse for the coup. Manley abandoned his plan after President James "Jimmy" Carter issued strong warnings against such a move and beefed up U.S. naval presence in Guantanamo. The Jamaica Defense Force destroyed the landing strip and shortly thereafter Manley lost Parliamentary elections amidst a wave of anti-Cuban popular resentment.

Young Jamaicans were being trained as terrorists in Jamaica in the late 1970s. One such young was, Colin Dennis. In his book "The Road Not Taken: Memoirs of a Reluctant Guerrilla", he details his training in Cuba in 1980. After arriving in Cuba, Dennis was taken to a remote camp where for eight weeks he was trained exclusively to urban terrorism in the use of an assortment of weapons and given instruction in assault techniques especially designed for police stations, banks, and prisons.

According to the Cuban Intelligence Officer Florentino Aspillaga, however, a total of fifty-seven flights were made between Havana and Costa Rica, for a total of 1.8-million tons (as stated) of arms. The Cuban military and security advisers who are reported to be stationed in Nicaragua, numbering between 2,500 and 3,000, are known to operate at all levels of the government and the Sandinista People's Army (EPS)[13].

Fidel Castro convinced the Soviets bosses that supporting revolutionary organizations, including terrorist groups, could be of strategic advantage. The Sandinista victory in Nicaragua touched off further turmoil in the rest of Central America and the Caribbean. Havana fomented armed revolts through a combination of urban terrorism and rural guerrilla warfare.

The Nicaraguan Sandinistas seized power in an insurrection against an unpopular dictator, Anastasio Somoza. Armed and abetted by Cuba, this action featured a high incidence of urban warfare with the consequent heavy loss of life.

In 1977-1978, the Intelligent Officer Armando Ulises Estrada, was a key element in organizing the anti-Somoza insurrection. Ulises concentrated on building a supply network for channeling arms and other supplies to guerrilla forces. Ulises Estrada conducted multiple secret trips to Nicaragua to facilitate the task of bringing together all of the groups that were to make up the Sandinista Front.

A Cuban secret operations center in San Jose monitored and assisted the flow of weapons. Large cache of arms was flown from Cuba to Panama, transshipped to Costa Rica on smaller planes, and supplied to Nicaraguan guerrillas based in northern Costa Rica, with the help of Panamanian strongman Omar Torrijos, and the Minister for Internal Security of Costa Rica, Johnny Echevarria.

Previously, in November 1975, Cuban Chief of spies, Manuel Piñeiro headed a high-level Cuban mission to Panama and met with top Panamanian government officials, including Noriega, then the G-2 (intelligence) chief. That year, Piñeiro was advising the late Panamanian dictator General Omar Torrijos in negotiating the Panama Canal Treaties[14].

Fernando Vecino Alegret, a major general moved to Managua arranging the shipment of 100 captured American 105mm howitzers from Vietnam, in a vessel operated under Lebanese registry by the Palestine Liberation Organization.

In early 1979, Cuba helped organize, arm, and transport an "internationalist brigade" to fight alongside FSLN guerrillas. Members were drawn from several Central and South American extremist groups, many of them experienced in terrorist activities. Plutarco Elias Hernandez a commander of the FSLN was the organizer of the Simon Bolivar Brigade, the 2000-man guerrilla force of various nationalities that fought with the Sandinistas.

The international brigade who included Palestinians, Montoneros, such as Emilio Gorriarán Merlo (who later executed Somoza in Paraguay), members of the Italian Red Brigade and Basque terrorist such as Francisco Larreategui Cuadra and Jesus Udendo Basterrechea. The Basque terrorists (the "Etarras") were the ones selected to carry out the attempt on the life of anti-Somoza leader turned anti-Sandinista, Eden Pastora, and against the Salvadoran Minister of Justice, General Jose Guillermo Garcia.

The Italian Premier Bettino Craxi declared that 44 of the most extremist Italian terrorists were working from Nicaragua, among them, Guglielmo Guglielmi, Roberto Sandalo, and Lauro Azzolini, the assassin of Aldo Moro[16].

The triumph of the anti-Somoza insurrection in July 1979 and the subsequent domination of the leadership of the Sandinista National Liberation Front (FSLN) were due by the Cuban-training programs. Behind the scenes, Cuba in disguise played an active role in organizing the FSLN and in training and equipping its forces, sending also military specialist to the field to help coordinate the war efforts. A minimum of 1 million pounds of arms moved to Costa Rica from Cuba during the Nicaraguan civil war, including anti-aircraft machine-guns, rocket launchers, bazookas, and mortars.

Cuba acted quickly to build up Sandinista military and security forces, and one of its star agents, Andres Barahona, became a top official of the Nicaraguan intelligence service, assisted by 1,500 military and security advisers.

At the Cuban Communist Party Congress in December 1980, Castro explicitly endorsed the Soviet intervention in Afghanistan and defended the Soviet "right" to intervene in Poland. He also reiterated that Cuba is irrevocably committed to support "national liberation" struggles around the world.

In the Congressional hearing on June 26, 1981, Robert Moss confirmed Cuba's massive involvement in international espionage and terrorism. He detailed Cuba's role in training and equipping groups, from throughout the world, in camps in Cuba, Algeria, South Yemen, Libya, and Africa. Finally, Mr. Moss referred to Philip Agee, a CIA turncoat. According to Mr. Moss, Agee has had more than 30 confirmed meetings in London with the local station chief of the Cuban DGI[17].

On July 26, 1980, Fidel Castro declared that the experiences of Guatemala, El Salvador, Chile, and Bolivia teach us that there is no other way than revolution, that there is no other "formula" than "revolutionary armed struggle." Castro's statement was an attempt to justify publicly what Cuban agents had been doing secretly since the beginning of the Revolution, stepping up support for armed insurgency and terrorism in target countries.

On the celebration of the first anniversary of the Sandinista revolution, a secret meeting was held in Monimbo, Nicaragua, with the participation of the upper echelons of the Sandinista regime, militant Central Americans, representatives of the KGB, the PLO, and Castro himself and with the Chief of the Americas Department of the Central Committee of the Cuban Communist Party, Manuel Piñeiro, as well as Antonio "Tony" de la Guardia, Chief of Information of Cuba's Special Operations Directorate (DO).

The purpose of the meeting was to discuss how to export the Nicaraguan Revolution and further weaken U.S. power and influence. In Monimbo, Castro asserted that he had planted enough agents in the U.S. to be able to unleash urban chaos[18].

In a hearing on June 26, 1981, the testimony of Robert Moss, a British journalist told of a meeting of Central American revolutionaries held last July in Monimbo, Nicaragua, to celebrate the overthrow of the Somoza regime. Castro boasted that his agents in the United States were so industrious and well placed that they had the capacity to create race riots at a moment of his choosing--race riots on a scale that, he said, would make the Miami troubles look like a sunshower.

Soviet intelligences cadres traveled to Panama in August 1981 to discuss with Cuban officials a strategy for Central

America. Allowing Havana to take the lead in Latin America, Africa and Middle East enables Moscow to maintain a low profile and cultivate state-to-state relations.

In order to exploit and control the revolution in Nicaragua, Cuba tried to induce the overthrow of the governments of El Salvador and Guatemala. Cuba also coordinated the development of clandestine support networks in Honduras, Costa Rica, and Nicaragua, sometimes using arms supply mechanisms established during the Nicaraguan civil war. The network established in Costa Rica and Nicaragua was later used to supply Salvadoran insurgents. Cubans accompanied the shipments.

In Managua, Cuban officer Fernando Comas Perez became the coordinator for the Salvadoran insurrection. The international brigades, who had been brought to Nicaragua, became the trainers of the Salvadoran, as well as the Guatemalan guerrillas, which were trained at Punta Huete, Nicaragua. A directorate was created, led by communist leader Cayetano Carpio, which included Manuel Ungo, Shafik Handal, Joaquin Villalobos, Roberto Roca, Eduardo Sanchez Castaneda and Ruben Zamora.

The Cubans frequently meet with Central American guerrillas in Managua to advise them on tactics and strategy, and training in scuba diving and underwater demolition. In El Salvador, several factions within the Cuban-backed rebel coalition, the Farabundo Marti National Liberation Front (FMLN), began as urban terrorist groups, several of which were trained and armed by Havana.

Havana orchestrated in addition a wave of propaganda to distort the realities of the Salvadoran conflict, stressing the theme of U.S. intent to intervene militarily in El Salvador.

When the Salvadoran Ranger forces cracked down in 1980, the FMLN concentrated its efforts in the countryside. Reversals in the rural areas, thanks to sustained U.S. assistance and a reformed Salvadoran military, have led the rebels back to urban operations with the apparent full blessing of Havana.

Between October 1980 and February 1981, took place a massive Cuban-directed flow of arms to Salvadoran and Guatemalan guerrillas from Vietnam, Ethiopia, and Eastern Europe through Nicaragua via clandestine surface and air routes, something that Castro later admitted.

In 1981, according to U.S. intelligence, the Cubans trained some 2,000 Guatemalan guerrillas and terrorists involving instruction in the use of explosives and heavy weapons such as 50mm mortars, rocket launchers, etc. Their weapons were provided by Nicaragua. As one result, the Guatemalan insurgency was rekindled in the 1980s and posed a serious and growing threat to the regime until 1985.

In June 1981, Guatemalan Paulino Castillo told reporters that he had undergone a seven-month training program in Cuba. His man group was divided into two sections. The first was trained in rural guerrilla tactics; the second in urban terrorism. After his training was completed, he returned to Guatemala via Nicaragua, but subsequently surrendered to a Guatemalan army patrol. A unit trained in Cuba places a bomb in a U.S. Eastern Airlines plane on July 2. The bomb exploded before being loaded, killing a Guatemalan airport employee.

Two thousand Guatemalan guerrillas were trained in Cuba before being dispatched to their native country. Their education involved traditional guerrilla tactics and bomb making. In August of 1987 FARC deserters revealed that various guerrilla fronts were still being trained by Cuban agents.

Cuban-supported guerrillas and terrorists attempted to wreck the March 20,1988, legislative and mayoral elections in El Salvador, just as they had six years earlier when Salvadorans went to the polls in that country's first free election. A former pilot of Panama's strongman Manuel Antonio Noriega said that planeloads of Cuban arms had been flown into that country.

While considering Honduras a useful support base for insurgencies elsewhere, Cuba worked to develop the capacity for insurrection within Honduras. Havana urged splintered extremist groups in Honduras to unify and embrace armed struggle. Incriminating documents confiscated, including notebooks indicated recent attendance in training course in Cuba, were also confiscated.

Though not a priority, Havana has helped forge a fighting coalition in Honduras from the squabbling extreme leftist groups in March 1983. Subsequently, both Havana and Managua have provided training and arms to several of these groups particularly the People's Revolutionary Liberation Movement, widely known as the Cinchoneros.

In September 1981, the Cinchoneros seized control of the Chamber of Commerce building in San Pedro Sula, and held several cabinet ministers and over one hundred business leaders as hostages while they demanded release of their jailed comrades-in-arms.

Since the 1960s, Cuba nurtured contacts with violent extremist groups in Colombia providing training to guerrilla leadership. Many leaders of the April-19 Movement (M-19), including the founder, Jamie Bateman -who also attended a Communist cadre school in Moscow- were trained in Cuba. Leaders of the National Liberation Army (ELN) and the Revolutionary Armed Forces of Colombia (FARC) also received Cuban instruction.

Cuban assistance to Colombian guerrillas was stepped up after the February 1980 seizure of the Dominican Republic Embassy in Bogota. Eighteen diplomats, including the U.S. Ambassador, were taken hostage by M-19 terrorists. As part of a negotiated settlement, the terrorist was flown on April 17, 1980 to Cuba, where the remaining hostages were released and the terrorists were given asylum.

During mid-1980, Cuban intelligence officers arranged a meeting of Colombian extremists, attended by representatives from the M-19, FARC, ELN, and other Colombian radical groups, to discuss a common strategy and tactics.

It is also during this period that we see the emergence of the so- called Colombian narco-guerrilla, the M-19 Movement which accepted arms negotiated by Castro with the narco-traders. Manuel Piñeiro would recommend to the M-19 that in order to obtain the financial resources, it should carry out kidnapping as well as assaults on banks and jewelries[19].

The M-19 had previously held talks with the Nicaraguan Sandinista on ways to achieve unity of action among guerrilla groups in Latin America. Although the meeting did not result in agreement by Colombian guerrillas on a unified strategy, practical cooperation among the guerrilla organizations increased.

In late 1980, the M-19 set in motion a large-scale terrorist operation in Colombia with Cuban help. In November, the M-19 sent guerrillas to Cuba via Panama to begin training for the operation, including the use of explosives, automatic weapons, hand-to-hand combat, military tactics, and communication. Cuban intelligence, together with the M-19, also created a money laundering and falsification unit using Panamanian banks[20].

In February 1981, some 100-200 armed M-19 guerrillas, upon completion of their military instruction in Cuba, re-infiltrated into Colombia from Panama by boat along the Pacific coast. The guerrillas' mission to establish a "people's army" failed. The M-19 members proved to be poorly equipped for the difficult countryside, and the Cuba-organized operation was soon dismantled by Colombian authorities. Among those captured was Rosenberg Pabon Pabon, the M-19 leader who had directed the Dominican Republic Embassy takeover and then fled to Cuba.

Cuba's propaganda support for Colombian terrorist has been impossible to deny. When a group consisting of M-19 dissidents kidnapped an American working for a private religious institute, Cuba implicitly supported the terrorists' action through Radio Havana broadcasts beamed to Colombia in February 1981, which denounced the institute workers as "U.S. spies." The American was later murdered by the kidnappers.

Cuban Vice President Carlos Rafael Rodriguez tactically admitted in an interview published in *Der Spiegel* on September 28, 1981, that Cuba was providing military training to Salvadoran guerillas and Colombian M-19 guerillas.

Colombia suspended relations with Cuba on March 23, in view of the clear evidence of Cuba's role in training M-19 guerrillas. President Turbay Ayala commented in an August 13 *New York Times* interview: "When we found that Cuba, a country with which we had diplomatic relations, was using those diplomatic relations to prepare a group of guerrillas to come and fight against the government, it was a kind of Pearl Harbor of us. It was like sending ministers to Washington at the same time you are about to bomb ships in Hawaii."

Cuban support of terrorism in Costa Rica, meanwhile, has had the lowest of profiles in Central America. Havana´s chief interest in Costa Rica was preserving the arms and agent network it established in the late 1970s for the overthrow of Nicaragua´s Somoza. This network was attempting to destabilize other more vulnerable Central American countries, El Salvador in particular.

On June 4, 2002, Miguel Mariano Ramos an explosives instructor and a Cuban intelligence officer was captured in Bogota. Terrorism in Colombia was on a par with the worst of terrorism in the Israeli-Palestinian conflict. And Cuba's fingerprinted it.

Terrorism had been virtually unknown in Costa Rica until March 1981 when the first terrorists trained in Cuba made their appearance in March when they blew up a vehicle carrying a chauffeur and three Marine security guards from the U.S. embassy in San Jose.

On occasion, however, Cuba has provided weapons and training for Costa Rican terrorists directly to the People's Revolutionary Movement, which it helped create in 1982. In March of this year, the police raided a terrorist safe-house in the Costa Rican capital, San Jose. The security forces arrested nine members of a Cuban terrorist arms-running network set up in the 1970s.

The terrorist belongs to the Argentine Montoneros, the Uruguayan Tupamaros, and Colombia's M-19, and to Cuba itself. The captured terrorist documents indicated that they received "ideological/military training" in Cuba and returned to work in the Atlantic coastal zone of Costa Rica. Some of the arrested terrorists are known to have belonged to the MRP, whose leader has traveled many times to Cuba to coordinate training to MRP elements.

With its renewed commitment to armed struggle and terrorism, Cuba's interest in the Dominican Republic has revived. Since early 1980, the Cubans have been encouraging radicals in that country to prepare for armed actions. Cuban intelligence officials, like Omar Cordoba Rivas, was in charge of all the operation, and make periodic visits to the island. Cuba also has given military instruction to many members of small extremist splinter groups like the Social Workers Movement and the Socialist Party.

In 1985 close to 700 Costa Ricans trained in Cuba returned to their country. Immediately thereafter, a wave of terrorist acts was unleashed in the country, with the participation of Montoneros, Tupamaros, and Members of the M-19 of Colombia. The Government of San Jose expelled Fernando Comas from the country and a few days later a car was blown to pieces with three American Marines inside.

Prior to the US invasion to Panama, Cuba dispatched large caches of arms that were stored in secret locations around the country. By mid-March 1988, Noriega and the Cubans reportedly were operating a secret arms airlift from Havana to three locations in Panama and outside the control of the PDF, with the intent of building an infrastructure for waging guerrilla war, according to Major Augusto Villalaz, a Panamanian Air Force officer who was granted political asylum in the United States that month. Villalaz revealed that he personally made three flights from Cuba into Panama to deliver weapons requested by Noriega; each flight carried sixteen tons of military equipment, including 100,000 AK-47 assault rifles, rocket-propelled grenades, hand-grenades, and ammunition. Villalaz added that a total of sixteen flights carrying about 500,000 pounds of weapons were planned[21].

At around this time, the Latin American groups working in Mexico were directed by Havana to carry out assaults on banks and jewelry stores in order to finance armed groups in Central and South America[22]. The coordinator for these activities was Cuban agent Armando Campos and the arms were received in Cuba through diplomatic valise.

Castro was forced to carry out a major restructuring of revolutionary strategy. On one hand, the regime was forced to settle for negotiated solutions to the more intractable revolutionary conflicts it was promoting in Central America and concentrate on Cuba's internal economic restructuring in order to survive the end of the massive soviet subsides that had prodded the regime for decades[23].

On the other hand, Castro rapidly moved to replace the Soviet protective umbrella by a major regrouping and re-strengthening of all the communist and radical groups in the Hemisphere that had been left in the cold by the collapse of the Soviet Union, as well as by strengthening Cuba's diplomatic and military ties with radical and anti-Western regimes throughout the Third World (especially Muslim countries).

Symbolic of these efforts was the "Fourth Latin American and Caribbean Meeting for Solidarity, Sovereignty, Self Determination and the Lives of our People" hosted by Castro in Havana on January 25-28, 1994. Over 1000 guerrilla leaders and radical Marxists from around the world answered Castro's summons to Havana and agreed to help save the "last bastion against U.S. imperialism" by mobilizing international campaigns of solidarity with the Cuban regime and against the U.S. embargo[24].

But, the essential elements of Castro's new strategy were to be channeled through the Sao Paulo Forum, formally founded on July 3, 1990 at the behest of Luis Ignacio Lula da Silva, head of Brazil's Workers Party, under the initiative of Fidel Castro. Around 68 eight radical political factions (including armed groups) from 22 different Latin American and Caribbean countries participated in the first meeting, with delegations from the United States, Canada, Spain, France and Italy participating as monitors.

Since that initial meeting, the Sao Paulo Forum, which was also a leading force in the radical anti-globalization movement, grew considerably. Its member organizations included Colombia's National Liberation Army (ELN) and the Colombian Revolutionary Armed Forces (FARC), Argentina's.

All for the Homeland Movement -the perpetrators of the January 1989 attack of the Tablada barracks in Buenos Aires as well as the Cuban Communist Party, the Sandinista National Liberation Front of Nicaragua, Aristide's Lavalas Party in Haiti and the Zapatista National Liberation Army of Mexico, among others.

Also noteworthy is the participation of ETA support groups. Venezuelan President Hugo Chavez, and his "Bolivarian Project", had also become an integral and major component of the Sao Paulo Forum.

The Forum was created with a new strategy to achieve power and obtain the "revolutionary transformation of society." It combines "various forms of struggle and organizations" reaching for power through electoral means when that was possible (such as the case of Hugo Chavez in Venezuela and president Jean-Bertrand Aristide in Haiti, as well as Lula's efforts in Brazil and Ortega's in Nicaragua) but affirming "the validity of armed struggle in the great majority of our countries."

However, the Sao Paulo Forum most important component was its region-wide approach to select targets of opportunity and channel regional and international support, including human and material resources to achieve its objectives.

Two important examples where this new approach has been used are: First and least known, the Ecuadorian coup d'état, for which the Foro channeled support from indigenous groups from throughout the Hemisphere. The second was that of the Colombian guerrillas, where the FSP and Cuba have been active in channeling international support. Former Defense Department counter-terrorism expert John More told UPI that Cubans, militant Palestinian, Hezbollah and even advisors from the leftist government of Venezuela were active in Colombia.

Also, in August 2001, Colombian officials arrested IRA members Niall Connelly, Martin McCauley and James Monaghan, and accused them of training the Revolutionary Armed Forces of Colombia (FARC). Connelly had been living in Cuba as the representative of the IRA for Latin America.

The sword and the *Pax*

During 1971-1972 Israeli general Moshe Dayan was trying strongly to reason with the political leadership that Egypt was taking steps for a military offensive into Sinai. At the beginning of 1973 was clear to many European countries and the United States that the Egyptians and Syrians were preparing for war; both had accumulated a huge arsenal of tanks, aircraft and Soviet rockets, who urgently readied anti-aircraft batteries in Egypt.

Despite all this, and various alerts that Israel received, their leadership was not yet convinced of the Arab intentions, and thought that they were large-scale maneuvers, persuaded that the lesson of 1967 was definite and that the Arabs were not at the height of an electronic warfare.

On October 3 in Jerusalem a long meeting took place of ministers, main military commands and military intelligence with the Premier Golda Meir; Yitzhak Hofi, chief of the armies of the north expressed his anxiety to the presents, especially in view that Syria had reinforced its front protrusion beyond the limits of a defense. Nevertheless, Premier Golda Meir maintained her optimism. On the following day, two days before the invasion, the CIA alerted the Mossad that the Arabs were going to throw an attack in all fronts[1]. On the following day the Soviet were launching to space a spy satellite, the Cosmos-596, which entered an orbit overflying Israel[2].

Several times outnumbered and caught completely by surprise, the Israeli army had to face a ferocious Syrian assault in the Golan Heights, where every Israeli tank had to tackle practically several Syrian armored squads. If reinforcement cannot arrive in time or the onslaught cannot be contained, the entire north of the country would be at the mercy of the enemy.

During 48 hours virtually what stood between the Syrian army and the destruction of Israel were the tactical skills of the general Yitzhak Hofi who developed a brilliant defensive campaign, until with sufficient reinforcements launched a counteroffensive that wiped out the best Syrian units in what has been considered the largest battle of tanks after the one in the arc of Kursk in 1943, between the Soviet tank armies and the Nazi German panzer units.

Meanwhile, after crossing the Suez Canal the Egyptian army occupied with impunity Bar-Lev -that Israeli wonder line of electronic fortification- and entrenched there in preparation for a frontal assault in the corridors of the Sinai aiming to the heart of the country. The Israeli air force was practically paralyzed since it could not protect its own troops against the barrier of Soviet ground-to-air missiles being assembled on the Egyptian side.

The assault took the Israeli army unaware; its reserves were not mobilized, the tank corps were in their parking spots, and the Bar-Lev line was guarded with fresh recruits. The regular army was on break for the religious holiday of Yom Kippur. For 36 hours, Israel was on the edge of defeat, which for this country would mean the first and last, with a new Holocaust.

Demonstrating his preparedness and the ability of its commands in those terrible hours, a quarter of its armed forces managed to contain the two huge Arab armies. United States established an air bridge direct to the Sinai providing vast amounts of modern weaponry to Israel. And then, finally they could move all its units to the battlefield and win an incredible victory.

When Egyptian defenses crumbled, the Soviet Union made it clear that they would intervene directly if the Israeli offensive were not stopped. Secretary of State Henry Kissinger pressured Premier Golda Meir to accept a ceasefire. Moscow knew that Egypt and Syria had been saved from total defeat at the last minute, not by the Soviet armament but by American pressure on Israel to stop its offensive.

Having continued Israel their counter-offensive, Syria would have collapsed and disappeared as a nation divided into its three territorial components; Egypt, after having lost his entire army, would had never recovered the Sinai, the PLO would have evaporated as an organization, and Tel-Aviv would have reorganized geographically and politically the Middle East to its convenience.

Yom-Kippur war was a victory for Israel in pure military terms, but psychologically was a terrible blow, especially because of their intelligence failure to anticipate the Egyptian-Syrian plan.

Access to American technology enabled Israel to create a modern air force capable of reaching all the States of the Arab League. This equation escalated the arms race in the Middle East, leading Syria, Libya and Iraq towards the Soviet Union.

US President Richard Nixon and his Secretary of State Henry Kissinger "the modern Machiavelli" as it is known in the Middle East, generated the idea of ensuring the control and stability of the area and the oil flow to the West implementing the strategy of "two pillars": The House Royal Saudi, and the Shah of Iran. To balance the region and guarantee of the security of the Gulf and Arab peninsula, United States began to provide sophisticated armaments to those allies.

This war contributed to strengthen the American idea of a political arrangement, despite the fact that the "Rogers plan" and "Jarring mission" had failed in the previous two years. In 1971 during the Mission of the UN to the Middle East led by Gunnar Jarring, Egyptian President Sadat promised the recognition and the normalization of relations in exchange for the return of Sinai.

What President Al-Sadat, and less clearly the Syrians and Jordanians, offered in 1971 was that the same thing Sadat formulated in 1973, and again proposed in Jerusalem in 1977:

peace with Israel and a Palestinian State from the dismantling of West Bank and Gaza.

At the beginning of the seventies Israel wasn't the center of attention of the United States despite the fact that aid levels were relatively high. The Egypt-Israel conflict, the Cold War, Latin America and Viet Nam still occupied the highest priorities. But this selective presence of the role of the United States in the Arab world morphed without discussion into what would become the more voluminous and crushing institutional presence of a foreign power in the modern history of the Middle East.

By negotiating the end of the Yom-Kippur war, Kissinger achieved a commitment from Israel to withdraw its army from the Sinai in 1975. This forged the foundations so that the Camp David agreements materialize. But Kissinger's diplomacy was not designed to implement a final and comprehensive solution to the Arab-Palestine-Israeli quarrel, but sought to reduce the tension in the Middle East. The ambiguity of this policy and the unrestricted support to the outdated and oppressive medieval structures of the Arab oil producers had disastrous consequences, including the displacement of Egypt as regional power *per excellence*.

The seventies saw Saudi Arabia emerge as a cardinal political force in the area, by being able to dictate the prices of oil, threatening simply to open its colossal reserves to the market. Its then Monarch Feisal Abdul-Aziz (The Desert Eagle) understood the need to stabilize the Arab-Israeli dispute to evade any danger of the ideological radicalism that was generating the Palestine struggle that would affect negatively in the legitimacy of its monarchy.

Faisal decided to warn the United States through the North American oil monopoly ARAMCO -which exploited the hydrocarbon of the peninsula Arab-, that its total alignment with Israel and the disregard to Arab interests was a blind strategy that made it impossible to achieve a negotiated solution to the dispute.

After the war of Yom-Kippur, Saudi Arabia, Kuwait and Iraq (with 50% of known world oil reserves), convinced the rest of the Arab countries to impose an oil embargo on United States and Holland for rendering partial with Israel. The embargo would be maintained until they would withdraw from Sinai, Gaza, Golan Heights and the West Bank, in compliance with the UN resolution No. 242.

For its part, France and England were not included in the embargo for having taken a neutral position in the conflict[3]. It would be after the Arab oil embargo that United States would lend ears to their big oil companies wrapped in the Middle East[4]. But it was too late; with the new Arab faculty to wield its oil as a weapon of political pressure, Western oil companies had already distanced from their governments not to be used as direct instruments of foreign policy.

In spite of the fact that from the mid-1970s until recently numerous unofficial contacts between the PLO and the United States took place, the same stagnated due to the Palestiniar refusal to accept the Resolution 242 of the UN and abandon terrorism, and the fact that for Washington the Palestiniar dilemma was secondary compared to its interests in the rest of the Arab world.

For the first time the Palestinians were being treated by the foreign ministries of the great powers as a separate entity from the Arab collective. Two successive North American administrations, those of Gerard Ford and James Earl "Jimmy" Carter, realized concrete efforts to settle the political problems of the Middle East.

The president Carter welcomed the Pan-Arabic design proposed by Syria to solve the Arab-Israeli conflict. In 1977 United States coordinated a peace conference in Geneva and the presence in it of the Palestinians, indicating the end of the "Kissinger era".

In October 1977 the Soviet Union and the United States signed a joint agreement where they undertook to resolve the

Arab-Israeli conflict. Soviet premier Leonid Brezhnev believed that this had assured American recognition to become involved in the peace process in the Middle East.

But Israel envisioned that a political agreement negotiated in the UNO, between the rest of the Arab countries, Palestine and the two big world powers would debilitate its position as negotiator. Like Israel, the Egyptian Anwar Sadat was in favor of separate agreements between each party with Israel, and was publicly opposed to the Soviet-United States release of 1977 on Palestine.

To the surprise of the whole world, in November 1977 Sadat travelled to Jerusalem changing the equation. It was also the era that Israeli politicians, among them Simon Peres, began talking for the first time about Palestinian rights. United States, with the favor of the Saudis, was forced to adjust to the new situation by reordering their priorities to give space to a peace agreement separately between Cairo and Tel Aviv and abandoning the path of the Palestinian solution through the UN.

From there, the President Sadat and Israeli premier Menachem Begin (who had been the head of the clandestine organization Irgun) met at Camp David under the auspices of President Carter, agreeing to an autonomy plan as the first irreversible step towards a final process of Palestinian self-determination.

Despite the 1979 Camp David Peace Treaty, the nub of the problem, the Israeli-Palestinian conflict, remained insoluble. After Camp David, a number of private initiatives produced confidential interviews between the administration of President Carter and the PLO in Beirut. By 1979, the PLO showed signs that he was capable of accepting the resolution 242.

Despite the fact that Mossad warned the CIA months in advance of the danger facing the Reza Shah Pahlavi regime, Western intelligence services failed to detect the crisis that toppled the Iranian monarchy[5] in 1979. This meant one of the most devastating blows to the American postwar foreign policy, since the balance of forces in the region was destroyed, and the Gulf countries, American allies, became more vulnerable to the forces of Islamic fundamentalism.

In 1980 the European Economic Community declared its support for Palestinian self-determination, presenting a serious divergence between the United States and European policy with regard to the conflict in the Middle East. What had begun after the Arab military debacle of 1967 and 1973, culminated in the agreements of Camp David and the fall of the Shah of Iran, realizing the nationalist ideologies of the Nasserism. the Baas and Pan-Arabism, and promoting Islamic fundamentalism.

The Iranian regime of Ayatollah (the Sign of God) Ruhollah (the Spirit of God) Musavi Khomeini entered in a broad articulation with the PLO that enthroned the state support of the condemned "non-Islamic" branch of the Iranian Shiism, which resulted in repudiation of the Emirates of the Gulf, Saudi Arabia, Jordan and Egypt. In the case of Egypt and Iraq, ups and downs were a constant, especially after the PLO's Alliance in 1991 with Saddam Hussein's regime.

Despite peace and negotiations and the "moderate" public position of Arafat, the PLO secretly still supported terrorism not to lose the support of the Arab Street. Moscow knew that many of the Palestinian terrorist groups "dissidents" of the PLO secretly were in accordance with Arafat. The KGB had information of many terrorist actions had been assembled with the help of the command of the PLO in Syria, Libya. A report written in 1981 about a training mission in the USSR relates to 194 officials from several Palestinian factions led by the Commander of the PLO Rashid Ahmed[6].

With the rise to power in Greece of the Pan-Hellenic Socialist Party of the first Minister Andreas Papandreou in 1981, viscerally hostile to Israel and the United States, the PLO earned a significant base of operations in Europe. The Chief of intelligence of Papandreou, Kostas Tsimas and the Vice-Minister of the interior Sifis Valyarakis were former terrorists who had been trained in military camps of Arafat on the South of the Lebanon, and maintained intimate relations with the Iraqis. Tsimas used his influence with Papandreou and his power to protect and promote the OLP violence[7]. There, the cupola of Palestinian terrorism moved with freedom: Abul Abbas, Abu Nidal, Abu Ibrahim, Abdullah Libi, Mohammed Rashid, Mohamed Boudia, Ahmed Yibril, and so on.

By the time Ronald Reagan is elected President of United States, in 1980, the situation was different. The status of the area was frozen and Egypt and Israel had come to a mutual understanding, and in 1981 the Soviet Union granted diplomatic recognition to the PLO. By 1982 the KGB was thwarted by intelligence reports indicating secret interviews between high figures of the PLO and American officials. Moscow suspected Arafat yielded to pressure from the West to exclude the Soviets from the agreements of the Middle East.

In 1983, the head of the Department of the Middle East for the Soviet Foreign Ministry, Oleg Grinevsky at a meeting in London said to diplomats that Moscow didn´t trust Arafat, and that long-term plans were forging for progressives Marxist elements of the PLO leadership circle to replace him[8].

As result of military encounters with Syria on North Lebanon in 1984 and siding with Saddam Hussein in the Gulf war, the PLO was extremely weakened Arafat's leadership began to crumble, as well as the maximalist of its policy against Israel. This cost him the suspension of substantial aid received from the Emirates of the Persian Gulf and Saudi Arabia, and losing grounds in Gaza and the West Bank in favor of Islamic extremists.

But at the end of the war with Iran, Saddam Hussein began to maneuver with the PLO, interested in introducing a Western-friendly face. The PLO had reached the conclusion that there was no possibility of a military victory against Israel. Also, there was a re-alignment with Egypt after Camp David and the acceptance of the proposals drawn up by the Secretary of State James Baker, the famous "Baker plan".

By the end of 1988 Egypt managed to persuade the PLO to denounce terrorism and abide the solution of two States in Palestine (one Jewish and another Arab) established by the UN in 1947. In a meeting in Algeria in that year, the Palestinian National Council ruled in favor of self-determination with a secular government in a part of the Palestine.

Another important change was the acceptance of resolutions No. 242 and No. 338 of the UN which had previously been rejected. By the PLO accepting the existence of the State of Israel, implied a big concession to their previous positions in an attempt to "All the Palestine expelling the Jews, or nothing at all."

In the fall of 1988, the Iraqis were among Arab States that supported the new moderate position from Arafat denouncing terrorism and accepting to dialogue with United States. In September, Jordan renounced administrative responsibility over the territory of the West Bank occupied by Israel, so a Palestinian State would be established. The fact of the Palestine tenacity for rebuilding an identity in exile, and that their struggle for self-determination was so well known internationally, such budget began to be handled in the American speech.

Palestine de facto

For more than six decades,
the Palestinian tragedy soars
over the Arab-Israeli future

United States has to immerse in the Islamic world, and precise political latitude to deal with Iraq and Somalia, to tighten dowels in Iran and Syria; but it cannot do so without first resolving the Israel-Palestine mess. From any angle or position it is necessary to analyze the Palestinian in Gaza and West Bank as the piece that is needed to understand and solve the Arab-Israeli crisis.

In a region where foreign powers come and go and the peace treaties formalize issues without solutions, United States must deliver a Palestinian State in tray to the Islamic States that have been identified with its anti-terrorism coalition, as shelter from the "divine mobs".

In the Islamic world authoritarianism has been accepted while it supports the 'Palestinian cause', as in the case of the Syrian Hafez Al-Assad, who died of natural causes thanks to not having 'collaborated' ever with the West. Contrary to what happened with Anwar Sadat, and with the Pakistani Pervez Musharraf because of their associating with the 'devil'.

Palestine is more a cause than a place, and the identity crisis is not only of the Palestinians for not having a State, but also the Israelis, who are soon sharing theirs. In contrast to the uncertain future of Iraq, Syria or Jordan, the outcome of the peace process is known and predictable; it will be the legal expression of what already prevails in the land.

In reality, a Palestinian State exists de facto since December 1987 the beginnings of the Intifada, and from the transfer of control of Gaza, in the West Bank, East Jerusalem, to the PLC. But Gaza (Egyptian enclave prior to 1967) and the

West Bank (former Jordanian territory) have neither common borders nor lineage links.

Therefore, the outcome of any negotiation is predictable and will be the legal expression of what already prevails in the land.

It will require an unlimited ability and ascendant by Islamic States to hold these two territories together. In fact, the peace process is a record of divorce for a couple who has been living separated for a long time and where in the most optimist scenario Jerusalem -impossible to chop- will require custody of two sovereignties.

West Bank and Gaza differ in their economic conditions, educational and cultural; they have different historical experiences and uneven inclinations with respect to Israel. The leaders of the PLO on both banks do not always agree on their tactics and strategies. It is not ventured to predict that, after some time, both parties could legitimize themselves with Israel separately, to transform in two mini-states without relationship with each other.

Israel is not a homogeneous country in ethnic or religious terms, but its long conflict with the Arabs allowed it to elude the inheritance of one million non-Jews citizens: Christian and Islamic.

The Palestinians of Israel, dotted by a different story mingled with the political, economic and cultural mode of the Israeli democracy -Western style-, organizing a much greater civil society than that of its Arab neighbors. Arab-Israeli youth dressed in the Western fashion, speaking more Hebrew than Arabic and dancing rock, differ from the rest of the Islamic world.

With a more reasonable intuition and greater opportunities for self-realization than its Fedayeen cousins, they initiated the peace and the recognition of the State of Israel. The Palestinian philosopher, Sari Nusseibeh has pointed out that Palestinians in Israel were slowly "turning Israeli".

They are culturally bilingual (Arabic and Hebrew) and as individuals mark their clear political disparity with its neighbor, while in community they proceed otherwise, being absorbed to the Israeli economic system and aspiring to succeed in it.

The Arab-Israelis are not inhabitants of "occupied Palestine", but citizens of the legitimate State of Israel, in which they fight for their equality. Israeli democracy has profiled their political perspective. Since 1992 no party could ignore their crucial vote as minority, which tipped the balance in the Knesset in favor of peace negotiations.

These Arab-Israeli parliamentarians where precisely the ones who opened the way for a regional consensus in favor of agreements with Israel, and the ones who persuaded the Egyptian Mubarak.

Although Israeli public opinion favors improving the conditions of the co-Israelis Arabs, on spite of the reflexive consciousness of that Zionists who were not looking to found a democracy, but a State for the Jews. To equalize the rights of Israeli Arabs with the Jewish majority will be unable to start until the achievement of reconciliation between the States of the region and the creation of a Palestinian State.

In addition, the current Palestinian situation illustrates the effects of an economic development unleveled. Palestinian farmers left the Earth to enter the Israeli labor market in the seventies and eighties, getting rid of the tradition of the old families and elders, which generated the *intifada* as an internal protest over Israel's control, in what can be described as a revolution with hallucinations.

All these movements surged without any connection with the PLO and the Palestinians from abroad. These Arab-Israeli handlers who fight for a state in the occupied territories, and supported the positions of Israeli politicians Simon Peres and Isaac Rabin, reject the terrorism of Hamas. Their agenda focuses on the progress of their community, to reach a political representation commensurate with its demographic weight in Israel.

At the end of the eighties with the *intifada*, Israel saw stained its image and universal admiration of a nation in pursuit of Peace, which had transformed an 'arid and empty land' in a modern society.

The PLO still sustains the obsolete flag, which was raised after the frustrated Arab invasion to Israel in 1948. The Palestinian case is then manipulated by Arab leaders, such as Gamal Abdul Nasser, on purpose keeping Palestinians in refugee camps, in order to create a mystical history and as an element of pressure in the crusade to expel Israelis into the sea.

This creed would shape for decades Arab politics, to the point that neither the deceased Arafat himself, nor anyone else in the area, has dared to homologate the Palestinians who in 1948 sought refuge in Lebanon, Syria and Jordan, with Jews expelled from Alexandria, Fez, Baghdad, Damascus and Beirut by the Arabs, after the creation of the State of Israel.

With Arafat occurred the symbiosis terrorism=Palestine, although in truth the bulk of the population was never involved in violent activities and always favored a peaceful solution. Arafat had refused constantly to cut its ties with the old clique of hardliners and long exile, and relegates the views of the Palestinians under occupation who were trying to achieve a final agreement with Israel.

Hamas, a branch of the Muslim Brotherhood, was organized as a result of the Intifada; its terrorist squads, active in Gaza and the West Bank, are funded by Iran. Hamas presents 'Zionism' as the personification of Satan and holds as irrefutable proof *The Protocols of the Elders of Zion*, the text manufactured by the Okhrana, the secret police of the Tsar.

In a strategic error, Israel stopped running to the fundamentalism of Hamas because it questioned the leadership of the PLO and Arafat, only to end up finding themselves as the target of their extensive levels of cruelty. If the tactics of the PLO were homicidal, those of Hamas would be suicidal; if the violence of the PLO were a method, it would be a means to an end for Hamas.

While the PLO aspires to establish a secular Palestine, Hamas is promoting the model of a theocratic state Taliban style, and offers as reward to the martyrs of their suicide missions a paradise of palaces of gold, delicious foods, beautiful women and good-looking male adolescents.

Hamas mixes religious motives with nationalism by advocating suicide for the 'cause', and the religious duty of freeing the Arab homeland; but the Quran does not recognize either suicide or homeland. Hamas has rejected the peace agreements and challenged the historical status of the PLO as 'legitimate representative of the Palestinian people', calling their leaders as drunken pork guzzlers.

It was in 1988 that the PLO had accepted the existence of the State of Israel. From December 1988 to mid-nineties dialogues between American diplomats and representatives of the PLO developed in Tunisia with views to implement a peace process in the region. While Israel was mired in the internal crisis of the *intifada* that entered its third year, and its premier Yitzhak Shamir yet persisted in his suggestions of a dialogue with the Palestinians, Saddam Hussein was erected champion of the Palestinians.

Arafat was frustrated by the lack of support of the Emirates of the Persian Gulf and the stagnation of the Egyptian peace operation. For the radical position, headed by Saddam Hussein, the Cairo Government was not reliable for being too identified with the West and, to make matters worse, maintained relations with Israel. Egyptian President Hosni Mubarak was accused by all Palestinian tendencies of having implicated Arafat in a strategy of "moderation" that ultimately, had accomplished nothing.

In May 1990, Arafat and Saddam Hussein convened an Arab Summit in Baghdad to discuss the settlement of Soviet Jews in the West Bank and ways of curbing the failure of the United States to prevent the Israeli policy. But in October 1991, United States managed to sit Israel and the Palestinians at the negotiation table, as well as Jordan, Syria and Egypt.

This negotiation resulted in a struggle of Palestinian factions where the moderate, led by Hanan Ashrawi who had managed to bring to reality the conference involving United States and the Russian Mikhail Gorbachov, relegated to the Conference.

The vulnerability of the PLO, being an extraterritorial organization with the embody a Palestine nation in exile and absent from the original territory, became patent during the *intifada*, and then with Hamas and the Islamic Jihad which settled in Gaza, and with its dramatic terrorist attacks would embrace the *martyrology* of Shiite Iranians.

In the fall of 1990, the PLO was hard pressed to launch its armed wing, Al-Fatah, against Hamas, as a result of its decision to play a part in the Madrid Conference with Israel.

During the Gulf war propaganda of the PLO in Gaza and the West Bank, and in the refugee camps in the Lebanon, Saddam Hussein was presented as the Arab hero who challenged militarily the United States and Israel "Crusaders". Arafat also served as international emissary of Saddam Hussein's regime. As a result of the international embargo against Iraq implemented by the UN, Arafat wrapped in extensive confidential negotiations with Iran looking for Tehran to allow the clandestine transit of Iraqi oil through its territory[1].

This irresponsible alignment precipitates disastrous results on all fronts of the PLO, undoing the advances in the peace negotiations, and costing him the suspension of the substantial tithe he received from the Emirates of the Gulf and Saudi Arabia, tilting the balance in favor of Islamic militants in the occupied territories.

Thus, Palestinians in the occupied territories faced economic and financial difficulties due to the precarious situation of Palestinians living in the Gulf, which previously sent their wages to their families. This antagonism of the PLO with Egypt, Kuwait, Saudi Arabia, and of course Syria is maintained until today day.

In September 1993, in full isolation, Arafat decided to go to Oslo, Norway, under the orbit of the *Pax Americana* to summarize long negotiations, which had been conducted secretly by delegations from the PLO and Israel, abandoning the Arab international diplomacy and entering in Israeli domestic politics.

There he undertook the promise to put an end to terrorism. Instantaneously Arafat lost his ascendancy with the Islamic militants. There he summed up to a peace agreement between Arafat and the Israeli Prime Minister Yitzhak Rabin, on behalf of their respective peoples, committing the Palestinian to put an end to terrorism. On one blow Arafat lost his ascendant with Islamic militancy, since the Palestinians attacked the peace agreements.

The fundamentalist Palestinian nucleated around Hamas, declared such agreements as the symbol of the end of the Islamic Palestinian, results of a plot by the United States and Israel, and consciously accepted by the PLO's Arafat, to whom they declared war.

Hamas challenged the historical leadership of the PLO as "the legitimate representative of the Palestinian people", calling their leaders pork gluttons and drunks. Hamas launched a campaign of violence against the PLO, maiming and burning Palestinians for "collaborating" with the negotiations.

In that year, the Sudanese Hassan Al-Turabi brought to an end in the Palestinian civil war, convincing Hamas to join forces with the PLO. A year later, the clashes between Hamas and the PLO spread all over Gaza. In September 1995 Tel Aviv withdraws from the cities of the West Bank and Arafat could appease, for the moment, the extremists.

The proof that the old autocrat has lost authority lies in his inability to liquidate terrorism. Israel's position has been clear: the more imperturbable Arafat remains before the human bombs of the Hamas and Islamic Jihad fundamentalists, the lower its political weight in the negotiations. This is precisely the dilemma written in the turrets of Israeli tanks: choose the wreck along with divine mobs, succumbing to their countless opponents or smoking the pipe of peace with the cavalry.

It is true that Arafat and his PLO have not assumed the risks of arranging the reconciliation of his people with their enemy. It took five disastrous wars and the humiliation of defeat to face the reality that the Israelites were so powerful that they could not be evicted from Palestine. Before such superiority, Palestinians can only hope in a short-period a supervised autonomy, and over the longer term to a mini-state in parts of the West Bank and the Gaza Strip, but without receiving the keys to Jordan.

While being forced to negotiate, but at the same time fearful of a total confrontation with Hamas, Arafat chooses invariably to withdraw from the negotiations at Camp David in 2000, rejecting the concessions obtained by Washington from Tel-Aviv, and returning to his familiar history of maximalist.

His traditional position of all or nothing responds to his inability to know what may or not be obtained in a world of nations, and his ignorance of the true scale of the international *realpolitik* of the world powers.

With the certainty that there will be a new day and a new peace offer, he made an effort to ignite the fire of the street insurrection and terrorism. Arafat no longer has time for drills; his position was made clear right away, under penalty of losing legitimacy to continue representing the Palestinians, or his own survival at the hands of his countless opponents.

In February 2002, a skilled, probably professionally trained sniper from the Palestinian terrorist group Tanzim methodically killed ten soldiers and civilians at a checkpoint in the West Bank. The sniper held the army and police down for more than an hour and then escaped undetected[2].

To launch his second Intifada, the PLO hoped that "the street" in the hands of Hamas, romanticized in the headlines of the suggestible European press, would force the *Pax Americana* to redeem their considered "unrealistic" claims.

But this strategy didn't help him regain the street, which was already in the hands of Hamas and the Islamic Jihad. Then he had no choice but to join strength with both, offering them even to integrate a Palestinian Government of "national unity". Then he merged his armed wing, Al-Fatah, with Hamas into a clandestine army, National Islamic Forces.

But perpetuating these marches and setbacks to accommodate, on the one hand, *Pan-Islamic* consciousness and, on the other hand, public opinion in the West, is resuming an old story of failures: the self-immolation of the Palestinian youth in an escalation against the oiled Israeli war machine.

It is the imaginary, described as an absurd by the Moroccan historian Abdallah Laroui, that one day the State of Israel will disappear by magic, to reconstitute in another totally-Palestinian nation from the Jordan River to the Mediterranean, where there will be minority settlings of Jews and Christians[3].

Nobody has managed to explain -Palestinians, Arabs or Israelis- how from the horrors of Black September until the current Israeli offensive in Gaza and the West Bank, the PLO has been able to survive to such terrible disasters. And now, while the Palestinian dilemma has internationalized and Israel's has been regionalized, geopolitics imposes to subdue the terrorist faction of Hamas in Gaza and the West Bank.

The truth is that the Palestinian leadership and his PLO have not been able, so far, to accept the risks to reconcile his people with a peace for which has not been prepared. That is the reason why an effective public policy is not implanted in Gaza and Jerusalem, fearing a bloody confrontation with Hamas, and that is the reason for his current blindness, not noticing all the momentums created by Washington to facilitate a treaty with Israel stating a Palestinian State.

Israel, meanwhile, has been at a crossroads: with peace it cannot continue to be defined as a fully Jewish State, with a central Christian-Israeli constituent and a current Arab-Israeli population.

Religiosity surrounding this conflict helps to forget the *realpolitik* that a balance of forces applies here as anywhere else. The fact they both sit opposite and neighboring creates an illusion of parity; but there is a huge asymmetry, since Israel has a formidable military arsenal and can strike down any combination of Arab States.

The solution of two states, coming from Hamas, offers no warranties to the common Israeli, and the Palestinians cannot thrive without access to the Israeli economy, which in turn needs them as labor. The PLO has insisted that to negotiate, Israel should freeze their "settlements" in the "occupied territories", previously commit to Palestinian statehood and accept its withdrawal to the pre-1967 borders. With their overwhelming material superiority over the Palestinians, no government in Jerusalem will grant these privileges.

Palestinians, who have lost each of their military clashes with the Jewish State, have to recognize their real position and negotiate from its real power and not from exaggerated claims. For the Palestinians, what was possible in 1947 is unthinkable today, and what they can get today, will be unattainable tomorrow. It is the price to pay (no matter whether fair or unfair) for more than five decades of belligerency and rejection against a state that has continued developing its military, economy and technology.

The Arab head of states and leaderships of the Islamic world, including the PLO, still has not apprehended in all its magnitude the determination of the world powers to establish, once and for all, the geo-strategic coordinates and the policy objectives that will govern the future of the area.

Pax Americana is not going to retreat from the oil regions to monitor it from a distance as it was done previously. It is a decision shared by all Eurasia powers without exception. Modern times are tearing apart the dual personality

Jekyll/Hyde style, with which the Islamic world has associated so far with the West.

The entire architecture of global power has changed. The issue is no longer which country is politically correct, but which is economically correct, since instead of military superpowers today supermarkets and stock markets dominate. No longer are governments but markets providing the financing for peace. Societies need to join the global economy and attract global investments in views to survive economically.

The global market rewards good economic management and batters or discards bad administrations -as Greece or Argentina- faster than ever. Today we are witnessing a global phenomenon of countries consolidating economically in blocks increasingly larger while fragmenting politically in smaller entities.

While there are emerging countries of the Cold War that seek to build computers, there are others who are renewing their ethnic and tribal fiefdoms. While in Japan, Taiwan, Singapore, South Korea, Maastricht and in Brussels, the future buries the past, in Sarajevo, Rwanda, Nagorno-Karabakh, Chechnya, Georgia, Kashmir, Sierra Leone, Cuba, Hebron and Gaza the past seems to be burying the future. In the Middle East the past always has buried the future and possibly, invariably, will happen as well.

The raise of the crusaders

The Levant, geographical name given to all the countries bordering the Eastern Mediterranean, where there has been a smart mix of Western ideas with Arab, Greek and Turkish native cultures; where people live simultaneously in two worlds without belonging to one in particular.

The words Lebanon and Syria were nothing more than geographical references. Beirut was never a city, but an idea that for a time represented the idea of coexistence and the spirit of tolerance. The dynamism of Beirut was a product of the Mediterranean.

Asia had its Hong Kong; Europe had Monaco and the Middle East the Beirut of banking secrecy, of casinos, the licentious nightlife. Christians and Muslims married, interacted, and associated in business. Lebanon became a sanctuary for political exiles and grounds of confluence of *avant–garde* Arabs.

The French increased the historical borders of Mount Lebanon including the huge population of Sunni Muslims, who were under the rule of the Christians Maronites, their French-speaking allies, and with its concordat with the Vatican. Lebanon gained independence from France in 1943. Muslims abandoned for a while their claims of append with Syria and accepted the notion that the Lebanon was an "Arab" country. Since then, Lebanon made its wealth from its position as bridge between the West and the Arab world.

Unlike other Arab States where the different groups were seeking secession, Lebanon is the only case where factions seeking to assume power want to maintain the unity of the country. The Levantine political idea grew naturally on these shores, and consisted of an original solution which persuaded the Lebanon citizens of various tribal communities that, sectarian, religious identities -Shiites, Sunnis, Christians and Druze- could mix, live and thrive in a city and even build a modern Republic.

Here was where politicians deposed by military coups were installed to write their memoirs, while artists, also, and Arab poets came to try their luck in this Middle East Broadway. For the rest of the Islamic world, there the rules didn't apply, sin was the norm and money could buy anything and anyone.

Impatient and intolerant Arab nationalists viewed with prejudice the heterogeneous cultures. In the thousands of shops in the bazaars of Beirut do business and lived side by side[1] the Maronite cobbler, the Druze butcher, Orthodox Greek moneychanger, the Sunni coffeemaker, the Shiite shopkeeper, and the Armenian jeweler.

It is true that there was a certain open society but, ultimately, Lebanon never had a democracy but a balance of sectarian power. Before the civil war, Lebanese democracy transformed the modern class conflict in an old religious-tribal feud. Democracy has been a mask for the Government's tribal mobsters and warlords, as the Gemayel (Pierre, Amin and Bashir), Camille (David) Chamoun, Kamal and Walid Jumblatt. Freedom was not such but an organized anarchy and the diversity of news media were subsidized by the Arab world voices.

Beirut published more books than the Islamic world and more newspapers than any country in the area. Among them, "An-Nahar" was the most famous in the Arabic language. Likewise, the American University of Beirut was the most prestigious in the Middle East. But Beirut was never the Switzerland of the Middle East, it is a city divided by ethnic and religious lines as the Tower of Babel; in it the symbol of its unity became their disunity, and where the only style of military battle that embroiled all these factions was that of massacre.

Lebanon, Syria, and Jordan were transforming into city-States, such as the Phoenician State-Cities. Damascus dominated the rest of Syria. Amman in Jordan grew as a Bedouin-Palestine city. South of Lebanon, managed by the Shiite ring, has been historically divorced from Beirut, and oriented toward Galilee. If the desert determined Syria, Mediterranean determines Lebanon.

The Lebanon antebellum was a quasi-democratic place that could tolerate the Christian Maronites with their autonomous province in Mount Lebanon, the Shiites and Sunni Muslims, and the Druze. The first demographic alteration in Lebanon, when the Maronites exceeded the Druze in number in the 19th century, had tremendous political implications; the same has happened with the second change, transforming marginal Shiites into the majority sect. If the history of the Lebanon was Maronite, its present and future is Shiite.

Bringing together two countries created the modern Republic of Lebanon, each dominated by a religious community: Sunni Muslims and Maronite Christians. The Islamic population of Lebanon (Shiite and Sunni) aspired to be part of Syria. The Druze is a heretical sect of Islam whose religious beliefs are kept secret.

There, everyone is primarily Druze, Maronite and Sunni before Lebanese, and always a member of the clan Druze of the Jumblatt before Druze, or a member of the Maronite clans, the Gemayel or the Franjieh, before Maronite. The civil war and the invasions of Israel and Syria would strengthen this trend, which condensed Lebanon in micro-clan families, villages or religious communities that tore the nation with their private armies and their different versions of reality.

The endless civil war in the Lebanon is part of a past. What happened in the Lebanon (apart from the new element of Syria and the PLO) was a repetition of what happened there in 1845 and 1860. Two main communities -Maronite and Druze- engaged in a violent dispute, dragging with it the international powers. The Christian Maronites would enjoy

European support in the 20th century; but here the term "Christian" has clouded as Maronites are a typical variation of Eastern Christianity, and their struggle would not include the Protestant or Orthodox Greeks or Armenians, or the Greek Catholic community.

It was precisely these Syrian Christians who knew the Arabic language, including St John of Damascus (675-749), who provided to European Christianity the doctrinal theology to challenge the Prophet Muhammad and Islam, stereotypes that flowed throughout the culture of the West (Muhammad as false prophet, hypocritical, and Muslims as violent, and so on).

This fear was understandable because the Islamic proselytizing religion based in conquering earned adepts in Christianity. It has been against this old and forgotten backdrop that in the Arab world (Lebanon), takes place much of the animosity between Christians and Muslims. That is why Lebanon didn't have a classic war, because foreigners and foreign invasions have been inseparable from the intra communal violence.

By 1970 the rapid population growth among Muslims turned the Lebanon inside out, reducing Christians to a third of the population. The Muslims began to demand reforms. In times that the Christian-Islamic relationship tensed in Lebanon, another phenomenon was added to the territory: The Jewish-Palestine conflict. In the 1970s and 1980s Christians fought against the Palestinians and Druze; rival Christian militias fought against each other, and Palestinian factions did the same.

The Lebanese unity was a political parable because the identity of the country was depending on which sect dominates it; the stretch to civil war was short. The reason why the cycle of violence began in 1975 and not in 1958 was due to the fact that the United States decided then to arbitrate militarily.

The war in Lebanon in 1975-1977 was not only due to the struggle between Syria and the PLO but it represented a microcosm of international politics, where the interests of the great powers, the history of minorities in the Arab world, the social revolution, and the tragic legacy of Westal colonialism were mixed.

Al-Sayyid Fadlallah, an admirable Shiite Lebanese essayist who has been published in the West, wrote in the midst of the fray of 1976 a theology of terror: *Islam and the Logic of Force,* which accentuated the intense fundamentalist debate. As a result of this war, the zone became the tactical hub of terrorist gangs, primarily of the PLO. After being expelled from Jordan, Arafat was received by Lebanese Muslims and Druze, with the hope that Palestinian fighters would unite them in their struggle against the Maronite Christians.

The PLO became strong in a section of Beirut and in southern Lebanon from where would launch their raids against the Northern Israeli population. In 1975 the Palestinian refugees supported by Lebanese Muslims, fought against Lebanese Christians. The Alawites of Syria and Lebanon Maronite Catholics need one another to survive before the numerically dominant Sunni Muslims, in both countries.

As a result of the Lebanese civil war, Syrian forces settled indefinitely in the area that became the operational center of terrorism internationally and especially of the PLO. The efforts of Washington to reach a conclusion of the Arab-Israeli conflict and the Lebanon through Arab mediation (Jordan, Arabia Saudi, Egypt), proved useless because Syria - underpinned by the former Soviet Union- daunted everyone with its military arsenal.

In 1976. the Syrian President Assad supported the Maronites in their war against the Palestinians, in order to reduce a possible war with Israel. This perception helped turn

Sunni Muslims within Syria and lunched the Syrians against the Palestinians.

On the other hand, the Shiites were represented by two movements: centrist Amal, headed by Nabih Berri and supported by Syria, and Hizb-Allah of Shiite militancy and headed by Hassan Nasrallah, which was propped by Iran. Hizb-Allah was nurtured of thousands of Iranian militants who filtered across the border in the 1980s, and their suicide bomb attacks and kidnappings against Israel and the West shook Beirut.

Lebanese Shiites hated the Palestinians for having transformed the Lebanese South on a battlefield; one of its most prestigious leaders was Adel Osseiran.

The balance was altered with the arrival of 300,000 Palestinians (Sunnis) fleeing the Arab-Israeli wars, and Jordan military repression. In Lebanon they constituted the terrorist organization Hamas with the help of Saudi Arabia. The slums of Fakhani, Sabra and Shatila in Beirut became a mini-state of the PLO allowing Arafat to keep the union between different factions.

Beirut provided Arafat and the PLO with bases, in order to launch direct attacks against Israel and to recruit and train operatives for their spectacular aircraft kidnappings and terrorist operations, which they hoped would maintain latent the Palestinian cause. The more important Sunni militias of Beirut, the Morabites, rather than a political party were a street gang with a Nasserist varnish, whose mafia boss was Ibrahim Koleilat.

The Christians could not accept the reality that they were no longer rulers of the Lebanon and to protect themselves decided to train their own militias with the support of Israel. The head of the militia would be Rashid Karami and his most relevant political character was Camille Chamoun, while Pierre Gemayel would be the founder of the Falangist militia.

In July 1980 Bashir Gemayel had eliminated his political rival Danny Chamoun and his armed corps, the Tigers; but not in a battle for dogma or sacred texts but because his private militia controlled illegal ports and racketeer patronage of East Beirut. In addition, the Druze of Walid Jumblatt, fed by Syria and always looking for opportunities, enters in the fight for power.

The fight between Lebanese Muslims and the faction dominated by the Maronites, known as Lebanese Phalange[2], broke out in 1975. The central Government stopped working while some factions of heavily armed militias reduced Lebanon to anarchy.

The Organization for the liberation of Palestinian (PLO) joined the Muslim side at the beginning of 1976 and Syria (worried about the Israeli reaction) intervened to support the Christians and against the PLO which had the back of the more radical groups.

So therefore, Beirut was divided with a "green line" from East to West, separating the Christian North of the Muslim South. In June the Arab League imposed a truce, entrusting the Syrians the maintenance the peace. Nevertheless, violence continued and the numerous attempts to reach peace agreements failed due to the continuous incidents by forces of one or another trend.

In 1978 Israel Defense Force enter the South of Lebanon in an attempt to eliminate the Palestinian bases. A UN force replaced Israeli troops, but continued assisting the Maronites and attacking the bases of the PLO. In June 1982, Israel, worry about the Syrian control in Lebanon and the increase of Palestinian act of violence against their border towns, invaded Lebanon.

By mid-August, after an intense American mediation, the cohorts of the PLO were compelled to leave Beirut evacuating to different Arab countries. Later in the same month, with Israeli troops surrounding Beirut, the Lebanese Parliament elected as President the leader of the Christian militia Bashir Gemayel. After his assassination in September by a

Palestinian squad, his brother Amin Gemayel was designated to replace him.

As revenge, the Falangist forces of Amin Gemayel launched a violent attack in the Palestinian refugee camps of Sabra and Shatila, slaughtering about 1,000 Palestinians. Because both camps happen to be in the section occupied by Israel, the PLO and Arab propaganda machine, and the liberal world press blame Israel as the perpetrator. To avoid an adverse profile, the Israelis retreated to the South of Lebanon, allowing the establishment in Beirut of an international peacekeeping force.

In late 1983, talks between the different formations of the country began in Geneva in order to pursue the peace process, but they failed. The Lebanese Muslims didn't put up with an international peacekeeping force that support a government led by Christians. As a result, on October 23, 1983 a terrorist attack was launched against their barracks with more than 300 American and French soldiers' casualties, precipitating the pull out of the international troops in February 1984.

In the resulting power vacuum, the fight between factions intensified until in 1985. In that year the Israeli troops withdrew almost completely from Lebanon, leaving a security zone in the South controlled by their Christian allies, the army of the South of the Lebanon (ESL). The Hizb-Allah Shiite[3] backed by the Iranians fought for this area against the ESL, having rejected a peace agreement, hosted by Syria, in December 1985. The main objective of Hizb-Allah was to control West Beirut.

In the south border with Israel, the PLO continued making their fierce raids, state of affairs who demanded the relentless retaliation of the Israel Defense Force against the facilities of the PLO in the South. To make matters worse a fast deterioration of conditions in Beirut enabled Syrian troops to occupy the Muslim sector in 1987 to end the hostility between the Lebanese and pro-Palestinian pro- Muslims.

Later, clashes followed between the factions at war, aggravated in 1988 by a new Israeli invasion on the South of the country and the end in September of the presidential mandate of Amin Gemayel, to whom General Christian Michael Aoun succeeded as head of the provisional Government. But Aoun was not accepted by the pro-Syria groups. As Lebanese factions were unable to come together in order to agree on a new President, the conflicting factions established their own administrations.

In October 1989, negotiators from all the Lebanese factions meeting in Saudi Arabia agreed to reform the Constitution of 1926 that gave power to the Muslims. Christian President Michel Aoun rejected the project, threatening with the permanent partition of the Lebanon. Then the struggle between the various Christian factions arose, and in October 1990, the Syrian troops positioned in East Beirut, troops defeated the forces loyal to Aoun.

On 5 November, the Lebanese Parliament, made up mostly by Muslim, gathered in Taif and ratified this reform electing as President the Maronite René Moawad. But, he was assassinated 17 days later by Moslems terrorist squads, and the Parliament had to elect in his place another Maronite, Elias Harawi.

The Lebanese army, backed by Syria, later regained control over a large part of the country, disarmed militias and expelled the PLO from its strongholds on the South of Lebanon. Then begin the withdrawal of the different militias from Beirut. The war had claimed the lives of more than 150,000 Lebanese since 1975.

In 1992 were held legislative elections, in which the pro-Syria Muslims were victorious. Shortly thereafter, Rafik Hariri formed a unity Government with Muslim and Christian members.

In July 1993, the Israeli launched airstrikes against bases of Hizb-Allah who were firing rockets against Israeli territory. The military encounter caused the emigration of 200,000 people from the South of Lebanon moving northward in search of greater security. The international community decided to intervene and in August, the Lebanese Army joined the forces of UN peacekeepers in the area, but without achieving the dispersion the Hizb-Allah units.

Continuous skirmishes between Hizb-Allah and the Israeli forces in the security zone between both countries generated numerous attacks between the two sides, making it difficult to carry out the peace agreements between Israel and the PLO enforced in September 1993.

Hizb-Allah once purchased 100 legitimate French national identity cards and 50 valid passports for cash from a corrupt French embassy official in Africa. (...) In 1998, a Lebanese citizen was arrested in Ciudad del Este, Paraguay, forging passports and U.S. residence and work visas (green cards) for Hizb-Allah operatives entering the United States[4].

In 1995, the Lebanese Parliament approved to extend by three years the mandate of President to the Maronite, Elias Harawi. A year later, were held legislative elections in which again won the pro-Syrian list, allowing Rafik Hariri to continue in his post as Prime Minister.

Lebanon became metaphor for barbarism and Beirut of urban jungle. The only thing that brought the Israeli armored incursion into Lebanon, and the consolidation of Syria in the Bekaa Valley, was to lessen the country and leave it at the mercy of the warlords who responded to Israel, Syria, Iraq, and Iran. Nevertheless, none of the Lebanese factions has desired a theocratic rinse.

The country will agree to a new demographic pattern, with a Shiite Muslim majority, dominated by a political elite submitted to Syria, where Hizb-Allah dominates. This new force estimated that Sunni Muslims (Gama 'a Islamiyah) have no legitimacy to govern the country. The Maronites lost the civil war and with it the right to handle Lebanon, since a Christian state means war with Syria. Christians had to approve Lebanon as an Arab country in exchange for Muslims to perpetuate the fiction of a numerical balance among all the sects and agree to share power.

In Syria

Syria is a political entity that encompasses three areas without something in common, and which hate each other and aspire to be separated. Without a defined national sentiment, the question has been whether Damascus will play the lead in a Levantine version of the Balkans.

Although it is frozen in time, its similarity to Lebanon and Iraq represent the risk that subsequent to the Alawite supremacy on their society, Syria could face the possibility of disintegrating as a nation.

Its leadership is terrified at the prospect of a new Yugoslavia, where the North would seek to reintegrate with Turkey; the Centre-East and the region of the Druze would amalgamate with Jordan and Southwest will join the Lebanon; and it would only remain an Alawite mini-state in the Northeast, as a refuge for the Assad clan.

It is very premature to assume as indissoluble the current partition in Arab Nations of this patch of land nestled between the Taurus Mountains and the sands of Arabia, which formerly surname Great Syria, and that for two millennia was anointed to the war chariot of Romans, Byzantines, Arabs, Mamelukes, Seljuks and Ottomans, and of which the bold English Scouts and Gertrude Bell and Freya Stark left wonderful testimonies.

Syria is a country that attracts the usual bands of tourists' hunters of monuments, since it is crowded with Greek temples, Roman amphitheaters, Crusaders, imposing architectures and Arab ancient castles. The city of Aleppo in the North and on the banks of the legendary river Euphrates is the Hal-pa-pa referred in the Sumerian tablets dating back

5,000 years. It is the second city in Syria and one of the oldest on the planet; destroyed by the Mongols of Hulagu Khan in 1260 and by Tamerlane "the Iron lame", in the year 1400.

With its multinational bazaars (Arabs, Turks, Armenians, Kurds), Aleppo is the entrance towards the Turkish Anatolian plateau, and preserves more historical links with the North, Mosul and Baghdad (both now in Iraq), than with the rest of the territory. The Sunni Muslim space of Hama, Homs and Damascus lies in the middle of the country. The Islamic community of the Druze occupies the southern region. To the west mountains and adjacent to the Lebanon, is the core of the Alawites, another Islamic sect which would take power with Hafiz Al-Assad and his current heir Basher Al-Assad.

In antiquity, Syria was the generic name of the region between the Anatolian peninsula, Turkey and the Sinai. The domain of that territory was a constant confrontation of the ancient civilizations, from the Egyptians Pharaohs, who considered it the gateway to their country, to the Persians, who saw in it a bridge on the road to the universal empire they projected.

In the central part of its coastline, between the XII and VII centuries BC, developed the Phoenician civilization, a society of sailors and merchants who created the first commercial economy of the planet, without worrying about the territorial expansion, not even for political unification. The Phoenician cities were always independent, although one or another temporarily exerted certain hegemony over the others.

Among the achievements of the Phoenicians are the invention of the alphabet, the ships suitable for the open sea, the manufacture of ceramics and fabrics, the expansion and systematization of geographical knowledge and the first circumnavigation of Africa.

The dissemination of these elements throughout the Mediterranean area is the origin of what would later be called "Western civilization", and whose main exponents were the Greeks. After the death of Alexander, The Great, his enormous empire was divided and Syria became the center of the Seleucid State (by Seleucus, one of his general), which extended as far as India.

In the Roman period the province of Syria was a frontier constantly agitated by the wars. The eastern part of the territory was already lost with the advance of the Parthians. Later, with the advent of Islam, the Umayyad Caliphs made Damascus the capital of the Empire, between 660 and 750, and laid the foundation for a strong national feeling, and carried out the "Arabization" of the territory.

By defeating the Umayyad, their opponents, the Abbasids, moved the capital to Baghdad, where the new Caliphs enjoyed more support. While it maintained its economic and cultural importance, Damascus lost its political clout, and in the 11th century has to face the invasion of the Christian Crusaders.

The defense of ancient Syria was put in charge of the local Emirs; but their internal rivalries allowed the triumph of the Crusaders, and the sustenance for almost 200 years of a small Christian kingdom, away from their support bases. Among the inheritance left by the Crusaders we can mention the strengthening of Christian communities in the region, especially the Maronites, who would serve as pretext for European interference from the 17th century.

The Egyptians started the process of expulsion of the Crusaders in the 13th century. This made Syria a virtual Egyptian province, and a theater of confrontation with the Mongol and Tatar invaders. In the 16th century the Egyptians definitely lost domination of the country that became controlled by the Ottoman Empire. When the Khedive of Egypt, Mehmet Ali, conquered Syria in 1831, he imposed heavy taxes and compulsory military service causing a popular revolt involving Christians and Muslims.

The European powers invoked the Islamic repressive measures against Christians as an excuse to intervene. They thus stopped the offensive of Mehmet Ali and entrusted to the French the "protection of the Syrian Christians". The process culminated in the complete withdrawal of the

Egyptian forces from Syria in 1840, the immediate restoration of Ottoman domain under the conditions that Christian missions and schools subsidized by the Europeans should be allowed.

In 1858 the Maronite Christians were well organized in communities that had been concentrating in the mountainous region between Damascus and Jerusalem. They broke with their ruling class, eliminating the feudal system of land tenure. Their Muslim neighbors -in particular the Druze- decided to suppress the movement in fear that it will spread in all the territory. The conflict between Moslems and Christians culminated in the so-called "massacres" in June, 1860.

A month later French troops landed in Beirut, to "protect" the Christians, and forced the Turkish Government to create a separate province, the "small Lebanon"; the province should be governed by a Christian -appointed by the Sultan, but with the approval of the European powers- and should have their own police. The Christians immediately abolished the feudal privileges. A social conflict was thus transformed into confessional groups´ confrontations, empowering the Christians of the "small Lebanon" with total dominance in relation to the local Muslim population.

So, through the Sykes-Picot agreement, Paris and London divided the Crescent Fertile Moon leaving Syria (with Lebanon) to France; while England remained with Palestine (including Jordan) and Iraq. Without knowing the agreement, the Emir Faisal was proclaimed King of Syria at the outbreak of the Arab revolt during the First World War.

In 1920, the French army occupied the country, forcing the Emir Faisal to withdraw. The Anglo-French rivalry spoiled all that made sense for that spot, the Great Syria, which was divided into six entities. Turkish Kemal Ataturk regained a piece of the North; the British Colonial Secretaries capriciously drew on a world map the mandates of Palestine, Transjordan, and Iraq. What's more the French turned their zone, later, into Syria and Lebanon. The part that kept the name "Syria", separated from Turkey by a Roman triumphal arc, the Bab-Al-Hawa today is far from being a nation, as it was under Istanbul.

Until 1932 the country experienced relative tranquility. In that year a President was elected with a Parliament, but France made clear its intention not to allow too much internal autonomy. This led to confrontations that ceased with an agreement where the French recognized the Justice of claims, the principal of which was the reunification with the Lebanon in 1936.

The Government of France never ratified the agreement, which caused more agitation culminating in the resignation of the Syrian President in 1939 and the suspension by the French administration of the Constitution of 1930 in Syria and Lebanon.

But, national sentiment does not constitute the foundation of the new Syria. The only patriotism that has existed there has been *Pan-Arabism* confined to Damascus. After all, like the Balkans, it is part of the same world that has not recovered from the collapse of the Turkish Empire, and the border conflicts that it generated.

Even though the territory has been cut off on all sides, Syria -like Lebanon- is a casserole of sects, religious brotherhoods and parochial tribal interests, enemies from each other and, worse yet, each one with its specific geographical location, which makes it a Levantine version of the Balkans.

Both Druze and Alawites[1] are the remnants of a wave of Shiism originated from Persia and Mesopotamia that a millennium ago spread above the Grand Syria. But the Alawites, 12% of the population, practice a faded version of Shiism, with dangerous affinities to the Phoenician Paganism and Christianity (Christmas, Palm Sunday, bread and wine in the ceremonies).

The Alawites sought refuge in Turkish secularism and the preventive umbrella offered by the multi-ethnicity of the great Syria to hide from the Islamic Sunni fundamentalism. From the Alawite minority -and the Druze- both the Ottomans and the French recruited soldiers and bureaucrats, obtaining the rancor that still lingers, from the Arabs of Damascus.

The Alawites embraced the Baas, a doctrinal corpus inspired by the German National Socialist Party of the 1930s, the Nazi, which gained momentum among Arabs of Damascus, Baghdad, Beirut and Palestine. In 1941, forces of France and England occupied the region.

Two years later Bechara El-Khouri in Lebanon and Shukri Al-Quwatli in Syria were elected as presidents respectively. But when the latter proposed to delete the clauses from the Constitution relating to the French mandate, the troops of this country took him prisoner along with his Cabinet.

The mutinies spread in both States, alerting the British who pressure the French army to act swiftly. The French occupation ended in March, 1946, when the United Nations ordered the withdrawal of all European forces and determined the end of the French mandate.

The Baas concluded as an intellectual pose that inflated the racism of the Sunni Arabs against Christians and Jews, and who bore the dictatorial regimes in Syria and Iraq, and influenced the Egyptian military which overthrew King Farouk and, also, the Yemeni officers who established the Northern Republic of Sanaa, in the 1960s.

In 1948, Syrian forces fought against the partition of Palestine and in 1956 sympathized with Egypt, after Nasser nationalized the Suez Canal, and provoke the conflict with Israel, France and Great Britain. In 1958, Syria joined the United Arab Republic, along with Egypt. The ambitious unifying project of Nasser failed in 1961 and ten years later returned, this time with greater elasticity in terms of links between its members, the Federation of Arab republics, of which Libya also participated.

The aspiration of its political class, including the Assad clan, has been the effort of redesigning all borders improvised by Europeans to restore the cherished Grand Syria. But, being this Syria smaller than the other Syria, it does not have political attractions for the unification of the Levant.

In 1958, the Syrian power elite embrace the Egyptian experiment of Arab unity, called the United Arab Republic, which was disbanded in 1961, given the deep disagreements between the Syrian Alawites and Sunnis Egyptians. The failure of that Arab union almost causes a military conflict. Two years later, an army composed mainly of Alawites, with the backing of the Bass party, assumed power in Damascus, by implementing a police state that, similar to the one on Iraq, destroyed the traditional political class and got rid of the civil society.

In 1963, a popular revolution brought to power the Arab Baas Socialist Party, founded in 1947 by the nationalist militant Michel Aflak of Christian origin. In November 1970 General Hafez Al-Assad took power and began a renewal movement, introducing reforms in the economic and social structures. The Fifth Regional Congress of the Party -the Baas believes that Arab countries are regions of the Arab nation- appointed Assad as Secretary General and proposed to "accelerate the stages towards the socialist transformation in different fields".

This orientation was institutionalized in the new constitution, adopted in 1973. Syria actively participated in the Arab-Israeli wars of 1967 and 1973, during which Israeli forces repelled their troops and occupied the Golan plateau. It joined together with Algeria, Yemen and the PLO, which objected to the U.S. policy in the region and also with the Camp David agreements. Its troops made up the greater part the Arab deterrent force, which intervened to supposedly avoid a partition of Lebanon in 1976.

In 1978, under an approach of the fraction Syria and Iraqi Baas party, progress was made towards the creation of a single state, but the project failed when attempting to unify the two branches of the Baas.

Syrian intellectuals (formerly at the forefront of Arab nationalism along with Egyptians) have been decimated, censored or exiled for opposing the heavy hand of both Assad. This has been the case with the eminent poet Ali Kanaap; also the Alawites, Mamduh Udwan and Saadallah Wannous dramatists, banned in Syria and published widely abroad; of the political philosopher Sadiqi Al-Azm, the staunchest defender of Salman Rushdie; the famed film director Duraid Lahham, proscribed in almost all Islamic countries for censoring religious fundamentalism and expose the irreversibility of the State of Israel.

The Baasist dynasty of the Assad of Syria has lasted more than any other not only because it was brutal, but for the reason that it has been extremely shrewd. As Middle East specialist Yossef Bodansky has stated: The majority of the urban population in Syria supports the Assad Administration (or, at the least, has demonstrated that it preferred them to the Islamist-dominated opposition). The economic élite has been dominated by Sunni urban families, as well as Armenian and Christian Orthodox families, in the main cities of western Syria; a strip between Damascus and Aleppo[2].

For them there are only agents and enemies; to stay in power they make use of the entire lethal arsenal the technology of war and espionage has to offer. The Muslim Brotherhood and the fundamentalists are sworn enemies of the Assad dynasty, and have done countless attacks and sabotage.

The Alawite elite that governs the country has built numerous mosques, as means to placate Sunni fundamentalists, whose aspirations for an Islamic State were bloodily drowned in the 1980s by Assad. Later on, the Syrian Fundamentalist Movement would opt to go semi-underground, while the regime outlawed Internet and mobile phones.

But that didn't prevent Syria from encouraging international terrorism since the 1960s. It uses the Shiites in the south of the Lebanon to attack Israel; it exerts control over Hizb-Allah settled in the Lebanese Bekaa Valley, while providing intelligence, money and international traffic to Al-Qaeda type organizations.

At the end of 1979 the Syrian section of the Baas censured the Moslem Brotherhood deeming them as "Zionist agents". The Moslem Brotherhood attacks continued. In 1982 the Government launched an offensive by the army; thousands of members of the Moslem Brotherhood were killed and the Syrian Government accused Iraq of having armed the rebels.

The border between the two countries was closed in April. Iraq responded with the shutdown of the pipeline that begins in Kirkuk and ends at the Syrian Port of Banias. In 1980 Iraq enters in an alliance with Saudi Arabia and Jordan in order to confront Syria, especially at the beginning of the war between Iran and Iraq.

The Syrian Government blamed Iraq of have triggered the conflict with Teheran to "divert attention from the central problem in the region", that is, the so argued Palestinian issue. At the end of that year, the tension between Jordan and Syria increased, when Damascus accused Amman of supporting the Moslem Brotherhood, putting both States on the brink of war. Only with significant efforts from Saudi Prince Abdul-Aziz that a military encounter was avoided.

On June 26, 1980 the fundamentalists launched grenades against Assad, the next day the Praetorian presidential guard entered into the prison of Palmira and executed more than one thousand Muslim prisoners[3]. The fundamentalists were strong in Aleppo and Hama, where they had their largest following, and Hafez Assad decided to give his punishment, because in this medium tribal Syrian game the rule is "you do or they do it to you".

Hama was the most beautiful city in Syria, located in the Central Plains, on the banks of the Orontes River, and was populated with Sunni Muslims. In a certain way Hama symbolized the tribal clash between the Alawite and the Sunni Muslim sect. The assault on Hama in the first week of 1982 was in charge of General Rifaat Al-Assad, brother of the then President, with its Alawite companies. In its report on Syria in 1983, Amnesty International estimated around 25,000 deaths in Hama[4]. That carnage is an example of an autocrat of the Islamic world that does not enjoy legitimacy among his people and that decided to crush a challenge to his authority by using weapons of the 20th century.

In 1981, erupted in Lebanon the so called "Arab missile crisis" when the troops of the Christian Phalange tried to extend their authority to the Lebanese city of Zahde. An Arab deterrence force -organized and commanded by Syria- tried to prevent this advance. At that moment Syria installed in the Lebanon Soviet surface-to-air SAM-6 missiles, which prompted an Israeli air-strike that wipe out the Syrian batteries. The crisis was eventually overcome, but in 1983 Israel invaded the Lebanon and destroyed the other bases of Syrian missiles.

The Damascus Government maintained its forces - estimated at 30 thousand troops- in Lebanese territory, conditioning its withdrawal to previous evacuation of all Israeli troops. In mid-1983 there was a serious crisis between the Syrian authorities and the leadership of the PLO, which prompted Syria to intensively support to Palestinian groups opposed to Yasser Arafat's leadership.

The fall of the oil price further aggravated the economic problems caused by the war, which forced the Syrian Government in 1984, to implement a tough austerity policy, which manifested in a strict control of financial activities, a shutting down of the borders to illegal trafficking of goods -

until then tolerated– and a substantial reduction of public expenditure.

In 1985, Al-Assad renewed his term as head of Government for seven years. In those manipulated elections he won 99.8% of the votes. Despite this set up, in 1987 there was a political calamity that forced the then Prime Minister, Abdul Rauf Al-Kassem to resign, accused of corruption. On November 1st, Mahmud Al-Zoubi, President of the people's Assembly, was elected Prime Minister of Syria.

In April 1987, there was an Arab Summit in which the majority of the countries attempted an alignment of Syria, in exchange for economic support, condemning Iran for the prolongation of the war. Syria didn't modify its stance towards Iran, vetoing a motion that allowed the re-entry of Egypt into the League of Arab countries at the same time.

But an unexpected element turns around the hostile Damascus position towards Cairo. The whole Soviet Bloc was in chaos and the particular Soviet Union was falling apart, and with that, the evaporation of military support from a super-power. So, in May 1990, Syria re-established diplomatic relations with Egypt.

Diplomatic relations with the United States improved markedly when Syria quickly aligned with the anti-Iraqi Alliance put together by Washington, on the event of the Iraq assault on Kuwait. Even Syria sent troops to the Saudi Arabia front.

In the context of the crisis, Syria took advantage and under the blind eyes of the whole world increased its influence in Lebanon and managed to strengthen an allied government disarming the majority of autonomous militias in that country. In May 1991, Syria and Lebanon signed a cooperation agreement in which Lebanon was recognized as a separate and independent State, for the first time since both countries achieved independence from France.

On December 2nd 1991, President Hafez Al-Assad was re-elected for the fourth time in an election where his candidacy was the only one ballot vote. Fifteen days later, by an agreement with international human rights organizations, the Syrian Government announced pardon for 2,800 political prisoners, all members of the Muslim Brotherhood.

In 1992, the Government abolished the death penalty and allowed some 4,000 Jews to emigrate. New legislation favored investments in the private sector, which grew significantly between 1991 and 1993. In the framework of a policy of encouraging the private sector of the Syrian economy, were opened to private capital state key sectors, such as the generation of electricity, the production of cement and the manufacture of medicines.

Meanwhile, Syria stayed away from the early stages of the peace process in the region, which allowed the establishment of the limited autonomy for Palestine and the signing of agreements between Israel and Jordan in July 1994.

In January a meeting was held between U.S. President Bill Clinton and Al-Assad in Geneva and, in September, the Syrian Foreign Minister was interviewed for the first time by Israeli television. In June 1995, in official negotiations with Israel, the return of the plateau of Golan to Syria didn´t materialized because Tel-Aviv argued that it was essential for its security a limited military presence in the region.

In October, an ambush by Hizb-Allah to Israeli troops in the southern border of Lebanon complicated the negotiations again. In mid-1996, Al-Assad played a part in a meeting of the Arab countries to coordinate a common strategy of negotiation with Israel.

Surprisingly, in November 1997, on the eve of the US military intervention in Iraq, Damascus intensified its relations with Baghdad. It was also a strategy against the ongoing Turk-Israeli Alliance in rapid consolidation. Their reason was that in case of a military conflict about the Golan Heights, Syria would be located in the middle of this new block.

The fear of Damascus was that in the event that Iraq would be razed it could be split in several states based on linguistic or religious criteria, making Turkey likely to control the colossal oilfields in Iraqi Kurdistan. The threat posed by the Turk-Israeli military alliance, which planned to produce thousands of new tanks for their armed forces, provoked also that Iran joined the Syria-Iraqi talks over security issues in April 1998.

Al-Assad was re-elected for his seventh consecutive five-year Presidency in 1999. During his election speech, the President said that the Government needed 'new blood' to boost economic reforms. In March 2000, each and every one of the 37 members of the Cabinet of the first Minister Mahmud Al-Zoubi presented their resignation to the President and Mohammed Mustafa Miro, a veteran leader of the Baas that served as Governor of the province of Aleppo, was appointed as the new premier.

The sudden death of Al-Assad on June 10th plunged the country in mourning for the sole ruler that most Syrians knew. Promptly, maneuvers were held to appoint the only alive son of the deceased, Basher Al-Assad who, after having been appointed commander of the armed forces, took over in July as the new President.

With the rise of his 35-year-old son, Basher Al-Assad, intellectuals and a faction of independent politicians, led by Riad Seif, thought they had before them an Arabic Mikhail Gorbachov who felt confident to emit criteria to reform the *ancient régime*, as the "one-party system", speed the privatization of the economy, allow more freedom of expression, and so on.

Among the first measures approved by the novel President, in April 2001 was the establishment of private banks and shortly thereafter enabled a private radio station to broadcast, although only music and no political content. But Basher, supported by the Baas old guard, disappointed the reformists when he described as "foreign intervention" the concept of civil society.

Although with Al–Assad father, the anti-Israeli rhetoric was intense, with Assad son it has reached levels of harshness that even the handful of Jews in Damascus do not dare to touch the Torah scrolls stacked in corners of the guarded synagogues. At the Arab Summit of that year, Basher Al-Assad stood out to vilify the Israelite Ariel Sharon, and announced that it would resume relations with Palestine, which his father had frozen, ensuring he would never follow the footsteps of Egypt and Jordan of a separate peace with Israel.

On the occasion of the pilgrimage of the Pope John Paul II by the footsteps of St. Paul, on the "road to Damascus", in May of that year, Basher Al-Assad in the welcoming ceremony launched a strong attack against Israel comparing the suffering of the Arabs with the persecution of Jesus Christ.

In addition, he asked the Christian Pope to remember in his prayers the people of Palestine and the Golan Heights, and expressed that he was a tolerant ruler in the religious aspect, but that this didn´t include the Jews, who had betrayed the Prophet Jesus and the Prophet Muhammad. At the end, Basher offered an anti-Jewish Alliance to a hesitant Pope. In response, John Paul II appealed to all parties to seek a lasting peace and a new attitude of understanding and respect between Christians, Muslims and Jews.

During the civil war in Lebanon in 1976, Syrian troops stormed to tilt the balance in favor of Muslims and Palestinians. But once in power, Basher Al-Assad realized the increasing vulnerability of his antiquated army in the Lebanon, especially after April 2001, when Israeli fighters destroyed its main radar stations.

With its tentacles in Lebanese domestic politics and economy, and controlling Beirut security apparatus, and with the complicity of the West, Basher Al-Assad had the luxury of removing his 25,000 soldiers in the Lebanese Bekaa Valley.

Syria, with unanimous support from Asia and Africa, obtained a seat in the United Nations Security Council in

October 2001, on spite of the opposition of Israel, and the requests of 38 US congressmen to the White House to oppose such appointment. But the official position of US was very mild due to their prevailed strategy to include the most influential Arab countries in their global campaign against terrorism.

International relations of Damascus were intense during 2001. After great pressure from the Lebanese Government, it vacated Beirut and redeployed their forces to other parts of the Lebanon. In August, the Syrian Premier Mohammed Mustafa Miro visited Iraq, in the first high-level trip to that country since relations stiffen because of Syrian support to Iran during the 1980-1988 wars.

As a result of the sabotage of September 11 in New York, Damascus moved away from Islamic bazaar mobs and offered his "'full support" to the Western Alliance and has maintained a self-protecting silence before the demons unleashed by Washington in the area.

The British Prime Minister, Anthony "Tony" Blair, also visited Damascus in November, to try to shore up the Syrian support to the anti-terrorist campaign driven by United States. However, the Prime Minister Blair and President Basher Al-Assad failed to agree on a definition of the term "terrorism" and the British leader returned to his country without concrete results.

After an imprisonment of more than two decades, the release in November of dozens of political prisoners belonging to the Moslem Brotherhood was greeted by Amnesty International as a "satisfactory step forward in respect for human rights in Syria". Almost all detainees remained in solitary confinement during their detention and were subjected to torture, ill treatment and degrading conditions.

In April 2002, the Syrian station radars in Lebanon were strike by Israeli aircraft, responding to an attack by the Hizb-Allah guerrillas, arousing fears of a military escalation that however didn't take place.

In May, the US Undersecretary of State, John Bolton, included Syria on the list of members of the so-called axis of evil countries, accusing Damascus of trying to obtain weapons of mass destruction. Washington threatened Syria with economic and diplomatic sanctions by stating that the regime was helping Iraqi fugitives. But the Syrian Government rejected the accusations.

In January 2004, Assad became the first Syrian ruler to visit Turkey, in a journey that marked the beginning of the thaw of relations with Ankara. On March 8 the Syrian Committee for the Defense of Democratic Freedoms and Human Rights organized an unprecedented demonstration in Damascus in demand of freedom for political prisoners and democracy. Two members of the Committee, Ahmad Jazen and Hassan Wattfa, were arrested and spent two months in prison.

The head of the Committee, Aktham Naisse, was arrested on April 14 after issuing a statement that accused the authorities of arresting over a thousand Kurds in an operation against this minority group and demanded the end of "terrorist and illegal practices" of the Government.

Also in April, after an explosion in a building that had been headquarters of the UN in Damascus (in unclear circumstances) took place a shootout that killed a civilian, a police officer and two of the four involved activists. The Government attributed the bombing to Islamic fundamentalists.

In May, United States imposed economic sanctions on Syria because of their support for terrorism and its refusal to prevent the entry of guerrillas in Iraq from its borders. Despite the decision by Washington, the European Union announced the shipping of a commercial delegation to Damascus to improve cooperation in the export of oil and gas to Europe.

After the assassination of former Lebanese premier Rafik Hariri in Beirut in February 2005, the pressure from Washington, Paris, the UN and the Lebanese opposition increased so that troops and Syrian intelligence agents would leave Lebanon immediately.

After meetings with Arab leaders, Basher Al-Assad announced in March an immediate removal of its troops placed in the Bekaa Valley, near the border. Following, in Summit with Emile Lahoud, his Lebanese similar, agreed to a partial withdrawal timetable; it established that, for the May general elections in Lebanon, all Syrian troops would pull out. Hizb-Allah in Beirut organized a mass demonstration of support for Damascus and rejection of foreign interference.

The apparent suicide in October of Ghazi Kanaan, Minister of Interior, aggravated the tension on the eve of the publication of a report by the UN that implicated him in the murder of Rafiq Hariri. Minister Kanaan and other officials in Damascus had been subject to an investigation by the UN; his deceased took placed after he had been interrogated by the enquire team sent by the World Forum, headed by German prosecutor Detlev Mehlis. "I think that this is the last statement I will make," said Kanaan hours before his death, which was listed officially as suicide.

A week later, the UN report said that Hariri's assassination was committed by a group with extensive organization, which had planned the attack for months and that it was unlikely that a complex plot could have been developed without the knowledge of their designated Lebanese and Syrian intelligence services.

Mehlis, the German prosecutor, added in his presentation that the Syrian Foreign Minister Faruk Al-Sharaa had affected his research by providing false information. While the Lebanese President, the pro-Syrian Emile Lahoud, rejected the allegations expressed in the report, according to which he would have received a phone call from a key suspect in the case, just a few minutes before the explosion that killed Hariri.

The Syrian Government also strongly rejected the conclusions, indicating that many tracks pointed directly to certain Syrian security individuals which had been involved in the murder. Damascus condemned the conclusions of the document, by being politically partial and for "containing false accusations".

It has been very difficult that the West would look beyond diplomatic pressures and one or another sanction to deal with the Syrian terrorist record, even when the Basher Al-Assad power elite is the most insidious in the entire Middle East.

But as Middle East specialist Yossef Bodansky has put it bluntly[5]: "The international community has been blindly following a jihadist-driven agenda for Syria; a solution the majority of Syrians reject, but which Turkey and Qatar have been driving. It begs the question: why are analysts in Washington -or Paris or London- not digging more deeply into what is really happening, given that the solution they have endorsed is so profoundly anti-Western? The US and West have allowed themselves to claim a moral imperative for intervention in Syria in support of non-Syrian objectives, and particularly objectives desired by Sunni radicals answerable to the Turkish and Qatari governments".

And Bodansky keep on as follows[6]: "Meanwhile, the West, led by the US, Turkey, and Qatar, is striving to repeat in Syria the legacy of the interventions in Bosnia and Libya, irrespective of the realities on the ground or the desires of the local population. To justify such an intervention, the US leads a media campaign to portray the Syrian National Council (SNC) and the Free Syrian Army (FSA) as westernized and democratic when Arab governments and the Arab media know that this is simply untrue. "

The roots of Islamic terrorism

During its 1300-year long history, from the theocracy established by the Prophet of Allah, Islam has been politically manipulated and presented in as many varieties as countries profess it. The unity of its world is as fictitious as its creed. Therefore, there is no Islamic or Arab nation, as there is not a Christian. There, the family, *clan* and the tribal interests always precede the nations; loyalty to the Islamic faith would also be stronger than to the state, which would fail to resolve this dichotomy.

That is the main reason why the Western-style *"partycracies"* do not prevail; a unique and unified Islamic Community and/or one Arab nation cannot be created even in the hypothetical case the purification sects lay down the quasi-secular governments of the Middle East.

The Islamic society -as all contemporary societies- is racist; its dogma is not democratic; and like its other Semitic relative, the Jewish-Christian, punishes an inferior status for women, whose role in society is at the heart of the Arab obsession with the honor. That is the reason why the current theocratic states sacrifice women to placate radicals.

The brutal ignorance of the West about the literature, the politics, and the credo of the Islamic space, has had disastrous consequences for the contemporary world. It is noticeable how the last years, crucial events both intellectual and religious passed unnoticed; type product of traditional analysis, which has always focused only on what is happening in the industrial poles of the planet.

The rise of the Middle East on the verge of international tension sits on several ingredients: The Arab-Israeli conflict with its sequel to Palestine; religious orthodoxy; ultra-nationalism of Egypt, Libya, Syria, and Iraq; the imperative geostrategic of oil; and the brand-new irruption of former Soviet Islamic States of Central Asia.

Obviating the thorny Palestinian matter -of course- the West from the "McCarthyism" era on was obsessed with the nuclear duel with the Soviets and suspicious of nationalist rhetoric and the survival of the State of Israel ruled out the Arab nationalist regimes of post-war. Seeking to establish a state of modern cut, those Arab pro-secular regimes proclaimed themselves against Islamic extremism and challenged the retrograde power of tribal underbosses transfigured by the grace of the oil sheikhs and Emirs.

With the exception of French President Charles de Gaulle, Euro-America never assessed the non-alignment of a Gamal Abdul Nasser of Egypt, of a Karim Kassem of Iraq, an Al-Salal Mohammed from Yemen, and a Mohammad Mossadegh of Iran, of a Houari Boumediene of Algeria or the Neo-Destour party of a Habib Bourguiba of Tunisia. At the time this Arab nationalism aborted on behalf of ideological crusades, the West polarized the region, helping the raise of fundamentalist theocracies and faction monarchies that bogged down, among other things, the Palestinian dispute.

Up to what point was a successful tactic of US and Europe to have played during the Cold War the "Islamic card" of the conservative monarchies and fundamentalist groups against nationalism and its ideology of Arab socialism?

One would have to imagine a plausible story for the Middle East if the existing alignment of certain Islamic Nations with the West had crystallized in the decade of 1950 or 1960. Right when the momentum of modernization and national emancipation was intense, bogged down by the Soviets and chastised by the European powers since the conflict of the Suez Canal in 1956.

As confirmed by the performances of Anwar El-Sadat, the Republicans of Yemen, and the Turkish military, Arab nationalism was much more receptive and malleable to negotiate any of these crises than Islamic oil-sheikhs, graced by London and Washington.

The resurrection of Islamic Puritanism is only the desperate gesture of an archaic religious design, threatened today in its basic pillars by the secular state, by the thrust of modernism, and by unbridled scientific and technological advance that cross the planet. Also, threatened by globalization: the drama of a dogmatic vision that refuses to renew itself and refuses to cede the ground of civil society.

Fundamentalism comes from the bottom Bedouin, religious and conservative, xenophobic and suspect of the outsider (beginning with Muhammad at Medina) contrary to the Islamic doctrinal marrow that starts from a commercial and urban culture (the Caliphate in Baghdad, Cordoba or Istanbul), more suitable for renovation.

Islamic terrorism in its multiple schools (either Black September, the Muslim Brotherhood, Hizb-Allah or Al-Qaeda) is the bloodthirsty corollary of this fundamentalism.

Active groups, including the Tamil Tigers (LTTE) of Sri Lanka, the Kurdish Communist Party (PKK) in Turkey, and Palestinian groups in Israel such as the PFLP, PLO, and DFLP, have not yet succeeded in their efforts to gain independent states, but have continued using terrorist tactics up through recent years[1].

There is no form of political expression, this is done "in the name of Islam," but primitive Islam (Christianity of the catacombs), a cult of nostalgia for the "re-Islamizing" of society.

The fathers of modern terrorism originated largely in Russia, where numerous groups, anarchists, and terror-advocating philosophers emerged, such as Sergi Nachayev and Mikhail Bakunin. Terrorism spread throughout Europe, where numerous heads of state were assassinated. It eventually came to the United States with the assassination of

President McKinley in September 1901 and the Wall Street bombings of 1920[2].

After the Russian Revolution of 1917, Russian terrorism further expanded and was encouraged by the communist leadership. Lenin, also known as the "Red Prince," encouraged collective terrorism. After World War Ist, the Irish Republican Army under the leadership of Michael Collins used terrorism to win independence for the southern counties of Ireland. Modern terrorism saw its greatest social and ideological advances after World War II, although its foundation was laid in the mid-1880s[3].

The emergence of the current Orthodox wing, type Osama Bin-Laden of Iranian Ahmadineyad, is unrelated to the traditional nihilism and anarchism of 19th century European misery city quarters. It is a philosophy of crisis of the educated and privileged segments of a society developed in the tumultuous decades of 1970s and 1980s in the heat of the "petro-Arabic" prosperity. The uncertainty of identity that was unleashed corrupted a generation of intellectuals and politicians.

The unfinished Israeli victory in the war of Yom Kippur in 1973 restored the "Arab honor" and brought a period of self-esteem and deep expectations, which resulted in the triumph of orthodoxy in Iran and Sudan, and the cry of holy war launched from Afghanistan. The Arab nationalist model also failed to free Palestine or raise the economic level of the Arab masses. These states will also be "confessional" in a sense, integrated by minorities and by a dominant sect that denied any ethnic diversity.

The collapse of oil prices in the 1980s and the inter-Arab wars produced a cynical and puritan reaction in a progeny of youth, discouraged and frustrated, in the Middle East street bazaars. They are the wretched of the Earth that the Antillean writer Frantz Fanon spoke about; rejected for good schools, null students, the "dysfunctional" abused in their breeding.

Prior to September 11, the words Osama bin Laden, al-Qaeda and pilot training in the same sentence should have spelled out suicide skyjacking to most people who worked the al-Qaeda mission. All of these words were found in one FBI agent's report prior to the attack. Al-Qaeda's global capabilities, matched with Bin Laden's personal animosity toward America and a previous skyjacking for this purpose by a group associated with al-Qaeda (the skyjacking of an Air France airliner by the Algerian GIA in 1994), should have made even the coolest intelligence analyst spill his coffee and issue a dire warning. Several did just that[4].

Terrorists trained by the foreign intelligence agencies of Chile, Cuba, Libya, Iraq, Iran, and North Korea have conducted assassinations, mass murders, and abductions, and have supplied other less skillful terrorist groups with weapons, training, and equipment[5].

With its promise of a more virtuous government, these militants crave power in nearly all Arab States; that is why the debate is no longer between the defenders of the secular order or the religious, but who will govern in the name of Islam. It is the absurd tension of every Islamic nation between divine law and *realpolitik* of the state.

The belligerence of orthodox Islam, not only has handhold in the mosques and the sermons of cadis, mullahs, imams and ayatollahs. There is an extensive political, philosophical, and literary work, a constant journalistic disclosure, which has served as ideological orientation to the militant. It would be the book of Egyptian Sayyid Qutb, *Signposts on the Road* -an Islamic version of *What is to be Done?* From Vladimir I. Lenin- which would give shape to the current trend of Islamic revitalization.

Sayyid Qutb Ibrahim Husayn Shadhili, a prolific and obsessive writer who covered novel, poetry and political and philosophical essay. The assassination of Hassan Al-Banna, the Supreme Guide of the al-Ikhwan al-Muslimun (Moslem Brotherhood), in February 1949 outraged Qutb. He set out from Egypt in early November 1950, this time to Saudi Arabia for Hajj. It was there in Saudi Arabia that he met, for the first time, the Indian Islamic scholar and author of fifty books in diverse languages Abu Al-Hasan Al-Nadawi.

Nadawi was the founder of the Muslim World League, and organized multiple Islamic conferences. At the time he was highly respected in the entire Islamic world.

On his return to Egypt in 1950, Qutb drew the attention of the Muslim Brotherhood both in the army and outside it to him. On 15 October 1954, the government dissolved the Organization of Muslim Brotherhood and 450 of its members, including the Supreme Guide and Qutb, were arrested. Qutb was tortured fiercely and executed by orders of Egyptian President Nasser in 1966, turning into the apostle of the Moslem Brotherhood and the modern militancy.

Qutb also would stand out as a devout disciple the Egyptian Mohammed Al-Ghazel, theoretician of Islam and a member of the Muslim Brotherhood, who roamed from Gaza to Algeria preaching this intolerant version of Islam.

Sayyid Qutb is widely considered the ideologue of the Islamic political movements of the modern world. His writings and, in particular, his theory of *jahiliyyah* have been viewed as one of his literary weapons and a threat to the nationalistic regimes in the Arab and Muslim worlds from Cairo to Tashkent and are now viewed as a threat to the West as well[6].

In his manifesto Qutb argued that every devout Muslim was obliged to declare Jihad against the infidel (jahili) societies, including Arab nationalist regimes; and he also considered the right to decide who was or was not a believer. In his pathological vision, Qutb judged the West as "synthetic" and depraved, by comparing it with the declining imperial Rome, and sentencing it to death in his book *Islam and the Problems of Civilization*.

Muslim thinkers claim that the constructs of nationalism, secularism, socialism, secular democracy and modernism, together with the sociopolitical movements they spawned, have taken hold in Islamic society at the expense of Islamic values[7].

In Qutb's analysis, this confrontational theory is certainly not separate from his concept of Sovereignty. These two concepts (*jahiliyyah* and Sovereignty) together form the hard core of the ideological and political tactics of many of the Islamic political organizations worldwide. It is for this reason that this book is paired with another book, *The Power of Sovereignty: The Political and Ideological Philosophy of Sayyid Qutb*, London, Routledge (2006), to analyze the religious-political and philosophical relations between the two concepts, the impact of their force and intent on the ideological and political establishment of nationalism, capitalism, socialism, communism and democracy as well as their influence on Egypt's Jihad groups, with whom Ayman Al-Zawahiri and his conspirators in what has later come to be called Al-Qaida were ideologically trained[8].

Generations of followers would refine his thought, as shown in the manifest *Philosophy of Confrontation*, of the organization Jihad Al-Benaa (Realization of the Holy war), and in the so-called Program of Islamic Action, of the Islamic group Gama'a Islamiyah, documents that were published in 1984 and both written by a group of the Moslem Brotherhood in prison.

According with Qutb, the world was divided today into two large blocs, the Communist bloc in the East and the Capitalist bloc in the West. That is what appears on the surface, what everybody is saying and thinking. But we believe that it is a superficial division and not a real one, a division based on interests and not on principles, a struggle for goods and markets and not for ideas and convictions. We should not be deceived by the fact that we see a strong and violent struggle between the Eastern and Western blocs, for both of them have a materialistic notion of life; each is similar to the other in its thinking, and neither struggles for ideas and principles but only for influence in the world and profits in the market. The real and profound struggle is between Islam on one hand and both the Eastern and Western blocs on the other.

Qutb's viewpoints about the conflict between the Church and science in the Western world. This conflict, Qutb asserts, has separated Religion from the State, and created a condition that Qutb calls 'hideous schizophrenia'. He stresses that Western civilization is exhausted and has no system able to guide human life. These features and properties, he says, belong only to Islam. Qutb stresses the end of the white man's leadership. The turn now is for the leadership of Islam. Islam is the religion of the future[9].

In Qutb's view, all social systems in the world are exhausted and have nothing to 'offer to humanity'. The 'turn' now is for 'Islam', but it cannot resume the 'leadership' without human effort (...) In this regard, Qutb stresses that there must be a group of people able to carry the responsibility to establish an Islamic society[10].

Qutb rejected nationalism, capitalism, socialism, communism and modernity, as well as those Muslim societies which did not practice the Islamic law (...) After Qutb enunciated his theory of *jahiliyyah* and *hakimiyyah*, a number of intellectuals sought out the Islamic movement, especially Islamic groups in Egypt[11].

For instance, in *Islam: The Religion of the Future*, published in 1961, Qutb writes: 'The purpose of life is not and never was only food, drink, sex and shelter as Marx believed. Marxism is completely ignorant of the human consciousness, human nature, and the nature of history[12].

Another of the eminent thinkers of radicalism was Egyptian intellectual, Wail Mohammed Othman, the Herbert Marcuse of the fundamentalist Islamic youth. His book *The God's Party in Struggle with the Party of Satan*, published in the decade 1970, divides the world in two social entities, and urges the believers to fight in order to restore the God's party to save to the Islam of its dangerous and constant exposure to the West. Same way, the Cairo newspaper Al-*Quds Al-Arabi*, the most prestigious and read in all Islamic circles, per years has encouraged the opposition against the elements and secular Moslem systems, and the violence against the apostate West.

To the dismay of the fundamentalists, the Egypt Emil Ludwig described, no longer exists; the country does not depend on a Nile of slimy banks scented with jasmines, and furrowed of feluccas with kerosene lamps. The coffee places with their water pipes and voluptuous dancers veiled in tulle are already archaeological species, since the Egyptians amuse themselves now with Star Trek, HBO, and Lady Gaga videos. The economy has grown thanks to strokes of oil and gas, with the money sent home by emigrants from the First World, the tourism and the customs of the Suez Canal.

Previously from Cairo, the power and thinking elites forced the Islamic world to confront its weaknesses in 1948 - after the dramatic Arab exodus from the new Jewish State- and in 1967, after the Six-Day War. However, at present, Egypt does not enjoy its past regional authority compared to the leading role of Iraq and Syria and the militancy of Saudi Arabia and Iran. The actual dilemma is if Egypt will shelter a revolution Iran-style or a Pharaonic boss since its settlers always expect that behavior from its rulers.

By the end of the 1970s, the writings of the radical Shiites thinkers in Iran, Lebanon and Iraq were expressing themselves in a way similar to the Sunnites of Egypt and Saudi Arabia, in its diagnoses and cures of the contemporary problems, and in its emphasis towards confrontation.

It was not difficult to imagine that this ideological *Corpus* would spawn a dynamic of action against the "infidels", especially when the idiomatic barrier of the Arab (Arabic) has prevented the West from defending its cause.

In 1996, the brilliant Egyptian journalist Mohammed Heikal, in its work *Secret Channels* —which went unnoticed in West— alerted about the deep fury and repulsion that against them was sheltered in all the Islamic horizon.

However, these ideals were as old as its own doctrine, and were embraced and spread by a Sunni group that would function as an international ideological party: The Muslim Brotherhood, much more feared and arachnid than Al-Qaeda and that since then would be in the background of all the extremist Middle East currents, including the Taliban.

The Muslim Brotherhood is the historical and spiritual mother of such groupings since the post-war period, and established what would become the leitmotif of Arab intransigence: destroy Israel and defy the West. The purpose of these schools of thought, and then the terrorist parties was the union of all Islam through Jihad or the supposed holy war, to replenish the Caliphate under a charismatic paladin, an emir chosen for its purity and virtues.

The Islamic revolution sponsored by the Muslim Brotherhood would be in favor of nationalism and would refuse the commitment to tribal traditional elites, with ethnic entities and with the feudal structure of Emirs and sheikhs. It preached –Taliban style-, the creation of an Islamic society similar to the one founded by the Prophet Muhammad, which covers the entire Muslim community: The *Umma*.

In this regard, Qutb said: We profess Islam as a State religion; separation between Islam and society is not in the nature of Islam. Qutb demonstrated how and why separation between religion and state was established in Europe. He emphasized that Christianity with its purity and denial of the material world crossed the seas to Europe, where it found the inheritors of the 'pagan' and 'materialistic Greek culture. Qutb claims that European systems and their laws were not as a whole derived from religion, but from the pagan Roman law rooted in the pagan Greek law.

According to its ideologists, the West has triumphed not for spiritual or philosophical reasons but because the Muslim world was frozen technologically. In Sudan, its branch committed horrendous crimes against Christians in Darfur. In the West Bank and Gaza, he organized the Hamas, its militant arm. In Jordan, his Army of Muhammad attacked the Royal family in 1993. In Tunisia, Rashid Ghannouchi spearheaded the movement.

Egypt, Saudi Arabia, and Syria have faced up in a brutal fashion these intolerant fanatics. In 1954, President Nasser tried to modernize the *ulemas*, and bloodily suppressed the members of the Muslim Brotherhood, which fled in panic. In 1982, Hafez Assad didn't hesitate to massacre close to 30,000 Sunnites in the city of Hama, only because there were sheltering followers of the Muslim Brotherhood.

In Algeria, the Muslim Brotherhood unleashed a vicious civil war since 1992, when the secular government of the president Chadli Benjedid refused to accept the electoral results and decided to crush them. The Muslim Brotherhood responded by cutthroat all women they found in the streets without veil, and same with any secular intellectual. The experience of Algeria and the repression that also they experienced in Egypt and Syria convinced them that the only recourse was the violent seizure of the power.

After the signing of the peace treaty with Israel in 1977, and in a gesture to their radical opposition, the Egyptian President Anwar Al-Sadat allowed the formation of groups and Islamic associations. The same way, it approved religious education, tolerating the fact that Islamists monopolized the primary education, where they were preaching against the notion of Egyptian nationalism, labeling the Pharaohs of corrupt race, and proposing to demolish graves, pyramids, and monuments.

Among them stood out the blind Abdel Hamid Kishk who was promising a pederast paradise to those who should immolate themselves for Islam: the eternal erection in company of groomed youngsters. On the other hand, the following Egyptian President, Hosni Mubarak, learned from the mistakes of the assassinated President Sadat. He was not so tolerant. But, unfortunately he was obliged to resign under the heavy hand of US and European powers, leaving his country open to the Moslem Brotherhood.

During the 20th century, Egypt focused an extraordinary cultural life that gave rise to what was called the "enlightenment" of the Arab culture, conceiver of his transcendent liberal and secular thought; with more than 200 newspapers, dozens of editorials, rich literature, a fabulous theater, and a film industry in progress. Their stellar writers would include Naguib Mahfouz, Nobel Prize winner and perhaps the most brilliant prose writer of the century, Tawfik Al-Hakim, Lewis Awad, Ahmed Baha El-Din, Yusuf Idris and Magdi Wahba, all world-class intellectuals.

The oil boom of 1970s had catastrophic effects for all the cultural chore of the Middle East. In possession of amazing wealth, ignorant and devout sheikhs and emirs of Saudi Arabia and the Gulf Emirates claimed for themselves the political and cultural agenda of the entire Islamic world. Hassan Hanafi, the well-known Egyptian intellectual has stated that from then on, the truth was swept away, the speculative discourse inhibited, and the intellect commercialized by this petrodollar culture of the sheikhs, the Iranian *fatwa's* and the yoke of a band of local despots in the style of Saddam Hussein.

According to Fuad Ajami, another talented Egyptian who sought refuge in the West, intellectuals in the Islamic world have been either beaten or seduced.

The books of Taha Husayn, an Egyptian Sorbonne Professor, marked the demarcation of Egypt from the Arab world and linked it with the Mediterranean. He proposed that Egypt should separate religion from politics, establish Western secular systems, create a liberal political domain and accept the values of European thought and culture. His thinking was derived to some extent from Ibn Khaldun and caused both, the university of Al-Azhar and the Manar to declare him an "apostate".

The powerful Cairo intellectuality was crumbling to evade confrontation with the interpreters of the Islam, putting its pen to the service of the dogma. Never the less, a small and hardened nucleus maintained its independence and the defense of the Arab nationalism. Yusuf Chaheen kept on producing provocative films. Adel Imam -an actor not less talented than Omar Sharif- continued mocking at the militancy in his performances and creations.

In 1992, Islamic extremists assassinated writer Farag Foda, defender of the Egyptian secular tradition and a persistent opponent to militant Islam. In 1994, Nobel Prize Mahfouz itself was the subject of an assassination attempt. By that date, the playwright and novelist Eli Salem decided to visit Israel at the price of being a pariah. These facts, together with the accusation of apostasy and the fatwa against Salman Rushdie, although they terrorized Egyptian intellectuals, failed to shut down the secular furious rebukes.

The country continued forging first rate intellectuals, harsh critics of fundamentalism and the previous Pharaonic rule of Hosni Mubarak such as Taha Hussein; impressive novelists, such as Yusuf Al-Qaid and Sonallah Ibrahim, who have delighted the Western literary critics; international economists, such as Galal Amin; World Jurists, such as Copts Boutros-Boutros. Sharp prose writers, like Rifaat Said, who continues to accuse militant Islam for the Foda murder.

Militant terrorism had its initial push in a fistful of Palestinian organizations at the beginning of 1960s. One of the first ones to distinguish that the Islamic violence was the wave of the future was the military ringleader of the PLO, Jalil Al-Wazir, and the fearsome Abu-Jihad. They mudded the area with the use of oil as a political weapon, with the erratic imprint of the former Libyan leader Muammar Al Kaddafi, and the collapse of Lebanon as a nation.

If the Arab-Israeli wars destroyed the Arab military mystic, that of Lebanon revealed the absurdity of Pan-Arabism, on having endured its agony without it being important to the rest of the Islamic world, only because "infidels" were not involved. The Greek Orthodox Lebanese novelist, playwright, critic and prominent public intellectual

Elias Khoury, in his piece The Cultural Amnesia, addressed this issue.

The immemorial antagonism between Baghdad and Damascus is more virulent than contemporary inter-Arabs rivalries. Syrian intellectuals (formerly at the forefront of Arab nationalism alongside the Egyptians) were decimated, censored, or exiled for opposing the heavy hand of the Assad's.

This has been the case with the eminent poet Ali Kanaap and Alawites playwrights Mamduh Udwan and Sad Allah Wannous, banned in Syria and published widely abroad, and political philosopher Sadiq Al-Azm, the staunchest supporter of Rushdie. Same case was famed film director Duraid Lahham, vetoed in almost all Islamic countries for censoring religious fundamentalism and exposing the irreversibility of the State of Israel.

As ironically expressed Egyptian Mohammed Heikal, "Allah deposited a vast financial power in the arid lands of the few, in the outdated and marginal Arab inhabitants of the desert." Output of the 19th century Wahhabi militant upheaval, quietly practicing slavery supposedly "abolished" in 1962, and condemning the heliocentric theory of Copernicus as a heresy to the Quran, Saudi Arabia has spread its conservative Islam throughout the Middle East.

This country, ruled by a Royal family assisted by a College of Ulemas, is the theocratic quintessence, with its legal Codex based on Sharia, its medieval justice, and its governmental edicts against women. These presumptuous princes, sitting on 30% of the oil world reserves, with a religious statement that does not enable them to operate an effective state management, have purchased the modern comfort without consequent modernization.

The Saudi House protects its legitimacy attacking all those who challenge their religious heritage; thus banning de books of his most celebrated intellectual value, the extremely popular novelist Abdul Rahman Mounif, and stripping him of Saudi citizenship. Mounif was the author of a total of fifteen novels. It is true that Iran and Pakistan have fanned Islamic terrorism; but the Saudi support and that of its relatives from the Gulf, although glassy, has not been less vital.

In March of 1975, members of the Royal family who sought greater openness to the West assassinated King Feisal. This fact would shake the Islamic world and would deepen the abyss that opposed the Saudi Royal House with fundamentalists and Shiite Muslims for the custody of the shrines of Mecca and Medina, and the alliance with the United States, seen as a harmful interference.

Years later, news was eroding the traditional values of Middle East society: Egyptian President Anwar El-Sadat, in dealings with the United Sates, made a pact with Israel in the Holy Land of Jerusalem. The affront reached inconceivable levels when the deposed Shah of Iran, Reza Pahlavi, took refuge in El Cairo; it would take little more to make Sadat's head roll.

On November 20, 1979, the Great Mosque of Mecca was assaulted by a contingent of 1,500 men under the command of Juhayman Al-Utaibi, who claimed the title of "Mahdi" (Messiah), placing himself in the gallery of Moses and Jesus. The bulk of the attackers had trained in Libya and South Yemen under Cuban and Palestinian instructors. The upraise of Mecca, aborted nothing less than by the "infidel" French Foreign Legion, gripped the Islamic world, among them Osama Bin Laden, for the allegations of corruption and conspiracy with the West launched by Al-Utaibi against the Saudi royal family, and his request for the return to the purity of Islam.

Equally, when the Soviets invaded Afghanistan, the episode reached the core of Islamic society, whose soil was trampled once again by the "Crusaders." Therefore, the Afghan resistance movement was made "in the name of

Allah", and not of nationalism. An Arab Legion was incubated, that transmuted into the Al-Qaeda of Bin-Laden. The Soviet withdrawal was viewed as a victory for Islam against a wicked super-power; and that is why fundamentalism was emboldened to stand up before the other super-power, the United States. We are thus on the crest of the fundamentalist revival in Egypt, Yemen, Saudi Arabia and Afghanistan.

Iran is a country the size of the United States, immensely rich in oil, with a mosaic of nationalities and twenty-five centuries of divine and absolute monarchs. Islam blends here with a distinctive Persian seal that would keep tense their relations with the "Arabs", whom they labeled as lousy primitives.

In 1953 there was an attempt to secularize the state, an incident that ended with a coup d'état promoted by British Petroleum against the premier Mohammad Mossadegh, accused of being too much leftist. Apart from the modernization drive, during the guardianship of the Shah, minorities in Iran were protected (Jewish, Christian, Zoroastrian and Bajai), and women obtained the right to vote along with family planning.

On February 1, 1979, Ayatollah Ruholla Khomeini -the Sign of Allah, the Spirit of Allah, the shadow of Allah- landed in Iran, expelled the Shah from his peacock throne, established a Republic, and kidnapped 63 Americans. The collapse of the Shah, like that of the Soviet Union, is one of those enigmas of history where the loss of legitimacy was the catalyst. Ironically, the two fathers of Iranian fundamentalism: Ali Shariati who created a strange mixture of Marxism with Islam, and urged religious *martyrology*; and Abdel Karim Sorush, a reformer to the Kemal Ataturk, who had no performance in this revolution.

The Shiite uprisings and the fiasco of the military rescue of United States were considered a triumph over the Western world and confirmed a hesitant Washington to orthodox eyes, which filled with pride the Islamic masses. Not only it disrupted the strategic equation of regional security, which was the most visible fact, but also precipitated a new and wide diversity of political groupings in the ranks of the Islamic militancy.

The regime of Ayatollah Khomeini marked a rupture with the Shiite rejection to the temporal power, by instituting a "State of Jurists" in which an enlightened clergy "persuaded by Allah" accepted to rule. The transfiguration of Islam into an ideology and an instrument of government and, consequently, failing in the organization of a modern and prosperous state, had counterproductive effects by undermining its credibility among a young generation distanced from the "divine mobs."

This undeniable distortion of faith found internal accusers within the own curate, and led to the arrest of the most prominent Shiite theologian, Ayatollah Shariatmadari, for his diatribes against the theocratic power established by Ayatollah Khomeini. Another Shiite prelate, Ayatollah Sabtu-Yazdi, in his book "The wisdom of the Government" trashed the claque of Ayatollah Khomeini.

Ethnic minorities, women, intellectuals, and Shiite theologians were a primary object of the Orthodox repression. The Decree of Ayatollah Khomeini forcing women to procreate men for the army had disastrous demographic effects, duplicating the population in just two decades.

Ayatollah Khomeini accused the minority Bajai of apostate and put a price on the head of Salman Rushdie for the *Satanic Verses*, a book that he himself confessed had never read. Saidi-Sirjani, a prolific writer and to the majority of critics better to Salman Rushdie, was imprisoned for demanding religion reforms and died because of the tortures.

The canons had to tolerate authors such as Karl Marx and Michel Foucault in universities, and not all serious rivals to the theocratic regime were eliminated.

Many Iranian artists, authors, and cinematographic directors, like the award-winning film director, writer and editor Mohsen Makhmalbaf, challenged the censorship with his film Kandahar. The movies of film director Bahram Beyzai, the most intellectual and conspicuous author in Iranian cinema, were prohibited because women played leading roles and Persian historical themes where used.

Feminist literate and editor Shala Sherkat would face the Shiite prelates from the Internet and her cultural magazine *Kiyan*[13], promoting civil and women rights within Islam, freedom of expression and of the press. *Kiyan* has taken as a flag the ideas of Soroush, Islamic reformer and a dangerous name to official ears.

However, the strong Persian tradition, the caliber of their culture since Biblical times, access to the professions and the modern world during much of the 20th century, are elements that far from having disappeared under a fanatical bark, are making a comeback and confronting the ayatollahs.

Iran has not been able to escape the dynamics of their own culture. Next to the "divine mobs", Coca-Cola is the national drink; jazz concerts swarm around, and alcohol is consumed at parties; Tehran is a forest of antennas and satellite disks; and the country is full of young people without a cause, avid users of the Internet.

Several paradoxes exist in present-day Iran, trapped in the blind alley of an increasingly unpopular fundamentalism, but stubborn in its agenda to hold on to the power, and without contingency plans for when the oil for export runs out. Perhaps we are doomed to another oil crisis in the Persian Gulf – not too far away- because the solution that Tehran entertains is the annexation of the Persian Gulf emirates, territories that vehemently has claimed as its own.

The year 1988 drastically changed fate in favor of Islamic terrorism. The plane carrying the President of Pakistan Zia-Ul-Hag and part of his Government team crashed in yet unknown circumstances, allowing the rise of Benazir Bhutto as premier and with it the most dogmatic group vision of Pakistan.

Premier Bhutto immediately entered into alliances with Syria, Iran and North Korea, in its attempt to intensify militant Islam across Asia, take over Kashmir, institute the Taliban in Afghanistan, and launch Osama Bin-Laden and his Al-Qaeda against "moderate" countries of the area. He did all this under the very noses of the West.

Just when United States dreamt with the stability of the new world order and the most powerful countries on the planet expected to reap dividends from the collapse of the Communist bloc, the most feared of the conflicts would explode: oil. Although the Near East held the potential to blow up the fragile relationship between the soviet Mikhail Gorbachev and NATO, the crisis in the Persian Gulf was one of those historic turns that outlined the way in which regional conflicts would ventilate from then on.

The disappearance of the Soviet Union disoriented the Islamic States, which took daily refuge in the bipolar fence. It has been argued that the concern about the Arab-Israeli conflict, the communist collapse, the east-west containment, the solution of the regional problems and the German unification distracted the big potencies of the Iraqi move on Kuwait. The first astonished one was the Iraqi Saddam Hussein himself, who was not expecting such a negative response from his, up to this moment, Western Allies.

The Gulf War was a traumatic experience for the Near East, after the sacred unity broke when several Islamic states closed ranks with the hated United States to defeat one of its pairs. The sides were integrated, on the one hand, with a coalition of pro-western countries led by Egypt, where they were converging Saudi Arabia, the petroleum emirates of the Gulf and even Syria; and, on the other hand, the fierce anti-western ones with Libya and Yemen on the lead.

The Islamic world would never be the same; the old behavior system of the Arab League was broken. While for Western coalition partners the Gulf War was consummated to defend control of oil reserves and liberate Kuwait, to the Middle East it took place to decide the political future of their religion, and what faction would remain with the power: Arab nationalism (Iraq, Syria, Libya, Algeria, Turkey) or the legitimacy of the Islamic theocracies (Kuwait, Saudi Arabia, Bahrain, Qatar, Oman, etc.).

The Iraqi incursion and the vast opening to the West of Saudi Arabia and the Emirates of the Gulf, with its new alliances with Egypt and Syria, have impacted these theocratic societies, impairing the authority of both Regent families. The invasion of Saddam Hussein was the latest chapter of a rivalry for regional preeminence between Egypt and Mesopotamia that sinks in the mist of times. When Iraq came out battered in the conflict, the Egyptian President Hosni Mubarak acquires a high prestige in the area, strengthening its role as mediator between Israelis and Palestinians.

It became evident the military defeat of Iraq didn´t bring stability in the region. The Arab-Israeli disagreement was still latent, so was the Palestinian issue, Lebanon, Syria, Islamic fundamentalism occupation, the Afghan mess and the polarization of wealth. The fundamentalists like Osama Bin-Laden demanded Saudi Arabia and the Emirates of the Gulf to choose between sanctioning the military permanence of the Americans –who they considered to be short-term security- or to request the immediate dismantling of the unbelievers, which would imply long-term Islamic legitimacy.

The Soviet Union evaporated; Israel has proven that alone can deal with the military challenge of all Arab states combined; Iran has unleashed and legitimized what secular nationalists ridiculed: religion made politics. Iraq, the most powerful Arab nation after Egypt, was humiliated by the military power of the United States. Even the PLO seeks peace with Israel and favors from Washington, like Jordan, while the "Arab spring" sweep the region.

On the other hand, the United States, the most formidable military power of the world, implements its right to create a new world order in his own image and likeness. Islamists argue that due to the "universality and centrality" of Islam for the believer, a secular legal system and political institutions Western-style cannot take root in the Middle East, unless the Quran suffers a renewal.

The cardinal hobble of this Islamic world overwhelmed by the violence is not Israel, but the authoritarianism that has paralyzed its economies and the absence of creativity and scientific and philosophical education.

The modernization scares and disorients; social hierarchies, values and traditions face immense changes to which the tradition serves as psychological blanket. There lays precisely the tragedy of the Arab failure to find realistic solutions, since the world that moves Islamic fundamentalism have been sentenced by the march of history.

How can such codified barbarism integrate in a more and more global and competitive world, if it excludes half of the population -the women- on having adopted the *Sharia* as its legal code? How can the economy bloom if the Arab woman is evaluated for being "bearer of men" and not for its intellectual capacity?

Nevertheless, Islamic militancy is not the solution. The Iranians have already concluded that there exists neither an "Islamic economy," nor an "Islamic sociology," nor an "Islamic" way to build cars, of stabilizing the monetary system, nor an Islamic miraculous way to development and alternative to the already covered by the Western world.

How sad it would be that after so much suffering the "Arab civilization" would embrace another utopia, one of some feverish religious prophet, who would prevent them from recovering the prosperity, the dynamism, tolerance and imagination that once characterized it!

The New Mahdi

The constant influence of the Pharaonic Egypt over the lands that they called Kush and the Greeks Nubia was one of the factors that prevented the formation of an organized state in the region from the 3rd millennium BC, until near the Christian era.

The Pharaohs preferred to have scattered tribes in the rearguard. That is why the Kingdom of Napata, in the south, arose in the 8th century BC, when the gravity of the Egyptian decadence allowed the country to be governed by foreign dynasties.

The last one was precisely Sudanese: The Kings of Napata dominated Egypt in the year 730 BC to become Pharaohs until 663, when the Assyrian conquest took place. The fall of the dynasty also meant that of the country which, without being occupied, disbanded. Soon, three kingdoms emerged instead: Nobatia, Dongola and Allodia, which would remain in place for more than 20 centuries.

Meanwhile, Persians, Greeks, Romans and Arabs were in the domain of Egypt. These kingdoms were kept politically and culturally autonomous, supported in its quality of commercial intermediaries between the Mediterranean market and sources of slaves, ivory, furs and other items of Equatorial Africa.

The great event of that long period, however, was the conversion to Christianity in the 6th century by Ethiopian influence and the Arab invasion a century later. All these events forced the King of Dongola, through a treaty to guarantee the territorial integrity of the neighbor Kingdom and Allodia, to provide facilities to Arab traders and allow the practice of Muslim religion. This treaty remained in force for more than 600 years.

The Egyptian Mamelukes destroyed the Kingdom of Dongola in the 14th century and of Allodia around 1500. The Mameluke incursions were constants, despite the formation of new kingdoms, this time Muslims, in Sennar, around the Blue Nile[1], Kordofan to the West and Darfur in the desert.

The Egyptian Pasha Mohammed Ali decided to exterminate the iron hands of the Mamelukes, and entered Sudan in 1820. Thereafter the Egyptian military presence, which established a base at Khartoum[2], became perpetual, culminating in 1876 with the total occupation of the country.

That domination meant a violent impact for the Sudan society. The unification of the country affected the autonomy of all small local chiefdoms. The introduction of new rites - even within the predominant Sunni orthodoxy- shocked religious media. Later, the prohibition of slavery by English pressure harmed a large community of traffickers who until shortly before controlled the country. Finally, the establishment of taxes, which affected especially farmers and ranchers, created a climate of deep and widespread dissatisfaction.

When in 1881 Mohammed Ahmad proclaimed himself Mahdi -Savior or Redeemer- and began a crusade for the salvation of Islam, he found immediate echo, particularly among Arabic people from the North. The direct intervention of the British, who in 1882 had occupied Egypt, failed to change the military course of the insurrection.

In 1885, the Mahdists occupied Khartoum, defeating British General Charles Gordon, and established the first native government. But British interests could not admit the existence of a state that was opposed to its strategy to unite Cairo in the North and Cape Coat in South Africa, with a continuous corridor of colonies.

In 1898, in a tweezers operation England mobilized troops from Uganda, Kenya and Egypt to attack the Sudanese Mahdi on two fronts. France, which had its own East-West transcontinental project, was also interested in Sudan and sent troops as a measure.

The Mahdi caught between three forces was defeated in September 1898. The later encounter of the colonial armies at Fashoda almost led to war between France and England, but the French ended up recognizing the British dominance over the Nile Basin, which was formalized as an Anglo-Egyptian condominium over Sudan.

England set out to prevent the real aspiration of Egypt of carrying out the unity alongside the Nile with the integration of Khartoum to Cairo. To do this, it threatened to create a federation and grant independence to the southern populations, inhabited by an Animist majority and a Christian minority, against the Arab and Muslim north.

The English began a policy of territorial isolates that prevented any kind of contact between the Sudanese South and the Egyptian North. In 1953, Sudan obtained a self-governing regime and in 1955 a full Sudanese parliament was elected, who proclaimed the independence of the country on January 1, 1956.

But the population of the southern Sudan could not find a solution to their problems since they had been displaced and had no real participation in the policy of the new state. Five months before the independence was proclaimed, a bloody civil war was unleashed, which lasted for 16 years on a continuous basis.

In 1969, in the midst of a civil war, General Jaafar Nimeiri took power and granted autonomy to the South. In 1976 Sudan and Egypt signed a mutual Defense Pact and the Nimeiri Government supported, at the beginning, the Camp David Accords, signed by Anwar El-Sadat, Jimmy Carter and Menachem Begin. However, when it became clear that this position isolated them from the rest of the Arab world, the Khartoum regime began to move away from Cairo to reach Saudi Arabia.

General Nimeiri then adopted a line that emphasized the Islamic character of his regime. On the other hand, such Islamization alienated the sympathies of the South of Sudan, who is not Muslim. In May 1977, general Nimeiri was re-elected President for a further period of six years.

Shortly after the government in Khartoum announced the start of a process of national reconciliation, which allowed re-entry to the country of some political leaders in exile and gave room to until then opposition parties such as the Ansar (Umma³ party), the people's Democratic Party and the Muslim Brotherhood.

However, the Sudanese Communist Party and the National Front's former Minister of finance, Sheriff Al-Hindi were left outside. General Nimeiri was re-elected for a third time in 1983, under accusations of fraud. In June of the same year, abruptly and violating the agreement of 1972, the Government split the southern provinces into smaller regional units, which generated immediate reactions of discontent in the affected region.

In September President Nimeiri imposed without prior notice the application of Islamic law (Sharia) in all the national territory, yielding to pressures from Saudi Arabia to obtain their financial aid. This measure caused the general protest of the animists and Christians in the South and the immediate reactivation of the guerrilla movement.

A rebellion surged in the town of Bhor, from which emerged the Popular Movement of Liberation of Sudan (SPLM), a political-military organization that gave the guerrilla faction from the South a new ideological base. The new movement had as objectives to carry out national unity and introduce socialism, within a framework of respect for the autonomy of the South and of religious freedom. The Popular Army of Liberation of Sudan, military wing of the SPLM, extended their actions to such an extent that foreign companies who were prospecting for oil in southern Sudan were gradually abandoning its facilities due to the war.

Meanwhile in the North, opposition parties and the Muslim Brotherhood increased their criticism against Nimeiri for using the Islamic law to punish Government critics. The international financial community also began to put pressure on the Sudanese President to not fully implement Sharia. External debt doubled, reaching 8,000 million dollars. Payment of depreciation and interest became systematically delayed and, at least in two occasions until the beginning of 1984, the country was considered bankrupt.

In 1985, the U.S. Government suspended aid and IMF forced a rise in food prices. The rebellion broke out even in the capital. In April 1985 Nimeiri traveled to United States for help, but could not return to his country; his Minister of Defense and General Commander of the army, Abdulrahman Suwar Al-Dahab had taken power. The coup didn't change the political situation. The Islamic bourgeoisie of the North began to settle, while the Popular Movement for the liberation of Sudan maintained its activities in the South, since the political and economic discrimination against the region didn't vary substantially. Political parties were disbanded and the division of the South was abolished. Dahab also began to study the application of the Sharia, and promised to call elections in 1986. The people's Party (UMMA), a grassroots Islamic organization, won elections in April 1986 and Sadiq Al-Mahdi was elected Prime Minister.

The Sudan Popular Liberation Movement (SPLM) requested the resignation of the Sadiq Al-Mahdi and the formation of a provisional government, while its 12,000 guerrillas surrounded southern garrisons loyal to the Government, keeping Sudan virtually divided in two, as hunger also had begun to wreak havoc in the region due to the air blockade created by the guerrillas.

The guerrillas agreed to let through the planes with food and medicines sent by the UN to the besieged towns of Juba, Wau, and Yirol. However, the economic, political and cultural contradictions between North and South were still unresolved, prolonging the conflict. Then, with secularism under attack throughout the Islamic world, Nimeiri reversed course and sought the support of the Islamists, nominating the Islamic fundamentalist spiritual leader of the Moslem Brotherhood Hassan Al-Turabi as Attorney General.

In 1983, the Sharia was imposed as the basic law for the entire country. Then, the discovery of oil in the southern regions exacerbates the conflict that responds to the attempt of the North to convert the South to Islam. Armed units composed of South tribe members incited mutiny precipitating a civil war, which, at a cost of more than one million lives in three decades, is still in force.

It was precisely Al-Turabi, mystical leader of the Muslim Brotherhood, and graduate from Islamic and European universities who would rise from the smoldering rubble of the Gulf War as a torch for ideological fundamentalism.

Sudan is a country where *efebos* and beautiful Sudanese women are sold, chosen especially for the pleasure to oil sheiks and African magnates, who live under the syndrome of the Mahdi.

At that point in time, in 1989, the head of the government Sadiq Al-Mahdi was going to offer the South a federal system within the context of Islam, but in June of that year, in the midst of the prolongation of the war between the southern guerrilla and the army, along with an increasing social tension, a group of Islamic fanatical soldiers led by Colonel Omar Hassan Al-Bashir, a disciple of Al-Turabi, gave a coup d'état[4]. Afterwards, Al-Turabi was catapulted to the headlines of the country and the Islamic international arena, making Sudan a base and haven for terrorists.

Al-Bashir dissolved the political parties, created a military directorate with 15 members and promised to end the war. Ten Months after assuming the military Government, there was an attempt of a coup d'état by discontent officers of the army.

Also the mediations of Ethiopia, Kenya, Uganda, Zaire and United States were dashed on that occasion to resolve the long-running internal conflict. Different peace initiatives failed, while Arab paramilitary groups financed by Al-Bashir and the Government troops harassed the peoples of the South.

Al-Turabi was intended to assume the mantle of the most important religious voice for the whole Islamic world. He sought to transform Sudan into the center of the Islamic Renaissance and the launch pad of the Jihad against the Judeo-Christian civilization, and was anxious to join the Sunnis with the Iranian Shiism, and thus shape the cherished Islamic Caliphate under his direction.

Cultural factionalism established by Al-Turabi made impossible any negotiation or reconciliation between the northern Islamic Sudan and the southern Christian Sudan. He decreed the arrest of Union leaders and abolished all civil society independent institutions. His regime would stand out for the tortures, executions, the prohibition of nightlife, banning the gathering for singing, dancing and drinking, etc. He sent thousands of orphans to Quranic schools -madrassas- to instruct them in the annihilation and death of non-believers[5].

The social support of Al-Turabi was concentrated in the Islamic intellectual communities coming from the Valley of the Nile and the University of Khartoum, as well as "modern" sectors such as the army, trade unions, and bureaucracy.

In 1991 he hosted in Khartoum, the Sudanese capital, what can be considered the highest Council of terrorist congregations from each country of the Islamic world, such as Al-Qaeda, Hizb-Allah, the FIS of Algeria, the FLS of Sudan, movements in Southeast Asia, the Egyptian Moslem Brotherhood. The purpose was to build training camps and to create a vast financial infrastructure in Europe and United States.

In words of Yoseff Bodansky[6]: "By 1992, Sudan's Hassan Al-Turabi adapted the Iranian jihadist tenets and adopted them into the Sunni neo-salafite doctrine, thus setting the grounds for the ascent of the jihadist trend now popularly associated with Osama bin Laden, Ayman Al-Zawahiri, and their supporters".

Al-Turabi persuaded the hard core fundamentalists from the Middle East that Islam was the most powerful ideological force in this post-Cold War; the only one capable of motivating uprooted young people and offer them a future, especially because the West was not aware of the current Islamic Renaissance.

For Al-Turabi world civilization and National Arab States were in full decline, while Africa sinks into tribalism, and even Iran, land of the triumphant Shiite Islam, does not present the hope of a new vision. Only Asia, with its "cultural solidarity" and their discipline gave him a bright future.

It will be Al-Turabi, and not Bin-Laden, the initial brain after the grandiose plans of Islamic terrorism; and Al-Qaeda, one of the many apparatus powered by the Sudanese. Al-Turabi commissioned Bin-Laden to be financial machinery, taking advantage of the largesse of the Saudi, Iranian, Pakistani secret services and the Gulf States.

Thereafter, the former members of the Arab Legion that had operated in Afghanistan would be dispatched to their countries of origin and to places where there were Islamic communities, with a mission to stand and wait for the attack signal. Several Sudanese sent by Al-Turabi participated in the plot to destroy the World Trade Center.

Al-Turabi helped Osama Bin Laden to build the lethal Al-Qaeda terrorist bloc. Al-Qaeda may have approximately 200 to 300 active leadership and terrorist operatives worldwide. It should always be presumed that there are at least a few dozen AQ operatives and supporters in the United States at any given time. The numbers of active supporters worldwide are conservatively estimated in the thousands. Their attacks include the 1993 World Trade Center bombing in New York City; the 1998 bombings of American embassies in Nairobi, Kenya, and Dar es Salaam, Tanzania; the 2000 bombing of the USS Cole in Aden, Yemen; and the September 11 attacks on the World Trade Center and the Pentagon[7].

The al-Qaeda organization's Mohammed Atta questioned agricultural pilots in southern Florida regarding the spray system and flight characteristics of crop dusting aircraft. Crop dusters and other industrial spray systems would have given these terrorists an excellent chemical or biological distribution system[8].

The fabric of destabilization for East Africa in 1992, whose purpose was the expulsion of United States from Somalia, was designed by Al-Turabi and executed by Bin-Laden. Somalia marked the crucial change of terrorism, their first victory over United States, consolidating Al-Turabi as the religious and intellectual mentor, and Bin-Laden as the avenging arm of a future Islamic fundamentalist empire, which would have its first territorial seat in all East Africa.

But Al-Turabi failed to attract the rural areas influenced by Sufism and the followers of the Mahdi (peasants and Bedouins). Many Islamic authorities opposed him as Yussuf El-Daim and Hashem El-Hadiya. Sudanese students would lose faith in Islam, which has ceased to generate new ideas, and whose thinking has fossilized.

On February 4th 1991, the Government established the federal system, and Sudan was divided into nine States, each administered by a Governor and a Cabinet of Ministers. On January 31 of that year, the Government of General Omar Al-Bashir in addition signed a new penal code based on the Sharia applicable in the North of the country, where the Islamic religion prevails.

In May 1994 the Government signed an agreement with two rebel groups, in order to allow assistance for the populations isolated by the conflict. But the situation continued to worsen and humanitarian organizations reiterated their complaints. African Rights accused Khartoum in July 1995 of being responsible for the genocide of the Nubians.

In the March 1996 elections, Al-Bashir was re-elected with 76% of the votes. After 12 years of war, with a million dead and a wave of refugees, the possibilities of coexistence between the theocrats of the North of the country and the Christian rebels of the South seemed increasingly lower.

In November 1997, disputes with Egypt for the administration of the triangle of Halaib -rich in phosphate, manganese and supposedly in oil- motivated Sudan to request the intervention of the Arab League. Under an agreement of 1899, the Halaib belonged to Egypt, but a new agreement signed in 1905, gave it to Sudan.

In January 1998, United States announced economic embargo to Sudan, arguing that it supported international terrorism training groups of opposition in neighboring countries to destabilize them, and lacking respect for human rights. A month later, the UN urged the international community to provide more than 100 million dollars to Sudan to assist 4 million victims of war and drought.

Sudanese guerrillas claimed responsibility for the attack that killed Vice President Zubair Mohammed Saleh in February 1998, when his plane crashed in the town of Nassir, 700 kilometers from Khartoum. According to observers, the Christian rebels of the PLA would have U.S. support through the collaboration of Uganda, Ethiopia and Eritrea.

The Catholic Church of Sudan decided to participate for the first time in the peace talks between the Islamic Government and the faction of the army for the liberation of the people of Sudan (SPLA) who agreed to engage in dialogue.

A meningitis epidemic ravaged the country on March 1999. Only in Khartoum 30 people died per day, being the most affected zones settlements on the outskirts of the city. Through an investment of 3 billion dollars, Sudan managed to inaugurate in June a 1,500 km pipeline that allowed it to exploit vast oil reserves that war and political problems had been postponed.

Towards the end of September, they began to produce 150,000 barrels of oil a day, figure they intended to rise to 250,000. However, given the high cost of investment, Sudan would begin to earn money for this concept after 2003. Meanwhile, hunger and war continued to ravage the country; thousands displaced people continued arriving at centers where international organizations operated.

Dress in military fatigue, Al-Bashir assumed once again the Presidency in February 2001, re-elected with 86.5% of the votes in the December elections, which were boycotted by most of the opposition parties. He attends a conclave with the tribal and regional rulers of the country, assembled in Khartoum to address the Group of the Sahel and Sahara States.

In December 2001, the authorities in Khartoum claimed having released more than 14,500 slaves after six months of campaigning by international human rights organizations.

In January 2002, the SPLA signed an alliance with its southern rival, the Sudanese force of Popular Defense, to craft a common front against the Government. In October, with the set in motion peace negotiations in Kenya between the Sudanese Government and the SPLA finally ended the two decades of civil war that had claimed the lives of two million people.

On that occasion, the Secretary of US State Colin Powell, whose Government team had declared access to African oil as a "matter of national interest", presented a proposal to triple US contribution to the SPLA to 300 million dollars, but at the same time threatened to maintain the embargo on Sudan, if peace was not achieved by March 2003.

The head of the SPLA, Col. John Garang, also requested to exercise the Vice-Presidency of Sudan, instead of Alí Osman

Taha. But, at the time, the Islamic government of north Sudan claimed that the southern provinces of Nuba, Abyei and Blue Nile, will fall under their jurisdiction, fueling the dispute.

Between April and December 2003, the Sudanese Government and the SPLA agreed to integrate their troops into an army of 39,000 soldiers in 2004, share of oil profits, draft a new Constitution, grant administrative autonomy to the South and convene a referendum for 2010, with a view to the independence of that region.

Also, the Islamist leader Hassan Al-Turabi, jailed for years, was released in October 2003, by lifting the ban on his party, the National Islamic Front (NIF). In 2003, 92% of the Sudanese were living under the poverty line. In January 2004, while peace was reached between North and South areas, government troops launched an offensive in the area of Darfur, in the West end of Sudan (range between northern and southern jurisdictions), against the army of the Sudan Liberation Movement (former Darfur Liberation Movement EMLS).

The EMLS had been founded the previous year, in response to systematic attacks to the Darfur region by groups of Arab shepherds66, expelled by the desertification of the Sahel (the region of origin), who wanted to evict the "Islamized" black tribes from their well irrigated lands[9].

Pro-Government Arab militias obtained weaponry, training and equipment by the Sudanese Government to perform the "scorched earth" operation. The campaign brings about a price tag of thousand human lives, destroyed 2,300 towns, and evicted a million people, who took to wandering the suburbs of cities across Sudan to seek refuge or crossed the border with Chad, without getting to escape torture, rape and looting, in the most complete impunity.

The world Organization against torture denounced the application of torture that year to Darfur refugee children. Since before 2003, according to the organization Human Rights Watch, in contradiction with the version of the governmental authorities, who were accused of carrying out an "ethnic cleansing".

In April, the UN Human Rights Commission refrained from applying sanctions to the Sudanese Government. However, the program of food aid from that agency denounced that hunger in Sudan amounted to three million people, in what they described as humanitarian disaster

The United Nations has described the Darfur conflict as the worst humanitarian crisis in the world. At least 10,000 people were killed in the last 15 months of fighting. According to the UN, murders and mass displacement of people reaffirm the will of a "campaign of ethnic cleansing".

Sudan's Government repeatedly denied accusations of supporting Arab militiamen who attacked villages. Humanitarian organizations denounced the Sudanese Government to put obstacles to the distribution of food and medicine.

In June, the American Secretary of State, Colin Powell, visited Sudan and attempted to end the attacks against the civilian population in Darfur. The clashes in that region took immense proportions. Washington warned Khartoum that the UN Security Council could interfere if the violence continued. Kofi Annan (Secretary General of the UN) said for his part that if Sudan does not protect the population of Darfur, the international community should act.

Mustafa Ismail, Minister for Foreign Affairs of Sudan, admitted that there was a problem in Darfur, but suggested that the magnitude was exaggerated, and promised that his Government would present a series of measures to address the issue before the end of the visit of United States representatives.

In July, the UN moved thousands of Sudanese refugees to safe camps. The Sudanese would continue fleeing to neighboring Chad because of continued violence in the Darfur region. According to UN, 15,000 refugees were transferred in those months to Chad. Humanitarian organizations accused the Janjaweed as perpetrators of displacement outside borders of 1.2 million Sudanese.

United States asked the United Nations to adopt sanctions against Sudan as it was considered that Khartoum demonstrated great passivity against the humanitarian disaster in the country.

By March 2005 it was estimated that 180,000 people had died in the conflict in Darfur in the last 18 months and two million had fled their villages, seeking refuge in major cities, while 200,000 had fled to Chad. The UN Commission assigned to the conflict, for its part, concluded that Sudan's Government was not guilty of genocide -figure that had forced the international community to intervene- but of "serious violations to human rights and international humanitarian law", which could be prosecuted as crimes against humanity.

The Commission recommended "especially" that the UN Security Council requested the International Criminal Court (ICC) to investigate thoroughly the situation. This quickly prompted a new disagreement with United States, which rejected the International Criminal Court, requested a court ad hoc to be installed in Arusha, Tanzania and the Security Council should punish Sudan, and the European Union, which argued that the International Criminal Court should take action on the matter.

Some political observers were alerted about a possible alliance between the armed groups of Darfur and Nuba, Abyei and Blue Nile anti-Government, and the spread of armed clashes through the territory of Sudan.

The Chadian army was attacked on the border by the Sudanese regular forces. Al-Bashir ordered the arrest of Al-Turabi once again and his political and military supporters.

At the same time, Vice President and Christian guerrilla leader John Garang, led a bloody armed struggle with Sudanese Muslim for more than 20 years died in a plane crash and the Government created a Commission of inquiry to determine whether his death was accidental.

Castro and the Islamic Terrorism

With regards to the Arab world, the Cuban government's support for radical and terrorist groups has been just as significant. Since the early 1960s, Castro's interest was centered on radical Muslims.

Cuban public opinion looked with sympathy upon the duel of the Algerian nationalists in their fight against the French to achieve sovereignty over their own territory. The first act of Castroism on the Dark Continent took place in connection with this anti-colonial struggle. Arms and equipment were immediately shipped to Algeria and this then became the first African undertaking.

He fostered direct links between the Palestinian terrorists of George Habash, the Egyptian Marxists of Henri Curiel, (later assassinated in Paris by a Cuban squad) the Iranians from the Tudeh party and the Iraqis. Over the protests of France, in December of 1961 Cuban ships unloaded U.S. military weapons in Casablanca destined to the Algerian guerrillas[1].

In 1959, Raul Castro and "Che" Guevara visited Cairo and established contacts with African liberation movements stationed in and supported by Cairo. Both Cuban leaders visited Gaza and expressed support for the Palestinian cause.

Cuba's military involvement in support of the Algerian National Liberation Front alarmed the French General Staff to the point where it triggered a reaction from the French government as noted in his report on Cuba's operations in Africa by Nobel Prize winner Gabriel Garcia Marquez[2]: "Even before the Cuban Revolution proclaimed its socialist character, Cuba had already rendered considerable aid to the fighters of the FLN (National Liberation Front) in Algeria in their fight against French colonialism. The administration of General de Gaulle, by way of reprisal, banned flights by Cubana de Aviacion (Airline Company) through French skies"

The Evian Accords, which signified Algeria's independence in 1962, were received with suspicion and reservation by Fidel Castro and Ernesto "Che" Guevara, both of whom were pushing for a military victory by the guerrillas over the French occupation army.

Algeria was the centerpiece of Cuba's relations with Africa in the sixties. It is well known that close personal relations developed between Castro and Ahmed Ben Bella. Both of them worked out a common strategy for Africa where Cuba would take care of the brainwork behind Algerian policy with special emphasis on the armed movements.

Major Jorge Serguera, the chief of finance of the Castro army, was appointed ambassador. Cuba had sent 50 Cuban doctors to Algeria shortly after that country's independence in 1962 as a gesture of internationalist solidarity.

Algerian President Ben Bella in turn proposed an understanding between Castro and the industrialized countries of Europe, especially France. He mediated between Fidel Castro and Nikita Khrushchev, between Indian premier Jawaharlal Nehru and Chinese Premier Chou En-Lai, between Indonesia and Malaysia, and between the rival factions of the Cameroonian UPC and the Angolan, Mozambican, and South African groups[3]. The intimate relationship between Castro and Ben Bella reached such extremes that, apart from the high-level Cuban-Soviet circles, the Algerian was the only one who was told in advance of the plans to base Soviet medium-range ballistic missiles with nuclear warheads on Cuba.

Along with this position Castro adopted the postulates of the faction from urban resistance, expressed by Ben Bella, to the detriment of the guerilla fighters who had rallied around Algerian military commanders Houari Boumediene and Ait-

Ahmed. The explainable aversion which existed during the Cuban struggle between the guerrillas and the urban underground, exploded in Algeria during a subsequent stage when the country was already completely independent.

The repeated attempts at that time, by the group of chosen Castroites to convince the Egyptian Gamal Abdul Nasser of the intentions and the tremendous importance of Castroism, turned out to be fruitless. Nasser considered Castro to be an extremist with a disjointed policy, while Castro, on account of ideological objections, refused to include Nasser among the "revolutionaries."

Cuban intelligence also knew that the Egyptian "rais" had regular contacts with United States intelligence. The dispute between Castro and Nasser became so troubled that the Cuban leader maintained diplomatic relations with Israel until Nasser died, despite the fact that this conspired against Castro's influence in the Islamic world.

This blind disagreement was one of the causes of the close relationship between Castro and Algeria and the emphasis on Ben Bella as a figure who challenged Nasser for hegemony in the region. The Castro-Ben Bella axis launched an anti-Nasser crusade at all levels. "Che" Guevara and Castro echoed the anti-Egyptian campaign of the Iraqi Baathist regime of president Karim Kassem, although Castro did not manage to lay the foundations of an understanding with the "strongman" of Baghdad.

The border conflict stemming from colonial days between Algeria and Morocco suddenly came to light in October 1963. It served as the first major Castro's military expansionist experiment in Africa. The conflict began in the Saharan districts of Hassi-Beida, which were claimed by both sides, and then spread to the South, to the sand flats of Tindouf and to the North, to the rocky area of Colomb-Bechar[4].

After Morocco became independent in 1956, the monarchy in Rabat proclaimed its right to recover the Sahara, including Mauritania, and expressed its displeasure with the concessions the French had obtained in Tindouf to prospect for petroleum. During the anti-colonialist struggle in Algeria, Morocco agreed with the provisional government of Algeria[5] to resolve the border problems through joint negotiations after independence.

The Algerian independence ceremony had not even ended when the first clashes took place in the districts of Colomb-Bechar and Zagdou. The ideological differences between monarchic Morocco and the left-wing balancing act of Ben Bella made the dispute worse.

In September, Moroccan units occupied Hassi-Beida and Tinjoub, both south of its Wadi-Draa boundaries. They were of strategic important because they blocked the two trans-Sahara tracks running from Colomb-Bechar to Tindouf. Morocco desperately needed Tindouf to legitimize its territorial claims in Mauritania and in the Spanish Sahara. Through this action, Rabat forced a decision in Algeria to resolve the entire border conflict.

Castro immediately offered his support and asked permission to send a "symbolic" volunteer force. In August, Castro sent a military delegation to Ben Bella, headed by "Che" Guevara and including his commanders Victor Dreke, Harry Villegas (Pombo), and Raul Suarez Gayol, who coordinated the aid that was to be given.

Cuban troops, advised by a Soviet general who had fought in the Spanish Civil War, were transported in the merchant vessels "Aracelio Iglesias," "Sierra Maestra" and "Playa Giron," arriving at the port of Oran on 21 October. Others carrying weapons and men followed these ships. Also used were Britannia turboprop aircraft flying the Havana--Prague-Algiers route.

The armored regiment was commanded by Major Efigenio Ameijeiras (a ferocious Castro's military leader), who headed immediately to the Algerian flank in the border conflict with

Morocco[6]. The Cuban shock detachment consisted of 3 motorized-mechanized battalions, 1 brigade with 50 T-55 main battle tanks, various artillery units (comprising 2,200 men), and around another 1,000 men as support personnel and crewmembers for the operation.

A Cuban tank battalion and other MiG-17 fighter aircraft arrived in the vessel "Gonzalez Lines" on 28 October[7]. The troops were under guerrilla commandant Ameijeiras, assisted by army officers Aldo Santamaria Cuadrado, Raul Diaz Arguelles, Samuel Rodiles, Lino Carreras, Joaquin Ordoqui, as well as officials from the guerrilla column of intrepid Ameijeiras.

This event was described in an article by the Colombian writer Gabriel Garcia Marquez[8]: "while Cuba was devastated by hurricane Flora, a battalion of Cuban internationalist fighting men went to defend Algeria against the Moroccans. At that time, there was not a single African liberation movement that did not have the solidarity of Cuba in the form of arms and war materiel and also in the form of training for technicians and military personnel as well as civilians and specialists. Mozambique from 1963, Guinea-Bissau from 1965, Cameroon and Sierra Leone, all received some expression of solidarity and aid from the Cubans at one time or another"

The Cuban military unit moved toward the zone of operations without waiting for orders from the Algerian high command. Algeria complemented this powerful nucleus with a unit of tanks and field artillery sent by the Egyptian Abdul Nasser. This combined Cuban-Egyptian presence was coordinated and approved of in advance by the USSR which authorized the shipment of war materiel and Egyptian units and which at that time supported a huge Egyptian expeditionary corps in North Yemen.

Before assuming operational command in Algeria, commandant Ameijeiras, accompanied by Cuban ambassador Jorge Serguera, passed through Cairo where he coordinated the details of the combined operation with the Egyptians.

Houari Boumediene and most of the Algerian military leaders disapproved of the Egyptian-Cuban military presence requested by Ben Bella[9].

The Algerian army rather hastily transferred reinforcements by land and by air and launched a series of attacks and counterattacks to control the piece of land involved in the conflict. The Cuban guests, supported by Algerian columns, breached the enemy forward defenses and penetrated deep into enemy territory, occupying the Moroccan towns of Ich on 17 October while bombing the region of Tindara. This caused confusion among the Moroccans and the conflict became generalized. Rabat's intentions to recover the region became fruitless.

On 25 October, Morocco went on the offensive further to the South, aiming at Tinfouchy; another Moroccan unit, deploying slowly, laid siege to Tindouf. In the diplomatic area, Rabat broke relations with Cuba and also withdrew its ambassador to Cairo.

The antagonism between Algeria and Morocco and the appearance of a Castro's military column caused anxiety among the states in the area, which then tried to prevent the international spread of the conflict, trying to move toward negotiations. Syria, Ghana, Iraq, Tunisia, Ethiopia, and Mali suggested various solutions and offered their official mediators to obstruct the Castro-Algerian machinery, which already threatened to spread the frontier clashes to the entire territory of Morocco. Except for Egypt, Syria, and Iraq -who were tilting toward Algeria- almost all of the African-Asian countries decided to be neutral toward the two contenders involved in the clash.

The Arab League adopted an emergency resolution calling for a cease-fire and created a mediation committee consisting of Tunisia, Lebanon, Libya, and Egypt, whose purpose was to secure the withdrawal of the forces of both countries to positions they had occupied before the war broke out.

On 28 October, negotiations were held in Mali between the two chief executives involved in the conflict. While these conversations took place, the Cuban-Egyptian "internationalist" brigade penetrated to Figuig and practically wiped out the Moroccan troops in the area. The Cuban troops did not come to a halt until 4 November, thus putting an end to the destruction.

Hassi-Beida and Tinjoub were set up as "no-man's land." Algeria was able to hold on to the oases of Tinfouchy. This was the first time the forces of Fidel Castro had participated in an operation abroad. After remaining in Algeria for a while -where they established training centers for African guerrillas- these forces were transferred to Congo Brazzaville for the next major operation on the continent.

During 1964 and 1965, "Che" Guevara had complete control of Cuba's policy toward Africa. On 18 December, "Che" Guevara arrived in the city of Algiers where he had talks with Ahmed Ben Bella, who was not enticed into lining up fully either for or against the USSR. Ben Bella's political and material support helped open the doors of various African states to the guerrillas.

"Che" Guevara tried to organize an international brigade in the Congo. He also hoped to include Cuban, Algerian, and Egyptian military units. "Che" Guevara made a short and secret trip to Algeria where he conferred with a group of Lumumbists and with Ben Bella's intelligence services. Training centers for African guerrillas with Cuban instructors were established in Ben Bella's Algeria under the control of the Castroist Major Jorge Serguera.

The Tunisian weekly "Jeune Afrique" printed an interview in which "Che" Guevara emphasized the positive value of the guerrilla focus in the light of conditions prevailing in Africa[10]. In turn, the Cairo publication "Akher" and the Moroccan publication "Liberacion" gave space to the first veiled attacks by "Che" Guevara against the passive attitude of the Soviets in Africa. This policy was called "revisionist" in those articles.

On 19 February, "Che" Guevara arrived in Egypt where he held a brief meeting with Abdul Nasser. Guevara tried to convince the Egyptian "rais" to make a greater commitment in terms of men and weapons in the Congo where he had offered to participate directly. But Nasser declined Guevara's request and tried to persuade him to the contrary. "Che" Guevara and Nasser discussed the position of Africa and the Middle East in the Chinese-Soviet conflict and the future combined African army, which at some moment could invade South Africa.

The idea of getting Egypt to link up with Algeria in an offensive in Africa fell through. In spite of the efforts to create an independent and nonaligned image, the Egyptians were cognizant through their direct connections with the USSR and the work of their intelligence services in Havana, of Fidel Castro's military and economic dependence on Moscow and the Soviet feasibility of obligating Castro (at any moment) to follow the course, which they thought he should take.

President Nasser knew that this was part of Castro's strategy to spread the revolution to parts of the Third World so as to make him look good in Moscow's eyes. This is why the Egyptians criticized Cubans during all meetings, both public and personal.

"Che" Guevara arrived in Algeria on 2 May 1965 where he conferred with President Ben Bella to finalize the details for the massive aid which the Congolese National Movement has getting through Lake Tanganyika[11].

Cuba welcomed the founding of the PLO, being the first contacts with Palestinian Fatah in 1965 in Algiers and Damascus. In Algeria, "Che" Guevara inspected the guerrilla school in Siddi-Bel-Abbes run by Algerians and Cubans and which specialized in giving military and political instruction to African and; Latin American insurgents. On the 7th of that month, "Che" Guevara met in Cairo with Christopher Gbenye and Gaston Sumialot, of the Congolese movement MNC, and Egyptian President Nasser.

The coups d'état in Algeria had harmful effects on Castro's subversion scheme in Africa. The USSR permitted Ben Bella to ship Soviet war materiel to the Congo, on the condition of replacing it. The Algerian military leaders, headed by Boumediene, rejected involvement in the African movements because they believed that the principal direction of Algerian foreign policy would have to be toward the Arab world and material support for President Nasser and Syria to confront Israel. The alliance with Fidel Castro was not at all accepted by that group.

More traditional relations with Algeria were developed after a brief cooling of contacts following the overthrow of the Algerian leader and Cuba's close friend, Ben Bella. Fidel Castro was one of Boumedienne's initial targets. The members of the DGI were expelled immediately and the presence of Cuban military instructors in the guerrilla training camps was terminated. Cuba agreed to cooperate with Algeria in the fields of education, radio, television, journalism, sports, arts and culture[12]. In the late sixties, cooperation with Algeria took a qualitative and quantitative step.

Some intelligence sources stated that "Che" Guevara had made a secret stopover in Cairo before going on to the Congo. He reportedly established contact there with members of the Congolese National Council who helped him in his trip and with the Egyptian intelligence services whose mission it was to get him to Tanzania to continue his trip to Burundi and to cross the region of Lake Tanganyika toward the Fizi-Baraka massif.

In June 1967 the USSR tried to stop military action by President Nasser against Israel. Soviet intelligence knew that Egypt and Syria were no match for Israel and they did not want to provoke direct intervention by the United States which could only trigger a conflict with Washington or a "shameful" retreat before the eyes of Moscow's Arab allies.

The Soviet decision to intervene directly at the sign of the imminent defeat and collapse of the Egyptians at the hands of

Israel impressed the Cuban leadership. The "Six Days War" changed the general Soviet policy toward the Middle East, to the point that it became the main supplier of armaments. Its new policy came in the face of Arab frustration as symbolized by the harsh recriminations of the Algerian leader Houari Boumediene because of the "lukewarm" response of the Soviets. This Algerian position also made a deep impression in Cuba which restored Algiers to the select group of "militants".

Together with the Algerians that were transferred to Cuba for training -1959 to 1960- were a considerable amount of AI Fattah Palestinians, who carried out the first commando attacks against the Israelis. Ulises Estrada, the man in charge of Africa and the Middle East in the Cuban DGI, was to be the key man in relations between Cuba and the PLO. In 1967 and 1968, the Cuban DGI through its office in Cairo, infiltrated a group of military personnel into the Palestinian organization called Al-Asifa.

Castro helped put together the terrorist commando of the pro-Soviet Palestinian group, the Popular Front for the Liberation of Palestine of George Habash, whose armed section is known as the "Boudiaf Commando" and which was under the leadership of Mohammed Boudiaf, an Algerian former follower of Ben Bella and a friend of Fidel Castro.

When the Israelis eliminated Boudiaf in Paris, the Cuban embassy in France was the link in the subsequent reorganization of this group which from then on was headed by the legendary Ilitch Ramirez Sanchez (Carlos, the Jackal), graduated from the terrorism school in Matanzas, Cuba[13].

The Tricontinent Conference was held in Havana in January, 1966. Cuba provided the organizational structure to support terrorist, anti-American groups in the Middle East and Latin America. Through the Tri-Continental Castro connected the PLO with various terrorist organizations, such as the Red Army of Japan, the IRA (Irish Republican Army), the Basque ETA, and the German Baader-Meinhoff. In 1968 Cuba and Syria developed a close alliance and supported Fatah and the Eritrean Liberation Front (ELF).

The rise to power of Colonel Muammar Khadafy in Libya aroused the curiosity and interest of Cuba who tried to get him to accept its positions. The Libyan, although a fanatical Muslim of undecipherable political bent, inspired the oil challenge against those Western countries that supported Israel and unleashed a wave of subversion and anti-Zionist terror in the area.

During the Sixties, Cuba did not have a definite policy toward the Middle East, partly because of its weak relations with Egyptian President Nasser and because the USSR was moving cautiously in view of the connection between Yasser Arafat and China. Starting with the Egyptian military collapse during the "Six Days' War" with Israel in 1967, the influence, financial and military aid, military training, and sanctuaries of President Nasser for the "liberation movements" of Africa began to decline. Likewise, the Arab League moved toward more moderate currents.

Soviet pressures to get Castro to break with Israel were expressed by the visit of Soviet Premier Aleksey Kosygin to Havana in 1967. Cuba resisted those pressures. On the other hand, Castro maintained secret relations with the pro-Soviet Palestinian faction of George Habash. Abu Iyad, one of the closest lieutenants of Yasser Arafat, commented that from 1966 on, the PLO was sending militants for training in Cuba and that Cuban instructors were teaching classes in Palestinian training camps[14].

The Cubans facilitated the cooperation between the Red Brigades and the PLO, where the latter agreed to provide weapons to the Italians. As part of that collaboration, the Red Brigades, together with a unit from Black September, trained by Cuba, carried out an act of sabotage in the Trieste refineries. In 1967 and 1968, the Cuban DGI through its office in Cairo, infiltrated a group of military personnel into the Palestinian organization called Al-Asifa.

The difference between Castro and President Nasser had forced Havana to maintain this ambivalent position with respect to the PLO and Israel. Although its official propaganda presented Tel-Aviv as a United States instrument, Israeli technicians were providing advice for Cuba's citrus crop plans. The Stalinist Old Guard in Cuba was obviously pro-Nasserist and anti-Israeli. But at the same time the "neo-Marxists," the armed forces, the Communist youth, and the population at large expressed their preference for the Middle Eastern "David."

Castro and Khadafy[15] from the very beginning combined their aid for the Liberation Front of Eritrea, providing impetus for the creation of a state independent of the Ethiopian monarchy. Castro, the USSR, and the Egyptian Abdel Nasser appreciated the value of this territory because of its ports[16] on the Red Sea. This initial position in favor of independence for Eritrea caused Castro political trouble when his armies went into action in 1978 in support of the Ethiopian Mengistu Haile Marian who was determined to put an end to Eritrea's aspiration for independence.

Starting in 1969, the "akid" Khadafy launched a furious campaign against Fidel Castro because of his relations with Israel and his "phony non-alignment." Among other things, Khadafy tried to displace Fidel Castro as a possible leader of the nonaligned movement. Castro then pushed the Cuban Algerian renewal which had been taking shape ever since the visit to Havana by the foreign minister and chief of intelligence services of Boumediene, Abdul-Aziz Bouteflika, in November 1968.

Because of the abrupt death of Egyptian President Nasser, Castro believed that it was now possible to fill the power vacuum left by the "Moor" in the Islamic cultural area. This was the start of a more pronounced "Arabic" projection and the effort was in the hands of Osmani Cienfuegos and his bureaucracy. Here were the objectives: to regain the ground lost with Boumediene in Algeria; to establish trade relations with Morocco; to raise the level of official contacts in Egypt; to call for help for the PLO and to get closer to Iraq and Syria.

The idea also was to establish the guidelines for relations with Syria and Iraq, giving aid to Yasser Arafat and the guerrillas of Oman, from where one might gain access to the Persian Gulf while operations were under way in Eritrea and Ogaden with a view to the dismemberment of Ethiopia.

The Soviets set themselves up at the southern exit of the Red Sea[17] now that the Suez Canal, with Egyptian President Anwar El-Sadat, was a firm bastion of the West. The USSR was present in the Indian Ocean while Cuba deployed military units between South Yemen and Somalia, thus securing the ports of Aden and Berbera; East Germany in turn organized intelligence operations.

On the other hand, a Cuban tank brigade[18] took part in the final fighting in the "Yom Kippur" War on the Syrian side, near the Golan Heights; this was the first coordinated act worked out with Moscow. Castro's right hand, Osmani Cienfuegos was in charge of this operation and the brigade was moved by air across Saudi Arabia. During these operations, the Cubans lost 180 dead and 250 wounded[19].

According to scholar Edward Gonzalez[20], the number of tank crew members dispatched to Syria fluctuated between 500 and 750, plus a group of pilots to train the Syrians. The Israeli sources, cited in the Western press, maintained that 2 Cuban brigades (3,000-4,000 soldiers) served on the Golan Heights[21]. The Israeli defense minister at that time, Moshe Dayan, estimated that there were 3,000 Cubans on the side of Syria[22].

It was also known that a group of Cuban pilots were present together with North Koreans who were sent to Syria on request of the USSR. Syria had several minor clashes with the Israeli Army from which it did not emerge in good shape. The Cuban presence on the Golan Heights, it seems, lasted until January 1975, on the occasion of a visit by Cuban Army Chief of Staff, Senen Casas Regueiro and Raul Castro, who determined that it was to be transferred secretly to Angola, across South Yemen[23].

The "Economist Foreign Report" printed the following story[24]: "the war of attrition began at 0500 on 4 February 1974, when the Cuban tankers opened fire on the Israeli positions. The most violent clashes between the Israelis and the Cubans took place in the middle of February, throughout March, in the middle of April, and in the middle of May. Throughout these encounters, the Israelis pressured the Americans to get the Russians to pull their Cuban legionaries out of Syria."

As researcher Damian Fernandez put it, "the Israelis noted an increase in the enemy's fighting quality," pointing out furthermore that the Cubans had suffered heavy losses, that they later on were relieved with fresh units that were finally sent to their bases in the Congo.

"In September, Raul Castro paid a visit to the Cuban units in Syria, accompanied by a group of high-ranking officers. The visit lasted an entire month and featured an extremely detailed inspection of the armies in training and the level of combat preparedness of the troops in general. At the end of the visit, there was a festive parade which was attended by the Syrian political and military leaders and in the course of which President (Hafez) Assad and Raul Castro decorated officers and enlisted men of the Cuban forces[25]".

The process in South Yemen, covered amply by Castroist propaganda, began to hold Castro's interest. The Egyptian intelligence services had tried to maintain control over events in South Yemen and offered little information about the decolonizing process going on there. President Nasser, on the other hand, was afraid of the FLNA because of the connections between the Yemenite party boss Abdul Fattah Ismail and the Palestinian faction of George Habash.

As a result of Egyptian disinformation, as well as President Nasser's interest in political organization FLOSY, the Soviet espionage instruments, and, with them, the Cubans, supported this opposition movement (one of the two that was fighting for independence), erroneously thinking that the political organization FLN of Abdul Fattah Ismail and President Robaya Ali was a pro-British organization that might fall under Chinese control.

In 1968 Castro sent weapons via Cairo, to the NLF in Southern Yemen. At the beginning of the decade of the Seventies, the critical point between South Yemen and the USSR (plus Soviet suspicions as to Chinese penetration) involved the military aid which Moscow had been giving to North Yemen, the enemy of the people in Aden, and which turned out to be much more substantial than what the South was getting.

It was to be George Habash who was to introduce the Cubans to the South Yemeni. At the end of 1971, the Cuban ambassador in Cairo, Jacinto Vazquez, had already established contacts with the Yemeni government. At the beginning of 1972, two Cuban officials (Francisco Laureano Cardoso and Ramón Pérez Yero) arrived in Aden, opening the way to a strong military mission of tankers, aviators, artillerymen, and security people who preceded them rapidly. This military presence was established furthermore on request of the Soviets so as to assemble weapons and to train the Yemenis in the use of these weapons.

At the Khormaksar air base near Aden, Cuban and Soviet pilots organized the small air force of the regime. Immediately, also, Cuba began to train the guerrillas of Dhofar (Oman) in the 6th Governorate, bordering on Oman, on request of South Yemen, the Iraqi Communist Party as well as the Communist Party of the USSR, as a flanking movement designed to push through to the Arabian Gulf.

During that same year, in 1972, MiG aircraft, piloted by Cubans, went into action during the border clashes with North Yemen. In October, the leaders of South Yemen, Abdul Fattah Ismail and Ali Nasser Mohammed (the Secretary

General of the Liberation Front and the Prime Minister, respectively), paid an official visit to Havana.

The number of military and civilian personnel was increased on the basis of these visits. By the time Western sources had spotted the beginning of the Cuban military presence in South Yemen (April 1973) as well as air force personnel (June 1973), Castro actually had been stationing both of these military specialty units which had even gone into action almost a year back, in that country.

In 1973 began a series of visits to Cuba (regular and secret most of the time) by the leader of Aden, Fattah Ismail, for treatment of a lung ailment. That year, Fattah and Castro, each by himself, had lengthy meetings with First Secretary of the CPSU Leonid Brezhnev. On Castro's urging, the Soviet Union terminated its old pledges of military aid to North Yemen which had interfered with relations with Aden.

The numerical strength of Castro's forces in South Yemen was kept secret. It is known that these forces were augmented considerably in 1973 due to the border clashes in Oman. Western sources estimated them at 600-700 soldiers, considering the reinforcements brought in by the vessel "Vietnam Heroico" in March 1973. Aid to the guerrillas of Oman was continued until 1977, since it was precisely the military defeat of those guerrillas at the hands of the British-Iranian forces that brought about the downfall of the pro-Chinese insurrection leaders in Dhofar, something that was of interest to Cuba.

During 1973-1977, the level of soldiers kept in South Yemen fluctuated around 1,200 men, including the personnel at the Omani guerrilla bases in the 6th Governorate, the Cuban General Staff, the military training units, the tankers, pilots, artillerymen, the personnel stationed in the Strait of Bab-el-Mandeb and near the border with North Yemen, plus the security personnel.

In 1972 at a time when the Soviet Union established itself strongly in Berbera (Somalia) and sent military equipment and personnel to South Yemen[26], Castro deployed the personnel of one armored division between Somalia and South Yemen, reinforced by MiG-21 fighter-bombers and rocket artillery. The military units stationed in Somalia were under a Cuban general staff in Aden, directed by General Waldo Reina. Castro's deployment in South Yemen extended along the borders with North Yemen, the Island of Perim, Saudi Arabia, and Oman, training camps in the 6th Governorate, and direct control over the militias.

This military complex, which later on was shifted to Somalia, constituted a single centralized force that could be moved from one side of the Strait to the other and that really represented the logistic, technical, and command support structure for rapidly assembling combat units that might be brought in by air (Odessa-Aden) or by sea. One must keep in mind here that outside of Europe and America, until the decade of the Sixties, the military bases of Suez, Aden, and Singapore were considered the most important bases of the West, both air and naval, that is.

But the presence of Castro's armed forces in South Yemen was not related only to the training of guerrillas of Dhofar. These Cuban forces also carried out a domestic function in support of the government of South Yemen plus a geostrategic function in relation to Soviet plans. In the port of Aden, the USSR had a naval base at the far western end of the Indian Ocean for the movements of its navy from the Kamchatka Peninsula and in the Khormaksar airport it had a transit facility for its reconnaissance or transportation flights to Africa and the Indian Ocean. South Yemen was Castro's most important military operations base until the invasion of Angola.

The Soviets in South Yemen had control of the armed forces, aviation, rockets, and military schools. The Cubans worked with aviation, they had control over the tanks, the artillery, and the militia training schools; they also led the military units in each province or governorate; the intelligence and security agencies were advised by the East Germans.

The 4th Summit Conference of the Nonaligned Countries was held in Algeria in September 1973 with the attendance of 75 full member countries and 3 invited guests. Cuba protested against the presence of the Sultanate of Oman which it said was "basically unable to comply with the principles and objectives of nonalignment."

During the Conference, Cuba pledge to help Egypt, Syria, and Jordan to recover the territories occupied by Israel. Castro was looking for a formula to create permanent institutions for the movement. Before the end of the Conference, Castro tried by all means at his command to restore the movement's confidence in him as a person. His advisers recommend him to break relations with Israel; in turn, it would help him negotiate certain financial loans with Iraq, Algeria, and Kuwait.

With respect to the Middle East, Castro accepted the Soviet idea of a negotiated Arab-Israeli solution which would benefit the pro-Soviet side. A unit of Cuban combat pilots was also to be stationed in Algeria to assemble Soviet fighters and to train the Algerians.

After South Yemen became independent and following the announcement of the dismantling of the British military facilities in the Indian Ocean, the USSR began to explore the possibilities along the coast while at the same time negotiating with Sekou Touré and looking into the construction of a submarine base in Cuba.

The USSR outflanked the United States naval forces in the area and with determination pushed toward the Continental Southern Horn. But while the Indian Ocean was not considered an area of essential interest to the Kremlin, the approaches, the naval passages, routes, and ports between Africa and India, as well as the West's petroleum lifeline from the Persian Gulf, obviously were included among Cuba and Soviet immediate objectives.

In South Yemen, the East Germans had the logistic responsibility for the Soviet military arsenal; the Czechs maintained the quartermaster supply setup and the communications services; the Cubans comprised the special fighting forces, while the South Yemenis made up the infantry; this is an example of how the USSR organized Cuba's action and presence in Africa and the Middle East.

According to terrorism expert Claire Sterling Barely two months after the Yom Kippur war, in December 1973, forty Cuban experts in terrorist warfare arrived secretly in South Yemen. With them was an East German specialist in the field named Hans Fiedler, who had been in Cuba since 1971. Landing in Aden, they were at once whisked upcountry to a Palestinian guerrilla camp run by the orthodox Communist Haif Hawatmeh. Second in importance only to Habash and Haddad, this network remains in business with the Cubans acting as one of its most active affiliates.

Frustrated by the low level of economic and financial aid from the Soviet Bloc, South Yemeni President Salem Robaya Ali (Salmin) approached Saudi Arabia, trying to "moderate" his ideological stridency, the commitment in Ethiopia, and attempting to stop the process in support of a "Marxist" party. The Saudis offered help in exchange for the Cuban-Soviet military withdrawal.

Starting with the secret conversations in 1975 between the foreign ministers of Aden (Saleh Muti) and Saudi Arabia (Saud Al Feisal), the Soviets reacted against President Robaya Ali who refused to "coordinate" his foreign policy. The USSR called on Khadafy to counterbalance the Saudis with financial aid. The Libyan proved interested in escalating the guerrilla war in Oman and, supported by Cuba and the USSR, he tried to dissuade Somalia and South Yemen in favor of a federation with his country.

Soviet Marshal Andrei Grechko met in November 1975 with representatives of North Yemen whom he offered military aid[27]; political forces in the USSR and Cuba (Carlos Rafael Rodriguez, Valdes Vivo) pressured Fattah Ismail to freeze negotiations of President Robaya Ali with the Saudis. The leaders of Aden immediately stopped their negotiations with Saudi Arabia. However, the Cuban diplomatic representatives in Aden, linked to the Africa Section of the Central Committee (Perez Novoa), individuals loyal to Osmani Cienfuegos, secretly supported the moves made by Robaya Ali.

The Saudis managed to neutralize the negotiations between North Yemen and the USSR, regaining the initiative in favor of a gradual union of both Yemen. The USSR as well as Cuba observed the Saudi maneuvers in consternation. In February 1977, the Czech foreign minister arrived in North Yemen, while Soviet Defense Vice Minister General L.S. Sokolov and General M. Kozlov, the deputy chief of staff, dropped in at Aden. Just a day later, a meeting was held between the presidents of both Yemen. At that point, the objective pursued by Castro and the USSR in the southern part of the Arabian Peninsula was to prevent South Yemen to get together with North Yemen and the Saudis.

But these negotiations continued in spite of Soviet pressures. In April 1977, the Saudi foreign minister visited Aden and at the end of the year Robaya Ali reciprocated by visiting Riyadh[28].

Radio Moscow, immediately expressed the Soviet concern[29]: "a region of great strategic importance with vast oil reserves, including the Suez Canal, one of the biggest and most important sea lanes of the world...Riyadh is not concealing his intentions to use his influence and attract progressive regimes of the region to the camp of the reactionary Arab countries with a view to wiping out the patriotic forces in the region of the Red Sea. To attain these objectives, we can see that the Saudi rulers are making generous promises of aid".

In February 1978, MiG aircraft piloted by Cubans downed four Saudi fighters in the Oasis of Wadis while Cuban instructors and Yemeni troops occupied a military line along the frontier with Oman, establishing contacts with the Dhofar guerrillas. Days later, the Yemeni Premier Ali Nasser Mohammed had talks in Moscow with Leonid Brezhnev, Aleksey Kosygin, Dimitri Ustinov, and Andrey Gromyko[30].

The USSR decided to support the pro-Soviet faction of Ali Nasser-Fattah Ismail, in opposition to moderate president Robaya Ali who refused to let the Yemenis participate in the campaign which the USSR, Cuba, and Ethiopia were planning against the Eritreans[31]. The rise of Fattah Ismail, as well as the presence of units of the United States Seventh Fleet, because of the Yom Kippur War, blocked the way of the Soviets and Cubans in the country.

The crisis in the African Horn precipitated the internal struggle in South Yemeni, causing a political realignment with outside factors (the USSR, Cuba, North Yemen, and Saudi Arabia). While, on the one hand, the extremist elite of Fattah Ismail, Ali Antar, and Ali Nasr Mohammed closed ranks with Havana, the nationalists, symbolized by Robaya Ali and Saleh Mutih tried to get out of the situation in the Horn and counterbalance the pro-Soviets.

In May 1978, the pro-Cuban wing of Fattah Ismail forced the establishment of a communist party. On 17 May, Soviet Vice Defense Minister Marshal S.G. Gorshkov talked in South Yemen with Defense Minister Ali Antar and Fattah Ismail. Ali Antar accompanied Marshal Gorshkov on his return trip[32] where he signed a secret agreement with the Soviets behind the back of President Robaya Ali.

Days later, Saleh Muti made a visit to Havana at the very moment when a Soviet delegation was discussing, with Ali Nasr Mohammed, in the United Nations, affairs of extreme importance concerning military activities in the Indian Ocean[33].

In June 1978, the internal crisis broke out in South Yemen; this had to do with two crucial points: the military involvement of South Yemen in the Horn of Africa under Cuban pressure and the Cuban military presence in the country. President Robaya Ali announced the decision to demobilize the South Yemeni forces in Ethiopia and to resume aid to the Eritreans[34]. The pro-Soviet faction of Fattah reacted virulently.

Robaya Ali established secret contact with President Al Ghashmi of North Yemen to unite their forces and oust the Cubans. Through a maneuver, the president of North Yemen was assassinated by an emissary from Fattah Ismail who had passed himself off as a secret messenger from Robaya Ali.

When the president realized this and that there was a conspiracy to send him to Ethiopia under arrest, he launched an armed operation with loyal troops. Fattah got Cuban ground units, with the help of militia and East Germans, supported by Cuban air units, to crush the president's forces after several days of fighting[35].

That was how the Caribbean "gurkhas" helped defeat the "moderate" president of South Yemen, Salem Robaya Ali, securing power for the extremist faction of Abdul Fatah Ismail, an ally of Habash[36].

The new team in power in South Yemen (Ali Nasser Mohammed, Abdul Fattah Ismail, Saleh Muti, Ali Antar and Al Attas) had strong relations with Cuba. After the coup, the secret agreement signed between Ali Antar and Marshal Gorshkov was disclosed; by virtue of that agreement, "the USSR will militarily assist South Yemen in case of foreign aggression and, for this purpose, Yemen will grant naval and air facilities on the Island of Perim which will be directed by the Soviet command[37]".

During the war unleashed in February 1979 by the general staff of South Yemen against the North Yemen, the USSR and Cuba gave logistic support although they told the Adenites that they were facing a tough campaign.

After the violent collapse of the Aden regime, the death of Fatah Ismail, and the reunification with North Yemen, Cuban authorities negotiated with the government of Sanaa from which bilateral relations continued to develop, including areas of economic and political cooperation[38].

Castro also developed a very intensive interest in the Libyan Khadafy. After the war in Ogaden, Cuba, together with Libya, trained and equipped the terrorist groups that infiltrated Somalia; it also helped establish a powerful radio station called Radio Kulmis which constantly urged subversion against Siad Barre.

Libya was another tentacle in Africa which the Soviets tried to use to their benefit. The position of the "mystical" Khadafy developed after the meeting of the nonaligned in Algiers where he attacked Fidel Castro and the USSR and demanded the decolonization of the Islamic states in the Soviet federation. Fidel Castro and Muammar El Khadafy consolidated their friendship above all as of the Cuban intervention in Angola. Diplomatic relations and official and secret political contacts were increased and Castro cleared the way for Khadafy in the Kremlin.

In March 1977, Fidel Castro paid Libya one of the biggest visits ever made by a statesman in Africa. During his visit to Libya, in 1977, Castro and Khadafy agreed on exchanging military training missions for Libya at a price tag of $250 million, a loan payable in the form of 1.9 million tons of sugar at current prices[39].

The final Cuban-Libyan declaration reflects total agreement on viewpoints regarding the continent and the world. Both declared themselves in favor of Ethiopia, criticizing the "maneuvers" of the "reactionary" Arab countries[4C].

In September 1978, Fidel Castro made a "working visit" to the "Akid' of Cyrenaica. At the time two thousand five hundred Cuban troops were stationed in Libya. An additional forty-five hundred troops from Havana arrived in Libya in November of 1978. The Cuban mission was to train them in espionage, commando operations and insurgency control within Libya.

This was followed a year later by a visit of Cuban Defense Minister Raul Castro during which they agreed on the construction of two highways to the South, heading toward Chad, as well as technical-military aid. On request of the Cubans, the Libyan granted considerable economic aid to Ethiopia. Khadafy's personal escort and security services were to be trained by Havana. Hassan Ashkal and Salam Jalloud, the latter being the head of the secret service in Libya, and a frequent traveler to Cuba, were to coordinate Cuban terrorist training.

The coordinator of Cuban-Libyan military aid and chief of its intelligence services, Abdesselem Jalloud[41] from then on frequently visited Havana. Libya was to have the biggest military inventory on the continent and the logistics and maintenance were handled by Cuban, Soviet, Czechoslovak, North Korean, and German military advisors. The latter instructed an auxiliary force to increase the Libyan army. In return for that, the Libya of Khadafy was to serve as a shore facility for the Soviet fleet in the Mediterranean which was trying to counter the effectiveness of the Polaris missiles.

On February 1, 1979, the Cuban organized a meeting in Benghazi, Libya, of "progressive revolutionary organizations" of Latin America which included Argentine, Uruguayan and other terrorist groups. In this conference the Montoneros issued with the PLO a joint declaration stating that they have formed a tactical alliance to attack Israeli and Argentine targets. As a result, the Colombian terrorist group, M-19, which included Tupamaros from Uruguay, established strong ties with Palestinian and other Arab terrorists, as had many Brazilian guerrilla leaders.

World Mathaba was a Cuban and Libyan project to promote political, financial, and military support for revolutionary movements throughout the world; some of which resorted to terrorist methods like the IRA and ETA. Insurgencies in Central America, like the Sandinistas and others, along with the African National Congress of Nelson Mandela, Polisario, and others

During the "attack" which the Libyan commandos carried out at Gafsa on 27 January 1980, the Tunisian intelligence services obtained proof, from the deserter Nourredine Dridi, that these commandos had been trained by the Cuban military personnel at the bases of Taruma, Maaten Biskra, Sebha, Aouzou, Okba Ibn Nafis[42]. Shortly thereafter, some of the prisoners who had attacked Tunis confirmed Cuban intervention on television on 3 February 1980.

Khadafy was present in the Sudan, in Ethiopia, after the African National Congress, and supported Idi Amin Dada of Uganda. It is known that Khadafy was eager to have nuclear weapons. His attempts to acquire them from China had failed; therefore, Khadafy's intentions to annex the northern part of Chad are due to the rich uranium deposits in the Azou strip; be was also looking to Niger which contained the mountain range of the Montez Air, with the biggest known uranium deposits in Africa, at the same time, it is the fifth-largest producer outside the Soviet Bloc.

On the other hand, the Libyan chief executive tried to work with Pakistan in projects concerning the production of U-235. Havana supported the attempts in an effort to establish the anti-Sudanese alliance of Libya, Ethiopia, and South Yemen. Castro promised to support Khadafy's plans which were likewise aimed at creating a vast federation of Saharan Islamic states with the Sudan, Niger, Chad, and Northern Nigeria.

In 1978, Cuban brigades initiated the construction of two military roads in Southern Libya, which Khadafy needed for his invasion of Chad[43]. At the end of 1980, Khadafy upset the balance in the Sahara by launching the invasion of Chad, advised by Soviet military personnel who, from a headquarters established in Kufra and supported by aircraft piloted by North Koreans, plus more than 200 T-55 tanks, pushed deep into the territory of Chad. On that occasion, under powerful pressure from France and the United States,

Khadafy withdrew his troops, not without however having left the political situation in his favor.

Khadafy had two military forces for his expansion plans in the Sahara; one of them was deployed in Sehba, near Murzuk, with the mission of covering the entire Southwest; the other one was based in Kufra (Chad), facing toward the Sudan and the south of the Sahara. Both staffs had African mercenaries (Sudanese, Central Africans, and Ugandans). There were around 2,000 Soviet military advisors, about 1,000 Cubans, plus 1,500 East Germans in Libya; it was believed that Khadafy used them to support and advise in his invasions of Chad.

A few years later, the Tunisian police published evidence that the Libyan commandos that attacked Gafsa in January of 1980 were trained by Cubans in the Libyan bases of Tarhuma, Maaten Biskra, Sebha, Aouzou, and Okba-Ibn-Nafi[44]. In this alliance with Khadafy, Castro also looked toward the South Pacific, assisting the subversive movement of Philippine communists, the Kanak Socialist Front of New Caledonia[45].

One of the more fruitful terrorist relationships would be that of the Sandinistas of Nicaragua and the PLO, which trained more than 150 Sandinistas in Jordan, Lebanon, and Libya, among them Patricio Arguello, Enrique Smith and Rene Villa. Several Sandinistas took part in the 1979 Palestinian attempt against King Hussein II of Jordan[46].

The Middle Eastern network which Cuba cultivates to secure support for the Nicaraguan government and the guerrillas in El Salvador was disclosed by Cuban defector Hector Aguililla. As first secretary of the Cuban embassy in Syria, he participated in the acquisition and transfer of weapons from the Middle East destined for those purposes.

Until the end of 1979, the Soviet position with respect to the Western Sahara bad been neutral; but Castro's position was more militant. Since the 1970s, the Castro regime has been a fervent ally and backer of the Polisario Front.

Cuba has supplied weapons and munitions and has trained children conscripts (who are forcibly taken from their families in the impoverished refugee camps inside Polisario-controlled territory and then sent off to be educated and indoctrinated in Cuba) in guerrilla warfare tactics. Havana's support has helped the Polisario to survive and operate in the desert[47].

The economic interests of the USSR in Morocco had priority in spite of pressure from Libya and Algeria. It was not until the USSR changed its attitude in favor of Tripoli and Algiers, in November 1979 in the United Nations, that Castro made his big trip, publicly committing himself to the Polisario Front and offering it diplomatic recognition. That marked the beginning of military training in Cuba for the militants of Polisario. King Hassan II of Morocco, in an interview granted "L'Express" on 26 June 1978, stated that he had evidence as to direct Cuban participation in the Sahara conflict.

According to the magazine "Bohemia", Morocco wanted to hold on to its territory and would not permit what it called a "hostile country" along its border, obviously referring to Polisario[48]. France came out in favor of a solution by peaceful means while Algeria and Libya resolutely supported the cause of the Polisario.

Here is what Cuban magazine Bohemia[49] had to say about the solution of a Saharawi state: "This formula has no room for the land-grabbing efforts of King Hassan II, although he has no intention of letting go. A military presence of the imperialist powers there would be a triumph for the most aggressive circles in NATO...along with economic benefits represented by phosphates; there are various strategic reasons that persuade the pupils of imperialism to reach for this African enclave."

In 1977, a big Cuban delegation, headed by Central Committee member and old guerrilla fighter Armando Acosta visited the camps of the Polisario. During that year,

Bashir Mustafa As-Sayyid, second secretary of the Polisario front, made his first trip to Cuba where he had long talks with Fidel Castro.

Bashir Mustafa made periodic visits to Cuban from then on; each time he talked with the country's top leaders. During one of those visits, in 1979, he said that the Cubans had been in the camps of the Polisario since the beginning of the struggle on that front[50].

During the 6th Summit Conference of the Nonaligned in Havana, Castro launched a violent attack against Morocco and urged the nonaligned to recognize the Polisario and to give it material and military cooperation. Morocco ended its trade with Cuba when it broke relations with the Caribbean island due to Castro's support for the Polisario Front in Western Sahara.

On 21 January 1980, Cuba established diplomatic relations with the Saharawi Arab Democratic Republic or the Polisario Front, recognizing it as an independent "occupied" state which led to the rupture of diplomatic relations with and constant accusations by Rabat to the effect that Cuba was providing military aid for the Polisario. On the occasion of the fourth anniversary of the proclamation of the Democratic Arab Republic of the Sahara, a Cuban delegation, headed by Deputy Foreign Minister Rene Anillo, visited the areas under the control of the Polisario.

Cuba is one of the countries that serve as a middleman for the shipment of arms to the guerrillas, using its civilian merchant fleet. On 12 July 1980, two Moroccan Mirage aircraft opened fire on two Cuban ships, the "Morogoro" and the "Guillermo Pico" which were within territorial waters of the Western Sahara, near the territory where the Polisario operating.

From Tinduf, an Algerian enclave that borders with Morocco, Cuban personnel trained and provided consulting services to the Popular Liberation Front of the Spanish Sahara, providing arms and introducing Saharan nationals trained in Cuba, by using its merchant fleet stationed in the Canary Islands[51].

On 11 December 1980, the Moroccan Coast Guard authorities captured two Soviet ships and the Cuban ship "Golfo de Tonkin" inside the territorial waters of Morocco. The Cuban ship, which appeared to be a fishing vessel and came from the port of Conakry, Guinea, in reality carried communications and monitoring equipment used in espionage work close to the coast where clashes were taking place between the Polisario and the Moroccan Army.

During the first years of the Eighties, Algeria began to reduce its military aid to the Polisario while Libya visibly increased its commitment to that organization; at the same time, Cuba began to step its support up slowly; it had begun with a medical team in Tinduf and with training of more than 1,000 Saharawi guerrillas in Cuba.

Mohamed Abdul-Aziz, secretary-general of the Polisario, arrived in Cuba in May 1982 on an invitation from Fidel Castro. As a result of this visit, a cooperation accord was signed on 6 May 1982 between Isidoro Malmierca, the Cuban foreign minister, and Mohamed Salem Ould Salek, the information minister of that organization and its intelligence chief; under the provisions of this agreement, it was hoped that consultations between both parties might be stepped up with relation to information on international affairs. Undoubtedly, Cuba intends to supply the Polisario with intelligence information which would benefit the armed operations of that organization.

In July 1982, Political Bureau member and African affairs chief Jorge Risquet Valdes said that Cuba was making its "internationalist contribution" to the military successes of the Polisario Front and that other forms of expanding Cuban collaboration were being studied[52].

Just 4 months later, in November, a military delegation headed by Ibrahim Ghali, member of the Polisario Executive Committee and its defense minister, visited Havana and held meetings with Army General Raul Castro, Division General

Senen Casas Regueiro, and other high military commanders. Polisario Foreign Minister Said Mansour Omar arrived in Havana on 2 May 1986, at the very moment when the existence of Cuban specialists advising the guerrillas became known[53].

The intentions of the Polisario in the Western Sahara have to do with the phosphate and the thorn which it represents in the southern side of NATO.

During the reign of Khadafy Libya was in favor of supporting the Polisario, leaving the situation in the Western Sahara in the hands of King Hassan II of Morocco; in return, the latter would help relieve the African pressure to which Khadafy had been subjected since his invasion of Chad. That wrecked the Cuban plans of getting Khadafy to inherit the nonaligned of Castro.

Around 2,000 Saharawis have been trained in Cuban institutions and today occupy important political, social, administrative and professional positions in the POLISARIO political and military structure. By the Cuban government s own account, there are currently 800 Saharawi at state-run boarding schools on the Isle of Youth, in southern Cuba alone[54]. And according to independent sources, as many as 5,000 Sahrawi minors are currently being educated in Cuba[55].

The Cuban government maintains a brigade of physicians, advisors, and intelligence operatives within the Polisario zone[56]. Given Cuba's historic ties to Algeria, Cuban personnel likely enjoy secure access to the area via the Algerian border with Western Sahara.

The Moroccan government accused the Polisario Front of coordination and cooperation with al-Qaeda, notably the GSPC [al-Qaeda in the Maghreb]. It is highly unlikely that the Polisario leadership would be doing so without the knowledge and acquiescence of Havana. Moreover, the Cuban brigade of advisors and intelligence operatives stationed within the POLISARIO zone may be directly or indirectly (via Cuban-trained Sahrawi) supporting al-Qaeda operations and training camps. At the very least, it would be unwise to assume that Cuba s sophisticated intelligence apparatus is not providing valuable information and guidance to Polisario with a tacit consent to pass it on to an enemy (al-Qaeda) of a mutual enemy (the U.S.).

Castro stayed relatively aloof from the PLO during the Sixties due to relations between Yasser Arafat and China and the irritation which this was causing in the Kremlin. On the other hand, there was common talk and gossip in high Cuban government circles about the presumed "homosexualism" of the Palestinian leader.

Since 1968 Cuba has participated extensively in the training of Palestinian terrorists (including Abu Nidal) different locations: Nicaragua, Lebanon, Libya, and Iraq. The "lobby" of the PLO was decisive in the Third World when it came to getting Castro accepted as chairman of the nonaligned; in return for numerous advantages, Castro introduced them in Angola[57].

Already as early as 1968, Cuba cooperated with Iraq in the preparation of Palestinian guerrillas, one of the groups trained by Cubans was later named Black September[58]. At that time, the Cuban DGI, from their facilities in Cairo, provided military personnel to the Palestinian organization Al-Asifa[59].

Most of the financial assistance and weapons for the PLO were handled through the embassy of Cuba on Cyprus. A high intelligence officer by the name of Miguel Brugueras (who then operated in Panama) was assigned to Lebanon to handle direct contacts with the Palestinians. Likewise, specially selected PLO members were taking military counterintelligence training courses in Cuba given by Cubans and Soviets and Cuban training centers for Palestinians were established in South Yemen.

Later on, in May of 1972, Castro became one of the promoters of the conference in Badawi, Lebanon, where along with Habash, Abu Iyad and Fuad Chemali, the main international terrorist organizations would convene to coordinate operations in the Middle East and Western Europe[60].

Likewise, Castro formalized the famous Revolutionary Coordinating Junta with Muamar Khadafy, which from its location in Paris would dedicate itself to expanding the international support of the PLO and the Sandinista Front[61].

At the end of 1974, a large PLO delegation, headed by Yasser Arafat, arrived at the "Jose Marti" Airport, concluding agreements on military aid and guerrilla training in exchange for the acceptance of Cuba as a nonaligned country. A1 Fatah trained Pedro Arauz Palacios of the Sandinistas and in 1974-76 trained more Sandinistas in its Mid-Eastern training camps.

A high-level PLO military delegation including the new head of Intelligence paid a non-public visit to Cuba. PLO leaders continue to have close relations with the Cuban leadership, having access to specialized military and intelligence training, both in Cuba or Palestinian territory, and in the sharing of intelligence[62].

Toward the middle of 1976, the Israelis detected a significant number of Cubans advisors in southern Lebanon, and during the Israeli invasion of Lebanon, the Cuban embassy in Beirut served as general headquarters and communications center to Yasser Arafat[63]. During the Israeli incursion into Lebanon in 1982, Israeli intelligence captured Palestinian documents which included Cuban training manuals.

In March of 1978 the PLO and Cuba entered into an agreement where Cuba would send additional personnel to Palestinian camps in Lebanon while at the same time Cuban intelligence in Beirut and Cyprus would coordinate the formation of a central PLO intelligence command. Miguel Brugueras, a seasoned Cuban spy chief, assumed responsibility for the mission. Brugueras would also screen candidates for espionage and terrorism.

In the same month and through George Habash, the Cubans created a secret alliance between the PLO and the Sandinista Front, whereby the Palestinians would train the Salvadoran guerrillas of Shafik Handal secretary-general of the Communist Party of El Salvador, and Cayetano Carpio, turned up as links between the Palestinians, the Syrians, and the Cubans[64].

In May of 1978, Abu Salah Khalaf (Abu Iyad), military chief of Al-Fattah, announced that since the 1960s many Palestinian fedayeens received combat training in Cuba and that Cuban militaries provided training in Palestinian camps as well[65].

In the island of Socotra, under Yemen jurisdiction, terrorist training centers were established, for Latin Americans as well as Arabs. There, alongside Cubans, Carlos the Jackal and Abu Nidal acted as instructors, and graduated militants from the Palestinian Popular Front, and the likes of George Abdullah, Salem Yibril and Jacqueline Esber of the Lebanese Revolutionary Front (the Larf).

Following the Palestinian debacle in Jordan, the largest Palestinian training centers outside Lebanon were to be found in the Isle of Pines, Cuba. At that time the Cuban Government also increased its presence in the Palestinian camps in Lebanon[66]. In Khadafy's Libya and in southern Lebanon, Cuban fighters trained the PLO. The Cuban intelligence centers in Beirut (under the command of veteran spy Miguel Brugueras) and Cyprus would channel contacts and military cooperation with the PLO and other terrorist groups.

Before the end of the year, about 500 Palestinians were sent to Cuba[67] for training; many of them attended the Nico Lopez School of the Central Committee of the Cuban Communist Party where they took political, propaganda, and economics courses. The Cubans also went to Jordan where they trained the groups of Al-Fattah.

Palestine organizations, with Cuban assistance, have reciprocated by training various Latin American groups in the Middle East. Libya, which boasted a meeting of Latin

American "liberation movements" January 25-February 1, 1979, also has trained some Latin American extremists.

In March, 1979, a group of Sandinistas met in Havana with the PDFLP, an affiliate of the PLO, which has offered to fight for the FSLN. The Cubans asked the PLO to help the Montoneros and the Tupamaros, and, according to Israeli intelligence, provided arms and training for them. Mario Firmenich, the leader of the Montoneros, was the main link with Iraq and Libya as well as with the Spanish terrorist group ETA. In July, 1979, a planeload of 30 tons of Chinese Communist military equipment to the PLO was discovered on route to the Cuban training camps in Costa Rica.

The Sandinista also cooperated in a joint effort by Cuba and Palestine groups to provide military training in the Mideast to selected Latin American extremists. Some Sandinistas were themselves trained by the Palestine Liberation Organization, which maintains an embassy in Nicaragua.

Cuba also assisted the Salvadoran guerrillas in contacts with Arab radical states and terrorist organizations to arrange military training and financing for arms acquisition. In September 1980, Cuba laundered $500,000 in Iraqi funds for the Salvadoran insurgents. In March 1981, the Salvadoran Communist Party Secretary General, Shafik Handal, visited Lebanon and Syria to meet with Palestine leaders. Cuba also coordinated the training of a relatively small number of Salvadoran guerrillas in Palestinian camps in the Mideast.

The Palestinian Intifada increases Cuba's support for Arafat and the PLO, both diplomatic and military. Not to be left out of any area, Castro engaged another one hundred Cuban military officers to train PLO guerillas.

In 1989, through Cuban intelligence coordination, the PLO agreed to and was brokering the provision of SAM-7, surface to air missiles, to Panama's Manuel Noriega. The purpose was to stave off an imminent American invasion.

After the negotiations leading to the establishment of the Palestinian National Authority, Cuban-Palestinian military cooperation was enhanced, including the areas of counter-intelligence and intelligence[68]. In 1998 a high-level PLO military delegation including the head of Intelligence paid a visit to Cuba.

Cuba developed closer ties with Iraq in various areas (medical services, construction projects, grants and loans). Cuban military advisory to Iraq in different fields began in the mid-1970s. A Cuban military delegation was sent to Iraq to learn and share what was considered vital information and experiences from U.S. combat operations in Kuwait and Iraq[69].

In 1972 The Cubans offered the Iraqis training in counter insurgency to be used against the Kurds. In 1974 Cuba began the training of Iraqi special operation commandos as well as the provision of military engineers to build roads to war fronts. Cuban military instructors remained and were providing intelligence, training and engineering support to Saddam Hussein and his budding regime.

Saddam Hussein's Iraq has had at its disposal Cuban military construction brigades and instructors with military specialties[70] During the Gulf War, Cuba electronically monitored maneuvers by U.S. troops for Hussein's benefit, and took on the diplomatic representation of Baghdad abroad[71]. A Cuban military delegation was sent to   Iraq to learn and share what was considered vital information and experiences from U.S. combat operations in Kuwait and Iraq.

The election of Abdul-Aziz Bouteflika (April 1999) as President of Algeria, opened new opportunities for Cuba in the Middle East, given Bouteflika's close relationship with the Cuban government for more than three decades. Cuba joined with Algeria and Libya on a diplomatic-political offensive in support of POLISARIO (People's Front for the Liberation of Western Sahara and Rio del Oro); later on provided military cooperation, and medical services.

Castro visited Qaddafi "six times" from March 6 to May 16, 2001. This last suspicious visit was after visiting Algeria, Iran, Malaysia, Qatar and Syria. On May 15, 2001, Fidel Castro arrived in Syria with the published purpose of strengthening ties with old allies in the Middle East. He was greeted by President Assad at Damascus airport. The subsequent conversations between the leaders included promises of future mutual support. Another one hundred and fifty Cubans were strategically coordinating foreign subversive activity in the region, based in Algeria.

Iranian-Cuban relations have increased after several high-ranking delegations from Iran visited Cuba, together with additional purchases of Cuban pharmaceuticals and biotechnology products.

The Shiite regime of the Ayatollah Khomeini in Iran recruited Carlos "The Jackal" for the mission of the assassination of the deposed Shah then living in Mexico. The Cuban DI was supposed to provide the intelligence information and logistic for the operation.

From 1990 Cuba sold Iran the technology to recombinant protein production in yeast and Escherichia coli, as well as the large-scale purification protocols for both soluble and insoluble proteins synthesized in or excreted by them. This technology could be used to produce lethal agents in biochemical weapons, like anthrax bacteria, or lethal viruses. Jose de la Fuente, who was Director of Research and Development at the Center for Genetic Engineering and Biotechnology in Havana from 1990-98 has stated that "Cuba sold to Iran biotechnology which could be used to produce biochemical weapons[72].

On May 7, 2001, the New York Times published an article which quoted Fidel Castro speaking at Teacher's Training University in Tehran said that, "Iran and Cuba together can bring America to its knees."

Castro had visited Iran, Syria, and Libya. On May 10, 2001, Reuter's reports indicate that Fidel Castro told Iranians during his visit to Tehran University on the previous day that, "the imperialist king is destined to fall soon."

Former Defense Department counter-terrorism expert John More told UPI that Cubans, militant Palestinians, Hezbollah and even advisors from the leftist government of Venezuela are all active in Colombia.

The travel routes of several Al Qaeda Lieutenants through Latin America had been helped by Cuba. Some of the propaganda had served Cuba´s policy effort to harm United States.

Castro´s Realpolitik

Accompanied by high executives and several generals as well as his team of "African affairs specialists" plus an impressive personal guard, Castro landed in Algeria on 1 March 1977; from there he went to Tripoli where, talking to Gadhafi, he questioned the commitment of both of them to the guerrillas of Eritrea in the light of relations with the Derg.

The Libyan Khadafy offered his good offices with the Arab countries to get the Eritreans to accept Mengistu; in turn, Castro promised him help for Libya's plans in the Sahara. Khadafy asked Castro to send combat units for deployment along the Egyptian border and for training.

After cancelling his visit to Iraq on the 10th, Castro flew to Aden where Fattah Ismail[1] briefed him on the situation in the area, agreeing to cede territory in return for interceding in the conflict between Ethiopia and Somalia. He also met with the Yemenis who were very receptive to the idea of supporting Mengistu against Siad Barre.

Fidel convinced Siad Barre to negotiate with Mengistu in South Yemen. The conference between Mengistu of Ethiopia and Barre of Somalia did take place secretly in Aden on the 16th in the presence of Fidel Castro, Fattah Ismail, Salem Robaya Ali, and Ali Nasser Mohammed.

Fidel suggested to Mengistu H. Mariam and to Siad Barre the Soviet idea of a federation[2], made up of South Yemen, Ethiopia, Somalia, Djibouti, and Eritrea within whose context the problems of Eritrea and Ogaden were to be resolved. Mengistu rejected the alternative of the "Arab Lake" and the "prior autonomy" proposed by Siad Barre and he was joined in that by Fidel Castro and his Soviet and South Yemeni allies.

In a speech explaining Cuban involvement in the Horn of Africa, Fidel Castro mentioned the Aden meeting once again: "we arranged a meeting of the leaders of Ethiopia, Yemen, and Somalia with us in Aden to try to resolve the problems pending between Somalia and Ethiopia and specifically to prevent a war". There were two forces in Somalia according to Fidel Castro[3] the left-wing forces; and a powerful right-wing reactionary group, in favor of an alliance with imperialism, with the Arab reactionaries, with Saudi Arabia, with Iran, etc.

Cuba developed a political blueprint to Yemen according to which officials linked to Osmani Cienfuegos would run the area and would be inclined toward a greater commitment to and more support for Robaya Ali, although looking with foreboding to Somalia.

The Cuban foreign policy "zar" Carlos Rafael Rodriguez and Valdes Vivo, disapproved such steps; in the end, the Yemenis Fattah Ismail and Ali Nasser were to be the men with clout in the Soviet-Cuban decision on Ethiopia.

The USSR and Castro strengthened their position in South Yemen in favor of the faction of Fattah Ismail. The strategic and political factors involving South Yemen and the personal clashes between Siad Barre and Fidel Castro worked in favor of the Soviet decision. The Soviets and Cubans wanted to increase the military presence of Fidel Castro on the western shore of the Red Sea, especially in Ethiopia.

After the end of the meeting, Cuba withdrew its military mission to Somalia; South Yemen quickly dispatched a ship with more than 30 T-34 tanks, armored vehicles, and other weapons to Ethiopia. Castro and the South Yemenis then agreed to give Ethiopia military support if a conflict should break out.

The agreement for this multinational operation took shape in Moscow during a meeting at the beginning of the year, attended by Leonid Brezhnev, Aleksey Kosygin for the USSR,

Raul Castro for Cuba, and the South Yemeni Premier Ali Nasser Mohammed.

In the middle of January, Western intelligence sources detected the presence of generals Raul Castro and Koliyakok (commanding general of the Soviet forces in Libya), accompanied by many high-ranking officers from their respective armies, East Germans, and the chief of staff of South Yemen[4]. This group of high-ranking military officers planned the combined counteroffensive.

The USSR established airlifts through Benghazi in Libya and Aden in South Yemen, using its logistic reserves in East Germany and Czechoslovakia. During the first 10 hours of the airlift, the USSR shipped equipment to furnish the Cuban 3 divisions through Iraq, Libya, Mozambique, and Aden.

The offensive began with 30,000 Cubans, plus 2,500 South Yemenis who were operating the armored vehicles, aircraft, artillery, and the command posts. The South Yemenis operated mostly in the areas around Massawa, Eritrea; there they assumed a more visible role in the campaigns of 1977 and in the spring of 1978, supported by Soviet naval artillery that blasted the positions of the Eritreans around Massawa[5]. They piloted the MiG aircraft; they operated the tanks and the artillery as well as the reconnaissance helicopters. In the middle of February 1978, the Eritreans took several South Yemeni prisoners, including some pilots[6].

Cuban personnel strength at its very height came to 30,000 soldiers. Although Somalis was getting financial support from Egypt and Saudi Arabia, the aid from the Soviet Bloc came more quickly. Soviet military equipment came to a figure of $1 billion while the United States refused to supply any weapons; from Egypt and Iran, Somalia received old Soviet equipment, 60 German tanks, and 43 Italian helicopters. Saudi Arabia provided money.

Ethiopia assumed greater importance in the eyes of the Cuban and Soviets after the invasion of Afghanistan which cut their distances in the Indian Ocean. But it was not until

Afghanistan that the United States took measures to create a "Rapid Deployment Force" for the Persian Gulf.

Cuba reconciled the USSR to the idea of having lost influence in Somalia because the other shore of Bab el Mandeb (in Aden) compensated for the air and naval facilities they had enjoyed at Berbera with its airfield at Khormaksar and its spacious port facilities. The Soviet air forces, with their base in Aden, piloted by Cubans, made reconnaissance flights over the entire adjacent area along the Red Sea. In Massawa, Eritrea, they also based a fleet of MiG-23 "Flogger-B" and MiG-27 aircraft with Cuban crews.

The gradual growth of the Soviet-Cuban expansion circle starting from Angola (Shaba I, Shaba II, Namibia, Zimbabwe, Ethiopia, Mozambique, Sao Tome, and Principe) now became more somber after the completion of the famous "Arc of Crisis" which extends from the African Horn all the way to Afghanistan. Countries in the area, such as Saudi Arabia and Oman, were worried about the Cuban military proximity in Ethiopia and South Yemen.

In January 1978, almost the entire territory of Eritrea was in the hands of the Eritrean Liberation Front (which was pro-Chinese) and the People's Liberation Front. The South Yemeni troops, supported by armored units and rocket artillery, kept these guerrillas on the defensive during the operations in Ogaden.

After taking care of the problem of Ogaden, the Cuba war machine assisted the Ethiopian Army with the problem of Eritrea. Propaganda in Cuba charged that domestic imperialist aggression, through Eritrea, was trying to cut off Ethiopia's access to the Red Sea[7]. Soviet warships systematically bombed Massawa and Assab[8].

Although Havana preached its neutrality regarding the Eritrean disagreement, around 3,500 Cuban soldiers debarked in Asmara on 16 March and began to operate against the

Eritrean guerrilla encirclements, at the same time providing logistic support for the Ethiopian forces that were stationed there. On the other band, MiG aircraft piloted by Cubans began to turn up[9].

The presence of Cuban troops blocked Eritrea's independence[10]: "the Cuban troops provided the Ethiopians with logistics and air support in their war against the Eritrean separatist movement".

Since the Eritreans resisted the initial push, Cuba decided to negotiate on a federation solution due to heavy Arab protests. Besides, they were also influenced by the preoccupation of the Arab allies (Libya, Syria and Iraq) concerning the Eritrean movement. The Cubans contacted the Eritrean delegates with a view to discussing an autonomous accommodation where Ethiopia was hoping to retain control over foreign policy and the Eritrean port of Assab[11]. Secret meetings took place between March and June of 1978 in East Berlin between the Eritrean representatives and the Derg[12].

The Cubans underestimated the depth of the Eritrean problem and believed that the ideological-political affinity between the Derg and Somalia would prevail over ethnic and nationalist feelings. They pressured Mengistu in an effort to arrive at a negotiated solution which would get them out of the Eritrean problem. Mengistu's survival depended on his ability to overcome the Eritrean resistance and that would be possible only with Cuban support and as a result of disunity among the guerrillas.

Mengistu quite on his own decided to visit Havana on 26 April in an effort to help him in staging a new offensive against Eritrea and to put an end to the negotiations in East Berlin[13]. Castro gave his approval; the Cuban general staff issued orders for 3,000 Cuban soldiers stationed in Ogaden to be transferred quickly to Eritrea to reinforce some key points and to facilitate the advance of the Ethiopian Army[14].

In order to launch the new offensive against the guerrillas by June, the USSR together with Cuba was building air and naval installations on the Island of Dahlak and the Makale Air

Base, in the southern part of Eritrea, where were positioned more than 50 MiG-21 and 23 fighters with their Cuban crews[15], a large part of the helicopter fleet, plus 50 T-55 and T-62 tanks also with Cuban and Yemeni crews.

By the middle of the year, the combined operation of Ethiopian infantry and Soviet-Cuban air, naval, and armored support forced the Eritreans to withdraw toward the mountains. The Eritreans were caught in a pincer movement staged by Cuban and South Yemeni tankers, supported by the rocket batteries operated by East Germans and South Yemenis[16].

Throughout 1978 and 1979, the Eritrean fighters faced five major offensives by the Derg, assisted by Cuba, employing modern war materiel, napalm bombs, defoliants, and especially helicopters dropping nerve gas bombs[17].

However, Cuba tries to conceal its direct participation (logistics, planning, training, pilots, and tank crew members) during the military offensives against Eritrea, afraid of a virulent reaction from the various Arab states, such as Algeria, Libya, Iraq, Syria, and the PLO.

On the other hand, Cuba was seeking a border conflict in South Yemen with North Yemen in order, through the military supremacy of Aden, to bring about a merger of both parts of Yemen, forming a state that would be a counterweight to Saudi Arabia, destabilizing Oman and the Gulf Emirates.

In the Middle East, the Cuban actions helped the Soviet to avoid finding itself outflanked by a totally pro-Western region; with this objective in mind, it sought Mediterranean ports for its fleet and the effort to hinder the presence of United States troops or military bases assumes significance in their agenda.

The targets here were energy resources (not forgetting their old claims to the oil wells in the northern part of Iran), the Indian Ocean and the Red Sea, where the USSR with the help of Cuba occupied the Dahlak Island Group to resupply its naval fleet. It also used the airports of Asmara in Eritrea and Khormaksar in South Yemen for its reconnaissance flights over the Indian Ocean[18].

Havana and Moscow considered the Persian Gulf, the African Horn, the Suez Canal, and the Eastern Mediterranean to be the four cardinal points of the future theater of conventional operations between the big powers. The gigantic training maneuvers that Cuba and the USRR held in the desert zones of South Yemen, in 1979, provide a very interesting lesson; there the Cuban and the Soviets tested their rapid deployment air-transported units, including 7 divisions with 50,000 men[19].

It was also debated whether the invasion of Afghanistan by 85,000 Soviet soldiers was part of a strategy of expansion toward the Persian Gulf and the Indian subcontinent. In point of fact, this operation brought them closer to the ports of the Indian Ocean, threatening Baluchistan and Pashtunistan, providing a springboard toward the oilfields of Kirkuk and the Persian Gulf.

Following its presence in Afghanistan, the USSR promoted subversion among the tribes of Baluchistan, conspiring, with the blessings of India, to destabilize Pakistan and supporting through Havana, terrorism in the small Arab emirates of Abu Dhabi, Dubai, Ras-el-Khaima, and Oman.

The Cubans has displayed great interest in conflicts between countries, the objective of occupying the power vacuum left by Portugal, the strengthening of Khadafy, of Libya, because of his interest in expanding into the Sahara, greater attention to the Southern Cone after getting a hold on Angola and Mozambique, controlling the Swapo and the African National Congress of Nelson Mandela, as well as cultivating Zimbabwe. Starting with the Seventies, the Cubans made progress in Guinea, Guinea-Bissau, Mali, Ghana, Somalia, Ethiopia, etc.

Cuba developed a campaign in which it pictured the Middle East as being unstable, with the PLO-Israel-petroleum equation, to alarm Europe and to persuade it to depend on Soviet oil.

Cuban policy in Africa and the Middle East was not analyzed properly by specialists and publication organs who did not consider its global tendencies, its overseas positions, and its sensitive areas.

The importance of the African continent furthermore grows with its international influence and its areas that are of obvious military interest. Havana convinced the Africans and Arabs that the USSR was a neutral extra continental power that it would never push beyond the borders of Europe.

The African and Middle East areas presents vulnerabilities which make it one of the world's current and future focus of conflicts: the imbalance between population growth, unemployment, and starvation; tribalism and border problems; agrarian communalism; technical-industrial illiteracy; the geostrategic projection of the great powers; armed conflicts and terrorist movements; the anti-Westerns and the subsequent refusal of the latter to engage in a major economic compromise.

From a marginal position in the area, Havana was transformed into a decisive power in the southern part of the Arabian Peninsula, in the Horn of Africa, and in the Southern Cone, filling the vacuum left by the British withdrawal from positions East of Suez, exploiting the hesitation of NATO and the crisis in the United States executive branch.

Africa, for example, learned the risks of opposing the Cuban intelligence and military machine, especially after the brutal repression which the Cubans unleashed in the northern and southern parts of Angola, Eritrea, Ogaden and South Yemen.

In the middle of the Sixties, Cuba had penetrated and controlled the ANC, SWAPO, MPLA, and ZAPU. Starting with the next decade (the 1970s), Cuban policy toward Africa and the Middle East was changed considerably; in this assault, the USSR invested in the Island armaments, material resources, etc., worth billions.

The change in Cuba, in terms of using, besides terrorism, a more direct presence, employing military personnel, technicians, and troops, was due to the managing and consolidation of the entrance to the Red Sea, the European oil artery, with South Yemen and Ethiopia, establishing also with Angola a secure base in the far eastern part of the Atlantic, a pivot for bringing the entire southern part of Africa down. In controlling the Horn of Africa, Cuba helped the USSR to shift its naval power to the Indian Ocean, balancing the Polaris submarines and the United States naval base in the Chagos Island group.

Through the Cuban presence in Mozambique and its subsequent influence over the military regime of the Malagasy leader Didier Ratsiraka, Moscow penetrated deeply into the Western flank of the Indian Ocean, projecting itself toward South Africa in a pincer move. With the Havana-Tripoli axis, it had the possibility of expanding toward the southern Sahara and with the Polisario in order to get close to the Atlantic entrance to the Mediterranean.

The West paid no attention to the moves of the Cuban and Soviet navies, their fishing agreements and port facilities which they are getting in Africa and the Middle East. Admiral Gorshkov had this to say in July 1975[20]: "maritime shipments and fishing and scientific research in the ocean are parts of Soviet naval power".

Starting with Angola, Cuba expanded its fishing agreements on both coasts of Africa. The regimes of Libya, Guinea=Bissau, Cape Verde, Benin, Angola, Mozambique, Ethiopia, and South Yemen. All of these gave the Soviet fleet flexibility and ships carrying electronic intelligence equipment and marine current research instruments showed up much more frequently.

With respect to Africa, Latin America and the Middle East, the propaganda put out by Havana tried to convince everybody that the correlation of world forces favored socialism; it presented the United States as being the enemy of the African and Arab peoples.

United States does understand that Cuba represent a fatal danger to the Third World and the West. One cannot consider Cuban involvement in subversion and terrorism as the result of temporary crisis but rather as the sum of a geo-political projection.

Cuba continues to actively undermine U.S. policies in the Middle East and North Africa in primarily three ways:

a) Portraying U.S. actions and diplomacy in the region as those of an aggressor, seeking to impose hegemony by force such as the recurrent attacked on Iraq and Lybia, violation of sovereign rights (no-fly zones), the perpetuation of unjustified economic sanctions to countries in the region (Iraq, Iran, Syria), open political intervention and the use of brutal force as acts of retaliation (the Bin Laden);

b) portraying the U.S. as the main obstacle to a peaceful settlement of the Israel-Palestine and the Gulf conflicts, and

c) discrediting U.S. policies, especially by gaining support for Cuba's agenda at the U.N.[21]

These Anti-American views and policies are conveyed as a systematic message through a network of Cuban embassies in most countries of the region, at the U.N. and its multilateral system plus Cuban embassies and missions throughout the Western Hemisphere and other significant non-governmental political and cultural channels.

The annual dry-season offensive planned by the Soviet and Cuban military that commenced in November 1987 in Angola was intended to inflict a crushing defeat on the UNITA guerrilla forces so that they would no longer be a factor. The Soviets provided some of the best weapons in their inventory to the Cuban forces, including helicopters MI-17 HIP and Mi-18 HIND, as well as the SA-16 surface-to-air missile.

The combined Cuban/Angolan offensive began successfully with a major battle developing during November at Mavinga, a strategic town in southeastern Angola held by Jonas Savimbi's UNITA forces.

Savimbi's lightly-armed guerrillas could not hold out against the Cubans; and so the South Africans committed a substantial force (estimated by the Angolans at 8,000men) of SADF regulars and troops from the Namibian Territorial Forces.

The defeated Cuban/Angolan forces retreated towards Cuito Cuanavale, which had a strategic airstrip that would allow them to be reinforced and resupplied. The SADF forces pursued them in an effort to capture the airfield and destroy the Cuban/Angolan force.

A clear indication of the sudden increase in the strategic significance of the fighting was the dispatch of Cuban General Arnaldo T. Ochoa Sanchez to Cuito Cuanavale to become the senior regional commander in charge of the Southern Front. Ochoa, one of Cuba's most experienced senior officers, was the architect of the Cuban military arrival in Angola in 1976. He directed the joint Cuban/Angolan forces against UNITA in the late 1970s, and subsequently held senior command positions in Ethiopia during the 1978 Ogaden War with Somalia and chief Cuban military adviser to Nicaragua's Sandinista People's Army (EPS).

Since the North African campaign of World War II, there was a major mechanized battle in Africa. In began early in December, when the South Africans began to increase the pressure on the joint force of Cubans and Angolan government forces (FAPLA) who had retreated through the rough bush country from Mavinga to Cuito Cuanavale.

Cuban reinforcements and technicians began arriving in Cuito Cuanavale early in December, bolstering the infantry brigades as well as artillery and tank units, and at the same time, the Cuban air force in Angola was reinforced with experienced pilots. From then on, the Cubans sought air and anti-aircraft superiority.

The major South African offensives took place on January 13, February 14, February 25, March 1 and March 23 1988, involving the 61st, 62nd, 101st and 102nd battalions and the 32nd Buffalo division. The intense artillery and tank fire played a major role in stalling the SADF advance.

The South Africans G-5 and G-6 cannon demolished the bridge over the Cuito River and blocked the Cubans, but were not sufficient to capture the airfield. The turning point had come when the South Africans lost their air superiority due to the Soviet radar-guided surface-to-air missiles that destroyed several Mirage fighters, and the Cuba's rain of artillery fire and air strikes,

While representatives of Angola, Cuba and South Africa, with the United States acting as mediator, have met to discuss possible solutions to the Angolan civil war, Cuba has been actively preparing for the possibility of a major escalation of military activities in southern Angola, which could result in Cuban forces crossing the border into Namibia.

Having undoubtedly won an important victory over the South African Defense Force (SADF) in the protracted battle for Cuito Cuanavale in southern Angola during the first three months of this year, the Cubans have realized that the South African government is unwilling to pay the "human cost" of a large-scale military confrontation in defense of northern Namibia and southern Angola.

They have decided to make the most of the opportunity with an on-going military drive in south western Angola down to the Namibian border to take control of the strategically vital series of dams on the Cunene River above the Ruacana Falls guarded by a light force of South African troops.

General Arnaldo Ochoa moved his strategic headquarters from Cuito Cuanavale to the southern Angola, near the Namibia border. Cuban General Patricio De LaGuardia Font, who had organized the defenses of the Dembo region where the South African thrust had been stalled, was named his deputy commander, in charge of the south-ward advance of the Southern Front force.

The Cubans established three major task forces, with 200 tanks and supporting artillery, based around the towns of Mupa, Cahama and Xangongo. The elite corps comprised units of Cuba's 50th Division, the best combined-arms division of Cuba. The Cuban forces established over-the-border shelling capabilities with multiple-barrel rocket launchers (MBRLs), as well as anti-aircraft capability and capacity for raids.

They comprise the "quality core" of a Southern Front, of General Ochoa. They were assisted by less noticed Soviet pilots and East German military specialists and technicians in communications and air defense.

From mid-April to early May, additional 8,600 Cuban troops, elite combat and special operations units, arrived in Angola, followed by another 3,000 troops, elevating to 54,000 the total amount of Cuban troops in Angola.

The Cuban force opened a second strategic thrust in southwestern Angola intended to recapture the region that formerly supported the SWAPO infrastructure, in order to destabilize Namibia and the South African forces there. There they integrated a mixed column, commanded by a Cuban officer, of Namibian SWAPO units that they trained as mechanized infantry attached to the Angolan forces.

Cuban advance units and patrols were deployed 25 miles from the Namibian border. General Patricio De LaGuardia column advanced southeast to Xangongo, where one task force then moved on to Ngiva. The Cuban advances have succeeded in establishing a bridgehead close to the Namibian border, breaking of the tacit status quo in Angola.

On June 29, an armored column of an estimated 1,000 Cuban troops attacked towards the Calueque Dam, and were met by the SADF. The Cubans sent in eight MiG-23s on a precision bombing run over the Calueque Dam and the SADF garrison.

The parameters of Cuba's policy were defined by Castro in February 1986. Seeing the increasing significance of Africa as choke points for sea lines of communication, and to the ability to deny strategic minerals to the West, Castro anticipated that Cuba's direct military involvement in the region was bound to increase substantially. Castro called for the removal of South African military forces from Namibia as essential to SWAPO taking power.

The Cubans have openly contradicted assurances by Angolan President Jose Eduardo dos Santos that Cuban forces would not cross the border into Namibia. Indeed, Cuban MiG-23s and Su-22s started fly reconnaissance missions into Namibia, and openly stating that they did not rule out the possibility of their forces operating inside Namibia.

The Cubans pursuing to a considerable extent the objectives to press hard along the Namibian border in order to consolidate their presence before the start of the Southern Hemisphere's winter rains [July-August] which will put an end to large-scale operations until spring arrives in October-November.

Angolan Defense Minister Colonel General Pedro Maria Tonha, along with Tanzanian Defense Minister Salim Ahmad Salim, arrived in Havana on May 22, to conduct a week of consultations. They met were Fidel Castro; FAR Minister Raul Castro and the principal army generals.

The Tanzanian defense minister focused on the expected role of his country in the anticipated military escalation in southern Africa, and asked for Cuban military and training assistance for his country. The African National Congress of Nelson Mandela immediately widened the scope of its activities in South Africa to include sophisticated forms of sabotage and military confrontation.

Once it became clear that Fidel Castro was planning a military offensive inside Namibia and subsequent in South Africa, Jorge Risquet, a member of the Cuban Politburo and

Castro's own man in charge of operations in Africa and the Middle East, left London for urgent consultations in Moscow. Afterwards, he went to Ethiopia to establish Addis Ababa as an important stopover for the future Soviet military transport aircrafts carrying logistics to General Ochoa´s Southern Front.

At his briefing for Non-aligned ministers on June, Castro depicted the military option as the most viable means for achieving the liberation of Namibia and indeed, South Africa, and added that a major and "decisive" confrontation of Cuban forces with South Africa might be inevitable.

He also disclosed that an air base was being quickly constructed further south bringing the aircraft closer to the frontline, and had achieved air and anti-aircraft superiority, and deployed the best Cuban anti-aircraft weapons in southern Angola. By this way, Castro threatens South Africa with "serious defeat" if it does not capitulate.

The Soviet Defense Ministry's "Krasnaya Zvezda" [Red Star] recently noted that the negotiations in no way are expected to interfere with Soviet and Cuban support for the goals of the African National Congress and Namibia`s SWAPO.

With the bombing of the Calueque Dam, the Cubans contradicted Angolan assurances that the important dam complex would not be targeted and that Cuban forces would not cross the border into Namibia. The Cuban reinforcements were brought in without the knowledge of the government and President Dos Santos was upset over because it clearly undermined the negotiating peace talks.

The Cubans had shown no indication of flexibility in the negotiations, but a move on the diplomatic front surprised Castro when it was announced on August 8 a cease-fire agreement. The Botha government under international pressure reached the limit of concessions it was able to make, and under this agreement, all South African troops were to be withdrawn from Angola by September 1, and a timetable was agreed upon for the withdrawal of Cuban troops from Angola.

The Havana Cartel

Cuba has been actively engaged in the drug trade since 1961. The extent contributed to the expulsion of Cuba from the Organization of American States (OAS) in 1962.

Cuba has also become an important way-station for the transfer of drugs from Red China to Puerto Rico and thence to the mainland United States. A break in one drug ring came in December 1964 with the arrest of Castroite Cubans Carabeo Nerev and two accomplices. Eugene Marshall of the Federal Narcotics Bureau in Miami revealed that the three had been back to Cuba several times since they entered this country under the cover of "exiles."

On September 24, 1964, the New York Times reported: "There are strong suspicions that Communist Cuba is making an attempt to flood Puerto Rico with drugs via Havana in an effort to undermine the economy of the island." On January 6, United Press International reported that marihuana was arriving in the United States from Cuba "in great quantities."

In an interview with New York police inspector Ira Bluth, UPI reported that "marihuana used to come to New York almost entirely from Mexico, but recently a large amount of drugs from Cuba have been discovered they have been introduced into this country from Cuba through Florida.

The United States Narcotics Commission publicly acknowledged the link. In June of 1967, a Cuban trained Venezuelan intelligence officer, Manuel Marcano established before the Organization of American States, the Cuban link of drugs for guerrilla weapons in the hemisphere.

In 1974, Fernando Ravelo Renedo, a top Cuban intelligence agent, was named ambassador to Colombia. By this time

Colombia's M-19 guerrillas were receiving weaponry and training in Cuba. Ambassador Ravelo negotiated the Cuban government help both to the guerrillas and to the drug traffickers.

In 1978 another Cuban intelligence department, the MC, became involved in narcotics to raise foreign currency for covert Cuban operations. The MC Department under the direction of Colonel Tony De La Guardia, created private companies in different countries through which illegal businesses, including drug deals and sales[1].

A fellow by the name of James Herring happened to be circumventing the embargo and running computer equipment to Cuba aboard speedboats at the time. Herring noticed that DGI intelligence agents were handling narcotics.

In 1979 Ambassador Ravelo met Johnny Crump, and Jaime Guillot-Lara, two Colombian drug smugglers, at a party in Bogota. Guillot-Lara would eventually marry Raul Castro's daughter.

Crump traveled to Havana as a formal guest of the Cuban government, to discuss the Crump, refueling of drug planes in Cuba. During his visit he dealt with Rene Rodriguez Cruz, a member of Cuba's Central Committee. The Cuban Admiral Aldo Santamaria told Crump that his naval vessels would protect drug shipments coming through Cuban waters in the future.

The Colombian voyage would head to Cuban territorial waters, and the Cuban vessels would direct the appropriate time and location for the safest passage in avoidance of United States Customs planes and United States Coast Guard patrols. By 1980 billions of drug dollars were flying across the Caribbean because the Cubans were providing safe havens, documents, fuel, radar services and escort vessels, among other benefits.

Jeff Karonis, Former Lt. Commander of the United States Coast Guard, has stated that Coast Guard personnel would observe air drops in the middle of the day going on inside Cuban territorial waters. The Cuban Navy allowed the boats and larger shipments to dock with escorts. The Air Force had responsibility for light planes, which generally landed at Varadero. Cuban Air Force General Rafael del Pino, was in a position to give overflight permission. The requests would usually come from Raul Castro, the Minister of Defense himself.

Admiral Santamaria, Rene Rodriguez Cruz, Ambassador Ravelo Renedo and diplomat Bassols, were indicted in US courts of law. One of the witnesses was Mario Estevez, a Cuban intelligence officer, arrested in 1981. His mission was to coordinate intelligence and drug trafficking operations. Estevez also rendered testimony before a Senate sub-committee about the extensive drug ring Havana had developed.

In November of 1981, Colombian M-19 guerrillas kidnapped Marta Ochoa, daughter of cartel leader Fabio Ochoa. Tensions skyrocketed as the cartel refused to pay a ransom. Havana intervened to settle the differences. Then a group of guerrillas were captured in Colombia implicating Cuban embassy personnel as contact points for weapons and drug traffic coordination.

By 1982 the Sandinistas in Nicaragua, the FARC, ELN and the M-19 guerrillas of Colombia had bonded, with Havana as the coordinator. Antonio Farach, a defecting Nicaraguan diplomat, testified before US Congress that Nicaraguan embassies had instructions to help the FARC, the M-19, and even the PLO guerrillas, any time they were needed. Diplomatic missions now provided a link to drugs, violence and terrorism.

In 1982 the notorious Robert Vesco was indicted in the U.S. for smuggling tons of cocaine through Cuba, where he lived under the protection of the Cuban government.

Carlos Lehder, one of the founders of the Medellin Cartel revealed the inner workings of the Cartel and his associations with Fidel Castro and Manuel Noriega of Panama, among others. Carlos Lehder acknowledged personal meetings with Raul Castro related to drug shipments.

Lehder testified at trial that he met with Raul Castro and other senior Cuban officials in 1982 to negotiate an agreement that would allow cartel pilots to fly drug laden planes over Cuba on their way to the United States. Lehder's visit to Havana prompted Fidel Castro to play a more active role in the drug trade.

In September of 1982 the chief of America's intelligence department, Manuel Piñeiro and Castro's right hand, Osmani Cienfuegos, arrived in Panama to coordinate intelligence and narcotic activities. Shortly thereafter Manuel Noriega assumed control of Panama. At the same time Fidel Castro was meeting with Eden Pastora, Tomas Borge and other Sandinista leaders in Havana. According to Pastora, Castro said, "Follow my example. What you need to do is to whiten America with cocaine in order to destroy it."

In July of 1983, Jose Raul Perez Mendez, a Cuban intelligence officer, defected. In his debriefings he linked Raul Castro directly to drug operations. He added that Cuban intelligence had over three hundred intelligence officers engaged in espionage and drug trafficking in the United States.

Dr. Rachel Ehrenfeld's 1988 paper "Narco-Terrorism and the Cuban Connection" refers to a secret report by the U.S. Drug Enforcement Agency (DEA) published by The Miami Herald in November 1983 corroborating and dating Castro's participation in drug-trafficking into the U.S. from 1961.

Fidel and Raul Castro's involvement was so deep that Cuba was called in to mediate the dispute in Havana between Colombian drug lord Pablo Escobar and Panama's Manuel Noriega over the destruction of a drug lab in the Panamanian jungle at Darien on May 21, 1984. Another individual present at the meeting, Panamanian Jose Blandon, has likewise confirmed Fidel Castro's direct role. Blandon defected in 1988.

Jose Antonio Rodriguez Menier, a defecting Cuban intelligence officer, pointed that at some point Cuba decided to get into the drug market as a seller. They wanted a greater portion of the profits, because they knew the producers and the distributors. On August 7, 1984, William French Smith publicly denounced Cuba for participating in drug trafficking and linked the nefarious activity to terrorism. Francis Mullen, head of DEA, likewise linked the drug trafficking activities to terrorism.

In 1987 the Cubans ran into trouble. The Drug Enforcement Administration was electronically monitoring the activities of two racketeering organizations operating between Colombia, Cuba and Miami: The Ceballos clan operating in Colombia and the Ruiz clan in Miami.

As part of the investigation DEA agents started videotaping Chang's office. Fifty hours of videos during the next few months iced the Cuba case. There were multiple discussions about high ranking officials and protection by the Castro regime.

In 1989 the United States was on the verge again of indicting the Castro brothers and General Jose Abrantes. A plan was conceived to pull Abrantes from Cuba in the hopes that his arrest would lead to additional information against the Castro brothers, this time from a part of the Cuban cartel triumvirate.

The plan was named Operation Greyhound. It involved the U.S. Attorney's Office in the Southern District of Florida, United States Customs, DEA, and DIA. The Navy and Air Force were to respond. An elite Seal Team, a squadron of F-16 and E3 AWAC aircraft, also were to engage. A destroyer and a submarine would play backup roles.

The U.S. plan was then to arrest Abrantes on the high seas. On June 12, 1989, while under the watchful eye of United States Customs personnel, Fernandez was picked up by two individuals in a motor vehicle and disappeared. That night Division General Arnaldo Ochoa and Colonel Tony De La Guardia were arrested in Cuba. Cuba's DI was obviously all over the operation. The entire project had been compromised.

In 1989 Division General Arnaldo Ochoa returned to Cuba. The most decorated Cuban military officer, a hero of the revolution since 1959, and a triumphant leader of Castro's engagement in Angola. General Ochoa's career included heading a guerrilla cell in Venezuela while "Che" Guevara was in charge of a Cuban led revolutionary campaign in 1965 in Bolivia. From there Ochoa had gone to the Congo Brazzaville where he commanded 1,000 Cuban troops defending the country's leftist regime. He trained soldiers from Namibia, Mozambique, and South Africa.

After an extended command of the army in Havana up to 1971 he headed off in 1972 to direct the 500 man Cuban contingent training the army of Sierra Leone. During the 1973 Arab-Israeli war he trained Syrian forces in the Golan Heights. In 1975 he led nearly 4,000 Cuban troops in Zaire.

By 1976 he organized the popular militia in Addis Ababa and led 9,000 Cuban troops in Ethiopia's fight against Somalia during the regional war. By December of 1977 he was setting up armed forces in Granada for Prime Minister Maurice Bishop, and later provided training to guerrillas and soldiers from South Yemen, Syria, Vietnam, Lybia, Afghanistan, Iraq, and Laos. In 1983 he was dispatched to Nicaragua for the top assignment as military advisor to the Sandinista regime.

On Saturday May 27, 1989, Raul Castro ordered the surveillance of Transportation Minister Diocles Torralba's house. Torralba was the former head of the army's air defense forces and retained good contacts within the army.

At some point General Ochoa, Tony De La Guardia and Diocles Torralba began to discuss the defections of Major Florentino Aspillaga from Cuban intelligence and of Air Force General Rafael del Pino. Ochoa commented on the benefits of perestroika and the changing position of his former Soviet comrades in Angola relating to a shift towards democracy. Unbeknownst to the people attending the party, everything was being recorded by Raul Castro's surveillance team.

Four days later, on July 13, 1989, General Juan Escalona Reguera directed the execution of Major Amado Padron Trujillo, Captain Jorge Martinez Valdez, Colonel Tony De La

Guardia, and Division General Arnaldo Ochoa. Admiral Santamaria and Manuel Piñeiro survived.

T\the Attorney General himself at the time instructed a United States Attorney to refrain from filing an indictment that was already drafted as to other conduct by Raul and Fidel Castro.

On December 31, 1990, Reinaldo Ruiz died of a heart attack while in federal custody. On January 21, 1990, General Jose Abrantes died of a supposed heart attack after having always enjoyed perfect health. Rene Rodriguez Diaz, Johnny Crump's co-defendant and his link to Castro, died in late 1989 in Havana of a mysterious illness. Mario Estevez, the Cuban intelligence officer who implicated Rodriguez Diaz, also had an untimely demise in an American prison shortly thereafter.

The United States Coast Guard continued to observe drops of cocaine in Cuban territorial waters, commencing again soon after the Ochoa trial. According to U.S. Coast Guard Lt. Commander Karonis, planes were detected flying over Cuba, making air drops of drugs, and several nights in a row.

In early 1995, the "Lord of the Skies," Mexican cartel leader Amado Carrillo Fuentes, visited Cuba again. Despite repeated requests to the Cuban government by Mexican authorities to surrender him for prosecution, the Cuban government declined.

In January 1996, Jorge "Gordito" Cabrera, was arrested and charged with smuggling 5,828 pounds of cocaine from Colombia to Miami through the port of Havana. According to the testimony of Cabrera and three other cooperating witnesses, these operations had begun a year earlier, had the personal approval of Fidel and Raul Castro, and were conducted with the assistance of high-level Cuban government officials, including Manuel Pineiro[2].

The informants also described a previous massive shipment of 13,200 pounds of cocaine from Colombia in a Havana bound shipment of toilettries. At the time of his arrest, Cabrera was carrying a recent photo of himself with Fidel Castro[3].

The sophistication of Cuba's drug trafficking continued to develop, so did the ties with Colombian guerrillas. Cubans are now engaging in cocaine traffic through small airports in the Colombian jungle. Cocaine stashed in travel boxes is being ferried in Aero-taxi of Colombia planes. The Cubans move the cocaine from the source directly onto the larger airports where they in turn move it on Cubana Aviation flights.

The annual Patterns of Global Terrorism reports also continue to identify a number of terrorist organizations associated with Cuba: In Latin America: Guerrilla Army of the Poor's, a Guatemalan insurgent organization trained in Cuba. The Farabundo Marti National Front in El Salvador. Colombian National Liberation Army, organized by the Castro regime. Its main terrorist activities include kidnappings and extortion; and the Revolutionary Armed Forces of Colombia, the oldest and best-equipped in Colombia. It has received financial and military aid from Cuba and many of its members were trained in Havana.

Cuba provided advanced weapons and demolition training to the Tupac Amaru Revolutionary Movement (MRTA) in Peru. The Tupac Amaru attacked the U.S. Embassy in 1984; bombed the Texaco offices in 1985 and attacked the residence of the U.S. Ambassador in 1985 all in Lima, Peru.

The Cubans and the Sandinistas have been linked to the MRTA, a rapidly expanding Castroite urban terrorist organization that specializes in anti-U.S. actions. The MRTA's suspected Cuban-Nicaraguan connection emerged soon after the group began operating in late 1984. Peruvian security forces raided an MRTA training camp near Cuzco on November 27 and claimed to have seized weapons, olive-drab military uniforms, and medicines identified as having originated in Cuba and Nicaragua[4]. Former MRTA leader

Luis Varese Scotto is reported to have fought with the FSLN against the Somoza regime and to have undergone guerrilla training[5] in Cuba in 1981.

In other continents: Basque Separatist Movement. They commit violent terrorist acts in Spain. This group has close relations with the IRA, Irish Republican Army, and the most dangerous terrorist organization of Northern Ireland. The two groups have offices and safe haven in Cuba. Fatah: the arm section of the PLO. The Eritrean Liberation Front, fighting for secession from Ethiopia, actively supported by Cuba and Syria. The Polisario (People's Front for the Liberation of Western Sahara and Rio del Oro) created to fight against the Spanish-Moroccan-Mauritanian. This group enjoyed active support from Cuba, and has strong ties with Al Qaeda.

Cuba's support for ETA terrorism is well documented. Spanish intelligence sources have stated that throughout the 1990s, numerous members of ETA sought by authorities for multiple killings in Spain were known to have found refuge and support in Cuba[6]. At least 20 are still in Cuba today[7].

After a raid of ETA hideouts in Northern France, French intelligence seized documents that detailed Cuba's links to ETA spanning years. The papers provided, among other information, details of a 1992 ETA delegation visit with the Cuban Ministry of the Interior and the Communist Party. Cuban officials referred to their relationship with ETA as "fraternal, constant and strategic-stronger than ever.[8]

The evidence also pointed to the involvement of two senior Cuban intelligence agents in assisting six members of ETA in an escape from the Dominican Republic, where they were due for extradition hearings to Spain. Furthermore, a crackdown by Spanish intelligence of ETA's international financial operations revealed an "ETA conglomerate" in Cuba.

This is particularly revealing, since these transactions would require the highest authorization from the Castro regime[10]. Finally, to further confirm the Cuban Government's support for ETA, Castro refused to sign a resolution denouncing ETA terrorism at the 2000 Ibero-American Summit in Panama[11].

The Cuban Government continues to support and work with the Irish Republican Army. In August 2001 three IRA operatives were arrested by Colombia's security forces as part of "an international terrorist web" directly implicating Cuba. The IRA team's leader, Dubliner Niall Connolly, has been the Sinn Fein's "representative" in Cuba since 1996, and is said to have worked for the Cubans for at least 10 years. He reportedly spent four years at special military camps in Cuba, training in sophisticated weaponry and commando tactics.

In 2001, the U.S. position on Cuba was expressed fairly succinctly by Edmund Hull, the U.S. State Department's acting coordinator for counterterrorism[12]: "Cuba does remain on the list of state sponsors. Our problems with Cuba relate to its continuing provision of safe haven to wanted terrorists. They also have some associations with terrorist groups, like the ELN and the FARC in Colombia."

Intelligence experts in Colombia have told journalists that Cuba arranged for the IRA men to enter Colombia to train guerrillas of the Revolutionary Armed Forces of Colombia (FARC) in rebel- held territory. The training, directed by the Cuban Intelligence Directorate, was to help rebels assemble high-powered explosives[13] and anti-aircraft missiles, train guerrillas in developing remote detonation circuits for car bombs and mixing high-powered synthetic explosives to extend the range of gas cylinder mortars.

A London Mirror report points to the seriousness of the connections uncovered[14]: "Even more damaging for Sinn Fein are the stunning revelations that Connolly has run secret terrorist missions for the Cubans in Panama, Venezuela and Nicaragua. He gets his orders from the Cuban Intelligence station in the Spanish capital Madrid, where a spy center is run from the Cuban embassy. The European connection provides secret communication codes, false identities and flight tickets without arousing suspicion."

The 2001 Overview from Patterns of Global Terrorism report adds[15]: "A number of Basque ETA terrorists who gained sanctuary in Cuba some years ago continued to live on the island, as did several US terrorist fugitives. Havana also maintained ties to other state sponsors of terrorism and Latin American insurgents. Colombia's two largest terrorist organizations, the Revolutionary Armed Forces of Colombia and the National Liberation Army, both maintained a permanent presence on the island."

The implication of the report is that Cuba continues to not only to provide safe haven and training to Latin American terrorists, but also refuses to provide real cooperation in the War on Terror. Across the globe the Cubans are still significant players in subversion, terrorism, drug trafficking, kidnappings, and bank and armored car robberies.

Since he assumed power in Cuba, in 1959, Castro has fomented, trained, armed arid protected Puerto Rican terrorists in United States. His support for these activities was ratified in a combined resolution between Cuba and Iraq, at the UN in 1980, where they expressed that the aid given to the independents forces of Puerto Rico was not negotiable.

The FBI also learned that the Castro regime has provided training and sanctuary for a variety of Puerto Rican terrorist groups over the years. Among the weapons given the terrorists are M-16 rifles and anti-tank rockets traced to stocks that the U.S. abandoned in South Vietnam in 1975.

Castro was pursuing two objectives by the use of these groups: to demonstrate, by means of these attacks and sabotages, the vulnerability of the internal security of United States, and to dismantle the strategic U.S. military bases in Puerto Rico, which maintain the naval, air and electronic defense of the Caribbean Basin.

Fidel Castro's regime was the first foreign government to organize grand scale terrorist attacks within the United States.

It was through the Puerto Rican movement, that Castro first promoted groups to carry out such activities. But Castro also lent support to the leftist and Afro-American terrorist organizations that promoted violence as a method to fight inside the North American territory.

Among the first elements linked directly to Castro figured the Puerto Rican communists Juan Antonio Corretjer, Juan Mari Bras, Narciso Rabell Martinez and Filiberto Ojeda Rios, an obscure trumpet player that with time would become the axis of Cuban terrorism in Puerto Rico and the United States.

In 1961, Ojeda traveled to Cuba where the Cuban Government created for him the false identity of Felipe Ortega with which he was able to penetrate U.S. bases in Puerto Rico. It was at this time that Cuba helped create the Puerto Rican Authentic Movement (MAPA). In April of 1964, Puerto Rican authorities confiscated an arsenal belonging to MAPA and found documents that linked Cuba to the group. One month later, there came evidence that Cuba supplied armaments to MAPA, using the airport in Ponce.

In 1966 Ojeda Rios, together with Rabell and Jose Todd Pagan (linked to the East German STASI) participated in the Tricontinent Conference in Havana, where Castro connected them with other international terrorist organizations. It was there in Havana, during those days, that the Revolutionary Independents Movement (MIRA) was founded. Havana organized the armed branch of the MIRA, specialized in the use of explosive and sabotages, for which Ojeda, Rabell and Pagan had trained.

In March of 1968, Rabell and Pagan returned to Puerto Rico, and together with Corretjer, Wilson Cortes, David Feliciano and Hector Rodriguez, declared armed revolution, announcing the targeting of North American companies and direct actions against the FBI, the CIA and the national police[16].

In July 1968, the commandos of the MIRA destroyed the Sears store in Bayamon. A bombing campaign against banks, hotels, police headquarters, and in the offices of the Secret

Service followed. After organizing secret cells in Puerto Rico and in New York, Ojeda led the act of sabotage against the public library in Manhattan on December of 1969, and a wave of subsequent attacks in Puerto Rico.

Rabell, Ojeda and Pagan instructed their commandos in New York, facilitating their contacts with the Cuban delegation at the UN for the purpose of obtaining weapons and explosives. The Cuban Government made available mini-factories for weapons and bombs to these groups, just as it had done with the Tupamaros[17].

Some of the funds that Cuba sent the terrorists were channeled through Mari Bras and communist party member Juan Bautista Marquez. When Ojeda was arrested, they found Cuban technical manuals on explosive artifacts that were later presented as evidence before a Senate Judiciary Committee in Washington. But, Ojeda escaped after posting bond, and reappeared in San Juan, organizing the November 14 bomb attacks against numerous establishments.

The Department of the Americas, at the direction of Manuel Piñeiro, began to train Puerto Ricans on an ongoing basis at Guanabo, Cuba. At one point there were six hundred receiving terrorist training to be carried out upon homeland targets.

The links between Cuba and the Puerto Rican terrorists were detailed in the FBI Annual Report[18], December of 1973: "approximately 135 leaders of subversive groups of Puerto Rican independents have traveled to communist Cuba for indoctrination and/or training. Many of them received extensive instruction in guerrilla war tactics, preparation of explosive artifacts and sophisticated methods of sabotage".

The Puerto Rican terrorist organization, Armed Forces of National Liberation (FALN), began its operations in 1974. Upon returning to New York in 1974, Ojeda publicly announced the decision to fight "the empire" from within with any and all weapons; he then regrouped, within the National Liberation Armed Forces (FALN), different terrorist groups on the advice of Cuban intelligence officers Julian

Torres Rizo and Alina Alayo Amaro (alias Adelfa), both specialists on the United States.

The Cuban officers oversaw the training of the FALN cadres in explosives and urban terrorism. In 1977, a former member of FALN was interviewed in "Time" magazine and stated that he had received guerrilla training in Cuba, that friendly contacts in Cuba and the Dominican Republic provided FALN with arms and explosives, and that funds for the terrorist group and from wealthy radicals, bank robberies, and drug smuggling.

Moreover, the governor of Puerto Rico pointed out that the FALN was working in coordination with black North American terrorists of the Weather Underground as well as with the Cuban DGI. The Puerto Rican connections to members of the Weather Underground, like Katherine Boudin, were confirmed by Corretjer himself in a press interview[19]: "FALN was operating in close association with Castro's DGI (General Directorate of Intelligence) to carry out a campaign of urban terrorism like the Tupamaros did in Uruguay."

The reopening of the Puerto Rican "second front" by the FALN took the form of attacks (49 in total) against banks, corporate offices, and department stores in New York. In September and October of 1974, the Cubans provided logistical support for the FALN movement to explode bombs in City Hall and the police station in Newark, New Jersey, as well as at five other sites, including Rockefeller Center in Manhattan, New York.

The most spectacular attack took place January 24, 1975 at the French Tavern restaurant in Wall Street, where 4 people died and 55 were wounded. It was not until November 1976 that the authorities caught up with the wave of explosions perpetrated by the FALN, when the Chicago police occupied their safe houses[20].

In an address to the press, President Gerald Ford sent a message to Havana[21]: "There are those who seek to distort the facts, to mislead others about our relationship with Puerto

Rico. Those who might be inclined to interfere in our freely-determined relations should know that such an act will be considered intervention in the domestic affairs of Puerto Rico and of the United States, an unfriendly act which will be resisted by appropriate means."

As for Ojeda, he remained hidden until 1976 at the Cuban U.N. mission, where he was detected, fleeing to Puerto Rico. There he founded another terrorist organization that became famous, the Macheteros. Under the guidance of the Cubans intelligence operatives Mario Monzon and Alfredo Garcia Almeida, Ojeda moved to Paris, where they introduced him to Ilich Ramirez (Carlos the Jackal), and to the terrorist branch of the PLO.

The extremist organization, the Dominican Republic Resistance, was also incorporated to Ojeda's circle, and some months later, several Dominicans were arrested in Puerto Rico[22]. One of them, Victor Moral admitted that he had been trained by the PLO, and that he operated with Carlos the Jackal, in Europe, who, following orders from Havana transferred him to the Puerto Ricans. Governor Hernandez Colon himself accused Castro in 1976 of being the hand behind the Dominicans who robbed banks in Puerto Rico in order to finance terrorist activities[23].

Castro also arranged for the Chilean MIR -at the time of President Salvador Allende- to train and arm gangs of Puerto Rican terrorists. After the fall of Chilean President Allende, the training was centered in Cuba. Around 600 Puerto Ricans were trained in Guanabo, and some of them participated in the Cuban invasions of Angola and Ethiopia[24].

In August of 1978 the Macheteros gunned down a policeman in Naguabo, and one month later, they stole 500 pounds of ammonium nitrate, tobex dynamite, irmenite cartridges, detonators and wicks.

After the Sandinista victory in 1979, Havana centralized all the Puerto Rican terrorists under the control of Ojeda, including Corretjer and Federico Cintron. Argentine born Cuban intelligence agent Jorge Massetti helped funnel Cuban funds to finance Puerto Rican terrorists belonging to the Machetero group.

Two months later, the Macheteros, armed with AK-47 rifles, ambushed a U.S. navy bus in Sabana Seca, killing two marines and wounding nine. In March of 1980, U.S. authorities detained a Puerto Rican commando that was planning to attack the electoral precincts during the George Bush and Jimmy Carter's presidential elections.

In January of 1981 the terrorists attacked the military airport at Isla Verde where they destroyed nine U.S. fighter planes. The active measure, planned in Havana, was executed in a total of seven minutes as part of a strike and flight objective.

On March 1 the Macheteros parked a car bomb in the basement of the convention center in El Condado, in order to blow up Secretary of State Henry Kissinger. Had a detonator exploded properly on March 15, 1981, the Macheteros would have killed Henry Kissinger[25].

Between 1975 and 1981 the Puerto Rican commandos perpetrated 260 acts of violence in the Island and a hundred in the United States. William Webster, director of the FBI, testified in Congress, in December of 1981, that the series of terrorist incidents suggested multiple types of support from Cuba to the independents Puerto Rican movement.

In February of 1982, the FALN reemerged under the leadership of Luis Rosado with four dynamite attacks in the Wall Street financial district. The Cuban secret services were able to coordinate the FALN with two groups of North American terrorists: The May-19 and the Black Liberation Army[26]. As part of their investigation the FBI confiscated a list of objectives, heading the list was President Ronald Reagan.

In August 1983, the FALN carried out an attack in Washington, against the Navy's computer center, and in of June of 1983, the leader of the Macheteros Carlos "Puma" Rodriguez was arrested for bank robberies totaling 2.5 million dollars. The "Puma" Rodriguez's passport showed two trips to Cuba, just before the assaults[27].

In one of the most daring attacks, on September 2nd of that year, the Macheteros stole $7 million dollars from the offices of the Wells Fargo in the city of Hartford, Connecticut, the second largest robbery in the history of the United States. The robbery was planned by Ojeda and Juan Segarra Palmer, who had visited Cuba on several occasions during that time.

After an FBI investigation of a 1983 Wells Fargo depot robbery, thirteen members of the Puerto Rican terrorist group, the Macheteros, were arrested in Massachusetts, Puerto Rico, and Texas. A federal grand jury in August 1985 indicted seventeen people for the Wells Fargo robbery and for shipping most of the stolen funds to Cuba. One of those indicted, Victor Manuel Gerena, has been given sanctuary in Cuba.

After the assault, Segarra Palmer crossed the Mexican border in an RV with double floors where Victor Manuel Gerena, one of the attackers, was hiding along with the first $2 million, to be sent to Cuba. In Mexico the Cuban intelligence officials Fernando Comas, Jose Arbessu and Jorge Masetti were expecting them.

In March of 1984, the FBI detected the same RV crossing the border with Mexico[28]. In an interview granted to the Miami Herald, Masetti, who defected from Cuba in the 90's, said that in February of 1983, Arbessu gave the Macheteros false passports and $50,000 to finance the operation; and that he personally issued false documentation to Gerena so he could escape to Havana[29].

On October 30, 1983, the Macheteros Luis Colon and the Gonzalez brothers fired an LAW-M-72 anti-tank rocket against the FBI offices in San Juan, in reprisal for the U.S. invasion of Grenada. The rocket serial number showed that it belonged to the armaments left behind by the United States in Vietnam, an arsenal that was transferred to Cuba.

An FBI recording of Ojeda, days after the incident, revealed a plan to introduce 30 kilos of plastic explosives through the Mexican border as part of a shipment of arms and grenades supplied by Havana[30]. In January 1985 the

Macheteros strike again when they attacked with rockets the U.S. Supreme Court in San Juan.

Again, the rockets had been supplied by Cuba[31]. Secretary of State George Schultz stated on November 11, 1986 that Cuba distributed those weapons to the subversive elements in Latin America. Also, William H. Webster, /director of the FBI, stated that[32]: "Cuba's aggressive support of terrorism has not gone unnoticed."

In September of 1985, the FBI was able to arrest Ojeda, together with twelve known Macheteros. The Grand Jury accused Ojeda of working with the Cuban services and for participating in the Wells Fargo holdup. The evidence produced by the Attorney General's office showed that several Macheteros, Ojeda among others, had maintained permanent contacts in Mexico with the DGI[33]. Under pressure from Castro, the Mexican government freed Machetero William (Guillermo) Morales, who departed for Havana immediately.

Cuba, 90 miles from the U.S., has two powerful spy stations in the outskirts of Havana. One built by the former Soviet Union and still updated and maintained, and another built by China. Both of these stations are actively engaged in collecting military, economic and civilian information and are certainly sharing their findings with terrorists worldwide.

Cuba has the ability to use "Imint", "Sigint", "Humint", "Masint", and open source analysis to develop all source intelligence products for Cuba's political and military planners.

Cuba has one of the most sophisticated "Sigint" programs in the world. The main facility is, of course, the Bejucal base, west of La Habana and less than 100 miles from Key West. The "Sigint" facility at Bejucal is one of the largest and most sophisticated "Sigint" collection facilities in the world. The complex is manned by approximately 1,000 Cuban personnel, and is capable of monitoring a wide array of commercial and government communications throughout the United States, and between the United States and Europe[34].

Bejucal intercepts transmissions from microwave towers in the United States, communication satellite downlinks, and a wide range of short-wave and high-frequency radio transmissions. It also serves as a mission ground station and analytical facility. It can monitor all U.S. military and civilian geosynchronous communications satellites. It monitors all White House communications activities, launch control communications and telemetry from NASA and Air Force facilities at Cape Canaveral, financial and commodity wire services, and military communications links[35].

The Cubans operate "Sigint" collection sites in over 30 countries from diplomatic protected embassies, consulates, trade delegations, and residences. These activities are prominent in Europe and the U.S. The Cubans used Russian "Elint" satellites. Presently, they are using Chinese satellites.

The PRC has a number of programs that can provide Measurement and Signature Intelligence "Masint" data. They use infrared detection capabilities similar to those provided by the U.S. Defense Support Program (DSP) satellite system. Cuba and China have signed an agreement, in 1999, to cooperate in all of these areas[36].

The engineer Manuel Cereijo who has been studying the Cuban capabilities in cyber-terrorism, biological weapons and espionage, Cuba has the capacity and the technology to carry out electronic eavesdropping, computer networks intrusion and destruction through electromagnetic radiation.

Also, according with the engineer Cereijo Cuba has done extensive studies on electromagnetic radiation weapons capable of destroying microelectronic equipment from a two miles distance radius; and regularly develops computer viruses "with the intent of using them to disrupt computer systems during time of war or crisis." Many Cuban Americans in the U.S. have had their computers damaged by made-in-Cuba viruses. In a September 1997 article by Jonathan T. Stride titled Who Will Check Out Fidel Castro's New Chemical/Biological Weapons Plant in East Havana, Castro's chemical/biological weapons factories are exposed – based on a Confidential Report translated from Spanish on February 1997.

Castro's regime has spent more than $1 billion to set up a scientific infrastructure that, former Secretary of Defense William Cohen said in 1998, could support an offensive biological-warfare program. In 1995 the U.S. Office of Technological Assessment included Cuba among 17 countries believed to possess biological weapons.

In 2000, Ken Alibek, former deputy director of Biopreparat, the Soviet Union's biological-weapons program, revealed that a few years after Castro's visit to the Soviet Union in 1981, Cuba had one of the most sophisticated genetic-engineering labs in the world.

In his summary Betancourt says, "It has been widely commented that the CIA has found that the genetic and bio-technology industry, one of Castro's pet projects, is nothing but a cover for developing biological weapons. This industry is housed in a complex of buildings in the Miramar zone of Havana, some of which are reported to have the usual security measures associated with biological weapons development[37].

Beginning as early as 1992 as part and means of the conspiracy, "trained officers of the Cuban Directorate of Intelligence (DI) took up residence in South Florida and carried out clandestine activities. The Cuban spy network was known as the Wasp Network.

The Wasp Network continued its operations which included efforts at penetration of U.S. military installations, including MacDill Air Force Base, in Tampa. But on September 12, 1998, the Wasp Network agents were arrested. Among the witnesses, Lt. General James R. Clapper, former director of the Defense Intelligence Agency, testified that the objective of the group was "to get their hands on U.S. national defense secrets."

Seized from the Wasp Network were some interesting documents. A decrypted document labeled as DF-101(e) AA (f1.WPD) and introduced at the spy trial, states that, "the general idea of all of this, which is under your control, is to operate in an area and be able to move persons as well as things, including arms and explosives, between our country and the U.S. for that concept, suggest other subjects that we might not have in mind."

Inevitably on January 14, 1996, Operation Scorpion was approved by Fidel Castro authorizing the downing of Brothers to the Rescue planes. On February 24, 1996, two Cuban Air Force interceptors, a MiG 29-UB and a MiG 23-ML, took off from the Cuban airbase at San Antonio de los Baños for a second time that day to carry out Scorpion. The first BTTR airplane was destroyed, twenty miles from the Cuban coast. The second plane was also destroyed in international airspace minutes later. A second set of Cuban interceptors then went up, and according to recorded radio transmissions, gave chase to the third plane. Fidel Castro later acknowledged to Dan Rather of CBS news, when interviewed, that he gave the order.

On a related front, on June 30, 2001, a high ranking immigration official in Miami was convicted of violating the U.S. espionage act and lying on national security forms. Mariano Faget's conviction was based on his disclosure of classified information, converting government property in the form of secrets to his own use, and lying on a national security form about contacts with a Cuban official.

On September 22, 2001, a couple, Marisol and George Gari, became the sixth and seventh spies convicted in the massive FBI investigation into the Wasp Network. Gari had been ordered to work at the U.S. Southern Command headquarters in Miami in an infiltration attempt directed by the Cuban DI. On May 30, 2002, another spy, Juan Emilio Aboy, was caught trying to infiltrate the U.S. Military Southern Command as

Castro's DI continued its activities despite the official government statement disseminated to the media and the world.

On September 19, 2001, the official declaration of Cuba relating to the World Trade Center tragedy suggested that the United States was going to "utilize the painful tragedy to impose methods, prerogatives and privileges, which would lead the most powerful tyranny in the world to impose itself on all the peoples of the world."

On the same day, Ana Belen Montes was arrested in Washington, D.C., only ten days after the national tragedy at the World Trade Center and the Pentagon. She was the highest ranking intelligence officer on Cuba working at the Defense Intelligence Agency (DIA).

The timing of her arrest was the result of increasing contact after September 11, 2001, between Montes and Cuban intelligence. Because of Washington's concern that Montes was providing information to the Cubans, which in turn was being passed on to Cuban intelligence allies (all enemies of the United States) the investigation was shut down and her arrest was effectuated.

She became the seventeenth Cuban spy arrested since September of 1998 on U.S. soil. She stood accused of an ongoing conspiracy to transmit highly classified documents to the Cuban government relating to the national defense of the United States and the fraudulent evaluation of Cuba's military and intelligence threat to America.

Montes had access to satellite imaging, foreign communications intercepted by U.S. intelligence activity and espionage in other countries. Montes had been sending information to Cuba since 1991 about US military maneuvers and naval exercises of the Atlantic Command. Cuba shared that information with other hostile governments and terrorist states, like Libya, Iran, Syria and Iraq.

As part of her active measures directed from Cuba, she prepared fraudulent reports and disinformation to the Southern Command, the Secretary of Defense, and U.S.

intelligence agencies, which downplayed the reality of Cuba's armed forces and their intelligence capabilities. Montes also acknowledged giving the names of secret agents that operated in Cuba on behalf of the United States.

On January 2, 2003, Brazil's newly elected president, Luis Ignacio Lula de Silva, announced a leftist alliance in Latin America which would include Hugo Chavez, the president of Venezuela, and Fidel Castro, the Cuban dictator. Lula characterized the association as the "axis of good."

Yet it is Cuban security at the direction of the Cuban Directorate of Intelligence, who provided protection for President Chavez. As part of the "axis of good" alliance an entourage of Cuban security arrived in Rio de Janeiro to protect President Lula de Silva and provide appropriate intelligence and security training. Commander Hal Feeney, U.S. Navy Retired, a special mission veteran and expert on Cuban intelligence, has often remarked, "the long arm of the Cuban DI extends across the globe."

As a result of Fidel Castro's ongoing activities we suffer at least two kinds of loss. Castro and his Directorate of Intelligence broker information to Iran, Iraq, Libya and Syria. The Cubans gather it; the terrorist states use it.

The psychopathology
of a despot

Being located at the conjunction of the Tigris and Euphrates rivers, the region of the present-day Iraq has been easy prey for any conqueror army. In that sense, the invasion of Hussein to Kuwait in 1991 was the latest chapter of an aged rivalry between Egypt and Mesopotamia for regional pre-eminence, sinking on the night of the human history.

After the breakdown of the Ottoman Empire in 1918, Iraq was invented by England, the "Perfidious Albion", from three provinces (Mosul, Baghdad, and Basrah) that had nothing to do with each other. This artificial state has survived to this day without bursting into pieces only because who fared it, (always Sunni rulers), did so on the basis of bloody repression.

The Iraqi´s central Government of the 20th century was the instrument used by an ethno-religious community to benefit from oil revenues and oppress the remaining.

The Iraqi population of 22 million inhabitants is divided into three basic groups: Kurds in the northeast, the Muslims of the Sunni stream in the Centre and the Muslims of the Shiite power in the South[1]. Turkmen, Armenian, Assyrian and Chaldean Christians, Yazd's syncretism, the Mandaeans and Jews constitute the rest.

The Shiites, although they reside mainly in the South, are most in Baghdad. The Sunnis, despite being a minority with respect to the other two fundamental ethnicities, had being in command of all aspects of the Government, the army, the economy, politics and society, exerting a discriminatory and exclusionary control.

The non-existent nation of Kurdistan in political or geographical maps is a reality much more stable than the states of the region officially recognized by the world community. Twenty million Kurds inhabit the Taurus and Zagros mountain ranges, ignored by negotiators from the postwar period that shaped the Middle East States.

Kurdistan is parceled out and its parts have fallen in various neighboring countries, such as the eastern Turkey, Iran, and the former Soviet Union, Syria and Iraq. Unlike other countries of Africa, the Balkans, the Middle East and Central Asia, Kurdistan has more than two millennia of geographical, economic, cultural, religious and demographic coherence. The Kurds do not accept the division of their nation at the borders.

Constituted in political party for the entire Arab world in 1947, divided into regional commands, the Baas could succeed in Syria and Iraq, thanks to two coups that decided to cover with the ideological mantle of such an organization.

Behind an ancient wall that borders the Iraqi town of Qurna, a small double trunk apple tree still lies, -one of the thousands who abound throughout the Middle East- which stands out for a bronze plaque which announces the visitor they are in the "Garden of Eden".

These Iraqi claims, and the biblical Eden were parts of the megalomania of Saddam Hussein. While a millennia back Iraq[2] was the center of civilization, this past urged her to play again such splendor.

The propaganda that Saddam Hussein manipulated, rather than glorified, that distant past (such as the famous eye for an eye, tooth for a tooth from the code of Hammurabi); manifesting a discrepancy between the current reality and the ancient Babylonian glories of the "thousand and one nights" of school textbooks.

Saddam Hussein sought to recreate those days of medieval Islam when Baghdad was the center of an empire that stretched from North Africa to Asia Minor. That's why in Baghdad there was a colossal statue of two hands that ragged a scimitar, copies of the hands of Saddam Hussein. His photos, in all corners of Iraq, were placed next to the effigies of the Babylonian King Nebuchadnezzar and Saladdin, the defender against the Crusaders.

Saddam Hussein was raised by his uncle Khair Allah Tulfah, who was a prominent member of an Iraqi Pro-Nazi Organization during World War II. From him he inherited his admiration for the Nazi principles, which led him to join the nationalist Baas movement, whose philosophy also rested in the national German socialism and Italian fascism.

It was the era in which student Saddam Hussein, an admirer of the Bolshevik Vladimir I. Lenin joined the clandestine Socialist Pan-Arab Bass Party in Baghdad. He then organized the party militia, headed by General Hassan Al-Baker, he was part of the group that machined-gun the then President General Abdullah Karim Kassem in 1963. After the elimination of the President, Saddam miraculously escaped with a wound, from which extracted the projectile in cold blood, and then sought refuge in Syria and finally Egypt.

After the uprising against General Karim Kassem, the Egyptian President Nasser allies dominate Baghdad until July 1968, when Saddam Hussein was part of the coup that overthrew General Abdel Salam Aref, being the real power after the throne.

After a coup in 1972, Saddam Hussein emerged as the number two figure, behind the General Ahmed Hassan Al-Bakr, assuming the head of the internal security services. The nationalization of oil and the boom of 1973 would give him the means to a policy of intensive development, in accordance with his ambitions.

But the handling of Iraq is in the grip of three protagonists, which erected a formidable military machine in the middle. The preponderance of the Tikrit clan in key army positions, party of Government and intelligence agencies led the Iraqi historian Hanna Batatu to show that it was not the Baas who ruled, but the Tikriti through the Baas.

During Saddam Hussein era, Iraq was a country that functioned in many ways as a subsidiary of whole ownership of his family. This tribal loyalty and blood ties formed a small plutocracy of allies and relatives who took over the high positions of the administration, army and security.

Saddam Hussein grouped his power around tribal loyalty and ties of blood; a small plutocracy of allies and relatives, especially of the paternal clan of Al-Mahid, the mother's Tufalh, and the Rashid clan of his cousins, hogged the highest administrative, army and security positions.

The intimate claque of Saddam consisted of the following. Qusay Hussein, his youngest son, responsible for repression and who headed the famous punishment in 1995 against the Al-Dulaim tribes, and the local Shiite rebellion in 1997. Uday Hussein, his eldest son, would be noticeable for his killer instincts and the rape of women and girls, responsible for smuggling in Iraq and illicit financial transactions. His brother-in-law Adnan Hairala occupied the position of Defense Minister.

His cousin, Hussein Rashid, would be the Chief of presidential security; another cousin, Ali Hasan Al-Mahid, head of the secret police, known as "Chemical Ali" or the "Butcher of Kurdistan" by the atrocities committed in the repression against the Kurds in 1987 and 1988 during the Anfal campaign.

Another of their relatives, Mohammed Hamza Al-Zubaidi, was highlighted by violently suppressing the Shiite uprisings in 1991. Also a relative, Alí Salih Numan, former Governor of the occupied territory of Kuwait, ordered the destruction of the Shiite Holy places. Others from his court were Tariq Aziz, Izzat Ibrahim Al-Duri, Barzan Ibrahim Al-Tikriti, and Watban Ibrahim Al-Tikriti.

Wrapped in a state of almost permanent war, Syria and Iraq were dominated by brutal military dictatorships, to which should be added that of the Baas. In both Baghdad and Damascus, the power rested not in Government or party, but in a sort of on top direction, cemented by friendship or kinship: in Syria, with the clan Assad's from the Alawite minority; and in Iraq, with the Tikrit the family of Saddam Hussein's tribal clan.

His aura was coming from his hometown, Tikrit, birthplace of Saladin, the legendary Kurdish Warrior of the Byzantine era who defeated the European Crusaders in Jerusalem.

Even though the political logic pointed to an alliance between the Syrian Hafez El-Assad and the Iraqi Saddam Hussein being members of the same party, the Baas, there was a rupture. In 1975, an element of friction would be born from the dispute of the Syrian project to build a dam on the waters of the Euphrates River, which runs through both countries.

This issue, and the deadly clash between both Baas sections, is the paradox of deadly confrontation that would face the Baas in Syria with the one from Iraq, where the age-old rivalry with regard to the Euphrates, of the benefits of the Kirkuk-Mediterranean pipeline, would explain it all.

Among the main elements of the grievance lies the demotion and expulsion from Syria of the Group loyal to Michel Aflak, founder of the Baas. Aflak then seek refuge in Baghdad, and likewise, the other powerful Baas leader and ideologue, Zaki Arsuzi, who was a member of the minority Muslim sect of Alawites, from where Hafez Al-Assad emerged.

Syria and Iraq were torpedoing a peaceful settlement in the area, where the factor of containment was a militarily more powerful Israel. Syria always longed control over of Lebanese ports, reclaiming the territories which formerly belonged to the greater Syria; i.e., part of the Lebanon, Israel and Turkey. But Syria, a historical customer of the Soviet Union, while openly didn´t seek annexation to the Lebanon - rather indirect control of domestic politics- has been the zone's most brutal and repressive regime.

Iraq, for its part, would incline more than Syria to the West, but always pointed toward the annexation of its neighbors and an outlet to the Persian Gulf. Paradoxically, the current crisis has led the West to improve relations with Syria, its mortal enemy.

There came together at a single site, under the heavy hand of a single despot, weapons of mass destruction, the state support for international terrorism, armed invasion to their neighbors, smuggling of petroleum and an ongoing assault on human rights.

Saddam Hussein was a preacher of Pan-Arabism and the Arab unity, but directed from Baghdad. This explained his desire to overthrow the Royal Saudi family and his constant aspiration to annex Kuwait, despite the defeat in the Gulf war, as a way to eliminate the artificial colonial borders and define more "modern" Arab States.

Also, he initiated two bloody wars and launched constant public threats, urging the overthrow of the rulers of Saudi Arabia, Kuwait and Iran. As an Orthodox Sunni, he found the perfect enemy in Iranian fundamentalism. Thus he rejected agreements that divided the strategic track of Chat Al-Arab, appointment of legendary rivers Tigris and Euphrates, starting the war in 1980.

Earlier, in 1975, the Iranian armies of the Shah defeated him on that same site and for that same reason. Iraq who then invaded Iran and captured the oil of the Khuzestan region was one of the wealthiest nations of the Middle East, profoundly anti-West and with military pacts with the ex-Soviet Union.

Having imagined Washington that the potential transformation of Syria in the regional superpower, with his anti-Israel crusade, and furthermore that the Iranian theocracy harbored designs to swallow the oil States of the Gulf, it accepted Iraq claims that the Gulf States should sustain him financially in its war with Iran.

Hussein was seen as a lesser evil, because it served the strategic interests of the West by wearing down the ambitions of the Ayatollah Khomeini and Syrian Hafiz Al-Assad.

In the words of the then Assistant Secretary of Defense, Richard Lee Armitage, "a cold calculation in favor of Iraq" to remove Soviet influence and promote its modernization and regional influence, and at the same time open a valuable market to the United States.

Despite Israeli alarms about the anti-Semitic intentions of Hussein, United States, Europe and Japan (pigheaded in their confrontation with the Libyan Muammar Gadhafi and with "la bête noire", the Iranian fundamentalism), lined up with Hussein, error they later will pay.

Thus, in Washington emotions against Shiite fundamentalism prevailed, giving credit to the Iraqi propaganda of Ayatollah's fanatical human waves who threatened to "break down" the civilized world. But this bloody conflagration of trenches between Iran and Iraq, in which Saddam Hussein was trying to appropriate an oil country and assume the political leadership of the Arab world, at the end favored an Iran with higher demographics.

By 1985, Saddam Hussein's Republican Guard was expelled from Iranian territory; desperate, he declared war on civilian facilities, platforms and oil tankers, introducing terror throughout the Persian Gulf. In the North, the Iraqis also gassed the Kurds, and finally fulminated Tehran and other Iranian cities with missiles and chemical weapons.

Thus, the war with Iran would qualify as the bloodiest after the II World War, in which the prisoners were sanctioned to die of hunger. The conflict he unleashed against Iran cost $60 billion dollars, more than 300,000 Iraqi casualties and a million dead in total, the destruction of cities and facilities, breach of Arab banks and the fall in oil exports.

Excluded from the American list of terrorist States, and suspended the criticism to his human rights violations, Saddam Hussein escaped international censure only because his enemy was the Ayatollah Khomeini.

It is curious that the profound implications of this war without precedent would not be understood at that time, which repeated in the Middle East the preamble of World

War II, for a leader "elected and pure" with Napoleonic plans, which violated prohibitions of the Quran, such as hostage-taking. Nobody raised their voice when Saddam Hussein destabilized the Lebanon arming the Maronite Christians, or when he illegally acquired components for his nuclear and biochemical weapons programs.

Baghdad was a nest of Palestinian terrorists and Saddam Hussein was not developing weapons of mass destruction to show them on display.

The interest of Saddam Hussein on chemical weapons dated back to 1967, when with the help of German experts raised a small plant. In 1976 the French built the Osiris reactor in Tammuz, and three years later the Israeli spy agency, Mossad, blew in Toulon two reactors destined for Baghdad.

A year later, the Egyptian physicist Yahya Meshad, head of the Iraqi Atomic bomb project, was gunned down at the Meridian Hotel in Paris. On June 7, 1981 an electrifying Israeli air strike demolished the nuclear center of Tammuz.

The careless laws of the former Federal Germany about the export of nuclear and chemical materials enabled the company Imhausen Chemie to give Iraq a powerful chemical arsenal[3], as well as the former East Germany. The Austro–German company SAAB-16 and German Messerschmitt developed his rocketry, and already in December 1989 Iraq experimented with rockets of medium-range with high-explosive warheads.

The German consortium Karl Kolb and the signing of Hamburg WET formed part of this traffic of horror. In June 1990 Iraq acquired the Swiss company Chmidt Mechanics, specializing in high technology to process uranium. Meanwhile, the English TDG provided them with accuracy machinery for metal components of rocketry, and the nuclear program.

A group of French corporations, which features companies such as Protec, LeVide, Carbone Loraine, De Dietrich France, SVCM, Pirep and Prevost, formed part of the network where chemical materials have journeyed through. The United States Customs seized a shipment of potassium fluoride destined for Iraq in April 1985, decisive element to create nerve gas. By 1988, ALCOLAC of Baltimore sent him finally the chemical ingredients to manufacture mustard gas, while New York's Nu-Kraft assessed the manufacturing technique.

The administrations of Ronald Reagan and George Bush (father) challenged the military sanctions that Israelites demanded to Iraq. It was a result of the invasion of Kuwait that this American *realpolitik* varied sharply. France, Germany, Switzerland and Great Britain being silent accomplices of the Iraqi nuclear and chemical weapons infrastructure, got alarmed.

Iraq weaponized the lethal botulinum substance and reported to the United Nations that it had more than nineteen hundred liters in its possession, including a hundred bombs (five hundred pounds each) filled with the agent. Botulinum toxin is considered by USAMRIID to be the most lethal substance known to humankind. It is easy to find and cultivate in a laboratory environment. It was used in World War II to assassinate the Nazi leader Heydrich[4].

The Iraqi move for regional hegemony was predictable. With a war debt by $100 billion dollar, a huge army unoccupied and disappointed, and not receiving from his "Islamic brothers" economic benefits after 8 years of bloody clashes against Iran, the bitterness of Saddam Hussein headed against the rich sheiks of the Persian Gulf.

Saddam Hussein considered that the Arab-Israeli dispute, the Communist collapse, the German unification, the evaporation of the Cold War and the East-West rivalry in regional conflicts would distract the international powers from his run against Kuwait.

He was hoping to solve his economic problems with a brutal military-financial transaction appropriating Kuwait, suddenly becoming regional military power and, with half of the oil reserves on the planet, dictating the behavior of the global economy. Months earlier, he had negotiated the spoils of his future conquest with the Danish firm Volker Stevin, to dredge an exit channel to the Persian Gulf.

One of his vulnerabilities was his tendency to over-extend and cling to positions difficult to sustain, as the invasion of Iran in 1980, or his attacks on tankers in the Persian Gulf in 1984, or the use of weapons of mass destruction, or to deny see himself defeated by Iran. In the same category we can include his decision to remain in Kuwait at all costs or else his obstinacy in the development of biochemical and nuclear weapons.

It was the military and political preeminence of Saddam Hussein in the Arab world, sculpted with the help of NATO, that contributed to his schematic and simplistic vision of a "paralyzed" West, being that his erroneous calculation in relation to Kuwait.

In 1990 he invaded Kuwait, establishing in the short time of his occupation a regime of terror, looting and burning across the country. In a ruin without sense and large-scale environmental, it burned more than one thousand oil wells, while deliberately opened pipelines that spilled 11 million barrels of oil in the waters of the Persian Gulf. A spot of 40 kilometers long and 12 wide, in what was the single largest ever oil spill, with incalculable damage to the marine ecology.

Saddam Hussein's Iraq had the means and requirements to master its environment, and remaining in power without international control would again recover such hegemony; especially if his plans to strengthen his military capability with weapons of mass annihilation had crystallized in the absence of a powerful regional opponent.

The Iraqi invasion to Kuwait proved that force was the only instrument of solution to any conflict in the Arab world. His neighbors encouraged a military Alliance against Baghdad convinced that Saddam Hussein would continue his expansion throughout the Arab Peninsula, to Syria, Lebanon, and eventually Israel and Iran.

Hussein manipulated the televised images of Iraq that the world saw; manufacturing tragedies and suffering, blaming them on the West, like when attributed hunger and medical crises, caused by himself, to the United Nations, United States and its allies. He also placed simple citizens in dangerous military points, as human shields during the Gulf war, locating military equipments nearby mosques and cultural monuments.

The majority of the Iraqi population was contrary to the Government of Saddam Hussein. His Government was autocratic and violent, and his political police famous for the tortures. There was neither organized nor rival opposition of consideration. Saddam Hussein murdered his mentor, who he knew from childhood, arrested his brother and hanged his cousin. It was customary to engage their Ministers and senior officials in the platoons of execution of political prisoners, to secure their loyalties.

The discontent didn't end with the Shiites from the South: it spread to the ethnic group of the Kurds in the North, which had been repeatedly suppressed. Such was the cause for the challenge to his personal power, with more than 15 assassination attempts, and far from what the visual media presented.

Saddam Hussein could not stand competition; thus, in 1969 came to order the assassination of Yasser Arafat to discover that many members of the Baas adhered with more fervor to the Palestinians than to his person. On one occasion Saddam Hussein sent a group of religious sheikhs to confer with Kurdish leader Mustafa Barzani. One of the sheikhs plotted to bring to the meeting a recorder with a bomb, which exploded when Barzani himself pressed the button, killing the religious sheikhs, but miraculously sparing the Kurdish leader.

Also in 1969 took place the famous hanging of Jews in Baghdad, and in the middle of the war with Iran, he ordered the execution of officers who stood out, like his cousin, general Maher Abdel Rashid, the conqueror of Fao. What's more, during the Kuwait invasion he shot 200 officials who questioned his decisions. His faithful Nazim Kzar, who also took part in the famous hanging of Jews in Baghdad in 1969, was eliminated by his instructions in 1972.

In 1979 Saddam Hussein unleashed a bloody repression on its opponents within the Baas party and army, and managed to expel from power the then President Ahmad Hassan Al-Bakr. In those events he personally directed platoons firing squad, which executed 34 figures of the Government and the army, as well as intimate collaborators, accused of conspiring. From that moment, no one questioned his legitimacy. To legitimize his regime, Saddam Hussein added to his team the Baas party, with Michel Aflak on the lead.

According to Max van der Stoel, former Special Reporter of the UN for Iraq, the Baghdad Government was "the dictatorship and the most ruthless totalitarian regime that ever was in the world since the Second World War". The Commission on human rights of the UN, Amnesty International and Human Rights Watch, denounced for many years this relentless machinery of imprisonment, torture and executions to disaffected, clerics and military, relatives of political dissidents and defectors.

Saddam sparked a crusade against supporters and religious leaders of the Shiite Muslim majority, and tried to undermine the identity of minority Christian (Assyrian and Chaldean) and Yazidi.

"Ethnic cleansing" operations contributed to deploy throughout the country an estimated one million people, and raised the number of exiles to four million Iraqis, becoming the second largest refugee population on the planet. The West didn´t echo the shock of horror and dismay that swept the Islamic world at the time of the persecution, killings and executions of Shiite clerics and their followers, among them the most prominent ayatollahs, unleashed between 1998 and 2000, personally directed by Saddam Hussein.

Between 1987 and 1988 Saddam Hussein launched attacks with gas against Iraqi Kurdish targets, which left thousands dead. In February 1988, he unleashed "operation Anfal" against the Kurds and to a horrified world, on 16 March 1988, attacked the Kurdish village of Jalabja, in which more than 50,000 people perished from the lethal gases.

After the insurrection of 1991 in the South, the offensive unleashed by Saddam Hussein caused the death of about 60,000 Shiites. The use of deadly mustard gas in Halj Umran, in Panjwin, in the Majnoon Island and Umm-ar-Rasas is well documented; Tabun gas, in Al-Basrahm, in the Hawizah marshes, and Al-Fao; and neuro-toxic gases in Sumar-Mejran and Jalabja.

In December 1996, he arrested his own wife Sajida Khairallah Talfah and her daughters Raghad Hussein, Hala Hussein and Rana Hussein, at the suspicion that they had conjured up to assassinate his eldest son Uday Hussein. According to Amnesty, the heads of the decapitated women were exposed in stakes in front of their homes for several days.

In Saddam Hussein's Iraq it was a crime to possess a typewriter, and any critic of Hussein ended up in the gallows. But with 200,000 political opponents imprisoned there was no organized or rival opposition of consideration, and half a million exiles would never have the receptivity of the Arab world. It is estimated that Saddam Hussein's personal fortune exceeded 6 billion dollars, and among the characters he most admired were Joseph Stalin, Mao Zedong, Fidel Castro and Joseph Broz Tito.

In 1997 Saddam Hussein solved the problem of the overcrowding in prisons by executing 3,000 prisoners at once, and in 1995 around 1,600 common prisoners were used to refine the biological and chemical weapons. In May 2000 his

Government tortured to death the mother of three deserters in retaliation.

He manipulated the delivery of food to the population, rewarding those who supported his regime, and denying it to opponents. It not only manipulated the freedom of expression, of the press[5], and didn´t tolerate political opposition, but criticize him was punishable with the death penalty, and the personal or ethnic identity was the subject of arbitrary attacks.

The UN had documented more than 16,000 cases of missing persons. In August 2001 Amnesty International described the systematic use of torture against political opponents, and the practice of beheading women accused of prostitution, the torturing of prisoners with hot irons, with electric shocks, beatings and fractures of limbs, violations of women, spilling acid on the skin. The women in the families of detainees were raped, and the cost of executions had to be paid by the closest relatives.

Saddam Hussein never ceased to compete with Damascus and Tripoli in an effort to manipulate the army of terror, within the nebula of small groups, which changed their name to the rhythm of its operations on behalf of the Palestinian resistance.

Saddam provided intelligence information to terrorist organizations for their operations in Europe, as well as the specialized training in the manufacture and setting of explosives, infiltration of sensitive areas, not to mention extensive resources in money, false documentation and communication codes.

His intelligence services created the Arab Liberation Front, headed by Waddi Haddad. Hussein facilitated the ascension of the sinister Abu Abbas. Around the same time, he hosted renowned terrorists like Ahmed Yibril, Salem Abu Salem, Abu Iyad, head of the deadly "Unit 17", Abu Ibrahim the "explosives magician", etc.

Iraq would serve as the headquarters of Abu Nidal, author of countless terrorist attacks in more than 20 countries with more than 900 deaths. Black September, headed by Mohammed Yussuf El-Najjar, would receive training and advisory from the Iraqi secret service, Cuba and the KGB.

In the months prior to the First Gulf War, Saddam restored his ties with terrorists such as Imad Mugniyah, the brutal operative of Hizb-Allah, as well as the Marxist Palestinians George Habash and Nayel Hawatmeh located in Jordan, and threatening to strike with terrorist groups Darkhan and Saudi Arabia.

In 1993, Saddam Hussein mounted an assassination attempt that failed against former US President George Bush and the emir of Kuwait using a car loaded with a large quantity of explosives. In June of that year, President Bill Clinton authorized a military offensive against Iraqi military positions in retaliation to the attempt.

In April 2002 Saddam Hussein personally publically increased to $ 25,000 the sum to compensate the families of the Palestinian suicide bombers in Israeli territory. When the Coalition evicted the Taliban from Afghanistan, Abu Mussab Al-Zarqawi, Lieutenant of Osama Ben Laden, moved the command structure and camps to the northeast of Iraq, and from there Al-Qaeda training camps would coordinate the entire movement of the network.

France, Germany, Ukraine and Russia were accomplices of Iraqi rearmament, and benefited from its illegal trade with oil, violating the embargo and violating its own resolutions as members of the Security Council of the UN, and therefore topped the list of those who once again rejected to restructure the Coalition ally in the Middle East.

There was no "moderation" or "civilized" vision in his foreign policy. Saddam Hussein permanency in power brought more painful surprises. Countries and political forces that rejected the Iraqi disarmament by force overlooked that the sanctions and inspections didn't halt his repressive nature, his terrorism support and rearmament. The consequences were too serious to relay only in "containment" measures that never worked with Saddam Hussein.

Saddam Hussein lived constantly in his underground control posts scattered throughout Iraq. That is why when he granted interviews did it through a TV, so that intelligence agencies could not locate him. Therefore, in their televised public lectures during the Gulf crisis he used hostages as personal safety, thus preventing any attack on his person.

Saddam Hussein would be seen in the West as a lesser evil because it would serve their strategic interests to wear down the ambitions of the Ayatollah Khomeini and Syrian Hafez Al-Assad. The administrations of Ronald Reagan and George Bush (father) challenged the military sanctions to Iraq that the Israelites demanded.

It was a result of the invasion of Kuwait that this American *realpolitik* varied abruptly. United States, together with France, Germany, Switzerland and Great Britain, were silent accomplices of the Iraqi nuclear and chemical weapons infrastructure, which caused the U.S. to be alarmed.

But the military and political preeminence of Hussein in the Arab world, sculpted with the help of NATO, contributed to a schematic and simplistic vision of a "standstill" West and this calculation erred in Kuwait. Saddam Hussein considered that the Arab-Israeli dispute, the Communist collapse, German unification, and the evaporation of the Cold War and the East-West rivalry in regional conflict would distract the international powers of his run against Kuwait.

Ultimatum to Baghdad

The air assaults on Iraq during the Gulf war of 1991 didn´t destroy the two plants erected by the French for processing enriched uranium. The location of such plants was never known accurately, the illegal network of their foreign suppliers, nor the existing before the war. These centrifuges were much more advanced than those built by the United States for the bombs of Hiroshima and Nagasaki.

After the Gulf War of 1991, designers of nuclear and biochemical factories were still in Iraq, and it was unknown for certain until what level had improved the accuracy of its ballistic missiles that a decade ago fell on the roofs of Tel Aviv, and the foreign technicians who secretly in Baghdad managed to perfect solid fuel for missiles. The documentation for the same was never found, nor was handed over to the UN. Scientists and technicians in charge of Atomic programs disappeared from public life, from research institutes, and universities.

Held by the centers of intelligence and political decision in the West existed overwhelming evidence of the efforts of Saddam Hussein to poach and manufacture weapons of mass destruction. The "proof" that the weapons were available to him was in the hands of those who, precisely without shame, demanded them from Washington.

The question that was supposed to be asked was which countries had the technology to promote in Iraq the production of such sophisticated weapons, and the response would leave us only with three or four options. Such tests were not aired because the international public opinion would have astounded to know who was the partner in crime in the "civilized world" -especially in Europe- that such monstrosity of horror in the hands of Saddam Hussein had as final objective the same as the Führer: the annihilation of the Jews.

The French position was too cynical to erect a moral mantle against the politics of Washington, when "moralists" had just obtained a huge concession for oil exploitation in Iraq. Overt was the position of the Kremlin with the colossal sum of $ 40 billion tied to the oil concessions of Mosul northern province.

And it was sordid also the German reaction, when they termed the American leader as a "Modern Hitler", above all having been the German consortiums which built in stealth the Iraqi industry of poison gas[1], which was intended to be used again against the Jews of Israel.

The German imputation affected the politic relationship with the United States, as noted State Secretary Colin Powell. It was inadmissible that the Germanic consortia and its Government were so innocent, that they were not aware of the intentions of Saddam Hussein of gassing Jews.

In the times of the German Chancellor Konrad Adenauer, Israeli leaders David Ben Gurion and Golda Meir were horrified of the participation of thousands of Nazis technicians and high SS officials who secretly worked on the ballistic missiles and biochemical plans of Egypt and Iraq.

When American diplomacy "tightened" the Russian ruler Vladimir Putin, he admitted that his country participated in the construction of chemical installations in Iraq, but only as a minor partner of the French-German consortia, hinting to Washington to focus their grievances toward the West.

The German intelligence sources sounded the alarm in Washington by warning that Saddam Hussein had scientific personal knower of all secrets to compose atomic bombs

Hiroshima type, and industrial infrastructure to process the fission material in a period of three to six years.

Iraqis technical experts in nuclear and biochemical weapons were not eliminated by the Gulf war, and it was known their scientific level was high. If they managed to acquire about 20 pounds of enriched uranium[2], the deadline to build two or three atomic bombs was reduced to months, since Baghdad had solved all the theoretical and technological problems of nuclear fission.

Also, the scandal broke out in the intelligence network when news spread that strategic components for the making of radiation artifacts for an asymmetric war had "disappeared" from Ukrainian inventories, and that there were traces of a very strong and fast illegal traffic to the Middle East of very special aluminum tubes for nuclear factories.

In addition, an aircraft or a rocket is not the only vector for atomic weapons. There are several ways to scatter reactive material, apart from the explosives, which were devised by the former Soviet Union. Russians even confessed that they didn't know certainly how many nuclear warheads were produced in Soviet times, what the exact number in its arsenal was, or how many landed in Ukraine or Central Asia.

They could not control throughout the south China border to the Balkans. All this was aggravated by the deterioration of their security system and the corruption that had corroded their armed forces and its nuclear program. An Iraq with power of nuclear and chemical annihilation in three or six years was able to enthrone the uncertainty in the Middle East and unleash a regional mega-conflict, even nuclear, with Israel.

It is not only the danger of the spread of terrorism against the West, the implosion of four skyscrapers or the blackmail of Baghdad over its neighbors of the Crescent and the scimitar what has been at stake in the Middle East. For Tel Aviv, there was no doubt that Iraqi rearmament under Saddam Hussein had as first point the destruction of their

State in the short, medium or long term. For Tel-Aviv, there is no time to waste when one of his Arab neighbors try to develop weapons of mass destruction.

For more than one decade, Israel was warning Washington that Saddam Hussein had them as their next target. Israeli fears were not unfounded. In 1981, Israeli aviation attacked the atomic reactors at Osirak, which Saddam Hussein installed with French complicity, and by that date the Mossad sent to paradise the technicians who built a famous "super-canon" capable of reaching Israel.

In a private telephone communication between the Emir of Qatar and King Fahd of Saudi Arabia, the first commented that Yasser Arafat and Saddam Hussein sought to provoke a new war with Israel, noting that this would be disastrous for the Arab world, since Israel counted with hundreds of nuclear warheads and 47 atomic bombs.

The cold froze the Israeli cervical, since it was unknown if this watch of the three years had freshly activated, or it was approaching zero hour; and, above all, the variable that no sophisticated technological means in the hands of the West, including the intelligence satellites, was able to detect 20 pounds of enriched uranium.

Israel, the main factor of all crisis of the West with Saddam's Iraq, almost never was mentioned. Although it is not easy to prove it, the decision of President George W. Bush was not an electoral game or an impulsive action, but that it fell within the framework of the preventive.

Although in the media was not perceived as well, everything indicates that it was Israel who, convinced and alarmed by the advancement of Iraqi weapons of mass destruction, and put President Bush against the wall in a "you or us", establishing the dilemma that if Washington didn't resolve this mess, the tanks of Ariel Sharon would.

If Tel Aviv acted against Saddam Hussein, in case the West or United States did not, or proceed later on, it would sweep Syria first to allow their armored raid into Iraq, where they would leave no stone standing, in a deadly and bloody occupation and victory, where Israel, then a dominant regional power, would reorganize the Middle East in its image and likeness.

For United States and the West was not permissible that such was the way to solve the Iraqi dossier, because the region, full of explosive components, could go to hell. They couldn't allow Saddam Hussein to acquire nuclear and biochemical weapons with impunity due to the precedent that this would set for Iran.

An Iraqi nuclear blast against any fragile neighboring Arab State would destroy these societies irreversibly. Israel, moreover, was not going to contain itself if Iraq launched any rocket, because there was a coalition with the Arabs in 1991, and in power were the Ariel Sharon "hawks".

Jewish-American political forces already warned their congressmen that they objected George Bush plans against Iraq and that if the reasons that forced the President to this decision were not clear, they would have to opt to permanently withdraw their financial support.

The Atlantic solidarity crumbled because United States, the sole military super-power was the only one who could act on its own. So therefore, given the formidable American military deployment, the Gulf crisis restated the necessity of NATO which showed the military limits of the European to defend their vital interests and the feebleness of any military alliance that exclude the United States. That was the reason why the only thing that Paris, Rome and Berlin always propose is the formula of global embargo as the mechanism to deal with regional crises.

Long-since England and France ceased to be empires on the beaches of Normandy in the Second World War, once again, the Iraq crisis showed that the Western European countries were second rank powers lacking real world foreign policy, and whose international positions were curdled precisely of those vices they blamed American foreign policy for: domestic partisan bickering, interest hucksters, and provincial political eyesight.

Because, let's not forget, the European low down powers were precisely those who pressured intensely Washington to be involved from head to toe in Asia, in the Balkans, and in the Middle East.

They waited for United States to take out their chestnuts from the fire in Kosovo, their back courtyard, who requested that United States mediate the emerging influence of the Arab world and the political clout that Saudi Arabia and Egypt acquired, and who demanded from Washington the safety of the Arab oil fields.

The US policy and the use of its war machine will be dictated by the protection of the oil producers from the Middle East region in which any crisis can put in danger that vital world resource. That is why, according with new rules of global behavior, the West cannot allow that any Islamic country, such as Iran, moves to a nuclear power category.

In the swamp of Iraq

The interests of all current powers collide in the Middle East and Central Asia, especially those of Russia, China and Japan, main future competitors of United States in the global distribution.

American geopolitics thinker and former Presidential Advisor Zbigniew Brzezinski[1] wrote two decades ago about the strategic imperatives of United States in which the Middle East region stood as a central theme. Around 70% of the world oil reserves are located in the Persian Gulf-Caspian Sea area.

For the reason that Europe, Japan, South Korea, and China are already dependent to sustain their growth on tap oil in the Persian Gulf and the Caspian Sea, Brzezinski evaluated the political consequences of any power game by Russia if the main gas and oil pipelines from the Middle East to Europe pass through Russian territory, on the Black Sea in Novorossiysk.

In this case, the region will remain a political dependency of Russia who will be in a strong enough position to settle on how their new resources should be shared. The only way to avoid that a single power monopolizes the access to the resources2, from Brzezinski´s point of view is that other gas and oil pipelines passed across the Caspian Sea to Azerbaijan and thence towards the Mediterranean Sea via Turkey, reaching one of them the Arabian Sea through Afghanistan.

It was actually after 1979 that the area was transfigured into an element of national security for the United States, due to three cardinal events: The Soviet invasion to Afghanistan, the overthrow of the Shah of Iran by an Islamist movement led by Ayatollah Ruhollah Khomeini, and the revolt of the Islamic fundamentalists in Mecca.

It would be President James Earl "Jimmy" Carter who established the famous "Carter doctrine" that put together a geo-political vision to the region. The criteria of President Carter were: "Any attempt by a hostile power aimed at achieving control over the Persian Gulf was considered an attack on the vital interests of the United States and therefore repelled by all necessary means, including military action".

The "Carter doctrine" was backed with the creation of Rapid Deployment Joint Task Force on every continent, consisting of elite military units. This formed six regional unified commands, and one of them was the United States Central Command (USCentcom) to conduct all military operations as a theater-level Unified Combatant Command in the Middle East, with a forward headquarters in Qatar and base areas in Bahrain, Diego Garcia archipelago, in Oman and Saudi Arabia. Centcom task region comprise the Middle East, North Africa and Central Asia.

The National Energy Plan released in May 2001 by an advisory body led by Vice President Richard Bruce "Dick" Cheney, which was called "global oil acquisition strategy", is the guidebook to understand the economic, military and diplomatic actions undertaken by Washington in the Middle East.

The Plan sets out three main issues: United States must import a growing part of its demand for oil to safeguard its reserves. To acquire supplementary oil United States cannot depend on exclusively traditional sources of supply such as Saudi Arabia, Venezuela and Canada. It must obtain any additional quantity from new producers such as the States of the Caspian area, Russia and Africa. And, United States cannot rely exclusively on market forces to access this additional capacity, but it would need a significant effort from the Government authorities to overcome a resistance from the American oil companies.

Apart from Al-Qaeda the US invasion of Afghanistan relates to American plans of extending pipelines from the Caspian Sea, across Afghanistan, something that the Taliban had stubbornly rejected. This project conceived by the American oil consortium Unocal, torpedoed the plan designed by the Russians and Iranians.

No doubt that one of the considerations is the weakening of OPEC by means of a pipeline that will pass through Afghanistan and the overthrow of the Iraqi Saddam Hussein. After the occupation of Iraq, the British magazine, *The Economist*[3] raised the possibility of a flood of Iraqi oil on the world market, due to the Government's need for huge sums to rebuild the country, fact that would affect OPEC.

On the occasion of the Iraqi invasion to Kuwait, the U.S. administration reacted mainly to protect Saudi Arabia and not only for the conflict in Kuwaiti territory. The then Secretary of Defense "Dick Cheney" expressed that the reason was to prevent Saddam Hussein from capturing oil from Kuwait and Saudi Arabia, thus acquiring a "capacity of strangulation" on United States and the world economy.

United States would apply a double "containment" to Saddam's regime[4] until in the late nineties lost its effectiveness due to the strengthening of the economic relations of France and Russia with Iraq. The only formula on hand, according to Washington and London, was to intensify air shocks to soften the regime, and later to invade.

In order to consolidate the American supremacy and close the path to possible rivals, the administration of President George Bush son displayed diplomacy without patience to build consensus and coalitions in its foreign policy. Not being able to legitimize its military action in Iraq, the UN was cast aside by Washington and remained a spectator. Even those key allied states such as Egypt and Saudi Arabia didn't joined the war chariot.

Although in geopolitics term the action cannot be called incompetent by its long-term perspective, in their tactics there are irrational considerations of how to deal with the consequences of a military campaign.

It was as a result of the decomposition of the Soviet Union than the United States proposed a "common market of the Middle East", with the Emirates of the Gulf as financiers, Israel as a techno-center, Egypt providing qualified human resources and the rest of the countries supplying labor. The project has counted with the resistance of Syria, Iraq and Iran, although after the demolition of Saddam Hussein, the same became praiseworthy.

But it cannot be denied that the war that topples Saddam Hussein set the advantageous position of United States in the Euro-Asiatic mega-continent, while it provides bases for any future military action in the Middle East, thus ruining the plans of China, Russia and Europe as those of Syria and Iran. The domain of these sources of energy and power granted control of the world economy and a higher category against any force competitor.

Such military action in Iraq enthroned a debate among leading American politicians, especially the confrontation of the republican advisor teams of George Bush father and George Bush son. Thus, James Baker, Brent Scowcroft and Lawrence Eagleburger, from the Bush father team, were opposed to a unilateral action against Iraq that would divert the United States from their crucial mission in that area, that is the solution of the Israeli-Palestinian conflict. Former relevant officials from the William "Bill" Clinton administration, such as Madeleine Albright and Richard Holbrooke have been added to this group. Also, figures like Zbigniew Brzezinski issued their criticism.

Historically, the authoritarian Arab regimes have adopted superficial reforms without resulting in real change in the political structures and this has not been an obstacle for Washington to maintain economic and security interests (oil, anti-terrorism and the Arab-Israeli peace) that require a friendly relationship with such autocratic regimes.

After overthrowing the Taliban, United States crosses the threshold in a complex area, which has been characterized as the graveyard of Empires. After the war in Iraq, United States sought a democratic government model for the Arab world, which for the Islamic people was just an excuse, an interventionist policy, and an attempt to impose Western values.

The American Administration hoped that liberating Iraq from Saddam Hussein and sponsoring democracy not only would eliminate a major military threat in the region; at the same time, it would send a message to the Arab world that self-determination as part of the modern world is possible.

The paradigm of a unified and democratic Iraq as an archetypical for the Middle East, inducing democratic reforms in other Arab countries is accompanied with insurmountable obstacles: on the one hand, a unified state in Iraq is not feasible, not even an ethnic democracy, and by such it is not exemplary for the area.

In Iraq, the mistake has not being the inability to govern them peacefully. This accusation does not take into account that it is an artificial country, split into ethnic groups, religions and tribes, which were maintained thanks to the dictatorial force.

A laical-democratic Iraq is an aberration that the religious guides reject, boycott and condemn for being heretic. Moreover, Arab intellectuals consider it a hypocrite postulated, due to the backing of the West to despotic regimes such as Pakistan, Saudi Arabia, Kuwait, Bahrain, Qatar and Oman, among others.

Also, it does not consider that after the military victory, United States destroyed the Sunni social fabric that maintained control of the country. The timetable that was set up to choose a Government, designing a Constitution, build an army and an Iraqi police force was unrealistic, not only by the small timeframe proposed but because it didn't address the central issue of ethnic balance, and abandoned the Sunnis to their fate.

The U.S. strategy has been really aimed at achieving a democratic Iraq and Middle East without ceasing to be Islamic. Simply, this is a paradox because the *a-confessionalism* is a *conditio sine qua non* of any democracy. In Iraq and Afghanistan people vote in accordance with what they are ordered by their religious and tribal leaders or their military superiors.

The fact is that Islam and its Sharia are not compatible with democracy. Sharia, or the "Act of God", is an amalgam of rules from the Quran and the Hadiz[5]. Sharia considers adultery as a felony punished by stoning, and grants broad powers to the husband over his wife and children allowing polygamy as well.

For this reason, from the very beginning, the Coalition Provisional Authority led by the US diplomat Lewis Paul Bremer was opposed to establishing *Sharia* law as the main legal source.

The Constitution drafted by the Shiites and Kurds ignored the objections of many Sunnis. The Constitution managed to introduce the Islamic confessional concept, where this constitutes a source of law, pointing that the laws may not be contrary to Islam principles.

There are points on the North American agenda that hardly can be accepted by some or other members of three different ethnic groups, as that of a democracy out of balance by the ethnic factor, the women's rights, and control over the oil area of Kirkuk in Kurdish territory.

A central, democratic state is a fantasy in an Iraq composed of three disparate ethnic groups in dispute. And there lies the persistence and the root of the violence, and the legitimacy that the foreign terrorists and the Sunni guerrillas tried to keep their agendas in force.

The "federal" Government of Iraq headed by Prime Minister Nouri Al-Maliki wanted to negotiate with tyrannical Syria and fundamentalist Iran to achieve regional peace, but they are prevented from doing so by the American geo-political considerations.

International support for the "reconstruction of Iraq" faded because NATO European countries preferred to perform the peacekeeping tasks in safe areas, and did not want their forces mixed in the fighting.

All through the first years of occupation, influential US individuals, like the members of the Baker Committee[6], former Secretary of State Colin Powell, and former Secretary of Defense Donald Rumsfeld had advocated for the modification of the strategy in Iraq and minimize the expectations facing the reality that the strategy is not working. In a similar way have spoken General William Odom, former director of the National Security Agency, and General John Abizaid who was head of the CentCom during the Iraq campaign.

Even Senator John McCain had argued the need for more troops to achieve a quick victory over the internal resistance, in order to avoid a war that has become unpopular.

Henry Kissinger defended U.S. policy in Iraq, arguing that any reduction in troops would spark a public pressure would force the withdrawal of all troops. But Kissinger forgets that this is a war that ended up being political and the annihilation of a greater amount of Shiite militiamen or Sunni guerrillas does not grant victory.

With ignorant candor it was thought in Washington that the overthrow of Saddam Hussein, the eventual transfer of power to an Iraqi interim Government highly centralized and the American military presence would end violence and terrorism.

United States lost the chance to crown its flashing military victory with a fast dismantling, leaving a pacified country if it would have just created three ethnic states.

But Washington, involved by "Wilsonian" doctrine, has never believed in partition. The administration of Bill Clinton, in turn, didn't want to apply a partition in the multi-ethnic Bosnia, and was forced to maintain a permanent military presence in this powder keg. However, decentralization of Government and a sharing of oil revenues was part of the agreement that ended the Sudanese civil war, which already drew millions of victims.

Regardless of the positions that were found before the invasion, Europe has accepted United States to defend its vital interests: oil. That is why the West has been deaf to the growing Iraqi outcry in favor of the partition, the idea to redraw the map of Iraq, under the criterion that a separation leads to an increase of violence and sectarian exclusion. Critics of the redevelopment point out that Shiite militiaman with ties to political parties in the Government have been as responsible for terror as the Sunni insurgents.

The Baker Commission dismissed the idea of dividing Iraq into autonomous regions and of distributing the oil wealth among Kurds, Shiites and Sunni Arabs alike, arguing that it would incite civil war. However, the current vice President Joseph R. Biden Jr., endorsed the solution to separate Iraq into three autonomous States when serving as one of the leading voices on foreign policy of the Democratic Party, Member of the Senate Foreign Relations Committee.

The Iraqis do recognize they are wrapped in an undeclared civil war, and that de facto, there is a partition. After the US military withdraw, Iraq will head to its dismemberment, in which each of the three ethnic seeks to drastically eliminate the central Government so it won't become an instrument of oppression to those who are not in power.

Iraq is already disjoint because the Kurds do not want to be part of the country. Local governments and their ethnic and religious militias are those who actually control the different regions. Recognizing the full autonomy of its three ethnic components could then develop more durable pockets of political and economic freedom.

A fragmentation of Iraq in three autonomous enclaves with its own armed forces, its intelligence, its Prime Minister and oil Minister (with the Kurds to the North, the Sunnis to the Center and Shiites in the South) would at least limit Iranian influence on the South side.

The Kurds and their militiamen have their own quasi-country in which central Government and its symbols do not exist. The Kurdish militia constitutes the heart of the Kurdistan[7] security forces. The Kurdish experiment has inspired many Shiite leaders. The Kurds would have the best chance of creating a relatively free society in their area, because at present they are unsure that their current autonomy can be preserved after the American departure.

Perhaps most disturbing is that Turkey rejects Kurdish autonomy due to the negative effect on the Kurdish population living in its territory. For this reason, several times has threatened to intervene militarily, to proclaim an independent Kurdistan.

But the independence or the state autonomy within a Federation, supported by the Kurds and Sunnis reject Shiites, since the territory they inhabit, the central, lacks oil. The Constitution grants the Kurds and the Shiites a greater share of oil revenues than to the Sunnis. Another unfounded fear is that the Iranian Shiites (Persians) could assimilate the Iraqi Shiites (Arabs).

The Arab-Persian dispute is so deep that it exceeds the coincidence of Islamic sect, apart from the disagreement over the separation or not of religion and the State. In addition, Iraqi Shiite clerics are considered with more prestige and authority than the Iranians as the shrines of Shiite Islam are found precisely in the southern region of Iraq.

The Shiite and Kurds were brutally suppressed under Sunni regimes of Karim Kassem and Saddam Hussein, reason why once they reached power have managed to weaken the Government with a Constitution that includes the option of decentralization.

The Shiites, historic defenders of southern autonomy, like the Kurds in the North, have their own defense forces and control over oil exploitation. The bloody struggle of factions involved Sunnis versus Shiites and Sunnis versus Kurds, and also between Shiite sects. The three communities have stockpiles of armaments, which were never confiscated.

Shiites constitute 60% of the population and seek to vindicate the decades of oppression they were subjected by the Sunni minority. Unlike what is thought in Western capitals, Shiites have transformed the south in a fundamentalist state, with their alliances to Shiites from Iran. They control also the security forces and the Ministry of Interior.

The Shiite government postponed the disarmament of their militia responsible for massacres, and advocated for United States to keep on training security forces, in preparation of necessary combatants for the civil war that everyone guess will develop after the total American withdrawal.

The main political Shiite figures like Grand Ayatollah Ali Al-Sistani, the most revered Muslim cleric, promoted the plan to divide the country as a way of separating the warring sects. Abdul-Aziz Hakim, one of the leaders of the Islamic revolution, supported the creation of nine provinces in the South, where 60% of the oil reserves are found.

Hakim had designed proposals for rights and the territorial limits of a Shiite Independent State. "Federalism will separate all areas of the country that are incubating terrorism from those that are evolving and improving," said Khudair Khuzai, the Shiite Education Minister. "We will do the same as Kurdistan: to post soldiers along the borders."

The central Government dominated by Shiites and Kurds has not provided incentives to Sunnis, especially after their belligerence, and undergo the decentralization of the Iraqi State. The reconciliation with Sunnis (20% of the population) has not worked properly because the Shiites that effectively control the Government fiercely oppose the Sunnis.

The Sunnis are the only ones who want a unified territory (but not the current, dominated by Shiites and Kurds), since in a free Confederacy of State, or partition, they would obtain little oil. One of the reasons why the Sunni insurgents were fighting in the first years was because they fear being left in an area poor of resources.

The West and Northwest territories populated by Sunnis is a desolate desert, devoid of oil and gas. Sunni leaders do not receive the benefits of democracy and see only that Shiites are taking advantage of the escalation of violence to seize oil.

"The control of these areas will generate a huge fortune they can exploit," said Adnan Dulaimi, a prominent Sunni Arab politician. "Their motivation is that they are thirsty for control and power".

The only alternative in Iraq to prevent a civil war that encompasses all the ethnic groups is a controlled partition in which the Sunnis govern themselves and a viable oil partnership agreement is negotiated.

It is no surprise that the main acts of violence occurred in the so-called "Sunni triangle," in which terrorism had, and still has popular support. The anti-American terrorist attacks involved former officials and military of the downed Baas regime whose goal was to achieve the military withdrawal from the Coalition to regain power.

Thousands of them lost their duties and many others are waiting for be tried. It should not be forgotten that thousands of members of Saddam Hussein's repressive apparatus were experts in clandestine operations. It is even rumored that General Ezzat Ibrahim, who was number two in the regime, was at the forefront of many attacks.

But it is unknown for certain who was preparing the attacks; nobody took responsibility and Iraqi and American authorities had not been able to clarify it. Although terrorist and guerrilla attacks were the result of painstaking preparation and coordination, it can be deduced that they had dissimilar backgrounds: Shiite extremists, Sunni former military, former Sunni Baas and foreign Jihadists who revered

Osama Bin-Laden and infiltrated the open borders with Iran and Syria.

It was difficult to convince the Sunni minority, disaffected and armed, to abandon the fight against the central Government, since they considered themselves controlled victims of a tribal Alliance between Kurds and Shiites.

The Western press featured the actions of foreign jihadists and minimized the dominant and most voluminous uprising of Sunni, only to prove that fundamentalist foreigners were the only cause of the problems, and not the Iraqis. Another notion mentioned was that Sunni nationalists, representing nearly 90% of the insurrection, were no longer related with foreign jihadists.

With decentralization the violence was isolated and foreign terrorists lost support in the population. The peace was achieved when the Sunnis stopped unleashing terror. It has to be understood that involved in violence were also Sunni fighters, fearful of reprisals by a Shiite theocratic government.

Also the actual central, federal, rather symbolic state don`t have the means to impose itself above three ethnic states quasi-independent. On spite of Iraq Constitution, elected Government at the polls, armed forces and security police, the Sunnis has being adamant in their consideration that the only way for Iraq is to remake the country they just built.

It is noted that after the American withdrawal, autonomic decentralization would have difficulties in certain cities, in which, as in Beirut, the boundaries between ethnic-religious communities are not defined.

The provinces of Baghdad, Diyala, the Northern Babil and Southern Salah Uddin are completely heterogeneous, often patchwork of Sunni and Shiite people. Basrah in the South includes a substantial Sunni minority, while Mosul in the North encompasses significant numbers of Shiite Arabs, Kurds and Tucuman.

The Sunnis has recommended to divide Baghdad, with the Tigris River as a sort of Berlin wall, thus to distance the east of the mainly Shiite town from the West in its Sunni generality. Sunnis and Shiites already proclaim that the Baghdad division will be the solution.

From the moment the American presence disappears, with the current structure of State, Government and Constitution, the outbreak of a civil war could wrap the three communities, for the reason that the current Constitution promoted by United States is full of incongruence. According to it, any of the provinces of Iraq, or a group of them, can carry out a referendum to form a federal region.

To make sure such a thing does not happen again it is imperative to reach an eventual political agreement between the three ethnic groups that smother the violence, complemented with a better relationship between Iran, Syria and Turkey. For its part, United States would have to accept a Government other than the Western democratic model that forces now in Iraq.

The dilemma of Iraq is endless: a democracy plan rejected by all the Iraqi political forces and inconsistent with Islam; three armed ethnic groups that do not recognize or want a central or federated state and are only awaiting the departure of the last American soldier to declare their national independence; three territories, two in possession of enormous reserves of hydrocarbons and one without oil; Turkey to the North, prepared not to allow a Kurdish State in Iraq; Syria in the Northwest, supporting the Sunni faction against Kurds and Shiites; Jordan eastward, with aspirations of recovering the lost Sunni girdle, to redo the Hashemite monarchy; Iran to the East, supporting the South Shiites in their aspirations.

That is why the strategic error of the American campaign, both in Afghanistan and in Iraq was not military, but it has resided in the objective to seek the establishment of a democratic model supported by occupation forces of the "Christian West", in an Islamic environment.

In the bazaars and cafes of the Islamic world, democracy is associated with the military occupation of the "infidels". For the Islamic citizen there is another contradiction of the West when it repudiates the Government of the ayatollahs in Iran, but it supports an Iraq dominated by a militant Shiite with close ties to Tehran, and promotes elections in which Shiite religious parties take part financed by the Iranian theocracy.

Washington believes that it must sponsor democracy throughout the region; an agenda of promoting freedom, not far from the utopia of the former President Woodrow Wilson, with idealistic altruisms, in benefit and as the best means of defending the national security of the United States and throughout the West, under the notion that dictatorships are breeding grounds for terrorism.

But this is a goal not shared by all the elites who rule in the Middle East, which are already despotic. Islamic societies today repudiate democracy as a political system. In its yearning for "spreading democracy" United States does not realize that the term means something different in those countries with not an iota of democratic experience, such as Afghanistan and Iraq.

The consummation of democracy has arisen for populist autocratic regimes, as it did Iraq and Syria, but Washington is careful not to propose them to the Allied Islamic monarchies, like Kuwait or Qatar, which they qualify curiously as "moderates". This sets the paradox of breaking lances against anti-Islam autocratic regimes while strengthening relations with the archaic oil monarchies.

In theory, several states in the Islamic world have liberal constitutions, but lack political culture, civil society and the institutions required to sustain an open political system.

The obstinacy to enforce a democratic model rejected by the whole Islamic world has only given legitimacy to the defeated Iraqi Sunnis and Afghan Taliban, to launch a struggle "against the occupation".

Both in Afghanistan and in Iraq there is a false trade-off between security and liberties, balance that only occurs in developed democratic societies.

It is common criterion that the Iraqi rebellion was not defeated by force of arms. It is nothing new that the wars engender civil wars and insurgencies. American general Donald Alston referred to this situation in the following terms: "this insurgency is not going to be calm, terrorists and terrorism in Iraq will not be placated through military options or military operations".

The unruliness in Iraq and the obstinacy of the United States by implementing a rejected guideline cannot be denied. The instruction of a national military and police force has collided with the reality that they are training units which, in the end, will end up fighting the civil war for their religious-ethnic side, not for their country, and act as death squads, as in the case of the Shiites against the Sunnis.

It is noteworthy that senior U.S. officers on the ground have tilted towards the withdrawal of their 140,000 troops, due to the failure to establish democracy in a fragmented society and lacking of any experience or prior democratic culture; aware, moreover, that the increase in troops is not sustainable long-term, both in the military and the political sense.

In Afghanistan, the authority of the central Government of Hamid Karzai is weak in much of the country, which is in the hands of the local warlords. In synthesis, Afghanistan and Iraq are not yet prepared for the democratic exercise, since before the existence of democratic institutions (division of powers, multi- party system, civil society, elections, freedom of opinion, and so on), a democratic culture is required.

At this point, policymakers in Washington know that democracy is impossible in Iraq, without the support of Shiite religious leaders, and in Afghanistan without the support of the warlords.

Without a doubt, geo-regional US policy applied to the Middle East has found the same pitfalls the British faced during their colonial time in the region. The dilemma was, and is today, the task of management and peacemaking. It was not expected in Afghanistan the recovery of the Islamist Taliban.

The approach to the Hizb-Allah Muslim in Lebanon has only brought the increase of its influence, once more endangering the stability of that multi-ethnic country. Thus, the fledgling independence of Lebanon from Syria occupation, and it´s so called democratic experiment, is so fragile that it could be extinguished on any civil war.

In the case of the Palestinians, by forcing democratic voting, they removed the authority of the Al-Fatah secular organizations, the only ones capable of imposing internal order and external compromise, instead resulting in the election of the Islamist Hamas, the nemesis of Israel.

We cannot forget the failure of democratization effort of President "Bill" Clinton in Somalia. That mistake made in order to counteract the Islamists, supported the bloodthirsty warlords who in fact were no longer a decisive force in the country. This led to the strengthening and popularity of the Islamic fundamentalists who took control of the South, involving Ethiopia in their scheme.

Already in Kosovo United States had assumed a military policy of unilateralism, when decided to use NATO club dismissing the UN. Washington alleged the right of the "civilized" powers to liquidate the barbarism in the name of democratic values, no matter if they violate sovereignty.

Democracy, apart from the human and political rights, implies also the opening of a society of information and economic opportunities, points almost impossible to match in the Islamic world. Only 1.6% of the population has access to Internet; and no countries in the Middle East reaches consideration of "free society" since all are organized around Islam.

The Islamists consider that Christianity does not hold the monopoly on the 'right way', the appropriate model to evolve towards a more humane regime, as it showed by Japan after

1945 when it founded a democratic society, with its own characteristics, from a non-Western archetype.

We should consider what sense has to promote democracy in Iraq or any other country in the Middle East if it begets a hostile anti-American Government, or if it is better to forget the construction of democratic Nations and let the loyal dictatorships such as Saudi Arabia.

Not without reason Zbigniew Brzezinski points that Islam is not more hostile to democracy than Christianity or Judaism were at a certain time.

The Warlords

Afghanistan is a country with 20 million inhabitants, which is cut in two by the monumental Indo-Kush Mountains, and corridors, as the passage of Khyber, where all conquerors including Alexander, leaked into India.

The famous Hindu poet, Mohammed Iqbal, characterizes Afghanistan as "the heart of Asia", while Lord George Curzon, British Viceroy of the India, termed it his "Kettle".

In the North live several ethnic groups which include Uzbeks and Tajiks; in the East the Persians professing Shiism; in the South, reside the Pashtun, a majority in the country and that have been for nearly 300 years, as well as some ethnic conglomerates of Persian language.

It is estimated that the current Afghanistan territory was inhabited in the Neolithic, one hundred thousand years before Christ. Fragments of a skull of a Neanderthal man were found in the cave of Darra-i-Kur, in Badakhshan. In the Bronze Age, between the third and second millennium BC, with the drive of the active trade with Mesopotamia and Egypt, the main producers of the lapis lazuli were in the mines of Badakhshan.

Also, the first urban centers were developed there[1]. As the plateaus of Persia, the steppes of Central Asia and the Indus Valley saw the significantly grow in their populations, the region became passage for frequent displacement of peoples.

It is not new for Afghanistan, land of fierce warriors, to be the epicenter of conflict, such as the current. Their ancient monarchs considered it the center of the world and such illusion has persisted to the present day. The taliban[2], in its attempt to oppose such credo to the West and generate a new clash of civilizations, were just the latest in an extensive inventory of conquerors, warlords, Apostles, righteous and sophists which have walked this worldly corridor, mercilessly destroying old cultures and theologies.

Throughout its history, the territory has known three major denominations: Ariana, when arias tribes settled two millennia before our era, Greater Khorasan in the middle ages, and Afghanistan in modern times.

In its bend upper right, raise the mountains of Pamir, which Marco Polo called "the roof of the world". Its geography has determined its policy, the nature of its people and its history, which is made of routes like the Silk Road, crossroads of Empires, as that of Alexander the Great, nomadic avalanches as the ones of Genghis Khan and Tamerlane (the iron lame), of religious convulsions such as Zoroastrianism, Manichaeism and Buddhism.

The English created another mess, composing Afghanistan from pieces of Iran, from the Asian Republics and Pakistan, where the Pashtun people were divided. For its part, the Soviets never understood Afghanistan and that is why they bogged down in an ethnic revolt armed by the United States, China and Saudi Arabia.

In 1919, after a third Anglo-Afghan war, which this time lasted four months, Afghanistan was freed from the British protectorate. The leader of the independence was Amanullah Khan, grandson of emir imposed by the British. Since the Government was proposed to modernize the country, propelled a relatively liberal Constitution and was the first state in the world to establish diplomatic relations with the Soviet Union.

This was the beginning of a 'special relationship' that would last for seven decades. Ousted Amanullah Khan in 1929 by the descendants of the dynasty dethroned in 1879, which crowned Mohammed Nadir Shah, a new constitution was designed in 1931 to appease Islamic leaders, recognizing the power of local chiefs.

The new Shah was assassinated in 1933 and the Crown fell on his son Mohammed Zahir, who, during the first twenty years of his reign, attempted to consolidate the nation, increased foreign relations and encouraged the internal development with funds from the country.

After the Second World War (in which Afghanistan remained neutral while its two powerful neighbors, the Soviet Union and Great Britain were allies), when Pakistan became independent in 1947, the old dynastic Durand line confronted the country with the problem of the political status of Pashtuns who lived on the Pakistani side.

Since that year, Afghanistan and Pakistan have maintained a political dispute because of the right to self-determination of the Pashtun tribes that live along the borders between the two States. From the early 1950s the leadership of lieutenant general Mohammed Daud Khan stood out, who was cousin and brother-in-law of the King and was appointed Prime Minister in 1953.

Daud Khan nationalized the social services, built irrigation systems, roads, and schools and with financial support from United States constructed hydroelectric dams, reorganized the armed forces with Soviet aid and manifested himself neutral in the Cold War. He also abolished the mandatory the use of the veil for women[3], and lifted the prohibition for women to be seen in public[4].

During the onset of the Cold War, for the reason that was inserted in an area of high conflict, Afghanistan tried as much as possible to keep equidistant between United States and the Soviet Union. However, gradually the country was forced increasingly to depend on the Soviet Union due to the sustained support from United States to Pakistan.

From 1955, thousands of Afghans regularly were sent to study to the Union Soviet, mainly to receive military training. The Pashtuns desire for independency forced Daud Khan to take repressive measures and this compel Pakistan to close the border in 1961.

Soviet influence began to be reflected in some Marxists manifestations in the press and the Government. In Afghanistan, then an Islamic Kingdom ruled by Quranic law, those closed to the King saw this process with displeasure.

In March 1963 King Mohammed Zahir "accepted the resignation" of Daud Khan and two months later, Pakistan reopened the border, even if no solution to the problem of the Pashtuns had been given. A new Prime Minister was appointed, who didn't belong neither to the aristocracy or the Royal family.

The designation fell on Dr. Muhammad Yusuf, who proposed a Cabinet of technocrats and intellectuals and propelled a new Constitution based on the principles of individual freedom, which, at the same time, maintained the values of Islam and the monarchy. Adopted in 1964, the Constitution allowed the formation of political parties and elections for the first time, but indirectly prohibited the participation of Marxists parties.

As a result, the Communist People's Democratic Party of Afghanistan (PDPA) was founded secretly, and in 1965 was able to organize its first anti monarch demonstrations. Soon the Communist People's Democratic Party was divided between two wings: The Jalk Group (made up of tadjiks or Afghan-Persia ethnic) which advocated a revolution based exclusively on the worker, and the adherents of the Parcham or "flag" (from the Pashtun ethnic) who sought a broad popular union with the participation of intellectuals, the upper class, the urban middle classes and the military corpus.

The influence of both parties grew every year. In the urban and industrial areas, workers and students began to organize themselves actively, as well as the trend of demonstrations with increasingly open criticisms to the monarchy.

Moscow, which had not accepted the replacement of Daud, willingly supported that state of affairs in 1973. Therefore, taking advantage that King Mohammed Zahir went abroad for medical reasons, they exert their influence so that Daud Khan would be designated as President.

The Republic was proclaimed with support of the Communist People's Democratic Party and right away the Constitution of 1964 was annulled. The new one-party Constitution, based on the model of Algeria and Nasser's Egypt, was approved in April 1977 and Daud Khan, who had previously deposed the communists' ministers of his cabinet, and had lost the support of Moscow, was now their golden boy and elected President for a period of 10 years in a dubious election with minor domestic backing.

Daud Khan, as new President, devised a socialist program, almost identical to the one published four years ago, in the first issue of the newspaper *Parcham*. The Five-Year modernization program put in force a land reform, the nationalization of banks and industries, and the implement of social justice.

Daud Khan mended fences with Pakistan and put distance himself from the communists who supported him in the coup. He also tried to re-conquer the traditional ties with the Islamic world. He made official trips to Kuwait, Saudi Arabia and Egypt, where he signed a military treaty, and, in a desperate effort, tried to reconcile with the Shah of Iran in 1978. But these foreign policy schemes anger the Soviets who feared that Afghanistan would tilt to the West, and eventually precipitated his downfall.

The Pashtun political organization, the Parcham who were in control of the Ministry of Interior plotted with the army and organized on April 27, 1978, a coup d'état killing in cold blood President Daud Khan along with his family.

Then, a communist politician, Nur Mohammed Taraki initiate the so called "Saur Revolution" and was appointed as President, and confirmed as Secretary General of the Communist People's Democratic Party. Hafizullah Amin, leader of a rival Communist faction, and Babrak Karmal, leader of the Parcham, were appointed Deputy Prime Ministers.

The struggle between Babrak Karmal and Hafizullah Amin ruled in favor of the latter who in April 1979 ascended to the post of Prime Minister until then vacant.

The fate of Taraki was sealed in Havana, during the Non Aligned Movement conference in 1977. In Havana, Taraki was advised by Fidel Castro and Andrei Gromyko to get rid of Hafizullah Amin, considered a pro-Chinese.

But in his return, Taraki tried to dismiss Amin as Chairman of the Council of Ministers, reporting his meeting in Havana with Fidel Castro and Andrei Gromyko, but his suggestion was rejected, and in September was deposed and suffocated with pillows by orders of Hafizullah Amin, action ironically approved by the Soviet Leonid Brezhnev.

Amin introduced several changes such as the elimination of the "dowry", a literacy campaign, equity for women and a radical agrarian reform that shook the cultural patterns of the country. While he tried to convince that in his tenure Afghanistan should be a Non-aligned country, everyone who were familiar with radio Moscow broadcasts, knew that Hafizullah's Government was Marxist, pro-Soviet and, therefore, atheist.

In February 1979 Adolph Dubs the U.S. Ambassador in Kabul was abducted and murdered. United States considered that the plot to assassinate his Ambassador was known by the President Amin who did nothing to stop it. Then, United States interrupted their economic aid programs and increased their hostility toward a Government that qualified as pro-Soviet.

On spite of being a communist, the relation of the President Hafizullah Amin with the Soviet Union was very difficult. He knew that by suggestions of Fidel Castro and Andrei Gromyko he was sentenced. Also, he was not implicated in the killing of the US Ambassador Adolph Dubs, and suspected that the Soviets had used cronies of Babrak Karmal in order to fan the flames between United States with his Government, and Washington in fact has fallen in the trap.

The rivalry between Babrak Karmal and Hafizullah Amin split the PDPA, and he was accused to be an agent of the CIA. The Soviet decided to intervene using the Twenty-Year Treaty of Friendship. Hafizullah Amin was killed by the KGB meanwhile Soviet troops entered the country "for strategic reasons" in December 1979, and imposed Babrak Karmal, who occupied the seat of Prime Minister, President of the Revolutionary Council and general Secretary of the people's Democratic Party.

In various parts of the country began to grow resistance to the Soviet invaders and Muhaideens guerrillas5 were organized. Islamists traveled to Afghan land to combat "Satan" in volunteer expeditions financed by Saudi Arabia. At the time, millions of Afghan peasants took refuge in neighboring Pakistan and Iran. The Mujahedeen guerrillas, divided into various factions, supported by different countries (United States, Iran, Pakistan, Saudi Arabia) coincided with growing divisions in Kabul.

In May 1986, Babrak Karmal was replaced as Secretary of the PDPA by Mohammed Najibullah, a young doctor of Pashtun nationality, who in January 1987, announced a unilateral cease-fire, accompanied by guarantees for the opposition leaders who wanted to negotiate with the Government, amnesty to insurgent's prisoners and the promise of a speedy withdrawal of Soviet troops. The mujahedeen, however, continued to fight.

After six years of negotiations, an Afghan-Pakistani agreement was signed in Geneva with warranty from United States and the Soviet Union. That agreement established conditions for relations between both States, specified principles of non-intervention and guarantee the voluntary return of the refugees, who by then amounted over 4 million. Another document, signed by Afghanistan and the Soviet Union provided for the withdrawal of Soviet troops, which started to become effective a month later. The PDPA changed its name to the Watan Party6.

In September 1991, United States and the Soviet Union agreed to stop sending weapons to the Government and the Afghan guerrillas, leaving the confrontation between Saudi Arabia and Iran, and groups of mujahedeen that both countries financed. Once the Soviet Union vanished, the regime in Kabul ran out of external support and Najibullah took refuge at the headquarters of the UN in Kabul in April 1992 marking the fall of the Communist regime. Then, the Government remained in the hands of four Vice-Presidents.

Authorities announced their willingness to negotiate with the rebel groups, but their interview, at the gates of the capital, with Commander Ahmed Shah Massud, provoked protests by Mujahedeen groups of Pashtuns majority in the South and East of the country[7].

From Pakistan, Gulbudin Hekmatiar, head of an Islamic group[8] threatened to start bombarding the capital if the Government didn't give up. In the following days, forces of Ahmad Shah Massoud and Hekmatiar entered Kabul within same combat. The Alliance of "moderate" Muslim groups headed by Massoud, appointed Defense Minister in the new Government, gained control of the capital, expelling the fundamentalists led by Gulbudin Hekmatiar.

In May, the interim Council formally dissolved the Watan Party and established a special court to prosecute former Communist officials who had violated national or Islamic laws. The Khad, the secret police and the National Assembly were also disbanded. Some changes showed the Government's intention of reintroducing Islamic law in the country: it banned the sale of alcohol and tried to impose new regulations that forced women to cover their heads and wear the traditional clothes of Islamism.

Hekmatiar continued fighting Kabul, demanding the removal of Massoud and the militia of Abdul Rashid Dostum, who had been a member of the Communist Government, from which withdrew to join the Muslim guerrillas who seized power. By then, the economy of the country was paralyzed, and 60% of the productive apparatus destroyed.

The Pakistani Government decided to cut food and weapons smuggling across its border with Afghanistan, to weaken Hekmatiar, whom it accused of damaging relations between the two countries. From 1993, the president in Kabul and the leader of Jamiat-i-Islami, Buranuddin Rabbani, jointly with Hekmatiar and the lord war Dostum would be the main leaders of the fight, which was marked by covenants and betrayals.

The Taliban

In 1995 emerged the Taliban armed group in the South of Afghanistan, which changed the course of the war. These guerrillas, trained in Pakistan, were aimed to create the Islamic Government in Afghanistan and had the support of broad sectors of society. Since its proclamation, above-mentioned leaders formed a "traditionalist-communist Alliance", which attempted against Islam.

With no memory of the past or plans for the future, the Pakistani madrassa students took refuge in their dogma. The Afghan dilemma lies on this point: four powerful ethnic groups of different Islamic tendencies, which have been enemies for centuries. When it comes to exercise power, each has been relentless with the rest.

Taliban-prone Pashtun was not the only ethnic group that has carried out genocide; for this reason, in Afghanistan coalitions, pacts, and the 'representativeness' in Government have never worked. This country has always operated from cruel hegemony of one ethnicity over another.

The Taliban is not an indigenous movement with historical roots, but a creature of the extinct former first Minister Pakistani Ben-Azir Bhutto and her bodies of intelligence (ISI), to bring power to the Pashtun (for being components of Pakistan and majority in his army) and reopen and stabilize commercial land routes and smuggling with Central Asia, especially with Turkmenistan.

The Taliban, Pashtun tribes, received financial support from Afghan traders -former camel jockeys, today truck carriers- who approved the design of Bhutto. Only a handful of Taliban followers had fought against the Red Army in the

1980s, and another small group did so against the regime of President Najibullah, after the withdrawal of Soviet troops.

But the vast majority of these Islamic warriors had never fought; they were young students of the Quran, hatched from hundreds of madrassas[1], which were reproduced as mushrooms in the fields of Afghan refugees in Pakistan. Most were very young, orphaned by the war, indoctrinated by crude mullahs[2] about an ideal Islamic society; and see themselves as 'purifiers' of a way of life that has been slid to the corruption and excesses. But they do not know their country; have no memory of their past or plans for the future, only the present of their dogma.

Iran, Turkey, India, and Russia, jointly with four republics of Central Asia[3] supported the Northern Alliance, in contrast with Pakistan and Saudi Arabia who were inclined in favor of the Taliban. For its part, the hostility between Iran and the Taliban will be a historical animosity that will respond to old desires of the Shah, embraced by the ayatollahs, to convert the fervent Sunni Pashtuns to Shiism Islam.

This foreign intrusion on Afghanistan sparked a fierce regional conflict where even Iran has been repeatedly ready to invade the territory. At the heart of this struggle lies the intense rivalry of neighboring States and oil companies from the West for the last, unexploited and vast reserves of oil and gas from the planet (Central Asia), to determine the possible transit, mounting and terminal pipelines for transporting this energy to markets in Europe and Asia.

Russia, with its old Tsarist dream of achieving a window to the Indian Ocean; Pakistan favored the Pashtun, with the Taliban territory firmly under its orbit; Iran assisting Afghan Shiites; Saudi Arabia affiliating with the Taliban to control future crude oil prices; Washington who supported attempts by the oil giant Unocal to build a gas pipeline from Turkmenistan to Pakistan, through Taliban territory.

But it was not the battle for oil pipelines from Central Asia that concerned the economies of the most develop nations and part of the Islamic world, but the Taliban fundamentalism, which, after conquering Kandahar and capture Kabul, in September 1996, crushed the armed tribal groups, triggering a bloody ethnic cleansing against the Shiites.

In the name of Allah, they tortured, castrated, flayed alive and hanged the enemies that fell into their hands, starting with the former President Najibullah, doing so with two-thirds of the country. The Taliban poisoned water wells, destroyed irrigation systems, wiped out towns and cities, precipitated droughts and divided the country into Pashtun and non-Pashtun. Along with the destruction of the two colossal Buddha's, the most brutal act was the blockade to the Hazara region in the middle of Afghanistan, which brought hunger to more than one million for the simple fact of women refusing to comply with its prohibitions.

After the victory, Mullah Mohammed Omar Akhunzada a one-eyed, mysterious and elusive man of little education, without pedigree or connection with the family of the Prophet with a harem of three concubines, was legitimized as head of this brotherhood in April 1996, by perching on a minaret of Kandahar, wrapped with the supposed sacred mantle of the Prophet Muhammad before the eyes of a delirious crowd of Taliban who proclaimed him in the territories of the Taliban, as the Commander of the believers[4], title which had only assumed Omar, the first Caliph in Islamic history.

The extreme application of the Sharia -Islamic law- by soldiers of Allah and through a religious police, spread panic in the region, especially in Islamic communities through Pakistan and Central Asia. All kinds of recreation were prohibited, from listening to music to children flying kites, setting as social entertainment forced attendance to the public executions.

Under the Taliban regime, the use of the Internet by those who didn't belong to the Government was punished with the death penalty. In this context of transition and despite the demise of the Taliban regime, the situation of women remained painful. Outside Kabul, women with intentions to study and work were pursued, girls were forced to marry, and a large number of Afghan children -even under four years of age- were abducted and sold abroad as sex slaves or for labor.

The Taliban, in sum, assumed all the characteristics of a religious military order that recalls those of the Christianity of the Crusaders, or the Turkish janissaries. Its absolute male society supposedly challenged by the other half of the human race –hate toward women- led them to prohibiting women from education, work, public life, covering her from head to toe.

These orphans, servants and eunuchs, without knowing the company of women, mothers, sisters, cousins or friends, who received from their mullahs the notion of the tempting female that obstructed services to Allah, that have mitigated their carnal desires in homosexual relationships, didn't see anything unusual in the dreadful proscriptions of genre they instituted.

The cost of the Taliban regime has been the generalization of the hunger, a tide of refugees to all points, the exacerbation of divergences ethnic, plunging the country into chaos, turning them back in history, polarizing the regional States into two hostile sides. With the Taliban drug trafficking expanded and international terrorists like Osama Bin-Laden and his Al–Qaeda were protected. The way in which the Roman historian Cornelius Tacitus described the Roman conquest Britain fits them: "the Roman army created the desolation and called it peace".

In addition to Pakistan, Saudi Arabia and United States supported the intervention of the Taliban army. In September 1996 Kabul fell into their hands, while the Government was heading to the North of the country. The Islamic National United Front for the Salvation of Afghanistan mostly composed of Tajiks, Uzbeks and Hazaras factions, known as the Northern Alliance (AN) was formed in June 1997.

Once in possession of Kabul, following their rules to govern according to his interpretation of the Quran (the ascetic neo-banditry, popular among mountain pastors), the Taliban eradicated women from the public sphere, removing them from the educational system. At the same time, music and singing (except religious hymns), cinema and theatre, and alcohol were forbidden, by declaring them "un-Islamic".

The Taliban decision-making body was the Shura - Council- composed of 25 to 30 members and an expanded council of hundreds of members. By the end of 2000, the Taliban army controlled more than 95% of Afghan territory.

On 3 September 2001, Massoud, leader of the Northern Alliance, was killed allegedly ordered by Mullah Omar, what would have constituted a deadly blow to the aspirations of the opposition if it wasn't for the mediation of the September 11 terrorist attack on New York and Washington, which triggered the United States campaign against the terrorist organization Al–Qaeda directed by Saudi Osama Bin Laden, former Mujahedeen who lived in Afghanistan with thousands of his men protected by the Taliban.

That same month, the Council of elders meeting in Kabul, asked the Taliban Government to persuade Bin Laden to voluntarily leave the country. The Council decided also to call a Jihad (holy war) in the event that United States would attack Afghanistan. On October 7, aerial bombings of United States against Afghanistan started, within the framework of the campaign initially called "Infinite Justice" and then "Enduring Freedom" by U.S. President George W. Bush.

The coalition against Afghanistan was attended by the direct involvement of United States, United Kingdom, Australia and Canada and the support of the EU and NATO (including Turkey), China, Russia, Israel, India, Saudi Arabia and Pakistan a former ally of the Taliban. Iran and Iraq condemned the attacks. Rabbani has not only welcomed the Western military intervention but linked the future of Afghanistan with the "destruction" of the Taliban.

As the evolution of the war was clearing the political future, the leadership of Burhan Uddin Rabbani as President of the Islamic State of Afghanistan declined noticeably and the ruling triumvirate composed of Abdullah Abdullah, Minister for Foreign Affairs and spokesman main front, Yunus Qanuni, Interior Minister, and Mohammed Kassem Fahim, Defense Minister took shape.

The first two, Abdullah and Qanuni, embodied new generations of leaders trained abroad and with a notorious secular trend, while Kassem Fahim -right hand of the murdered Massoud- replaced him in office. After an aerial punishment that lasted several weeks, the Northern Alliance regained two-thirds of the country.

Finally, on November 13 it entered Kabul, breaching its commitments not to do so until the formation of a transitional Government, causing the reaction of the former monarch Mohammed Zahir, the United States and the UN. A good part of the population welcomed their arrival, since it meant the ending of both the Taliban regime and the U.S. bombing. The collapse of the Taliban was imminent when, between November 27 and December 5, place the Inter-Afghan Conference in Bonn took place.

The Northern Alliance had the biggest delegation with 11 of the 25 power figures, with Yunus Qanuni as Chief, followed by the delegations of the Group of Rome (of Mohammed Zahir confidence), the Cyprus Group (supported by Iran) and the Assembly of notable Pashtuns in Peshawar (Pakistan-supported).

The newly reinstated Governor of Nangarhar, Abdul Qadir, withdrew in disagreement with the role reserved to his ethnic group, the Pashtun. For the first time two women participated in the discussion. An agreement creating an interim administration of 30 members, for whose presidency the pro-monarchy Pashtun Hamid Karzai was appointed, was finally sealed.

A timetable of two years and a half was agreed until general elections, before which a *Loya Jirga* would formed as an emergency, an authority of transition and a constitutional *Loya Jirga*, assisted by a UN international security force.

The Northern Alliance was granted 18 of the 29 ministries. Abdullah, Qanuni and Fahim were confirmed in the functions they already played in the Alliance Government, while it was tasked to Mohammed Zahir the symbolic inaugurating of the *Loya Jirga*. Rabbani accepted the decisions taken recently on December 12, even though -according to him- Hamid Karzai was a President "imposed from outside".

On December 22, it was issued the transfer of power to Hamid Karzai. President Bush gave the order to restart trade with Afghanistan in February 2002, after 16 years of interruption. These had been suspended in January 1986 after the Soviet occupation took place. In April the former monarch Mohammed Zahir returned to Afghanistan, expressing that he would not claim the throne.

Yet the struggle between various factions continued and neither Osama Bin-Laden nor Mullah Omar had been found, target of the global anti-terrorism hunt headed by United States.

In July, Vice-President Haji Abdul Qadir and his driver died under a hail of bullets at the gates of the Ministry of Public Labor in Kabul. Abdel Qadir was a Pashtun who had collaborated as Commander of NATO in the fight against the Taliban North of Afghanistan; his murderers were never caught.

In September, President Karzai survived an assassination attempt in Kandahar, perpetrated by a member of the Al-Qaeda network. The attacker -later identified as Abdul Rahman- fired at the car of the representative. The Kandahar Governor, Gul Agha Sherzai, and a bodyguard were wounded. The attack occurred just a few hours after a bomb car exploded in Kabul and killed at least 10 people.

Towards the end of 2002, most of the country was controlled by powerful commanders -also called warlords- who exercised their power without great interference from the central Government and supported by the United States.

The authority of President Karzai was limited mainly to the country's capital.

In August, NATO launched a peace mission in the country, its first outside Europe in 54 years of history. NATO would be responsible for the planning, monitoring, command and control of the ISAF security in Afghanistan, with UN mandate. That same month, as first step towards elections in June 2004, the United Nations and the Government of Afghanistan signed an agreement for the adoption of a program of voter registration in preparation for the first national elections in 30 years.

In November of that year, the Constitutional Review Commission delivered a new draft Constitution for Afghanistan to President Karzai and Lakhdar Brahimi, UN Special Envoy. The draft establishes the creation of an Islamic Republic in which all citizens have equal rights. There is no reference to Sharia or Islamic law, but it was expected that no laws would contradict Islam.

However, Amnesty International warned that this draft didn't protect the rights of women by not prohibiting discrimination based on gender and not fully recognizing equality between men and women. Amid a growing instability, the UN suspended in November all its activities in the province of Ghazni in the East of Afghanistan, after the assassination of an official from its refugee agency.

That same month, were postponed to September the first democratic elections, after the Taliban hegemony. President Karzai announced that presidential and parliamentary elections would be made at the same time. Although the initial schedule, held in Bonn (Germany) in 2001, had contemplated presidential elections for June, they postponed it because of security problems and the delay in the registration of voters.

During the same period, the Afghan President said that his country was rising from the ashes of more than 20 years of war and requested international aid for the construction of schools, hospitals and roads. President Karzai warned that the country would need at least $ 28 billion over the next seven years for reconstruction.

The United States Army liberated 80 prisoners suspected of belonging to the Taliban movement in January 2005. More than 30 people were killed in January 2006 in a series of suicide attacks in the southern province of Kandahar.

In February there were clashes between government troops and suspected combatants Taliban in Helmand province, also in the South. That same month, a meeting of donors in London pledged to send more than 10 billion dollars, over the next 5 years, to help the reconstruction of the country. At the end of July 2006, NATO took over control of the southern region of the country, traditionally dominated by the Taliban and the druglords[5]. This transfer of control (of the United States to an organization composed of 37 countries, which increased its presence from 3,000 to 9,000 effective in the territory) coincided with an increase in violence in the area, where sometimes has more daily bombings than Iraq.

Dictatorship with atomic weapons

Pakistan means land of the pure. It was religion (Islam) the unifying element for people of different ethnic communities and with diverse languages.

The early Muslims who arrived in the Indian sub-continent were merchants of Arabia and Persia. The first permanent Muslim conquest was Sind, accomplished by Mohammed Ibn Kassim, in the year 711. In the 13th century the Muslim Kingdom of India were laid, with wide borders and capital in Delhi. After the conquest, the region was ruled by various Muslim dynasties, the last one of which was that of the Mongols.

The problem of Muslim identity, however, acquired great importance with the decline of Muslim power and the rise of the Indian middle class during the British colonialism. At the beginning of the 20th century Muslim leaders agreed on the need to have an effective political organization.

In October 1906, a delegation of Muslim leaders met with the British viceroy[1] and demanded a reform of the electoral system with a separate regime for Muslims. That same year was founded in Dhaka (Bangladesh) the Pan-India Muslim League which aimed to defend the political rights and the interests of the Muslim Indians.

The first to express the concept of Pakistan in its most elemental form was the philosopher Mohammed Iqbal, when in 1931 he proposed the formation of a state for the Muslims of India.

During the 1930s grew among Muslims the awareness of their own identity, together with the need to preserve within

386 The roots of Terrorism

separate territorial limits. Led by Mohammed Ali Jinnah, the Pan-India Muslim League continued its campaign in Pakistan, a land apart within British India.

After the general elections of April 1946, the League called a Convention of the newly elected parliamentarians Muslims in Delhi. The Convention reiterated the demand for and independent Pakistan. The Hindu-Muslim relationship was severely affected by the tensions and protests in different parts of the India between both communities.

This situation convinced the leaders of the National Congress of India to accept an independent Pakistan as a solution to the problems between both communities. On June 3, 1947, after the British withdrawal from India, they announced a separation plan, accepted by both the Muslim League and the Congress.

On 14 August of the same year the new State of Pakistan was born, including Eastern Punjab, Sind, Baluchistan, (northeastern frontier province) and East Bengal, surrounding India through the Northwest and Northeast.

From its birth to independent lifestyle Pakistan suffered permanent political crisis. Between 1948 and 1949 Pakistan waged a war with India and managed to annex one-third of the territory of the border province of Kashmir. The Muslim-majority territory had been under the control of India in 1947 after which local Kashmiri Government chose its annexation to that country in exchange for military support to fight an invasion of Pakistani tribes.

On October 27, 1958 General Ayyub Khan emerged as strongman, introduced a basic democracy, which was a system of local self-government with indirect presidential election. Martial law was lifted in 1962 and a new Constitution was drafted, which gave absolute powers to the President and Pakistan became an Islamic Republic.

Ayyub Khan had to resign on March 25, 1969, after massive protests. Martial law was declared again and General Yahya Khan was appointed President. In the period from

October to December 1970 General elections were held for the first time.

Two political parties, the Awami League in East Pakistan and the Party of the People of Pakistan (PPP) in the Western part triumphed. However, in the parliamentary elections the absolute majority in all Pakistan corresponded to the Awami League, which the federal Government granted. But the Parliament session was delayed and in March 1971 the village in Eastern Pakistan, led by the Awami League, began a movement for the liberation of Bangladesh.

A civil war began and the Awami League formed a Government in India from exile. The Indian army intervened, and on December 16, 1971 and Bangladesh attained its independence.

Zulfikar Ali Bhutto, leader of the Party of the People of Pakistan, formed a civilian Government in 1972, after the resignation of General Yahya; it promoted the participation of the public sector in the economy, developed a foreign policy of non-alignment and introduced a radical land reform.

Again, in 1977, General Zia-ul Haq overthrew the Government of Ali Bhutto and proclaimed martial law. Ali Bhutto was sent to jail and a court found him guilty of conspiracy in the assassination of a political leader of the opposition and sentenced him to death.

In 1988 destine changed drastically for Islamic terrorism. The plane in which traveled the President of Pakistan, Zia-ul-Hag and his Government team, crashed under still unknown circumstances, allowing the rise of the daughter of Alí Bhutto, Ben-Azir Bhutto as the first woman to preside over a predominantly Islamic country, and with it the most dogmatic group vision of Pakistan.

Ben-Azir Bhutto immediately entered into alliances with Syria, Iran and North Korea, in her attempt to revive militant Islam across Asia, obtained Kashmir, and installed the Taliban in Afghanistan. Also, she launched Bin-Laden and his al-Qaeda organization against "moderate" countries of the area. All this was done under the noses of the Western powers.

In Pakistan the army has always been an institution of great power. The country joined the Organization of the Treaty of Southeast Asia (OTSEA) in 1954 and the Central Treaty Organization (OTCEN) in 1955, two powerful military alliances led by the United States. Although Pakistan withdrew later from these alliances, ties with the United States didn't change.

Relations with India have always been strained. Both countries maintain claims on the territory of the State of Kashmir. India considers it an integral part of the country, while Pakistan has been asking the realization of a referendum so that the people of Kashmir decide their own destiny.

Pakistan faced India in the 1948-49, 1965 and 1971 wars. After the latest conflict the two States agreed in the creation of an area of ceasefire on both sides of the Kashmir borderline, which meant in addition to the territorial division, the separation of the local population. Since then, Kashmir nationalist groups have demanded the creation of an independent State in the region.

Pakistan strongly objected to the 1979 Soviet intervention in Afghanistan. In mid-1990, there were approximately three million Afghan refugees in the country, which also supported the struggle of the Mujahedeen, the groups of Afghan resistance against the pro-Soviet regime in Kabul.

It was during the rule of general Zia-ul-Haq, (1989-1997) and the Government of Ben-Azir Bhutto that a network of nearly 2,500 madrassas financed by the Saudi regime was created. The madrassa had only one objective: the production of fanatics (225,000 of them) on behalf of a gloomy cosmopolitan Islamism.

Their only truth was "the divine" and anyone who rebelled against their Imam did it against Allah. They were willing to kill and die for their faith if their religious leaders asked for it.

The Taliban creed, as an ultra-sect variant, was inspired by the Wahhabi sect that governs in Saudi Arabia.

The Sunni clerics of Cairo mosque, Al-Zahra, and the Shiia theologians of Qum, denounced the severity of the Afghans Mullah as a disgrace to the Prophet.

Those young Quranic students, Talibans, were then deployed along the border by the Pakistani army, and were sent to Afghanistan to fight as Mujahedeen.

During the years of the Soviet intervention in Afghanistan, United States used Pakistani territory to supply with arms the rebel groups. This situation turned Pakistan into an indispensable ally in the Washington policy for the region, which obtained from then on a vital US economic aid.

On August 6, 1990 Pakistani President Ghulam Ishaq Khan laid off Prime Minister Ben-Azir Bhutto on charges of nepotism and corruption. He dissolved the National Assembly and on October 24 Nawaz Sharif was elected to the post of Prime Minister, with the support of the Muslim League, a coalition formed against Ben-Azir Bhutto.

In addition to economic reforms, the Government of Nawaz Sharif began a weathered process of re- Islamization, introducing the Sharia (Islamic law) portraying the previous Government of Ben-Azir Bhutto as a period of religious regression. The application of Sharia law brought as immediate consequence a clear decline in the legal and social situation of women. The Government banned in the media any kind of mention on the right of divorce for women.

At the outbreak of the conflict in the Persian Gulf, Pakistan sided with the United States. It sent troops to Saudi Arabia after the Iraqi invasion to Kuwait, but under heavy public opinion pro-Iraqi sympathy, the Government announced that its forces would be limited to defend the Holy places of Islam and would not participate in combat or enter into Iraqi territory.

Besides the clashes between Government and opposition, Pakistan suffers, for years, periodic outbreaks of inter-ethnic struggle, especially among former refugees from India[2].

Violence has mainly affected the region of Sind and the city of Karachi, the main industrial center. In February 1992, the ancient dispute over the Kashmir border nearly triggered a new armed conflict between Pakistan and India. Pakistani-backed Islamic terrorists frequently crossed the border between Pakistan and India's Kashmir.

United States announced his displeasure at the Pakistani development of a nuclear weapons program made public this year. Washington suspended the financial aids and the arms sales to Islamabad. In response to these measures, Pakistan managed to get the economic and technological support of China for its nuclear research program.

Ben-Azir Bhutto returned to power after winning the elections of October 6. The efforts of Ben-Azir Bhutto for the democratization of the country and the equal rights of gender, were tainted by political and ethnic violence in 1994 and 1995, the bloodiest years since 1971, when the separation of Bangladesh.

One of the main political adversaries of Ben-Azir Bhutto, her brother Murtaza Bhutto, died in a clash with police on September 20, 1996. Murtaza Bhutto led a guerrilla group demanding the resignation of the Prime Minister. The Bhutto siblings were confronted since their father was toppled, in 1977. In November 1996, Ben-Azir Bhutto, accused of corruption, was relieved from her duties as Prime Minister, so that new parliamentary elections were issued.

Military confrontations between India and Pakistan continued registering in the Kashmir region. The negotiations that took place between New Delhi and Islamabad were still deadlocked: while India held that this area belonged to them, the Pakistani Government demanded a referendum for self-determination. The tension deepened in May 1998 when India conducted a series of nuclear tests, to which Pakistan responded by conducting its own nuclear tests.

On 12 October 1999, General Pervez Musharraf, who had been in charge of military operations in Kashmir, gave a coup. The Prime Minister Nawaz Sharif was imprisoned accused of hijacking, terrorism and attempted murder.

General Musharraf assumed the head of State and was appointed President of Pakistan on June 20, 2001, announcing that it would retain functions as Chief Executive, and would remain the Commander of the General staff of the army. Pakistan became the first nuclear power history in being led by a military.

After the terrorist attacks of September 11 2001 in New York and Washington, the United States announced the lifting of the economic and military sanctions that had been imposed on India and Pakistan after the 1998 nuclear tests. The measure was motivated by the support of General Musharraf to the U.S. military operation in Afghanistan against the Taliban regime and Saudi terrorist Osama Bin Laden.

The Taliban regime or Kabul had been directly supported military, economic and ideological by Pakistan, who considered the Taliban triumph as their first "victory".

Why Pakistan, which had willingly accepted the funds and weapons from the United States during the Cold War, had become violently anti-American overnight? According to the Pakistanis, many of their officers who had faithfully served the United States since 1951 felt humiliated by Washington's indifference.

The new "coalition against terrorism" headed by US needed the services of the Pakistani army, but general Musharraf walked the razor's edge. Too explicit a support for Washington could provoke a civil war in Pakistan and split the army.

Many things have changed in the last two decades, but the ironies of this story continue to multiply. In the same Pakistan, Islamism has expanded with the patronage of the State, not by popular support. The ascendancy that enjoys religious fundamentalism is the legacy of the previous military dictatorship of general Zia-ul-Haq, who received strong support from Washington and London during his 11 years of dictatorship.

When the American Secretary of State, Colin Powell, visited in October Islamabad, Musharraf asked the support of United States in the conflict in Kashmir, as well as economic aid to deal with the economic consequences caused by the flood of Afghan refugees crossing the border.

For the elections in October 2002, the Government imposed restrictions and proscriptions on important leaders, including Ben-Azir Bhutto and Nawaz Sharif. The Pakistan People's Party, which favors the military, received a slight majority; however, the most notable result was the growth of Islamist parties -especially in the border areas with Afghanistan-, growth that would make them key in any coalition Government.

Sharia law was introduced in June 2003 in the northeastern border province. Pakistan declared the ceasefire in Kashmir, in November 2003, which was immediately imitated by India. In December, President Musharraf miraculously survived an attempt on his life when a bomb installed under a bridge exploded seconds after the passage of his car.

In the Western Province of Baluchistan, nationalist forces had begun guerrilla's attacks in claims of greater autonomy, and part of revenue derived from the reserve of gas in the region.

In February 2004, the main nuclear scientist of the country, Doctor Abdul Kader Khan, admitted having worked in secret development of nuclear weapons and said that the technology had been transferred to Libya, Iran and North Korea.

Colin Powell, US Secretary of State, declared in March 2004 that Pakistan, besides NATO was the greatest ally of his country in the fight against terrorism, after the intense action against the Al-Qaeda networks, carried out along the border with Afghanistan.

The Sublime Porte

The ashes from the Ottoman Empire...
¿Will they re-ignite?

After the Pharaonic era, the Ottoman dynasty is the most stable in history, with an army whose roots reach the Roman legions. Heirs of the Baghdad Caliphate and the Mongol Khanates, they took Constantinople in 1453, turning the Mediterranean into a Turkish Lake.

In reality, they only varnished with Islam the Byzantine Empire. Its sultans were mere Byzantine emperors and their mosques, copies of the old architectural style of the Orthodox churches.

The big difference between the Turkish Caliphate with the rest of those who forged the Islam is that Turkey was a direct continuation of the odd Greek and Byzantine monstrosity, where *Pax Ottoman* also marked the marriage of Euro-Christian civilizations and the Asian, in the midst of a multiethnic and multicultural environment that held three monotheistic faiths.

The Turkish Empire approached in geographic coverage that of Alexander the Great. Like the imperial Macedonia, the state and the army were fused into a military theocracy that has lasted, and governs the country behind the curtains.

Another Ottoman merit was that the Caliphate was the intractable religious authority in which all tradition schools (Sunna) were personified.

But this multinational structure project opposed the European minimalism of nation-state in vogue and the ominous intrusion of Russia by raising the range of Nations to tiny ethnic groups in the Balkan Brazier.

The fate of the Ottomans was sealed with the error of allying with Germany, the loser of the First World War; and by seeing the regions of their empire (the Balkans, Caucasus, the Great Syria, Mesopotamia, and the Arabian Peninsula) transformed into a hotbed of artificial Islamic States that formed a still unstable political chess-board.

While it is true that on the threshold of the 20th century the Ottoman colossus was sick, the winds of reform and renovation rushing the Young Turks were not accepted by the West. It was a mistake because the Young Turks were a core of officers aware of the military and economic ascendancy of the Western civilization and the need to modernize their conservative Islamic world.

Thus, Paris and London derailed the work of the Young Turks, seeking to forge a modern multinational secular State of almost all the articulated Islamic world until Europe, which were governed by a professional middle class, and that encompass all the oil of the Middle East.

Only the political and military skills of Mustafa Kemal (Ataturk), the hero of Gallipoli and the brightest of the nationalists of the century, was able to save the plateau of Anatolia, founded on secular pillars to the Republic of Turkey.

In Turkish democracy, established after the Second World War, the military theocracy has been reform and has been the revolutionary fiber of society -heritage of the reformers of Ataturk- supported behind the scenes by the financial communities of Armenian, Greek and Turkish Jews, the erstwhile Byzantine Istanbul elite.

The Ottoman Caliphate had such confidence in its authority and legitimacy that never considered the possible rivalry of other religions or ethnic groups. The Islamization in Turkey was very different from the rest of the area, with little reason for the germination of a fundamentalist trend Taliban style.

The destruction of the Ottoman Caliphate abolished the institutional legitimacy, which until then enjoyed the Muslim tradition, creating a vacuum that the extremists have tried to fill. That is why we are still dealing with a reality that comes from the Turks, without the merits of the Ottoman Empire where the minority religions had self-governing territories under the patronage of the Sultanate.

The postmodern Turkey, dotted with a flagrant individualism, has outbid the traditionalism of the Middle East. Women enjoy more freedom and rights than in other Islamic societies and the percentage of the professionals is larger than in many countries of the West.

Today, the Army General Staff led by General Hussein Kivrikoglu, actually manages Turkey and its foreign policy. The struggle between the new Islamic rich and the wealthy Jewish community, has not however, originated an identity crisis, because the clear separation of the state and the Islamic religion is recognized by all, to the point that it was as recently as 1996 when an Islamic, Necmettin Erbakan, assumed the position of Prime Minister.

The renewed Turkish Islam, organized in the Party of Virtue, rejects fundamentalism and is not nourished by the declassed (as in Algeria or Iran) and the most ardent of them hates the rest of the Arabs.

In the past two decades, Turkey has undertaken an offensive into the territories once part of its empire, although it takes advantage of every occasion to accuse of treason the Arabs for subordinating to England and France during the First World War.

Turkey drags the Kurdish complication, the only minority group that ran out of state after that conflict. Syria, which maintains a complaint with Turkey for the diversion of the river Euphrates, claims the Turkish southern portion of Hatai and encourages Kurdish terrorism. With Armenia remain a huge conflict for the massacre of a million Armenians in 1915, and the expulsion of Anatolia, which remained alive.

Istanbul convinced NATO to intercede in favor of the Bosnian Muslims, and its merchants have once more invaded the Balkans. The military campaigns of NATO in the Balkans, the strikes of United States against Iraq, against terrorism and Afghanistan, found in Turkey a military valuable and strong springboard, but at the same time, a socio-political cunning that once again becomes the key and the door of the West to the world of Islam.

In the case of Iraq, Turkey has not ceased in its claims about the oil province of Mosul, hoping to recover it if the Iraqi's central unity collapses, purpose to which they have contributed.

Although the Syrian Arabs, Greeks and Armenians were their traditional victims, the Jews, the Hashemite and the Azeri[1] were always linked to their spheres of power; hence, its excellent relations with the Jordanian royal family and Azerbaijan.

A scenario that threatens to become a nightmare is the coalition between Turkey, Israel, Jordan and Azerbaijan, as opposed to Syria, Greece and Armenia.

Turkey feeds a long-term strategy in Azerbaijan, where dived into the economy and train the army. There it seeks to build a thousand-mile pipeline from Baku to the Mediterranean port of Ceyhan, project endorsed in 1999 by the U.S. President Bill Clinton, and that competes with the other alternative through Iran. The Caspian can produce four million barrels a day of oil of high quality, twice more than Kuwait.

Israelis perceive that Turkey has a bright future and that their hostility toward Judaism is warmer than that of the rest of the Middle East; that is why, up to recently, they formed an Association of commercial, military and intelligence between Tel Aviv and Istanbul, a dangerous combination in the Middle East.

Now that the Soviet Empire was gone, the Black Sea[2] can transform in its hinterland. The rivalry for the Caucasus -with oil reserves exceeding those of Iraq and Iran combined- promises to have as main actors Turkey and Russia. The Christian West again recognizes in Istanbul their wall of containment of a flamboyant and aggressive Russian Orthodox autocracy.

In the same way the States of the Middle East, likely to explode into ethnic pieces, are precisely adjacent to Turkey: Syria, Iraq, Armenia, Georgia and Azerbaijan. The fate of Iraq also passes through Istanbul.

It is an exaggeration to say that a modern Byzantine-Ottoman Empire is born on the Bosporus, but the reality cannot be ignored that Turkey can project its powerful silhouette in the Middle East and Central Asia, altering the political equation of all that tangled geography.

That is why the geography that for centuries conferred the Ottoman Empire to be the "Sublime Porte'" to Asia could assign actual Turkey with the same role in the 21st century.

Notes

Archeology of a geo-strategy
1 Secret agreement reached between the British and French diplomats, Sir Mark Sykes and Georges Picot.
2 Lesch, David W. (1996), *Middle East and the United States: A Historical and Political Reassessment*, Boulder, CO: Westview Press, p. 92, 94.
3 $12.8 billion dollars.
4 At 10 minutes from the Soviet Union.

Cuba: Terrorism within the Revolution
1 For example, from the early involvement in Angola to the January 1988 siege of Cuito Cuanavale, Cuban military activities in Africa were practically ignored by the Cuban press.
2 In 1960, Brazil's president Janio Quadros embarked on a dynamic policy toward Africa. Like Cuba, Brazil supported the self-determination of the remaining African colonies and attempted to find new markets in Africa.
3 Jaime Suchlicki, Director of the Institute for Cuban and Cuban-American Studies. Miami, September 2001.
4 Idem.
5 Orlando Hidalgo Castro. Spy for Fidel. Miami: E. A. Seeman Publishing, Inc 1971 pp. 39-40.
6 Suchlicki, Jaime. Castro and Terrorism: A Chronology. University of Miami, September 2001.
7 Castro's 26 of July Movement began the pattern of airplane hijackings - 1958 with the assault of a Cubana Airlines plane that crash-landed in the western province on November 2, 1958, by the Preston sugar mill on the northern corner of Oriente. There was only one American survivor. See Wayne S. Smith. The Closest of Enemies (New York, London; W.W, Norton & Company, 1987); 31-33).
8 Hugh Thomas, *The Cuban Revolution* (New York: Harper & Row Publishers, 1977), pp. 218-219.
9 Claire Sterling, The Terror Network: The Secret War of International Terrorism; New York Holt, Rinehart and Winston, 1985 p. 253 7.
10 Zoo, 1967-1969: The Cuban Program and Other Atrocities, on "Honor Bound: American Prisoners of War in Southeast Asia 1961-/973," by Stuart I. Rochester and Frederick Kiley, Naval Institute Press, 1998. See also "Faith of my Fathers. Senator John McCain, Random House, 1999. See also "El piloto de Vietnam identifica a su torturador", Pablo Alfonso, El Nuevo Herald, September 9, 1999.

A religion of war
1 The *Shahada*.
2 Indian, Chinese, Japanese.
3 Baget Bozzo, Gianni. Baget Bozzo, *Di fronte all Islamm. Il grande conflitto*. Marietti, Genova, 2001, 51.

4 2001, 51.

5 Baget Bozzo, 2001, 87.

6 Baget Bozzo, 2001, 90.

7 Baget Bozzo, 2001, 56.

8 The Zoroastrianism or Mazdeism is the name of the religion and philosophy based on the teachings of the Prophet and Iranian reformer Zoroaster (Zarathustra).

9 Gnostic dualist religion founded by Mani.

10 The Sharia.

11 The Jihad is an essential Islamic concept; an obligation imposed by Allah on every Muslim and cannot be ignored or circumvented; it represents a struggle to do the right thing. While for some it is a holy war against the infidel, a majority of Muslim intellectuals insist that Jihad should be understood as a fight without weapons.

12 Tariq Ramadan is the nephew of Hassan Al-Banna, who founded the Islamic integral nationalism group Muslim Brotherhood in 1928. He has studied Islamic theology in Cairo, and is honored in French literature and a specialist in the work of philosopher Friedrich Nietzsche.

Islam: tribe and plutocracy.

1 Karl August Wittfogel. *Oriental Despotism. A comparative study of Total Power*. Yale University Press. New Haven. 1957.

2 The Blue Nile and the White Nile.

3. Islamic north and Christian south.

4. Gerard Chaliand. *Revolution in the Third World*. Viking Adult. 1977.

5. Nabucodonosor II, the Great, is probably the best-known ruler of the Chaldean Dynasty of Babylon. He reigned between 605 and 562 b.c. He is famous for the conquest of Judah and Jerusalem, and the famous hanging gardens of Babylon. Infamous in Jewish tradition, he has been glorified in the Iraq of Sadam Hussein.

6. Daryush Shayegan was born in Tehran in 1935. He studied at the Sorbonne, and has worked as Professor of philosophy at the University of Tehran. He has directed the Iranian Centre for the Dialogue of Civilizations. Considered one of the intellectuals and leading contemporary thinkers of his country, he is the author of ten titles, notably *La Mirada mutilada. Barcelona, Peninsula,* 1990.

7. Against Islamic Extremism: The Writings of Muhammad Said Al-'Ashmawy, Carolyn Fluehr-Lobban editor. Publisher: University Press of Florida. Gainesville, FL, 1998.

8. Ahmed Salman Rushdie. Satanic Verses. Viking Adult. 1988.

Islam: State and Nation

1. Calipha: dogma and sword.

2. The Umma.

3. The Khademul and the Hár Amíne.

4. In 1922 he abolished the Sultanate and in 1923 declared the Republic of Turkey, of which emerged as leader. From the first moment, his Government policy was aimed towards a single objective, based on the construction of a Turkish nation in the image and likeness of the Occidental countries. For this, he issued a decree in favor of the secularization of the Administration and introduced important reforms, such as the implementation of monogamy, an education system and a secular legislation, and the introduction of the Gregorian calendar and the Latin alphabet.

5. Malek Bennabí. *Le Probléme des idées dans le monde musulman.* El Bayyinate, Algiers, 1990 edition.

A Jewish State

1 Theodor Herlz. The Jewish State. Editor Jacob M. Alkow. 1896. Kindle Edition.

2 The Balfour Declaration was a formal document from the British Government posted in November 1917, in which England favored the creation of a Jewish national home in Palestine. The letter was signed by the Secretary of Foreign Relations, Arthur James Balfour, and addressed to Baron Lionel Walter Rothschild, English Jewish personality, for his transmition to the Zionist Federation.

3 It is the part of the original territory of Palestine, which invaded Jordan after the Armistice that followed the declared war of invasion because of the establishment of the State of Israel. It is called in modern times the Latin Languages because is found on the side of the West Bank of the Jordan River.

4 The Kibbutz is an Israeli voluntary agricultural commune that carries a lifestyle based on the principles of socialism and secular Judaism; it is worth mentioning that there are also religious kibbutzim.

5 Aliyah Bet is the Hebrew term that refers to the illegal immigration of Jews to Palestine between 1920 and 1948, when Britain controlled the region. The Hebrew word 'aliyah' (literally 'ascension')

6 Bantustan is the term designated for each of the territories that operated as tribal reserves of non-white people in South Africa and actual Namibia, in the era of segregation during the apartheid.

¿A tribal conflict?

1 Eretz, Israel.

2 The West Bank.

3 Steven, Stewart. *The Spy Masters of Israel.* Ballantine Books, New York, 1980: 106 y 111.

4 The Teflon Warrior.

5 Eisenberg, Denis, Uri Dan y Eli Landau. *The Mossad Inside Stories.* Paddington Press Ltd., New York, 1978: p. 120.

6 Komitet Gosudárstvennoy Bezopásnosti, or the Committee for the Security of the State was the name of the services of intelligence, counter-intelligence and police of the Soviet Union.
7 McLane, Charles B. *Soviet-Middle East Relations. Central Asian Research Centre.* London, 1973, pag. 10.
8 Steven, 1980, pag. 319.
9 Steven, 1980, pag. 331.
10 Said, Edward W. *The Question of Palestine.* Vintage Books Edition, 1992, pag. 170.
11 Steven, 1980, pag. Xxii.
12 Steven, 1980, pag. Xxiv.
13 Darwish, Adel and Gregory Alexander. *Unholy Babylon: The Secret History of Saddam´s War.* St. Martin Press, New York, 1991, pág. 49.
14 Darwish, 1991, pág. 50
15 Eisenberg, 1978: p. 251.

The Guerrilla Foco

1 Thomas, Hugh. Cuba, *the Pursuit of Freedom.* New York: Harper and Row, 1971; Dominguez, Jorge I. To Make a World Safe for Revolution. Cuba's Foreign Policy. Cambridge, MA: Harvard University, 1989.
2 Braña, Manuel, *El Aparato.* Coral Gables, 1964, pp. 488-489.
3 Pak, Byung Koo. The Cuban Problem in the Organization of American States: A Model for Collective Decision-Making. Ph.D. Dissertation. Michigan: University Microfilms, Inc., 1965.
4 Notably, DuPont and Sears.
5 Vivanco, Juan M. *Subversion en America Latina.* Miami, p. 35.
6 Leyva de Varona, Adolfo. Cuban-Mexican Relations during the Castro Era: A Historical. And his, Ph.D. Dissertation. Michigan: University Microfilms, Inc., 1994. pp. 146-151.
7 See U.S. Congress, Senate, Committee on the Judiciary, Internal Security Subcommittee, *The Tricontinental Conference of African, Asian, and Latin American Peoples,* 1966.
8 Franqui, Carlos. *Diario de la Revolución Cubana.* Ed., by R. Torres, Barcelona, Spain, 1976, p.471.
9 Ernesto Betancourt. Is Castro Preparing for a Gotterdammerung? SOCICUBA, 1999.
10 Ernesto Betancourt, ibid.
11 Edward V. McCarthy, Diario de las Américas, 2-18-65.
12 Idem.
13 Idem.
14 Debray, Regis (1967). "Revolution within the Revolution." Monthly Review Press.
15 Miguez, Alberto. "Castro's Armies in Africa." (Paper Study) Cuban American National Foundation, Washington, 1985.
16 Perrault, Gilles. *Un Homme Apart.* Paris, 1984, pp. 474-475.

17 Alfonso L. Tarabochia, Cuba: The Technocracy of Subversion, Espionage and Terrorism (International Association of Chiefs of Police, 1976, 34.
18 Life Magazine, "Letters from Prison", George Jackson.
19 Tarabochia, 1976 pp 30-33
20 Federal Bureau of Investigation, Foreign Influence Weather Underground Organization (WUO August 20, 1976, p. 121 23. Ibid pp. 15-19. 24 G 17.
21 Idem.
22 Terroristic Activity Inside the Weatherman Movement: Hearings before the Subcommittee to Investigate the Administration of the Internal Security Act and Other Internal Security Laws, U.S. Senate, 93rd Congress, 2nd Session, October 18, 1974, p. 137.
23 Armando Correa. Veneno de Castro abre sospechas que Cuba oculta armas bacteriologicas. El Nuevo Herald, May 4, 1997, sec. a. p. 6.
24 Vivanco, 136.
25 Hernandez and Mas, who executed Dan Mitrione, were trained in Cuba. See "El Combatiente" Newsletter, Year VII, 6/12/74. No. 121.

Castro Africanus

1 These views were expressed in a series of conferences delivered by several high Cuban government officials between 1959 and 1960. La Revolucion Cubana ante el Mundo. Havana, September 1960.
2 The Afro-Asian term was used in the early sixties to refer to the recently independent countries in Africa and Asia. They were the founders of the Non-Aligned Movement.
3 Robert K Furtak, Cuba 25 años de politica exterior. Foro Internacional, Vol. 25, No. 4, April-June 1985, pp. 343-361.
4 These views were expressed in a series of conferences delivered by several high Cuban government officials between 1959 and 1960. La Revolucion Cubana ante el Mundo. Havana, September 1960.
5 Guillermo Jimenez, Chief of the Regional Policy Department of the Ministry of Foreign Relations, on" The Cuban Revolution and the Solidarity and Cooperation with the Afro-Asian Countries in the Common Struggle for National Liberation. La Revolucion Cubana ante el Mundo. Havana, September, 1960, pp. 21-60.
6 In the lectures delivered by Foreign Minister Raul Roa shortly after the Soviets pledged support for Cuba in case of a US Aggression, it seems the Cuban leadership was pleasantly surprised with the support offered by the Soviets.
7 Ministry of Foreign Relations. Fidel Castro: This is Our Line. Havana: no publication date.
8 Television Cubana Network, Havana 20 February 1989, in FBIS-LAT, 17 February 1989, p. 7.
9 Ministry of Foreign Relations. Fidel Castro: This is our Line. Havana.
10 Serapiao, "Mozambique-Cuba relationship 1960-1986." Conference in the Seminar about Cuban Internationalism in Sub-Sahara Africa. USIA.

Washington, DC, January 23 1987. The author participated, jointly with Pablo Rivalta, in the coordination of the camps in Tanzania. The training camp located in Algeria (Siddi-Bel-Abbas) was directed by Henry Villegas, today a General in the Cuban Armed Forces.

11 "Ché" Guevara fought in Africa, Cuban Colonel says, "French Press Agency, *Washington times*, October 6, 1987, p. A9.

12 Ernesto "Che" Guevara. "Obras Revolucionarias." Ediciones ERA, Buenos Aires, pp. 441 and 457. Ahmed Ben Bella; interview with Luis M. Gonzalez Mata in "Las Muertes del Che Guevara." Barcelona, 1980; pp. 94-95. Conversation of the author with Ernesto "Che" Guevara. Dar-es-Salaam. 1964.

13 The "Community".

14 Singleton, Seth. CSIS. "Notas sobre Africa"; Washington, 26 de abril, 1983.

15 In 1985, Angola's debt with Cuba amounted to 47 million, the eighth largest for Angola. See Sabado, Lisbon, 3 December 1988, in FBIS-AFR, 11 January 1989, p. 18-19.

16 The author was present in an Embassy conference delivered by General Arnaldo Ochoa; Aden, April 1976; Aden, May 1976.

17 Alfonso Iglesias. Internacionalismo: ayuda y colaboración. Colaboración Internacional, No. 2, April-June, 1986, pp. 16-18.

18 Damian Fernandez. The Duty of a Revolutionary: Cuba's Foreign Policy as a Third World Model. Harvard International Review. January 1987, pp. 29-32.

19 Marina and David Otaway. Afro communism. New York: Africana Publishing Co., 1986.

20 See also Olga Nazario. Cuba's Relations with Africa in the Eighties: Scope and Limitations; in Cuban Foreign Policy: The New Internationalism, edited by James Suchlicki and Damian Fernandez, Miami, Fl., University of Miami, 1985, pp. 68/98.

21 Radio Rebelde, Havana, 17 October, 1987.

Castro's offensive in Latin America

1 Crozier, Brian. *Occidente se Suicida.* Buenos Aires, 1979, p. 9.

2 U.S. Department of State, Bureau of Public Affairs, *Cuba's Renewed Support for Violence in Latin America*, Special Report No. 90, December 14, 1981, p. 11.

3 James Theberge, "Kremlin's hand in Chile." Soviet Analyst, August 15, 1974. As reprinted by U.S. Congress, House, Committee on Foreign Affairs, *United States and Chile During the Allende Years*, 1970-73, 1975, p.636.

4 Robert Moss, *Chile's Marxist Experiment* (Newton Abbot; David & Charles, 1973.

5 Intelligence Activities Committee, United States Senate. Plan Z. Covert Action in Chile, 1963-1973. Dec. 18, 1975, p. 20.

6 Brian Crozier, "Soviet Support for International Terrorism," Unpublished 41 42 Paper at the Jerusalem Conference on International Terrorism, 1979, p.

1. See Boris N. Ponomarev, "The World Situation and the Revolutionary Process," World Marxist Review, no. 6, June, 1974.

7 Reuters, 6-08-86.

8 Grenada Documents. 1983. Personal letter from Desire D. Bouterse to Maurice Bishop.

9 Don Bonning, "Suriname: Denies It's Edging into Havana's Caribbean Orbit," *Miami Herald*, January 19, 1983.

10 James LeMoyne, "Strongman Finds Suriname Isn't Easily Subdued," *New York Times*, January 19, 1984.

11 Edward Dew, "Did Suriname Switch?" *Caribbean Review*, vol. 12, no.2 (Fall 1983), p. 29.

12 Jackson Diehl, 'Suriname Keeps Foreign Policy In Balance, " *Washington Post*, October 13, 1983, p. A28.

13 U.S. Departments of State and Defense, *Background paper: Nicaragua's Military Build-up and Support for Central American Subversion*, July 18, 1984. p. 11.

14 *FBIS*, vol. 6, June 12, 1975, p. N1.

15 Jack Anderson. U.S. Concerned About Castro Spymaster. The Washington Post. 5 March 1981.

16 Oggi, Audizione del onorevole Bettino Craxi, Rome, 20 gennaio 1983.

17 U.S. Senate, Subcommittee on Security and Terrorism, Committee on the Judiciary, *Washington, D.C.* The Role of Cuban in International Terrorism and Subversion. Intelligence Activities of the DGI, Friday, February 26, 1982.

18 Moss, Robert. U.S. Congress, Senate, Committee of the Judiciary, Subcommittee on Security and Terrorism. Terrorism: The Role of Moscow and its Subcontractors, 9th Cong. 1st sess.; June 26, 1982, pp. II, (19--).

19 Masetti, Jorge. *La loi des corsaires*. Paris: Editions Stock, 1993, pp. 186-187.

20 Masetti, 1993, pp. 205-206

21 James M. Dorsey, "Cuba Helps Plant Seeds of War," *Washington Times*, March 21, 1988.

22 Masetti, p. 138.

23 Gonzalez, Edward and David Ronfeldt. *Cuba Adrift in a Post-Communist World*. Santa Monica: RAND, 1992.

24 FB1S- Latin America, 1-29, 1994.

The sword and the Pax

1 Eisenberg, 1978: p. 251.

2 Steven, 1980, pag. 365.

3 Darwish, St. Martin Press, New York, 1991, pág. 49.

4 Idem.

5 Steven, 1980, pag, xxvii.

6 Gordievsky, Oleg, and Christopher Andrew. *KGB, The Inside Story*. Harper Collins Publishers, New York, 1990, p. 546-547.

7 Emerson, Steven A. and Cristina del Sesto. *Terrorist*. Villard Books, New York, 1991, 136.

8 Gordievsky, 1990, p. 548.

Palestine de facto
1 Darwish, 1991, p. 301.
2 Malcolm W. Nance. *Terrorist Recognition Handbook*. CRC Press Taylor & Francis Group. Second Edition, p. 140
3 Larui, Abdallah. *La Crisis de los intelectuales árabes* (The Crisis of the Arab Intellectuals). Prodhufi, S. A., Madrid, 1991.

The raise of the crusaders
1 Friedmann, Thomas L. *From Beirut to Jerusalem*. Anchor Books, New York, 1990, 215.
2 Kataeb.
3 HizbAlláh: Party of God.
4 Nance. CRC Press Taylor & Francis Group. p. 38.

In Syria
1 Alawites, followers of the Martyr Ali.
2 Yossef Bodansky. Why the West is Supporting an Anti-Western Solution in Syria. Fri. 20 April 2012.
3 Friedman, 1990, 79.
4 Friedman, 1990, 77.
5 Bodansky. 20 April 2012.
6 Idem.

The roots of Islamic terrorism
1 Nance. CRC Press Taylor & Francis Group. p. 59.
2 Nance. CRC Press Taylor & Francis Group. p. 49.
3 Idem.
4 Nance. CRC Press Taylor & Francis Group. p. 5.
5 Nance. CRC Press Taylor & Francis Group. p. 14.
6 Sayed Khatab. The Political Thought of Sayyid Qutb. The theory of jahiliyyah. Routledge. Taylor & Francis Group. London and New York. 2006; Introduction
7 Khatab. London and New York. 2006.
8 Khatab. London and New York. 2006; 2.
9 Khatab. London and New York. 2006; 164.
10 Khatab. London and New York. 2006; 169.
11 Khatab. London and New York. 2006; 9.
12 Khatab. London and New York. 2006; 68.
13 Kiyan or Essence.

The New Mahdi
1 The Blue Nile: Al-Bahr Al-Azraq.
2 Jartum: Al-Jartum.
3 Islamic Community: Umma.

4 Viorst, Milton. *In the Shadow of the Prophet*: Westview Press, Colorado, 2001, 127.
5 Non-believers: kafir.
6 EconoMonitor.com
7 Nance. CRC Press Taylor & Francis Group. p. 20.
8 Nance. CRC Press Taylor & Francis Group. p. 155.
9 The Masal, fur y Zaghawa.

Castro and the Islamic Terrorism

1 Serguera, Riveri, Jorge. *Caminos del Che*. Mexico: Plaza y Valdés Editores, 1997, p. 55.
2 Gabriel Garcia Marquez; *Operation Carlota*; Prensa Latina, Moscow Azul Editores; Peru, Lima, 1977.
3 Idem.
4 About 80 miles inside the Sahara on the Atlantic side of Africa.
5 Agreement put into effect by Yousef Ben Khedda.
6 Dutch, William J. Studies in Comparative Communism. XIII and 2. Spring-Summer, 1978, pp. 31-74.
7 Dutch. Spring-Summer 1978; 34-74 page 44.
8 Marquez; Operacion Carlota; op. cit.
9 Author's conversation with Abdul-Aziz Bouteflika in Dar-es-Salaam, Tanzania, February 1964.
10 Algeria, Libya, Mauritania, Mali, Sudan, Ethiopia, Somalia, the African Central Republic, Nigeria, Dahomey, Togo, Ghana, Upper Volta, Liberia, Zaire, Congo Brazzaville, Gabon, Burundi, etc.
11 In the region of Fizi-Baraka.
12 Jorge F. Perez-Lopez and Rene Perez-Lopez, Calendar of Cuban Bilateral Agreements 1959-1976. Pittsburgh, PA: University Center for International Studies, 1980.
13 Kopilow, David J. *Castro, Israel and the PLO*. The Cuban American National Foundation, Washington, 1984, p. 6.
14 Cited by writers, 30 May 1978, David J. Kopilow; op. cit., page 8.
15 Plus the USSR, the Sudan, and Egypt.
16 Assab and Massawa.
17 Ethiopia, Somalia, North and South Yemen.
18 From the Cuban Eastern Army.
19 Kopilow, ob. cit. pag. 9.
20 Edward Gonzalez; ob. cit. p 4.
21 Durch; ob. cit. p. 53.
22 Ibid. p. 5.
23 Damian J Fernandez. PhD Dissertation. La política exterior cubana en el Medio Oriente. Universidad de Miami, 1986.
24 Idem.
25 Idem.
26 Pilots, technicians, and general staff personnel.
27 Novik; ob. cit. p. 12.

28 Idem.

29 Moscow Radio, in Arab. 04-21-1977. Quoted by Nimrod Novik; ob. cit. p. 13

30 Novik; ob. cit. p. 15-16.

31 Newsweek. 07-10-1978. New York Times; 06-27, 1978.

32 Novik; ob. cit. p. 17.

33 Moscow Radio, in Arab. 04-21-1977. Quoted by Nimrod Novik; ob. cit. p. 18, 68.

34 Weekly Review. Nairobi, No. 156; 02-13-1978.

35 Author interview with Cuban diplomatic officers in Yemen.

36 Ayoob, Mohamed. *Conflict and Intervention in the Third World*. New York, 1980, p. 86.

37 MENA, 8 July 1978: MEED, 30 June 1978, quoting Al Watan Al Arabi, Nimrod Novik, op. cit., page 19.

38 Domingo Amuchastegui. Cuba in the Middle East, a brief chronology. Foreword by Haim Shaked, Director Middle East Studies Institute. July, 1999.

39 Durch, op. cit., page 72.

40 Afrique-Asie, No. 135, 16 May 1977.

41 Mestiri, *Les Cubains et L'Afrique*. Paris: Editions Karthala, 1980, 63.

42 Mestiri, op. cit., pages 59-60.

43 Mestiri, p. 63.

44 Ibid. p. 9.

45 Miguez, 1985.

46 The author was present in a meeting with Osmani Cienfuegos Gorriaran, Secretary General of Tricontinent Organization, and responsible for Cuban policy towards Africa and the Middle East by that time. Also, conversations of the author with officials of the Africa and Middle East Section of the General Department for International Relations of the Central Committee of the Cuban Communist Party. Havana, 1973-1974.

47 R. M. Holley, "Cuba and the Polisario Front." Washington, DC: Moroccan American Center for Policy, 2005. On children's experiences, see "Aid Child POWs," The Washington Times, September 25, 2005.

48 Bohemia, Havana, October 1978.

49 Idem.

50 BBC, Thursday, January 24, 1980.

51 Bohemia, Havana, 1977, p. 76.

52 BBC, Saturday, July 17, 1982.

53 New York Times, June 9, 1985, page 9.

54 Prensa Latina, "Saharawi Parliamentary Leader Visits Cuba," Havana, 12 March 2007.

55 Holley, Moroccan, 2005, pp., 5, 9.

56 Ibid., p. 6.

57 Kopilow, op. cit., page 10.

58 Interview of the author with Palestinian George Habash, chief of the FPLO, and with Abdul Fattah Ismail, Secretary of the South Yemen Party. Aden, July 13, 1977.
59 Idem.
60 Perrault, 1984, pp. 474-475.
61 Idem.
62 Amuchastegui. July, 1999.
63 Interview of the author with officers of the Cuban Embassy to Cyprus at that time.
64 Perrault, 1984, pp. 474-475.
65 Reuters, May 30, 1978.
66 Kopilow, p. 8.
67 Kopilow, p. 36.
68 Amuchastegui. July, 1999.
69 Idem.
70 Etinger, Yaakov. New Times, No. 39, 1981.
71 Washington Times, July 20, 1998.
72 Jose dela Fuente. Wine into vinegar - the fall of Cuba's biotechnology. Nature Biotechnology, October 2001.

Castro´s Realpolitik

1 First Secretary of the Vanguard Party of South Yemen, pro-Soviet; personal friend of Fidel Castro, was assassinated during the internal crisis in South Yemen in May 1986.
2 Novik, op. cit., page 31.
3 Bohemia, Havana, No. 52, 29 December 1978.
4 New York Times, 5 April 1976.
5 Izvestiya, 29 March 1963, quoted by Nimrod Novik, "The Bab-el-Mandeb Coast" (Soviet Diplomacy and Regional Dynamics), Foreign Policy Studies Institute, Philadelphia, Monograph No. 26, 1979, pages 25 and 69.
6 John K. Cooley. East Wind over Africa. Red China´s African Offensive. Walter and Company. New York, 1965, page 37.
7 Pravda, 15 March 1978, quoted by Nimrod Novik, op. cit., page 51.
8 New York Times, 16 May 1978.
9 Bereket Habte Selassie. Conflicto e intervención en el Cuerno del Africa. Monthly Review Press, New York y Londres, 1980, page 142.
10 Edward Gonzalez, op. cit., page 12.
11 David Lamb, "Critical Moment in Ethiopian Aid During the War in Eritrea," Los Angeles Times, 29 May 1978, page 7. "Eritrea in the Struggle," Volume 3, September-November 1978, Richard Sherman, op. cit., page 110.
12 Africa Confidential, 7 July 1978, 3 Sudanow 4, February 1979: 17.
13 Author's conversations in 1978 with Cuban officials stationed in Ethiopia.
14 Daniel S. Papp, "The Soviet Union and Cuban in Ethiopia," Contemporary History, 76, March 1979, 113.
15 Foreign Report 1.547, 16 August 1978, 2.

16 Idem.
17 Mestiri, op. cit., page 42.
18 Jay Malin. The Washington Times, 20 November 1984.
19 Avigdor Hazelkorn, "The Foreign Function of the Soviet Armed Forces," Naval School Review, Vol. 33, No. 1, January-February 1980, page 41.
20 Vanneman, Peter and W. Martin James III. Soviet Foreign Policy in Southern Africa. Problems and Prospects. Pretoria, 1982, page 41.
21 Amuchastegui. July, 1999.

The Havana Cartel

1 According to Manuel De Beunza, a Cuban intelligence officer that defected in Canada; Interview, March 2001.
2 Betancourt, Ernesto. Fidel Castro and the Drug Trade. Cuba: Assessing the Threat to US Security. Endowment for Cuban American Studies. 2001, p. 53.
3 Idem.
4 *Oiga* [Lima], December 17, 1984, pp. 13-18.
5 Idem.
6 Spanish paper says ETA members seek refuge in Cuba. Madrid, Reuters, November 17, 1997; M. Arostegui, Ibid. Miguez, Ibid. Europa Press, Ibid.
7 Arostegui, El Nuevo Herald, 12, 12, 1997.
8 Idem.
9 Dos activistas de ETA eran los hombres de Cuba de Gadusmar," El Pais, Madrid, 29, 1998. Fernando Lázaro, "ETA intenta extender su red financiera a Suiza," El Mundo, Madrid, July 19, 1998.
10 López-Fonseca. "ETA se refugia en Cuba," Epoca (Madrid) 10 de diciembre 2000.
11 "Flores y Castro chocan por Posada Carriles," El Diario de Hoy, Panama, November 18, 2000: Pablo Alfonso, "Trifulca en la Cumbre," El Nuevo Herald, November 19, 2000.
12 Transcript: State's Edmund Hull on Global Terrorism Report, U.S. Department of State, 05/01/2001.
13 A napalm-like device.
14 The Mirror, 8-17-01. Colombia Provo is Top Man for Castro and IRA in Latin America.
15 Overview of State-Sponsored Terrorism, Patterns of Global Terrorism - 2000.
16 The Cuban American National Foundation. "Castro's Puerto Rican Obsession." Washington,1987, p. 14.
17 Cuba provided these mini-factories to numerous subversive organizations.
18 FBI. Annual Report. 1973.
19 U.S. Congress, 90th Congress/2d Session, 1368-1373.
20 The Cuban American National Foundation. 1987, p. 14.
21 Ibid., p. 31.
22 Tarabochia, 1970, p. S3758.

23 Diario Las Americas. January 1, 1982, p. 1.
24 Turner, Harry. The San Juan Star. May 20, 1976.
25 US Congress, Senate. Subcommittee on Security and Terrorism, Committee of the Judiciary. The Role of Cuba in International Terrorism and Subversion, 9ff 17 Congress/1" 1 Session.
26 Bittman, Ladislav. Testimony, Document 2, Hydra of Carnage; op. cit., p. 579.
27 Ibid.
28 The New York Times, August 31, 1985.
29 The Miami Herald, -03-1991.
30 The Cuban American National Foundation, p. 6.
31 Ibid, p. 18.
32 FBI. Press Advisory. August 20, 1985.
33 The Cuban American National Foundation, p.5.
34 Manuel Cereijo. An overview of Cuban Intelligence Collection Capabilities. INGMCA@aol.com.
35 Idem.
36 Idem.
37 Agustin Blazquez and Jaums Sutton. Castro and International Terrorism. 2001, ABIP.

The Psychopathology of a despot
1 Kurds (20%), Sunni (15%) and Shiite (60%).
2 Ancient Mesopotamia.
3 Mustard and nerve gas.
4 Nance. CRC Press Taylor, p. 178.
5 About 500 journalists executed.

Ultimatum to Baghdad
1 Sarin and tarim, experienced in the concentration camps of Treblinka and Auschwitz.
2 Illegally, of course.

In the Swamp of Iraq
1 Zbigniew Brzezinski. *El nuevo tablero mundial*. Barcelona, Paidós, 1998, p. 145: American Primacy and Its Geostrategic Imperatives). Basic Books. 1997.
2 Idem.
3 January 30, 2001,
4 military and sanctions.
5 The hadeeth is the relationship of the events and actions of the Prophet Muhammad.
6 The Baker Commission directed by the former State Secretary, James Baker.
7 Peshmerga or Kurd Militia.

The Warlords
1 Mundigak y Deh Murasi Ghundai.
2 Taliban: Persian word meaning 'student of Islam'.
3 The chador: woman's veil.
4 La pudra.
5 Muyahedeenes: Persian voice to designate Islam warriors.
6 Watan Party: Party of the Country.
7 Del Jamiat-i-Islami.
8 Hezb-i-Islami.

The Taliban
1 Madrazas: theological Islamic schools.
2 Mullahs: religious guides.
3 Uzbekistan, Kazakhstan, Tajikistan and Kirghizstan.
4 Commander of believers: Amir-al-Momumin.
5 The South of Afghanistan, which includes the provinces of Day Kundi, Helmand, Kandahar, Nimroz, Uruzgan and Zabul.
Sindhis and the mohair's.

Dictatorship with atomic weapons
1 Chief Representative of British imperial rule in India.
2 Sindhis and the Mohair's.

The Sublime Porte
1 Azerí: from Azerbaiyán.
2 The Black Sea, the Colquis of M.

www.ingramcontent.com/pod-product-compliance
Lightning Source LLC
Chambersburg PA
CBHW060332290526
45793CB00003B/598